HARVARD HISTORICAL STUDIES

Published under the direction
of the Department of History
from the income of the
Henry Warren Torrey Fund

Volume CII

THOMAS J. WILSON PRIZE

The Puritan Moment

The Coming of Revolution in an English County

William Hunt

Harvard University Press
Cambridge, Massachusetts
London, England

Library of Congress Cataloging in Publication Data

Hunt, William, 1944–
    The Puritan moment.

    (Harvard historical studies; v. 102)
    Includes index.
    1. Essex—History.   2. Puritans—England—Essex—
History.   3. Essex—Economic conditions.   4. Great
Britain—History—Civil War, 1642–1649—Causes.   I. Title.
II. Series.
DA670.E7H8   1983   942.6′7062   82–11992
ISBN 0–674–73903–5 (cloth)
ISBN 0–674–73904–3 (paper)

For my mother and father,

who never despaired

Contents

Preface

In the past thirty years local history has ceased to be the province of eccentric vicars and has become a major theater of English historiography. A host of regional and municipal studies have substantially modified our picture of seventeenth-century England.[1] The organizing concepts of earlier generations—such as the rising (and/or falling) gentry, the Puritan (and/or Bourgeois) Revolution, even the "rise of the House of Commons"—have all been subjected to searching and often destructive criticism on the basis of careful, tightly focused scholarship. It has become fashionable to insist on the essential stability of Stuart society, to stress its hierarchical structure and its intense provincialism. Local concerns, we are told, consistently predominated over national issues. Ivan Roots, the author of what has been called "the best one-volume account of the Revolution," writes that "in Dorset, Somersetshire, and Lancashire it was local rather than national politics that men revelled in . . . Rebellions, including the Great Rebellion itself, were emphatically local movements." Alan Everitt, the author of seminal studies of Kent and Suffolk, agrees. The members of the Long Parliament, he insists, were not revolutionaries but "angry countrymen." They rode in "from their estates in Cumberland, Cornwall, and Kent" concerned only to end the increasing interference of the central government in their local communities. Everitt remarks, plausibly enough, that "there was nothing revolutionary in this attitude of mind."[2]

The localist thesis has gained wide acceptance in the past decade. It is current orthodoxy. A highly acclaimed recent study of the Civil War period by J. S. Morrill bears the title *The Revolt of the Provinces*. But it is worth looking more closely at the examples adduced in support of the localist interpretation. Roots cites the gentry of Dorset, Somerset, and Lancashire; Everitt cites those of Cumberland, Cornwall, and Kent. J. S. Morrill's specialty is Cheshire. Now, it is perfectly true that there was "nothing revolutionary" about the gentry of such counties. In every one of these counties the vast bulk of the gentry were Royalists in the Civil War. The localist thesis helps us to see more clearly why revolution on a national scale was extremely unlikely in seventeenth-century England. It does not do much to explain how such a revolution nevertheless occurred.

The problem, I would suggest, is that scholars have lately devoted too little attention to the regions and social groups from which Parliament drew its decisive support in the Civil War. I have tried in this book to help fill the gap. The rationale for devoting so much space to the coming of revolution in a single county is not that Essex was somehow typical of England as a whole, but that it was the revolutionary county par excellence. John Hampden called Essex "the place of most life of religion in the land"; an Essex Royalist lamented that his county was the "professed stage of rebellion," and the "first born of Parliament." Clarendon observed that Essex was the county in which the Parliamentary leaders "most confided." Early in 1647 the county's deputy lieutenants and justices of the peace boasted that Essex had been "by God's acceptance, more than ordinarily instrumental in the suppressing of the common enemy."[3] If we want to understand why the English Revolution happened, we need to take a long look at Essex.

In attempting to account for the radicalism of Essex, I assign a major explanatory role to that complex phenomenon known as puritanism: hence my title. The words *puritan* and *puritanism* have fallen somewhat out of favor in recent years, owing to their admitted ambiguity. I trust that my reasons for retaining them, and indeed for seeking to rehabilitate, to some extent, the notion of a puritan revolution, will become clear as the argument unfolds, but it may be useful to provide a summary definition at the outset. I understand by *puritanism* a body of opinion within English Protestantism characterized by an intense hostility to the Church of Rome as the incarnation of Antichrist; an emphasis on preaching and Bible study rather than ritual as the means of salvation; and a desire to impose a strict moral code, which I term the culture of discipline, upon society as a whole. These attitudes were generally accompanied by an aggressive, imperialist conception of England's national vocation.

These attitudes were not necessarily peculiar to the people I consider Puritans, but Puritans were distinguished by the intensity with which they held them. This intensity earned them the hostility of more complacent Protestants, not to speak of Catholics, as well as

those who placed a high value on ceremonial splendor and uniformity. The very word *Puritan,* which implies factiousness and spiritual
pride, expresses this hostility. That is why those to whom it was applied disliked it. They referred to themselves instead as the godly,
the Saints, or, less hubristically, as professors. Adherents of puritanism so defined might disagree on many matters and might ex-
hibit a wide range of personality types; but down to at least 1642
they perceived themselves, and were regarded by outsiders, as form-
ing a distinct cultural community.

Any competent account of the origins of the English Revolution
will attempt to do justice to both its material and ideological causes.
But I have sought to do more than merely juxtapose them as discrete
factors; I have tried to demonstrate their interpenetration. More
specifically, I have aimed to present religious thought and feeling
as both reflective and creative of social reality. I make no claim to
have settled anything. The perception of patterns in the historical
carpet is inevitably governed by personal temperament and cognitive
style. One historian's gestalt is another's hallucination. Psychological diversity would alone suffice to keep historians quarreling.
But as Etienne Gilson once said, it is not to be rid of history that
we study it.

Acknowledgments

I hope that my specific debts to the many scholars on whose work I have drawn are sufficiently acknowledged in the notes to this book. But I must express my general gratitude to three scholars without whose fundamental, and still largely unpublished, research a work of interpretive synthesis would have been impossible: Felix Hull, B. W. Quintrell, and N. C. P. Tyack. Special thanks are also due my two former advisers at Harvard: the late W. K. Jordan, who first suggested to me a study of the county of Essex, and Wallace Mac-Caffrey, who provided counsel and encouragement over a distressingly long haul. My archival researches were greatly facilitated by the staffs of the Essex Record Office, the Institute for Historical Research, the British Library, the Public Record Office, the London Guildhall, Colchester Castle, the Dr. Williams Library, the Bodleian Library of Oxford, the Fitzwilliam Library of Cambridge, and the Houghton Library of Harvard. I am particularly grateful to Mr. Arthur Searle of the British Library for his help with the Barrington manuscripts. Mr. Stephen Schultz produced a fine county map on very short notice, and my typist, Dorothy Foster, has been both efficient and forbearing.

My greatest personal debt, after that recorded in the dedication, is to the poet and novelist Norman Macleod, who has taught me by his own example persistence in rash undertakings. To my late friend H. J. Balthazar I owe my appreciation of the ironic confusion of spiritual values with material needs. For advice, help, and support of various kinds I am obliged to the following friends and colleagues: Marvin Becker, David Bien, Penelope Butler, Susan Cahn, Elizabeth Clark, Laurie Colwin, Robin Jacoby, Norman Owen, and Paddy Quick. Thanks, finally, to Kathleen Stein for helping me to retain a few of my wits.

The power of Essex is great, a place of most life of religion in the land, and your power in the county is great too. The difficulties of this war need the utmost of both.

— John Hampden
to Sir Thomas Barrington, 1643

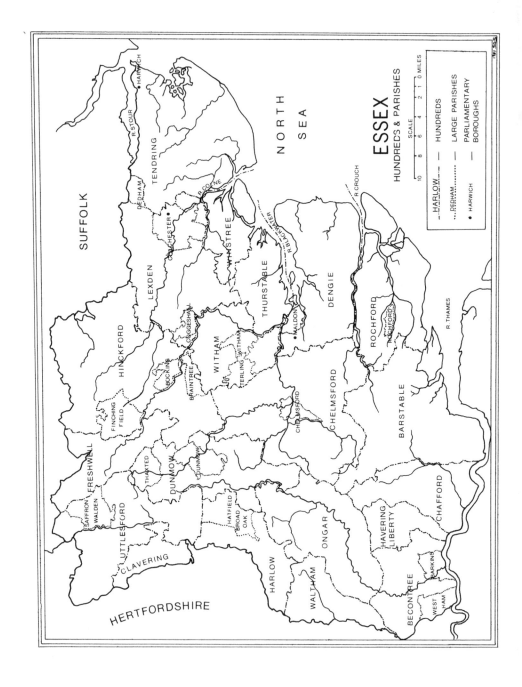

ESSEX

HUNDREDS & PARISHES

SCALE

10 8 6 4 2 1 0 MILES

HARLOW ..... — HUNDREDS

DEDHAM .... — LARGE PARISHES

— PARLIAMENTARY

• HARWICH — BOROUGHS

SUFFOLK

NORTH SEA

HERTFORDSHIRE

• HARWICH

R. STOUR

DEDHAM

TENDRING

R. COLNE

COLCHESTER •

LEXDEN

WINSTREE

HINCKFORD

COGGESHALL

BOCKING

BRAINTREE

WITHAM

TERLING WITHAM

THURSTABLE

R. BLACKWATER

• MALDON

DENGIE

R. CROUCH

CHELMSFORD

ROCHFORD

ROCHFORD

FINCHING FIELD

THAXTED

DUNMOW

DUNMOW

CHELMSFORD

BARSTABLE

R. THAMES

SAFFRON FRESHWELL

WALDEN

UTTLESFORD

HATFIELD BROAD OAK

ONGAR

HAVERING LIBERTY

CHAFFORD

CLAVERING

HARLOW

WALTHAM

BECONTREE

BARKING

WEST HAM

PART I

The County Community 1570–1620

The laboring man that tills the fertile soil,
  And reaps the harvest fruit, hath not indeed
The gain, but pain; and if for all his toil
  He gets the straw, the lord will have the seed.

The mason poor that builds the lordly halls
  Dwells not in them; they are for high degree;
His cottage is compact in paper walls,
  And not with brick or stone as others be.

—*Edward de Vere, Earl of Oxford and a native of*
Essex, written ca. 1576

1 / The English Goshen

This shire . . . deserveth title of the English Goshen, the fattest of the land; comparable to Pal-
estina, that flowed with milk and honey.
—*John Norden, in* Speculi Britanniae Pars, *1840*

The county of Essex comprises a little over one million acres, or roughly 1,570 square miles, to the northeast of London. At the death of Queen Elizabeth rather more than one hundred thousand men, women, and children lived there, the vast majority of them in rural hamlets and villages. The only town of any real consequence was Colchester in the northeast, with nearly nine thousand inhabitants, followed, at a considerable distance, by the twin clothing towns of Bocking and Braintree, with a combined population of about 2,500. No other town contained as many as two thousand souls, and only eleven held more than one thousand.[1]

Yet, Essex was "exceeding rich," according to William Camden, writing in 1607.[2] The Privy Council agreed. In the Ship Money assessments of 1636–37 Essex was rated at £8,000 along with Kent, Somerset, Suffolk, and Lincolnshire. Only two counties were assessed more heavily: Devon, at £9,000, and Yorkshire, with thrice the population of Essex, at £12,000.[3] Since the county was overwhelmingly rural, most of this wealth was naturally drawn from its fields and pastures. Not that Essex was an exclusively agricultural county. Indeed, compared to the rest of England it was relatively industrialized and thus subject to the vicissitudes of the clothing trade. But, as a glance at Tables 1 and 2 will suggest, most adult males worked on farms, whether as owners, tenants, or agricultural laborers.

Table 1 gives the additions—the designations of occupation or status affixed to each individual for legal purposes—that were claimed by or assigned to a random sample (surnames beginning with *A* and *B*) of male testators of known status from Essex, between

Table 1. Wills of men (surnames A–B) by status of testator, Essex, 1570–1619

Addition	Number	Percent of all male wills (N = 2,071)	Percent of wills of males of known status (N = 1,356)
Gentlemen	55	2.7	4.1
Yeomen	439	21.2	32.4
Husbandmen	445	21.5	32.8
Laborers	57	2.8	4.2
Clothiers	17	0.8	1.3
Weavers	34	1.6	2.5
Other artisans	210	10.1	15.5
Food/leather trades	59	2.8	4.4
Wives/widows	378	—	—
Spinsters	40	—	—
No status and singlemen	715	34.5	—
Others	40	1.9	2.9
Total	2,489	99.9[a]	100.1[a]

Source: F. G. Emmison, Wills at Chelmsford (London, 1958), I.

[a] Rounding errors.

1570 and 1619. Table 2 gives the additions of a sample of accused felons at the Essex Assizes. These tables cannot provide us with an accurate class map of Essex society. Alas, we have nothing comparable to the occupational census compiled by John Smith in 1608 for the county of Gloucestershire.[4] The two samples are socially skewed in opposite directions. Only about half the population—generally speaking, the richer half—left wills. It is probably safe to assume that accused felons were drawn disproportionately from the strata of the population that did not make wills. But taken together, the tables are adequate to confirm the predominance of agriculture in the county's economy.

In Elizabethan England people who worked the soil were called neither farmers nor peasants. The addition accorded to a substantial farmer, whether a tenant or an owner-occupier, was yeoman. He was the English equivalent of the Russian kulak or the French coq du paroisse. The smaller subsistence farmer received the humbler title of husbandman, while the landless or dwarf-holding cottager was simply called laborer. (In 1600 the word laborer was almost invariably reserved for agricultural workers; other wage earners received the

Table 2. Sample of accused felons by status, Essex Assizes, 1570–1610

Addition	Number indicted	Percent
Yeomen	90	15.0
Artisans and tradesmen	191	31.8
Husbandmen	37	6.2
Laborers	274	45.7
Others	8	1.3
Total	600	100.0
Total nonagricultural	199	33.2

Source: Essex Record Office, Chelmsford, Assize File, 1570–71, 1580–81, 1590–91, 1600–01, 1610.

designation specific to their craft.) Table 1 refers to 1,356 wills left by males of known status. Of these, 69.4 percent, or 941, bear agricultural additions. In Table 2 we see that slightly more than two-thirds of the accused felons were identified as yeomen, husbandmen, or laborers.

The countryside in which these men and their families worked was uncommonly bountiful. In 1594 John Norden described Essex as "most fat, fruitful, and full of profitable things, exceeding (as far as I can find) any other shire for the general commodities and plenty." He called it "the English Goshen, the fattest of the land."[5] Michael Drayton was equally effusive. "Essex is our dower," he sang in *Poly-Olbion,*

> . . . which greatly doth abound
> With every simple good that in the isle is found.[6]

A century later John Brome remarked that the county was beautiful as well as fertile, "of as great variety as delight . . . full of woods and shady groves, enriched with all kinds of grain."[7]

Few modern travelers, rattling through Essex on the express from Liverpool Street to Ipswich, find the county particularly delightful or remark on its variety. Outside its northwest corner, Essex is probably the flattest county in England, and much of its landscape, particularly in the south, is blighted by urban sprawl. But the relatively monotonous landscape conceals a complex geological structure that fostered, in medieval times, a varied pattern of settlement and cultivation. In the words of an eighteenth-century agronomist, "every species of soil from the most stubborn to the mildest loam" is to be found within the county.[8] The stubbornest of these soils is the London clay, which covers most of southern Essex. Brown and brittle on the surface, blue and viscous underground, it lends itself admirably to the production of bricks and oak trees. But it was less tractable to the medieval plough, and in 1600 much of this area was still densely wooded. Further north the clay mingles with chalk and other glacial debris, becoming lighter, more friable, and hence easier to till. In the seventeenth century the best arable land in Essex was to be found in the uplands of the northwest, on the border of Cambridgeshire, where the belt of chalk that encircles the London clay basin breaks to the surface. The coasts of Essex, along the Thames and the North Sea, were fringed with marshes, remarkably fertile and notoriously unhealthy. Norden complained of the "cruel quartain ague" he had contracted while visiting them.[9] The mildest loams of all were to be found in the shallow valleys of the Colne, Stour, Blackwater, and Chelmer, flowing in roughly parallel courses from the chalk upland to the North Sea, and of the Lea and Roding, which run south to join the Thames.[10] The precious meadowland along these streams fetched the highest rents in all of Essex.[11]

The distribution of soils conditioned the agricultural history of Essex. In the Middle Ages the forest still covered most of the county's million-odd acres, but by 1600 the woodland proper had dwindled down to Hatfield, Hainault, Epping, and Waltham Forests on the western fringe. The piecemeal assarting of arable land from the primeval forest gave rise over much of Essex to "the pattern of hamlets, isolated dispersed farms, and enclosures characteristic of districts colonized from woodland" rather than to the nucleated villages and open-field system that developed in less thickly wooded regions. The northern half of the enclosed district, which also contained the clothing villages, was an area of mixed pastoral and arable farming. While affording "many good feedings" for cattle and sheep, the hundreds of Lexden, Hinckford, Dunmow, and Freshwell also produced, according to Norden, "corn in reasonable measure," particularly around the Rodings in Dunmow. (In English usage, of course, *corn* means any kind of cereal—not maize). Hops were also widely grown in these hundreds. In the northeast the hundreds of Lexden and Tendring contained a number of furze-covered heaths around Mistley, Ardleigh, Thorrington, and Lexden village. To the southwest, in Thurstable hundred, lay the largest such area—Tiptree Heath. The flocks of sheep pastured on these heaths were modest in size, but the wool was renowned for its quality.[12]

Chelmsford hundred, in the heart of the county, was a district of mixed husbandry (Norden found it "reasonable apt for corn"), and the county town of Chelmsford was an important grain market. But the region was also "much interlaced with woods and rugged grounds," so that arable farming had to be combined with cattle rearing. Further south, on the tougher London clay, husbandry became more purely pastoral. The hundreds of Waltham and Ongar, the half-hundred of Becontree, and the liberty of Havering were densely wooded. Sheep and cattle grazed in the clearings, while lean, self-reliant swine rooted for mast in the oak forests. Along with native bullocks and sheep, the woodland pasture of southern Essex fattened store animals, brought in by drovers from the Midlands and from the north and west for the fairs at Brentwood, Romford, and Epping, which supplied the London market. On the estates of the Petre family in Chelmsford hundred, the sale of forest produce—ash for the coopers, bark for the tanners—brought in a considerable supplementary income.[13]

In all of these regions the pattern of enclosed fields and dispersed hamlets prevailed. But in the chalky uplands of Freshwell, Uttlesford, and Clavering hundreds in the northwest corner, the familiar medieval open-field system predominated. Here, the individual peasant holding lay not in a compact block surrounded by hedgerows but in dispersed strips, intermingled with the strips of other tenants in large, unobstructed fields surrounding a nucleated settlement. The typical open-field village (found more often in theory than in fact) possessed three great fields. One was sown with wheat in the autumn, another with barley or rye in the spring, while the third remained fallow; the crops were rotated on a three-year cycle. In practice, however, local custom and conditions produced a more complicated pattern. The village of Clavering, for example, possessed no fewer than fifteen fields, and nowhere, according to the leading student of the subject, is there evidence of the classic three-field system, or the even simpler two-field alternation. One reason, no doubt, was the variety of crops grown in the fertile, rolling landscape of northwest Essex. Among them were peas, beans, and saffron, which was grown as a dye and medicine as well as a spice in the fields surrounding the old borough of Saffron Walden. (This labor-intensive crop eventually exhausted the soil, and saffron disappeared from the fields of Essex by the early eighteenth century.) The open-field system was largely, but not entirely, confined to the northwest. There were also open fields along the valley of the Stour, flanking the Lea from Stanstead Mountfitchet to Walthamstowe and the Thames between West Ham and Mucking. Smaller pockets were found around Colchester and between Chelmsford and Maldon.[14]

The marshlands along the Thames and North Sea coasts formed another distinctive agricultural region. They were famous for the production of veal, which Fuller called "the fattest, fairest, and finest flesh in England, and consequently in all Europe," and for "great and large cheeses . . . wondered at for their massiveness and thickness," made from ewes' milk. The lush grasslands also provided a rich pasture for horses, Welsh store cattle, and wethers from Lincolnshire and Leicestershire. There was money to be made in these unhealthy wetlands. As Fuller observed, the funeral effigies of butchers and graziers in the parish churches of southernmost Essex reflected their growing prosperity in the seventeenth century, and sixty years earlier the parishioners of West Ham complained that these entrepreneurs were monopolizing the pasture lands.[15] But in 1600 the reclamation and maintenance of marsh pasture was a difficult and precarious task, and the failure of landlords to maintain dikes and drainage systems led to recurrent flooding.[16]

While distinguishing broadly between the agricultural regions of Essex, between areas of arable, pasture, and marsh land, it should also be stressed that there was enormous local variety within each hundred, even within each parish. Virtually all Essex farming was in some sense mixed husbandry, since the vast majority of farmers combined, though in varying proportions, the growing of crops with the keeping of livestock. Swine, poultry, and, to a lesser extent, sheep were ubiquitous, and all quarters of the county probably contributed to the great flocks of geese, numbering in the hundreds of thousands, that were driven twice a year to the market at Epping. Grain, on the other hand, was grown in the pastoral marshlands as well as in the arable open-field districts.[17]

Agriculture was not the county's only source of food. Along the Thames and North Sea coasts many of the inhabitants made their living from the sea. Fishing was the principal occupation of the Thames-side town of Barking, and by its own account the little village of East Doniland, at the mouth of the Colne below Colchester, was entirely composed of "poor mariners."[18] Setting out from the Thames and the other estuaries and tidal creeks between Harwich and London, Essex hoys and skiffs risked the hazards of wind, tide, and the depredations of Dunkirk pirates to trawl for turbot, cod, mackerel, whiting, flounder, and "the finest soles in England." Sprats were consumed in such quantities in the cloth town of Colchester that they were known as "weavers' beef." Daniel Defoe held that "the best and nicest, though not the largest, oysters in England" were those taken from the Woelfleet Bank in the mouth of the river Crouch below Maldon.[19] ("New Wallfleet oysters," the cry of the London street hawkers, was incorporated by Orlando Gibbons into his vocal fantasia on "The Cries of London.") There were more rich beds in the mouth of the Colne below Colchester; they became the source of considerable friction in the mid-seventeenth century between fishermen and riparian landlords.[20]

Wild game, too, taken legally or otherwise, provided an important supplement to the food supply, and must have added welcome variety to a largely farinaceous diet. The coastal marshlands bred an abundance of fowl. Defoe tells us that Osey Island in Maldon Water harbored an "infinite number . . . of duck, teal, and widgeon," so many that the island seemed covered with them.[21] Inland, rabbits were captured with snares and haynets—legally on many wastes and common lands, more riskily on the private warrens and parklands of the gentry.[22] Essex was full of private game preserves, which were valued by the aristocracy not only for recreation but also for their increasingly valuable timber. William Harrison thought that as much as one-twentieth of the county's land mass was thus unnecessarily withheld from cultivation. But the stealth and daring of the poaching community did something to amend matters. Sausage flavored with poached Essex venison was a delicacy in the capital.[23]

In 1600 Essex farmers were not particularly innovative, at least not by comparison with their colleagues across the Channel in the Low Countries. There is little evidence of market gardening or of the introduction of revolutionary new crops like clover before the Civil War. Much land it is impossible to be more precise—was still wooded and supplied only fuel, game, and rough pasture. But the general quality of husbandry in Essex must have been high. The county's farmers, together with its fishermen and poachers, were able to support, without major subsistence crises, a population density of about sixty-four persons per square mile, while at the same time sending ever-increasing amounts of grain, cheese, poultry and eggs southward by cart and barge to feed the insatiable and recklessly expanding capital.[24]

After agriculture the most important activity in sixteenth-century Essex was the making of cloth. Of the eleven largest towns in Essex, three (Saffron Walden, Chelmsford, and Dunmow) were essentially market towns; one (West Ham) was a suburb of London; and a fifth (Thaxted) was a declining producer of cutlery. The remaining six, including the three largest (Colchester, Braintree-Bocking, and Coggeshall), were all cloth towns. The cloth towns accounted for 67.6 percent of the population of all eleven towns.[25]

The industry was concentrated in the northern hundreds of Hinckford and Lexden, where fulling mills dotted the banks of the slow-moving Stour, Colne, and Pant.[26] Cloth had been made here since at least the thirteenth century. Edward III had fostered the modernization of the industry in the fourteenth century by encouraging the immigration of highly skilled artisans from the Low Countries.[27] But by the beginning of Elizabeth's reign the manufacture of traditional broadcloth was in decline. In 1566 an unemployed weaver of Colchester lamented that the "weavers' occupation is a dead science nowadays." The obituary was premature.[28] The industry was revived by a second wave of Flemish immigrants, many of them fleeing the religious persecution of the Duke of Alva. The refugees, whose community in Colchester grew to 1,297 between 1565 and 1586, introduced the manufacture of the lighter and cheaper textiles known as New Draperies, which revitalized the local industry. These "bays and says," as the new stuffs were called, were shipped each week by boat or carrier's cart to the halls of the London merchant companies for export to the Netherlands, Spain, Portugal, and the Baltic. By 1623 the clothiers' great six-wheeled carts had wrought such devastation to the road between Sudbury and Chelmsford that carts of more than two wheels had to be banned, despite the anguished cries of the carters that two-wheeled carts were always toppling over.[29]

In the principal clothing towns of Colchester, Coggeshall (thought by Norden to produce the finest white cloth in England), Braintree, Bocking, Halsted, Dedham, and Witham, it seems that the majority of the population participated in the industry. In 1580 the departure of twenty Dutch clothiers from Halsted, where they felt they had been mistreated, produced acute economic distress in all the surrounding parishes. In 1597 it was reported that 120 of Dedham's two hundred households were totally dependent on the local clothiers for their livelihood. In the same year the hundred of Hinckford protested against an increase in the charges for purveyance, on the ground that the majority of its population was engaged in industry rather than agriculture. The clothing industry, it was reported in 1618, provided employment for "many poor persons . . . which otherwise know not how to live, especially women."[30]

Though concentrated in Hinckford and Lexden hundreds, the cloth trade ramified throughout the county. There were at least a handful of weavers in places like Saffron Walden and Dunmow in the northwest, in Hatfield Broad Oak and Bobbingworth in the west, and in Billericay in the south.[31] Moreover, it took anywhere from five to ten spinners to keep the weavers' looms furnished with yarn. In most parishes women probably supplemented the family income by spinning for the entrepreneurs of the clothing towns.[32] As Fuller expressed it, the county of Essex was "characterized like the good wife described by Bathsheba: 'she layeth her hand to the spindle, and her hands hold the distaff.' " In 1629 it was estimated that the clothing industry supported as many as fifty thousand people in Essex, but this figure is surely too high. K. H. Burley's figure of twenty-nine thousand is more plausible, and in 1600 the number was probably lower.[33] Nonetheless, it is quite likely that almost half the adult population—and a very much higher proportion of the women—relied to some degree on the cloth trade, and the entire county was affected by its vicissitudes.

None of the other industries of Tudor-Stuart Essex merits more than passing mention. There were brick kilns here and there, making use of the county's abundant supply of clay; there were also a number of potters in the village of Stock. Along the Thames from Woodford to Bow Bridge the air was polluted as early as 1614 by the starch works at Stratford. At the time of the Restoration this same region was England's main center for the manufacture of gunpowder.[34] Most of the population not engaged in agriculture, clothing, or fishing were local artisans and tradesmen fashioning ploughs, wheels, and other tools for their neighbors, tanning hides, grinding flour, and brewing and selling beer. Moreover, many tradesmen and artisans were part-time farmers as well. Colchester, for example— more than three times the size of the next largest town—still possessed extensive common fields on which the townsmen pastured their sheep.[35]

Nevertheless, Essex in 1600 was, economically speaking, relatively advanced. Hinckford and Lexden were among England's principal industrial areas. The county's agriculture was stimulated by the pull of demand from the clothing towns and still more from the rapidly expanding metropolis. The marketing of produce was, to be sure, severely hampered by the county's execrable roads, bad even by contemporary standards. The Quarter Sessions rolls abound with complaints about rotten bridges, washed-out cart tracks, and unlopped hedgerows; the royal progresses of Queen Elizabeth were hindered by "broad pools of water and mud."[36] But the miseries of land travel were partially compensated by the county's excellent network of slow-flowing rivers and by its extensive coastline. The Crouch, the Chelmer, the Blackwater, the Stour, and the Roding were all navigable by shallow-drafted rafts and barges. The Colne admitted hoys and skiffs to the Hithe of Colchester, some eight miles inland, and ships of large burden could sail within three miles of the town. A little lower down, wrote Defoe, the Colne estuary could receive a royal navy.[37]

In 1565 an inquest into the customs jurisdiction enumerated sixty-four navigable creeks and lading places on the Essex coast; Felix Hull has identified no fewer than 130. The most important ports were Harwich, Colchester, and Maldon, although in 1565 the creek of Maldon was "in much decay by reason that the main channel thereof is delven up and divided into sundry parts with sand and great quantities of sea-ooze and shingle." Brightlingsea, at the mouth of the Colne, also played a modest role as a port, while Leigh-on-Sea in the Thames estuary was "a very proper town, well furnished with good mariners, where commonly tall ships do ride, . . . a common and special lading place for butter, all manner of grain, and other things."[38]

These ports were principally concerned with the domestic coastal traffic, with the export of corn from the marshlands of Dengie and Rochford to London. But the county's geographical situation made possible considerable traffic with the Low Countries, a fact of considerable consequence for the religious life of Essex. For our purposes, the most important cargoes unloaded in these creeks and inlets were the Bibles and Protestant tracts smuggled in from the Continent during the sixteenth century. This illicit trade in contraband heresy was a major force in English intellectual history; it is a testimony to the ingenuity of these Protestant smugglers that we know next to nothing about them.[39]

To the seventeenth-century eye Essex was a county of contrasts—almost a microcosm of England as a whole. The marshlands along the coast resembled the Lincolnshire fens; the nucleated villages of the county's northwestern corner belonged to the great open-field region of the Midlands; most of the rest of Essex displayed the pattern of enclosed fields and dispersed settlements typical of Kent and East Anglia. The southwestern quarter of the county was still largely covered by forest. Hinckford and Lexden hundreds in the northeast, together with the adjacent portion of Suffolk, formed an industrial area comparable to the clothing districts of Gloucestershire, Somerset, and the West Riding of Yorkshire.[40] Essex, to be sure, possessed no mineral wealth to compare with the lead of Somerset and Derbyshire or the coal of Durham and Northumberland. Nor did its forest zone harbor an iron industry like the Weald of Kent and Sussex. But otherwise Michael Drayton was not far wrong when he claimed for Essex "every simple good that in the isle is found."

It may be that Essex flowed, as John Norden asserted, with milk and honey, but if so the milk and honey did not spread themselves very evenly. Our best source for the distribution of wealth in early seventeenth-century Essex is the Ship Money assessment of 1637. Table 3 gives the distribution of some 1,300 taxpayers from twenty parishes.[41] The poor were exempt. Assuming that the same criterion of poverty was employed in the Ship Money assessment of 1637 as for the Hearth Tax of 1670—an assumption supported by the rough equivalence in the number of ratepayers in each assessment—then roughly 38 percent of the county's households would have paid no

Table 3. Essex Ship Money assessments, 1637

Tax rate	Number of taxpayers	Percent of total
Less than 10s.	1,056	77.3
10s.–£1	194	14.2
£1–£2	88	6.4
£2–£5	24	1.8
Over £5	4	0.3
Total	1,366	100.0

Source: Public Record Office, London, SP 16 / 358.

tax at all.[42] Of the taxpayers, 77 percent paid less than 10s. (A sub-sample of this group—597 individuals in six parishes—reveals that 438, or 73 percent, of those assessed under 10s. paid less than 5s.).

What these figures demonstrate most strikingly is the degree to which a handful of individuals towered over the mass of the population. The distribution by rate and title of all taxpayers assessed at £3 or more appears in Table 4. Only one-third of one percent of all rate payers owed as much as £5, yet four peers were rated at ten times that sum; another five paid from £25 to £40. After the peers come a handful of magnates of the second echelon, mostly knights and baronets, paying between £10 and £20, below whom the base of the pyramid broadens rapidly.

The 2.1 percent of ratepayers assessed at £2 or more included a handful of clothiers and merchants, but for the most part this group consisted of the armigerous gentry—landowners entitled to bear coats of arms by virtue of their allegedly purer breeding and their manifestly superior wealth. Assuming an overall equivalence between the total number of taxpayers in 1637 and 1670, there would have been 379 households paying £2 or more in Ship Money.[43] According to Clive Holmes, basing his figure on the Heralds' Visitations, there were 309 armigerous families below the peerage in Essex in 1640.[44] This estimate squares well with the evidence of surviving wills, 2.6 percent of which bear the style of gentleman or some more exalted title. If we accept the prevalent assumption that roughly half the population left wills[45] and that virtually all gentlemen did so, and if we put the adult male population of Essex at twenty-five thousand, we arrive at a cohort of gentlemen numbering 325.

The wealth of this aristocracy derived principally from their possession of land in the form of manors, those bundles of economic

Table 4. Status of Essex taxpayers rated at £3 and over, 1637

Status	Tax rate				Total
	£3–£5	£5–£10	£10–£20	Over £20	
Peer	0	0	1	9	10
Knights and baronets	10	16	15	0	41
Esquires	13	18	4	0	35
Gentlemen	13	6	0	0	19
"Mr."	20	7	0	0	27
None given	43	6	0	0	49
Total	99	53	20	9	181

Source: Public Record Office, London, SP 16/358.

claims and legal prerogatives that still formed the basic unit of agricultural society. There were about 1,100 manors in Essex, of which 780 have been identified as being in private hands in 1640. Most of these manorial lords were peers, knights, or gentlemen.[46] The greatest landlords in the county were the Riches, seated at Great Leighs. In 1630 Robert Rich, second Earl of Warwick, possessed sixty-four manors in Essex. Only one other family held as many as thirty manors—the Petres of Ingatestone—with profitable, well-run estates in the center and south of the county. Next came the families of D'Arcy and Wiseman, with twenty-six and twenty-four manors, respectively, and the Wentworths, Baynings, Mildmays, De Veres, Tyrells, and Radcliffes, each with between eleven and fifteen apiece.[47] Manors varied greatly in size and value, however, and a family's resources were not necessarily proportional to the number of its lordships.[48] For example, the compact estate that the Barringtons of Hatfield Broad Oak had carved out of Hatfield Forest on the county's western fringe consisted of only a handful of manors. Yet, they were among the county's indisputably dominant families, closely allied with the house of Rich.

Most of this landowning aristocracy was relatively new—either to the county or to gentility—and most older families, like the De Veres, Audleys, Tyrells, and Waldegraves, were in decline by 1600. Newer families, like the widely ramified Mildmay clan, the Petres, and most spectacularly the Riches, had profited from the spoils of court office and monastic lands. Others, like the Wisemans, the D'Arcys, the Dennys, and the Fanshawes, were consolidating their holdings into more manageable and profitable blocs. The Baynings had recently risen into the upper ranks of the gentry on the profits of the cloth industry, although their ascent was quite exceptional.[49]

The relative novelty of the Essex aristocracy is perhaps its most distinctive feature. According to Clive Holmes, only 15 percent of the county's politically prominent families had acquired their estates before 1485, as compared with nearly three-quarters of the Kentish gentry. By this criterion the Essex aristocracy was considerably younger than that of Norfolk or Suffolk, where the corresponding figures were 42 percent and 31 percent, respectively. Only in neighboring Hertfordshire does the aristocracy appear to have been more recently settled: there only 10 percent could claim to have been established before the battle of Bosworth. The novelty of the Essex gentry was accompanied by a lack of dynastic integration. Whereas 82 percent of the Kentish gentry married within the county, their counterparts in Essex were less than half as likely to do so. With the exception, once again, of Hertfordshire, the Essex aristocracy was the least endogamous in East Anglia.[50]

By and large, the manorial income of this Essex aristocracy came from rents rather than from direct production. Land held by the residual medieval tenures of freehold and copyhold—tenures that were becoming increasingly hard to distinguish from each other or from simple ownership[51]—was subject to rents and entry fines fixed by tradition. The price inflation of the sixteenth century had drastically reduced the value of these payments. By 1600 the bulk of the lord's income came from leasing the land that belonged to him directly—the demesne—at an economically appropriate rent. In 1600 it was already common to lease the demesne, which might be as large as 750 acres but was usually four hundred acres or less, to a few large tenant farmers, generally for a period of twenty-one years or longer.[52]

The pioneering researches of Felix Hull give us some idea of the distribution of land among the manorial tenantry. Disregarding regional variations for the moment, we can derive from Hull's figures the average holdings of tenants for the entire county.[53]

Now, what did this mean in practice? In any agricultural society not completely devoted to subsistence farming—and Essex was not—the important class divisions are between those who hold enough land to employ wage labor, those who farm only with the

Size of holding (in acres)	Percentage of tenantry
5 or less	46.0
6–20	24.7
21–50	17.3
51–100	6.7
over 100	5.2

aid of their own families, and those who are forced to work the land of others for wages to supplement the income from their own holdings, if indeed they have any land at all.

England's agricultural geography is too varied, even within the bounds of a single county like Essex, to permit confident generalization, but there are indications that, in normal years, farmers with fifty acres would regularly employ the labor of nonrelatives, while those with less than twenty would hire themselves out fairly frequently to others, especially during the peak periods of sowing and harvesting. The Statute of Artificers of 1563 provided that any man holding "a half a ploughland" was entitled to take on an "apprentice," which in agriculture meant simply a youth serving for "board wages"—that is, without a cash wage.[54] The ploughland was a notoriously variable unit, but generally meant about a hundred acres.[55] Thus, only farmers with at least half that amount were considered substantial enough to maintain steady employees. The acts for the "maintenance of tillage" in the fifteenth and sixteenth centuries forbade the destruction of houses possessing twenty acres of land or more, which would suggest that this was regarded as the lower limit of the viable peasant holding.[56] John Lilburne, when he proposed his scheme of land reform in the 1650s, hoped to assure every family between twenty-five and thirty-five acres, which he regarded as the minimum necessary to reverse "the decay of housekeeping."[57] So, on the whole, twenty and fifty acres seem reasonable boundaries.

One must bear in mind, however, that these are very crude categories, and the lines between them are purely theoretical. A small farmer, for example, may work for wages a few days a year or for months at a time, while a "strong" farmer may employ one or two servants or a score of day laborers. Above all—and this is especially pertinent to Essex—a man who appears in the manorial records as a small-holder may in fact be a prosperous artisan or merchant.

Of these three groups of tenants only the intermediate stratum—those holding from twenty to fifty acres—can be considered a peasantry in the strict sense of subsistence family farmers. Like peasants everywhere they were at the mercy of the weather. Peter Bowden has reckoned that in an average year the holder of a thirty-acre farm could just make ends meet. In a good year he might clear a profit of three to five pounds. But when the harvest failed, such a man would have to go into debt to buy food; a series of bad crops could drive him from the land. His richer neighbor, with more than fifty acres, could not only survive a year or two of dearth but actually profit from the inflation of food prices.[58]

The figures derived from Hull's researches suggest that barely 12 percent of the manorial tenantry belonged to this fortunate last category. It is interesting, if hardly conclusive, to compare these figures with the evidence of the surviving wills. Twenty-one percent of these were left by men described as yeomen. On the assumption that half the adult male population left wills, and that virtually all those entitled to the addition of yeoman did so, then yeomen would have made up 10.5 percent of the adult male population, a figure that squares tidily with the 11.9 percent of the tenantry holding more than fifty acres.

Another 17.3 percent would have been family farmers, holding between twenty-one and fifty acres. Thus, just under 30 percent of the tenantry possessed more than the twenty acres that represented the threshold of independence. (It is worth noting in passing that, according to the accounts of the highway surveyors, about the same percentage of households in eleven rural parishes possessed their own carts and draft animals, an important criterion of economic independence in rural society.)[59] Meanwhile, 77.7 percent of all tenants held less than twenty acres and would therefore have been at least partially dependent on wage labor or some nonagricultural occupation. Nearly half of the rural population, 46 percent, lived on less than five acres, and in most cases, Hull tells us, quite a bit less. These tenants must have been very dependent indeed on other sources of income.[60]

The average figures for manorial holdings, however, almost certainly understate the percentage of tenants possessing only minute

parcels of land. On Hull's sample manors from the open-field district in the northwest, and from the clothing region of the northeast,
the percentage of tenants holding less than five acres rose to 56.7
percent. Yet, these areas were far more densely populated than the
center and southeast of the county, where the percentage of small-
holders fell to 33 percent. Moreover, the manorial records used by
Hull underestimate the number of dwarf-holdings, since they fail to
record subtenancies. For example, in the northwestern parish of
Heydon in 1625 fifteen households were listed as holding less than
four acres, but only nine of these appeared in the manorial survey
taken five years later; the rest must have been subtenants.[61] Many of
these small-holders were artisans for whom farming was perhaps a
secondary occupation. In the Quarter Sessions rolls one frequently
reads of bricklayers, glovers, and coopers who kept hogs, sheep, or a
hive of bees.[62] Above all, many of the smaller tenants, and even
more of their wives, participated in one or another aspect of the
cloth industry.

Most of those for whom cloth making was a full-time occupation
were poor. Weavers and other textile workers probably formed at
least 15 percent of the adult male population,[63] yet as Table 1 discloses, they left only 1.6 percent of surviving wills. Robert Reyce,
across the border in Suffolk, observed that "it is by common experience tried . . . that in those parts of this shire where clothiers do
dwell, or have dwelled, there are found the greatest number of
poor."[64]

While wage rates for weavers were not set by the justices in Quarter Sessions, the clothiers of Bocking made the following estimate in
1636 of their employees' income: in good times, a weaver "if industrious" could earn between 10d. and 12d. a day, or about the same
as an agricultural laborer. But the laborer might have some land of
his own to tide him over periods of unemployment. Many weavers
did not. At Colchester, during the same year, the clothiers wrote to
the Privy Council that their weavers "cannot be without work one
week."[65] The industrious comber, according to the Bocking clothiers, could earn between 14d. and 16d., but there was probably only
one of these highly skilled artisans to every five weavers.[66] Spinsters,
who were five times as numerous as weavers, could expect only 5d.
to 6d., but they were more likely to belong to farming households.

At the other end of the scale was the clothier, who bought wool from the chapmen and fellmongers, put it out to the combers, spinners, weavers, and fullers, and then sent the finished product to the overseas merchants of London. Clothiers varied widely in wealth and scale of operation. J. E. Pilgrim believes that the average clothier worked on a small scale. This may have been generally true at Colchester, where clothiers were forbidden to employ more than five weavers. But these regulations did not extend to rural clothing towns like Coggeshall, Bocking, and Braintree.[67] Robert Reyce estimated that a clothier producing twenty cloths a week would employ five hundred persons, "for by that time his wool is come home, and is sorted, . . . what with breakers, dyers, wood setters, wringers, spinners and weavers, burlers, shearmen, and carriers, besides his own large family, the number will soon be accomplished."[68] Even in Colchester in the 1630s, despite the official restrictions, a clothier by the name of Thomas Reynolds employed, by his own account, "400 households of spinners, fifty-two of weavers, and thirty-three of others."[69]

Such clothiers were clearly moving into the ranks of the gentry, like Thomas Guyon of Coggeshall, who left an estate of £100,000 at his death in 1653, or Thomas Spring who, during the reign of King James, acquired great estates in Essex and Suffolk.[70] The Baynings of Essex also owed their extensive land holdings to the profits of cloth making, and in 1637 Paul Viscount Bayning was one of four peers in Essex rated at £50, the highest figure in the county.[71] Such men were the counterparts of the gentlemen-clothiers of Suffolk and Wiltshire and the gentlemen-ironmongers of Sussex.[72]

Far more representative, however, were the yeomen-clothiers of country towns like Braintree—men like Adrian Mott of Braintree, rated at £1 12s. 8d. in the Ship Money assessment of 1637, who dominated the local vestry for nearly half a century and left the sizable sum of £100 to the poor but who achieved only local prominence.[73] The median assessment for fifteen members of the Braintree vestry, most of whom were probably clothiers, was 14s. By way of contrast, a really wealthy clothier like Henry Ennew of Coggeshall paid £2 15s.[74] In 1670 the houses of most clothiers contained between five and ten hearths, whereas the home of substantial gentlemen would contain upwards of twenty.[75]

Essex, then, was hardly a peasant society composed simply of a

Table 5. Social stratification in early seventeenth-century Essex

Stratum	Components	Ship Money rate (1637)	Estimated percent of population
I	Peers and gentry: landlords, lawyers, civil servants, high ecclesiastics	over £2	1–2
II	Big farmers (owning or leasing over 50 acres), clothiers, wealthy tradesmen	10s.–£2	10–15
III	Small farmers, prosperous artisans, better-off weavers	less than 10s.	45–50
IV	Agricultural laborers, poorer artisans, including most weavers	0	35–40

handful of landlords dominating an undifferentiated mass of subsistence farmers. There are many theoretically valid ways of categorizing the members of a society, and a number of plausible classificatory schemes have been proposed for early modern England.[76] Table 5 offers a simple, indeed rather crude, hypothetical model of the social structure of Essex that may make the subsequent argument easier to follow. I have divided the families of Essex into four strata in descending order of wealth. It is no doubt somewhat evasive to number these strata rather than naming them. It is certainly safer. The roman numerals are colorless, but for that very reason they are free of anachronistic connotations. The estimated percentages represent no more than educated guesses based on a collation of Ship Money and Hearth Tax rates, with impressions derived from wills, criminal records, and contemporary observations. To offer a detailed justification of my procedures would be to impute to these figures more significance than I should like to claim. My largest assumptions have been that Ship Money, like the Hearth Tax, spared the lowest 38 percent of the population and that about one-half of the population left wills—generally speaking, the richer half.[77] My purpose in offering this table is to provide some general image of the society before we begin the discussion of social change. I feel reasonably confident that the model here proposed does not radically distort the facts.

Most of the members of group I were gentlemen, whom inferiors addressed as "Master" or "Your Worship," if not by some loftier title. This group constituted the county's political elite. From the greatest families were chosen the lords lieutenant and their deputies, who were the principal representatives of royal authority in the shire. From the middle ranks of the gentry came the bulk of the justices of the peace, whose responsibility was to superintend the day-to-day maintenance of social order and to see governmental policies implemented in their locality. The great merchants of Colchester dominated their town as aldermen, while the lesser gentry exercised a modest political authority as lords of manors and as occasional members of the county's grand jury. It would be reasonable to include the very richest leaseholders, perhaps those holding more than three hundred acres, in this dominant stratum as well. Such men rivaled or surpassed many of the landed gentry in wealth, if not yet in social status.[78] Even if they did not succeed in crossing the line into gentility themselves, their children were likely to do so.

Since this dominant stratum probably contained no more than 2 percent of the population, its members were thin on the ground; there would be no more than a family or two in most of the 416 Essex parishes. Local elites were composed largely of individuals from group II, working more or less harmoniously with whatever members of the dominant group were available. At the parochial level they constituted a ruling class of sorts, though their influence on national affairs was confined, in normal times, to the exercise of the franchise in parliamentary elections. Group II would also contain the majority of the parish clergy. There was a wide variety in clerical incomes, but even a relatively impoverished vicar or curate, provided he was morally respectable, would enjoy substantial prestige and influence. (Minor clerical functionaries, however, such as beadles, sextons, vergers, and the like probably belong in group III.)

Groups III and IV constitute the subordinate majority of the population: husbandmen, artisans, and laborers. These were the folk that William Harrison, an Essex man, referred to as the "vulgar and common sort." Harrison's neighbor, the courtier-diplomat Sir Thomas Smith, called them "the rascallity," a word that it is rather a pity to have lost and that conveys much about class attitudes. For Harrison and Smith the defining characteristic of the "rascallity" was political impotence. In Harrison's words, the lower orders "have neither voice nor authority in the commonwealth, but are to be

ruled and not to rule other[s]."[79] My criterion for differentiating between groups III and IV is the ability to make ends meet with a bit
to spare. Individuals in group III could accumulate a modest surplus
to pass on to the next generation; those in group IV could at best
meet their immediate needs and at worst were driven to beggary or
crime. The boundary between these two categories was both porous
and subject to fluctuation over time. The percentage of the population in group IV would shrink in good years and swell in times of
plague, dearth, or commercial depression.

Essex did not "flow with milk and honey" for the poorer half of
the population. The English Goshen belonged to the people in
groups I and II. Yet, the lower orders were also part of the county
community, and without some attempt to reconstruct their experience, even the history of the local and county elites will remain un-
intelligible.

2 / Make-Shift's Inheritance

At noon if it bloweth, at night if it shine,
Out trudgeth Hugh Make-Shift, with hook and with line,
Whiles Gillet, his spouse, is a-milking thy cow,
Sir Hugh is a-rigging thy gate or thy plough.
—*Thomas Tusser, in* Thomas Tusser . . . His Good Points of
Husbandry, *ca. 1570*

Essex in 1600 was being gradually but fundamentally transformed; its inhabitants were faced with novel challenges, opportunities, and dangers. To begin with the elementals: sex had gotten the
upper hand over death. An examination of the registers of eleven
Essex parishes between 1560 and 1599 shows that in nine of these
parishes there was a significant surplus of baptisms to burials. The
following list demonstrates that surplus per decade for the years
1560–1599.[1]

Parish	Surplus per decade
Doddinghurst	+41
Coggeshall	+182
Chelmsford	−1
Great Waltham	+118
Black Notley	+37
Ingatestone	+8
Dengie	−8
Barnston	+23
Earls Colne	+128
Chigwell	+40
Little Chesterford	+24

Alan Macfarlane observed the same phenomenon in Boreham and
Little Baddow and concluded that in both parishes, disregarding
migration, natural increase would have caused the population to
double during the reign of Elizabeth. Keith Wrightson and David
Levine found a similar pattern in the village of Terling. They have

suggested that the population of the entire county rose from fifty thousand to one hundred thousand in the century after the Reformation. The growth of London was even more spectacular—from about thirty-three thousand in 1500 to four hundred thousand in the mid-seventeenth century.[2]

The multiplication of hungry mouths stimulated commercial farming. In 1564 Essex shipped only 1,086 quarters of grain to the markets of London; by the end of James's reign the figure had risen to 12,765, and Essex was supplying about one-fifth of all of the grain that the capital received by sea.[3] There is no way to measure the amount of grain, poultry, cheese, eggs, and veal that was carted or herded into London, but the volume of land-borne trade was certainly increasing as well. So was the marketing of produce within the county itself. In 1600 the parish of Finchingfield petitioned to be allowed to license another victualing house; the town's one victualer could no longer supply the more than eighty households that had to buy their food. In the next few years similar petitions came from Langham, Great Oakley, Halsted, and High Easter.[4]

The expanding market for food is reflected in the proliferation of middlemen—higglers, badgers, poulterers, fishmongers, and the like. Only five wills survive for such individuals from between 1520 and 1569, but from the next half-century there are forty—an eightfold increase, while the total of all surviving wills merely doubles.[5] These middlemen were often regarded with suspicion and hostility, since their speculative activities were thought to drive up prices by creating artificial shortages. William Harrison of Radwinter claimed that landless artisans and laborers often found it impossible to buy a few bushels of grain on market day because the middlemen outbid them and cornered the supply.[6]

In 1608 the craftsmen of Chelmsford complained that "the loaders and badgers and millers, as soon as the market bell ringeth, presently sweepeth [sic] all away, and it is carried into their chambers, and we cannot get any corn or meal but at such a reckoning as it maketh the hearts of us all cold within our bellies."[7] This suspicion of middlemen was shared by the authorities. In 1574, a time of dearth, Justices Thomas Barrington and James Altham suppressed forty-one badgers in the county's western division. But the badgers and higglers served an essential function in meeting the widening market for Essex produce. As local fairs and markets declined in favor of the larger markets at Colchester and Chelmsford, these itinerant middlemen became indispensable.[8]

The growth of the market created new opportunities for farmers who were able to produce a surplus for sale. It provided the economic basis for the rising living standards that William Harrison observed among the Essex yeomanry. Harrison remarked on a "great amendment of lodging," the process that W. G. Hoskins has called the "rebuilding of rural England."[9] Harrison's impressions are confirmed by the architectural evidence. The Essex countryside abounds with farmhouses and mansions constructed during the late sixteenth century, and with older structures that received a new cross-wing or second story at about this time. Brick chimneys, another novelty mentioned by Harrison, became common after about 1570; the old open hearth was often replaced with a double-backed fireplace, capable of heating two rooms at once. The smoke from the old hearth had escaped through a simple hole in the roof; but now that the new chimney drew off the smoke more efficiently, it was possible to insert a ceiling under the rafters and thus create new rooms, called sollars, above the parlor and hall. The new floor afforded some additional measure of privacy in sleeping arrangements; servants and children slept in the sollars, while master and mistress had the parlor to themselves.[10]

In the small port town of Maldon, average house prices rose from £26 to £42 between 1571 and 1600.[11] Yet, William Harrison's neighbors were still able to replace wooden spoons and platters with tin, pewter, and even silver and to abandon the Spartan habits of their forebears in favor of sybaritic luxuries such as pillows and featherbeds. Like Robert Reyce of Suffolk a half-century later, Harrison observed that many yeomen were rising into the ranks of the gentry—buying the lands of "unthrifty gentlemen" and sending their sons to Oxford, Cambridge, and the Inns of Court.[12]

The problem of landowning gentlemen who wished to maintain or improve their own position was to secure their share of the rising profits being made by farmers and graziers. Those who could extract an economically rational rent from tenants prospered; those whose rents remained fixed at customary levels found their standard of living gnawed away by inflation. In extreme cases they, or more often their posterity, might be displaced by more ambitious or more fortunate competitors. Thus, the ancient family of De Vere watched a sizable proportion of their estate pass into the hands of the Harlackendens, their former stewards.[13]

On the whole, however, the Essex gentry did not suffer from any lack of commercial acumen; they were not inhibited from maximizing their revenue by conservative prejudice. In striking contrast to the gentry of Kent, which Alan Everitt has argued was "immemorially rooted" in the shire, most Essex landowners belonged to relatively new families—new either to the county or to gentle status—whose local prominence postdated the dissolution of the monasteries. It was, above all, a county of parvenus.

The family of Rich owed its rise from the ranks of the minor gentry to Sir Richard Rich, arguably the most rapacious and unprincipled of all of Henry VIII's servants. Rich obtained vast tracts of monastic lands for his services to the Defender of the Faith; he retained his estates under Mary by becoming an enthusiastic persecutor of Protestants. The fortunes of the Petres of Ingatestone also rested on monastic land acquired through royal service. The Petres, like the first Richard Rich, reverted to Catholicism at the time of Mary; unlike the Riches, they remained loyal to the old faith thereafter, but they kept the land. Their estates in the center and south of the county were run with notable efficiency. The widely ramified Mildmay clan also owed its prominence to the spoil of the monasteries.

The Baynings, who rose into the upper gentry on the profits of the cloth industry, were exceptional, but many landowners had mercantile or legal antecedents, and many more intermarried with City wealth. The rise of most gentry families—the D'Arcys, the Wisemans, the Fanshawes, the Wentworths, the Maynards, and the rest—was gradual and unspectacular, and was due more often to prudent marriage, genealogical good luck, and careful estate management than to the windfall of royal bounty.[14]

In contrast, most of the older Essex families—those who could trace their gentility back before 1500—were in decline by 1600. They included the Audleys, the Tyrells, the Waldegraves, the Radcliffes, and above all the De Veres. Earls of Oxford since 1142, the De Veres were ruined by the extravagance of their seventeenth Earl in the reign of Elizabeth and died out shortly thereafter. The only an-

cient family that retained its dominance was the Barrington family
of Hatfield Broad Oak, whose political power in the county was enhanced by a close alliance with the house of Rich.[15] In the 1620s the
ancient Barringtons and the parvenu Riches were also partners in
commercial and colonial speculation—further proof, if it were
needed, that genealogy does not determine economic mentality.

For the astute landlord one possible response to the inflation of
food prices might have been to engage in direct production for the
market, as the great lords of eastern Europe were doing. Seigneurial
exploitation of the demesne, or home farm, was not unknown in
Essex. It brought in £405 to the Tyrells in 1539 (the bulk of their
income) and £610 to Sir William Petre in 1556.[16] William Harrison
thought it necessary to denounce "men of great port and countenance" who became "graziers, butchers, tanners, sheepmasters,
woodmen, and *denique quid non.*" He held that such gentlemen were
unfairly encroaching on the livelihood of their tenant farmers.[17] But
Harrison does not claim that this practice was widespread in his own
county and admits that his information is based on hearsay. No
doubt many gentlemen continued to operate a home farm to meet
the immediate needs of the household, but there is no sign of any
dramatic extension of direct production on the Prussian or Polish
model. The eastern European latifundia required a servile labor
force and an agrarian economy of monoculture. It was ill-suited to a
land where the population was formally free and where agricultural
technique was varied and complex.

The Essex landlord was primarily a rentier. He received the bulk
of his income from leasing the demesne, which might be as large as
750 acres but was usually under four hundred, to a few large tenant
farmers.[18] To be sure, manorial lords still received payments from
tenants who held by the medieval tenures of copyhold and freehold.
Both classes of tenants paid an annual rent, while copyholders also
paid an entry fine upon assuming the holding. But these payments
had been fixed long ago by custom, and their value had been drastically reduced by the inflation of the sixteenth century. Practically
speaking, copyhold and freehold were becoming increasingly hard
to distinguish from each other, or from simple ownership.[19] In contrast, the demesne could be rented out for whatever the market
would bear, and the rent could be adjusted whenever a lease ex-

pired. Not that this gave the landlord an entirely free hand, however; most leases were for twenty-one years or more.[20]

To keep pace with inflation the rentier had to increase his rent
roll. One way to do this was simply to acquire additional rent-bear-
ing properties, by purchase, marriage, or inheritance. As has already
been suggested, many Essex families throve by just such means; they
bought up land, married sons to heiresses, and no doubt foreclosed
on mortgages as well. In the village of Terling freehold land was
passing steadily from yeomen and husbandmen to the gentry. On
the manor of Ockenden Fee, gentle hands held 14 percent of the
freehold land in 1601 but 67 percent thirty years later.[21]

There were also ways of increasing the yield from existing properties. To realize the potential value of an estate the landlord needed
to establish the extent of his assets, to recover prerogatives that had
slipped from seigneurial control in previous generations, and to extinguish customary practices that prevented the extraction of an
economic rent. These tasks were facilitated by the emergence of a
new class of professional experts: the surveyors. In the dedication to
William Cecil of *The Surveyor's Dialogue*, John Norden claimed that
"the true and exact surveying of land" was the best way to increase
the revenues of an estate.[22] The surveying of manors became increasingly popular in the late Elizabethan period. Of fifty-two surveys
surviving from prerevolutionary Essex, all but four date from after
1570.[23] There were no doubt many more surveys that have not survived, since in addition to highly skilled specialists like John Norden, Christopher Saxton, and the Walkers, there was a host of semi-
professionals. "As I have passed through London," observed a
character in John Norden's *Surveyor's Dialogue*, "I have seen many of
their bills fixed upon posts in the streets to solicit men to afford them
some services." Norden himself warned his readers against "me-
chanical men and country fellows" who set up as surveyors, even
though frequently illiterate. The popularity of Norden's own manual suggests that any competent steward felt himself obliged to acquire at least a smattering of the art in order to defend and advance
his master's interests. In addition to the surveyor and steward, there
was a host of freelance informers—"officious fellows," as the Farmer
in Norden's *Dialogue* called them, "that to procure the Lord's good
opinion will pry into men's estates."[24]

The surveyor was not popular in the countryside. The Farmer's denunciation of the Surveyor in Norden's *Dialogue* has an authentic ring:

You pry into men's titles and estates . . . whereby you bring men and matter in question oftentimes that would (as long time they had) lie without any question. And often times you are the cause that men lose their land; and sometimes they are abridged of such liberties as they have long used in manors; and customs are altered, broken, and sometimes perverted or taken away by your means: and above all, you look into the value of men's lands, whereby the lords of manors do rack their tenants to a higher rate than ever before.[25]

Norden protests that the honest and skillful surveyor would judge the claims of tenants and lords impartially, on the basis of law. But rival claims and rival conceptions of justice were in conflict throughout the long transition from feudal to modern property. It was the lord, not the tenant, who paid the surveyor's fee. The surveyor's task was to ferret out what Norden calls "abuses, encroachments, and usurpations" on the part of the tenantry, and he was likely to be offered the tenancy of any lands thus "recovered." On the other hand, the surveyor was legally liable for any mistakes that cost the lord money. There was no sanction, so far as we know, against errors to the disadvantage of the tenantry.[26]

As we have seen, the bulk of the landlord's income came from land held by leasehold, usually in fairly large blocks. By the late sixteenth century it seems that most of the agricultural land in Essex was held in this fashion. (In the village of Terling, Wrightson and Levine found that most of the land was in the hands of about ten leaseholding farmers by the early seventeenth century.)[27] Since leasehold rents could be revised when the lease expired, one of the surveyor's principal tasks was to determine the maximum rent that might reasonably be charged for a given farm. Not surprisingly, surveyors often discovered that the tenant was paying far less than the economic rent to which the lord was entitled. At Chrishall, for example, 167 acres leased for a total of £31 18s. were found to be worth £86 5s. 2d. At West Ham the surveyor estimated that 345.5 acres, which yielded the lord £25 10s. 7d., might bring in as much as £173 17s. 16d.

Leasehold rents had lagged behind the market value of land— thus affording the tenant an unearned increment—because they were frequently granted for extremely long periods, such as ninety-nine years, or the duration of three designated lives. But in the late Elizabethan period leaseholds tended to become standardized at twenty-one years—long enough to afford considerable security to the tenant while permitting more frequent adjustments. By the later seventeenth century virtually all leases were for twenty-one years or less. Of 402 leases on the Petre and Audley estates studied by K. E. Burley, only seventeen were for more than twenty-one years, while 144 were for less than sixteen.[28]

The shortening of leases allowed the law of supply and demand to drive rents upward. William Harrison observed that if a tenant failed to renew his lease at least six years before its expiration, "another man shall step in for a reversion and so defeat him outright." John Norden too spoke of the inflationary effect of competitive bidding by "rash and over-forward men," while a few years later Robert Reyce of Suffolk wrote that "this is the rule of farming at this day, where no owner can have anything, be it never so mean and small but . . . he shall have tenants enough, which will offer and give unreasonable rates for grounds."[29]

Statistical evidence on the movement of Essex rents is extremely scanty for the sixteenth and seventeenth centuries, but Felix Hull has concluded that "whenever a lease fell due after about 1580 it was usual for an increase to be made in rent." On the Petre estate a farm of 167 acres that was leased for £50 in 1579 brought in £140 in 1593. The rent of the farm of Ames in East Horndon rose even more dramatically, from £13 10s. 8d. in 1580 to £133 10s. 8d. in 1626. At Boxted, meanwhile, leasehold rents rose from 4s. per acre to 26s. between 1586 and 1612.[30] According to Lawrence Stone the average leasehold rent on the Petre estates rose from 1s. 10d. per acre in 1560 to 7s. 6d. in 1640, while total rentals on the lands of the Howard family increased from £564 to £2,451 between 1576 and 1641.[31] On the Barret estates at Belhouse Park leasehold rents rose from 2s. to 9s. an acre between 1566 and 1651.[32] In Terling, Wrightson and Levine found evidence of a substantial—perhaps as much as a fivefold—increase in rents during the reigns of Elizabeth and James.[33]

Some contemporary moralists were appalled by this enhancing of rents. To the vicar of Radwinter, William Harrison, it seemed that landlords were determined "to bring their poor tenants almost into plain servitude and misery."[34] George Gifford, the popular preacher of Maldon, observed that "the landlords set such rent of their grounds that the tenants labor and toil like horses, spend their strength and get nothing."[35] Richard Rogers, the minister of Wethersfield, complained that landlords now strove to "pill and strip bare their tenants," whereas "the predecessors of them both lived together before them in love and good will."[36]

These men were theologians, not sociologists; they had a vested interest in sin. Harrison himself elsewhere acknowledges that not all tenants were being ground down "to plain servitude and misery." In earlier generations, he recalled, farmers had lived with extreme frugality, and yet they were "scarce able to live and pay their rents . . . without selling of a cow or an horse or more, though they paid by £4 at the uttermost by the year." But now, even though the rent might have increased from £4 to £100, "yet will the farmer . . . think his gains very small toward the end of his term if he have not six or seven years' rent lying by him, therewith to purchase a new lease."[37]

There is no necessary contradiction between these remarks and the gloomier observations. The market-oriented yeoman, with over a hundred acres, could easily absorb a rent increase that might severely strain the resources of the family farmer. Many of these smaller farmers, however, held their land by customary tenure, often in the traditional medieval units of a yardland or half-yardland (about thirty and fifteen acres, respectively). Landlords had less discretion in dealing with such holdings, whose rents were fixed not by periodically renegotiated contract but by supposedly immemorial and immutable custom. On the manors studied by Felix Hull 50 percent of the tenantry held their land solely by copyhold, while another 18 percent held some copyhold land.[38] To what degree were these customary tenants shielded from the effects of inflation?

Since the rents of assize on customary land had remained fixed during more than a century of rising food prices, the gap between the lord's actual and potential revenue, as disclosed by the survey, was even wider on customary than on leasehold property. The real profit from copyhold lands came not from the rents of assize but from the entry fines, which came due when the land changed hands by sale or inheritance. At Rivers Hall in Boxted, for example, assize rents amounted to a mere £11 6s. 2d., while fines brought in £135

17s. 8d. These fines might in turn be either fixed by custom or arbitrable. In the latter case the lord might succeed in increasing them
in accordance with rising land values. In Essex, Felix Hull discovered that fines were arbitrable, and hence subject to upward revi-
sion, on at least half of twenty manors studied.[39] There were thus
two ways in which a lord might increase the return on lands subject
to copyhold arrangements: he might find a means of increasing the
amount of the entry fine, or he might discover a pretext for extin-
guishing the customary tenure entirely and let the land out by lease
at an economic rent.

William Harrison thought that both these practices were common. He wrote of "the daily oppression of copyholders" by landlords who were "daily devising new means and seeking up all the old
how to cut them shorter and shorter, doubling, trebling, and now
and then seven times increasing their fines, driving them also for
every trifle to lose and forfeit their tenures . . . to the end they may
fleece them yet more."[40]

There is little direct evidence of such activities, apart from the
Earl of Dorset's declaration in 1607 of the Crown's intention to raise
entry fines on its Essex properties.[41] But the silence of the documents
is inconclusive for two reasons. First, there are few surviving series of
manorial records yielding the same information for a given manor
over time; it is therefore impossible to determine the extent to which
fines were being raised and copyholds eliminated. Second, it may be
questioned whether the modification or destruction of traditional
tenurial arrangements is the sort of activity that lords would ever
have recorded with any precision.

What is clear is that landlords had every incentive to get rid of
small and commercially inefficient copyholders whenever they con-
veniently could. In 1589 an Essex man named Sir John Smith overheard two gentlemen joking that the recent military expedition
against Spain "would be worth unto one of them above a thousand
marks and to the other above £400 . . . by the death of so many of
their tenants that died in that journey: that the new fines for other
lives would be worth that or more."[42] There were less sanguinary
methods for eliminating copyholders, and *The Surveyor's Dialogue* is
full of them.[43] As Norden reminded his gentle readers, copyholds (or
indeed freeholds) might be forfeited if the tenant violated manorial

custom. One of the jobs of the surveyor, who in this respect resem-
bles the eighteenth-century French *feudiste,* was to establish the existence of neglected customs and identify offenders. Tenures might be
forfeited for ploughing meadow land, felling timber without authorization, or alienating or subletting a copyhold without license. (It
will be noted that these are all measures a small copyholder might
be pressed to adopt during hard times like the 1590s, when surveyors
seem to have been particularly active in Essex.[44] Norden himself,
who urged landlords to deal with their tenants in accordance with
the "law of love," acknowledged that "lords commonly know better
how to take advantage of such casualties than the tenants know how
to avoid them," and that many were "too forward in taking advantage of forfeitures upon small occasions."[45] One strongly suspects
that the "Indian summer" of the Essex manor—that revival of manorial court activity that Felix Hull has discovered in the late sixteenth century—may have had something to do with the attempt to
enforce obsolete customs and establish forfeitures. The mere failure
to attend the manorial court, for example, could entail the confisca-
tion of one's holding.[46] According to George Gifford the death of a
customary tenant provided unscrupulous landlords with an opportunity to reassert or extend seignurial rights. Such lords would
"pluck away from the widow and children that little which was left
them. If there be but a cock they will have it . . . If there be a little
commodity of house or land, what devices they have to wind it in,
and to wring it away!"[47]

Enclosure, whether of open fields under tillage or of common pasture land, was the most notorious device adopted by rationalizing
landlords to extinguish customary rights, and something must be
said of its incidence in Essex. Most of Essex had been enclosed
directly from forest before 1500, while the open fields of the northwestern corner were destined to survive into the eighteenth century.
These facts alone make it impossible to blame the encloser for the
dispossession of the small farmer; indeed, no Essex author cited enclosures among the abuses of the age. But they did occur, and they
provoked considerable local irritation. In 1563 the Privy Council
wrote to three Essex justices about "a certain disorder in Essex in the
breaking up of hedges and pales by women and boys," although
there are no further details.[48] In 1591 the poor of Colchester com-

plained against the town authorities for enclosing five hundred acres
of common surrounding the town. (The burgesses claimed to have
acted by permission of the lord, Sir Thomas Heneage, but the petitioners refused to believe "that good Sir Thomas would give such a
leave.")[49] In 1623 a scheme to enclose Tiptree Heath, the largest of
the county's unforested waste areas, produced complaints from two
hundred of the commoners.[50]

The most serious disputes, however, concerned the enclosure of
forest lands, where small-holders cherished traditional rights to set
snares, gather nuts and firewood, and pasture swine. In 1572 the enclosure of sixty-one acres in Woodford was resisted by a crowd of
three hundred, "who cast down 400 rods of hedge and ditch and
burned eight or ten loads of bushes and stakes." In a separate incident a crowd of women set upon the encloser, John Rigby, and his
workmen, "to beat them out of the woods." Rigby was injured "on
the face and on the head very sore, to the great hazard of his life."
The rioters threatened to kill both Rigby and the lord of the manor,
"although half a score of them should be hanged."[51] In 1611, 130 laborers, husbandmen, and artisans in Hatfield Broad Oak "riotously
assembled, forcibly cut, broke, and threw down 200 perches of the
hedges" around a new enclosure made by Sir Francis Barrington in
Hatfield Forest.[52] It was with such precedents in mind that Fulke
Greville in 1617 recommended that a royal survey of Waltham Forest be postponed because the inhabitants threatened rebellion in defense of their common rights.[53]

But these were the only important agrarian disorders before 1620.
The vast majority of enclosure disputes were trifling affairs, though
even small bits of pasture or right-of-way might be important to
those deprived of them. Thus, the inhabitants of Hadleigh complained in 1617 that the enclosure of half an acre of common was "a
great hindrance to the poor commoners." Most of the illegal enclosures recorded in the Quarter Sessions were in any case carried out
not by large landowners but by yeomen and husbandmen. In Upminster in 1612 it was a London scrivener who enclosed six acres of
common on Chafford Heath; in 1607 at Great Burstead the culprit
was the local rector, who had filched half an acre of common land
from his spiritual flock.[54]

There is little evidence, then, of any massive frontal assault on
customary rights and tenures in sixteenth-century Essex. But, once

again, the evidence is inconclusive. For example, 137 cases of disseisin (the wrongful seizure of land), many involving considerable violence, were presented at the Quarter Sessions between 1570 and 1610.[55] How many of the accused were resisting eviction on the basis of a more or less legitimate traditional claim to their land? In Staffordshire, it has been suggested, most disseisin cases resulted from the enclosure of common lands.[56] The impression that enclosure was a relatively minor problem in Essex might be modified if more of these cases could be reconstructed in detail.

Leaving aside the question of enclosures, many if not most of these disseisin cases must have involved a clash of real or imagined rights, as well as of economic interests. They involved, after all, a physical struggle over real estate. Assuming the relative sanity of all parties and a reasonably lawful state of society, it makes sense to assume that each contestant genuinely believed in the legitimacy of his or her case. So, when George Wheatly defended his forty-acre farm in Newport in the year 1585, with the help of some friends and "a bow and twelve shafts, a pitchfork, a pease hook . . . a piece of an old sword [and] . . . hot water cast out of the house," he must have thought he had some sort of right on his side. The same could be said of the Fryerning blacksmith who in 1583 led a crowd of sixty men and women to expel a recently introduced tenant from a messuage in Writtle. Certainly the blacksmith had substantial community support.[57]

Some later cases give us a little more to go on. In 1636 John Chawkes brought an indictment of forcible entry against his tenant, John Totman, and secured a writ of ejection from the Quarter Sessions. Totman appealed to the Earl of Warwick. Warwick appointed a board of arbitrators, which ruled in Totman's favor. They determined that Totman "had £10 worth of wrong in being thus thrown out of his house . . . violently, as if it had been a just cause that he owed rent. But we find that upon the account he owes never a penny." The arbitrators (themselves illiterate, and so presumably closer in status to Totman than to his landlord) commented that "for a poor man to be thus ruinated with his wife and eight children, we are much taken up withal." They asked relief for the family, now "harborless, waiting upon the charity of the township," and noted bitterly that the landlord, in addition to breaking his covenant, had spent £3 at the Quarter Sessions promoting "this uncharitable suit."[58]

This case reveals how much may be concealed behind the skeletal accounts of disseisin cases in the records. We know the background of Totman's case only because he somehow got the ear of the county's leading magnate. Not many tenants could count on such patronage. The rest were left to their own devices, like William Mosse of Theydon Garnon. Mosse was the tenant of a gentleman named Bailey. In 1664 Bailey found another tenant, one William Cockerton, who was willing to pay more. (Cockerton testified that, as to the rent, "because Mr. Bailey was his friend, he wholly left it to him, and was content to stand to his courtesy.") Cockerton coaxed the key to the farmhouse from one of Mosse's servants, and at Michaelmas (when rents were due and leaseholds changed hands) "did . . . carry a stool to it and there left it, being informed by his neighbors that if he did so he had thereby the actual possession of it." But a few days later Mosse returned with his servant and some friends, broke into the house, changed the lock, and refused to leave, thus disseising the new tenant.[59] Unlike Totman, Mosse was no doubt legally in the wrong—as perhaps were most of the thousand or so disseisors mentioned in the sixteenth- and seventeenth-century rolls. But what is legal may not appear legitimate to the victims of economic change.

The decennial totals of disseisin cases at the Quarter Sessions from 1570 to 1629 can be shown as follows:[60]

Decade	Number of cases
1570–1579	45
1580–1589	37
1590–1599	26
1600–1609	29
1610–1619	22
1620–1629	14

The general trend is downward, which would seem to suggest a slackening of conflict over time. But the trend admits of several interpretations. Relations between landlord and tenant may have become more harmonious, but it might also be that the smaller and uneconomic tenants had simply been thinned out, while those that remained were losing the will to resist. Tenants trying to resist or reverse an eviction were typically abetted by family and neighbors, and collective support for traditional rights probably declined along with the vitality of the manorial court.

Any conclusions on this subject must remain provisional, pending an examination of the records of the court of Star Chamber, which the Herculean labors of T. G. Barnes and his students are making feasible. Nevertheless, the evidence of the Essex county courts would suggest that Marxists, and progressive historians in general, have considerably exaggerated the role played by violence and fraud in the decline of the English peasantry. It must have been far more common, because far simpler, for lords simply to reassert control of customary land when a line of tenants died out—a process we can clearly observe in the manorial rolls of Coggeshall during the Interregnum.[61] Margaret Spufford has shown how, in several Cambridgeshire villages, the impersonal forces of the market virtually wiped out the subsistence holdings of fifteen and thirty acres. Harvest failure, particularly in the 1590s, drove the yardlander or half-yardlander ever deeper into debt for food and seed corn, until he was forced to sell his holding. The land would then be absorbed into a larger and more economically efficient unit of production.[62] There seems no reason to doubt that a similar process was at work in Essex.

It is important, however, to distinguish between the fate of copyhold tenure and the experience of the subsistence farmers who originally made up the bulk of copyholders. As Eric Kerridge has shown, we can no longer think of copyholders as constituting, in the sixteenth century, a distinct economic class.[63] Still less can we equate customary tenants with subsistence farmers of servile ancestry. While some copyholds were being quietly resumed by the lords, others were being purchased by men of substantial estates, who then sublet them to the actual farmers. In fact, such wealthy copyholders were themselves rentier landlords. Since they were fully capable of defending their interests at law, their copyholds became indistinguishable from freehold property. The persistence of customary tenure, in other words, does not imply the survival of the small peasantry who at one time held most customary land. We are gradually realizing that the whole structure of rural landholding, with its often complex hierarchy of sub- (and sub-sub-) lessees, is vastly more complicated than the familiar categories of freehold, copyhold, and leasehold can encompass.[64]

Still, the overall pattern is fairly clear: rural society was becoming polarized. Moreover, the concentration of land in the hands of larger farmers coincided with considerable population growth. The combination of these two processes made it increasingly difficult for the "vulgar and common sort"—our groups III and IV of the preceding chapter—to establish themselves on the land.

In earlier periods of demographic expansion landless families had pushed back the frontiers of cultivation, carving out homesteads from forest, heath, and marshland. The movement of internal colonization was still in progress in many parts of seventeenth-century England, as David Hey has shown in his valuable study of the Shropshire village of Myddle.[65] Even in Essex the amount of potentially fruitful wasteland, although much diminished, was by no means exhausted. Essex was "nowhere devoid of woods," wrote John Norden, and Felix Hull discovered that most manors possessed at least a few acres of woodland. Felsted, for example, had seventy-six acres, and Great Wakering and Woodham Ferrers sixty-one and fifty-eight, respectively, although none of these parishes was regarded as heavily wooded. In addition there were broad wastelands like Tiptree Common in Tendring hundred, and the heaths around Stanway, Boxted, and Danbury, not to mention the marshes along the Thames and North Sea coasts. Thousands of acres, moreover, were artificially withheld from cultivation behind the pales of the gentry's game parks.[66]

Some of this land was being improved. Crondon Park, for example, was acquired by the Petre family in 1545 and disparked for cultivation by 1556. The parklands and Chadwell and Little Thurrock were broken up for tillage on the eve of the revolution.[67] London merchants like Giles Vandeputt, a Dutch immigrant, were draining the marshes around Corringham, Mucking, and Fobbing.[68] Under the early Stuarts the Crown lent its support to plans to drain the coastal fens—for a time the great Dutch engineer Vermuyden was at work in the county—and to bring the barren expanse of Tiptree in Tendring hundred under the plough.[69]

There were also several factors retarding the extension of the arable area. The draining of the fens was a slow and immensely expensive process. The scarcity and rising price of timber encouraged the preservation of England's shrinking forests, as did the gentry's passion for the chase. It is even possible that the amount of land

withheld from cultivation by imparking increased in the late sixteenth century. John Norden's map of 1594 shows fifty-two principal parks, as against the forty-four plotted in 1576 by Christopher
Saxton.[70] The accession of an avid huntsman to the throne in 1603
must have made deer parks even more fashionable. James himself
built a new hunting lodge at Chapel Hainault in 1611 and thereafter rewarded several courtiers with licenses to enclose woodlands in
Essex for their own recreation. The Earl of Southampton was permitted in 1611 to "dispose at pleasure of woods in Essex" (as well as
in Somerset, Wiltshire, and Suffolk), while Sir Robert Wroth was li-
censed to add Benfield Wood and another three hundred acres to his
Great Park at Bardfield. In the early 1620s Sir Samuel Tryon enclosed a park at Halsted.[71]

Most important, such clearances as did occur failed to benefit the
small-holder. The new techniques employed in draining the fens required capital outlays far beyond the capacity of the peasant farmer.
Even where the new farmlands were above sea level, the movement
toward agrarian consolidation and the rise in rents put the small
farmer at a crippling disadvantage. As the steward of the Rich family informed his master, "some persons well learned in the laws"
held that entry fines on land recently granted from the waste were
arbitrable at the lord's will. It is not surprising, therefore, that the
increase in rents in the late sixteenth century was steepest on those
lands that had the lowest initial value.[72] The medieval clearances
had been encouraged by lords who were eager to increase the number of tenants bound to serve them in battle or to labor on the demesne. The new landlord was concerned merely with the size of his
rent roll, and it was the substantial tenant rather than the cottager
who could best fatten it. It was this conflict of interest that produced
the enclosure riots in Waltham Forest and the demisecular struggle
between landlords and squatters over the "improvement" of Tiptree
Heath.

In the long run, the elimination of the small-holder helped to raise
agricultural productivity, thus enabling the country to sustain population levels far higher than those that had brought disaster in the
fourteenth century. But this benign outcome was not fully apparent
until the reign of Charles II. In the shorter run, with which we are
here concerned, the cannibalization of subsistence farms interacted
with the natural population increase to swell the class of landless

wage laborers. The entire county, as Wrightson and Levine re-marked about the village of Terling, was "filling up at the bot-tom."[73]

As these landless families multiplied, they became economically superfluous. The abundance of rural laborers drove real wages down. The purchasing power of agricultural wages was 40 percent lower in 1570 than in 1450.[74] As a result, it became impossible to support a household containing young children or infirm adults on wage labor alone.

The Essex rates for 1612 set the value of a laborer's food at £9 per year. In 1599 seven "impotent" paupers in Sheering were each given a weekly allowance of 3s. 4d. "at the least," an annual sum of £8 13s. 4d. From allowances paid for the rearing of orphaned children, it would appear that the cost of feeding a young child for a year was reckoned at £5 2s.[75] According to official estimates, therefore, a laboring couple with two small children would need about £28 per year in order to feed their family adequately, and perhaps another pound or two for rent, fuel, and clothing. Now, a day laborer who succeeded in finding work for six days a week throughout the year could have earned, at the wage rates of 1611, a maximum of £14 6s. per year. His wife could bring in a few pounds spinning—perhaps even as much as £10, according to the Bocking clothiers—if she were industrious and steadily employed. That would bring their combined income to £24 6d., a good £5 short. Unless the couple could grow or catch roughly one-sixth of their food, they would need charity—or be forced to choose between hunger and crime. More-over, these calculations assume steady employment, which was hard to find in the seventeenth-century countryside.[76]

With more families dependent on declining wages, the boundary between groups III and IV, the threshold of modest economic security, was moving upward. In simpler terms, there were more and more poor people. "A great number complain of the increase of poverty," wrote William Harrison in 1577, adding that in many villages the majority of inhabitants were "very poor folks, often without all manner of occupying, sith the ground of the parish is gotten up into a few men's hands, yea sometimes into the tenure of one, two, or three, whereby the rest are compelled either to be hired servants unto the other, or else to beg their bread in misery from door to door."[77] Twelve years later George Gifford, the popular preacher of Maldon, spoke with dismay of "multitudes of poor men whose wives and children have scarce bread to put in their mouths," while his friend Richard Rogers, minister of Wethersfield in the clothing district of Hinckford hundred, puzzled over the causes of the "great beggary" he saw around him.[78]

How common was this state of affairs? As clergymen, Harrison, Gifford, and Rogers were all professional catastrophists, so to speak. But there is plenty of evidence to suggest that they were not hallucinating. In 1570, for example, the parish of Stambourne in the hundred of Hinckford declared itself unable to support its destitute inhabitants. Stambourne's plight had recently been exacerbated by the actions of one Henry Bigge of the parish of Ridgewell, just across the Colne. Bigge held six or more cottages in Stambourne, which he let to "such families as cannot elsewhere have any dwelling, but are shifted from other towns and places whenas they seem to come to that state that they must needs be chargeable to their town if they should there abide." Five years later, when the rate collectors of the half-hundred of Becontree, on London's outskirts, were ordered to account for the anticipated fiscal surplus, they replied that "there are so many poor people that there is no overplus to be spared." In the next year the parish of Henham, in the extreme northwest of Essex, sought permission to evict a poor woman and her children because the parish was already "very sore charged with poor."[79]

In 1581 Buttsbury, a village a few miles south of Chelmsford, was "charged with more poor than they can sustain." So, in the terrible decade of the 1590s, were Little Yeldham, Ardleigh, and Bocking in Hinckford hundred, Mountnessing in the hundred of Chelmsford, and Navestock in the western hundred of Ongar. Thundersley, a few miles from the Thames estuary, petitioned in 1590 that a man and his family be given a license to beg, as the town was already overburdened with paupers. In 1595 the once flourishing borough of Thaxted—as famous in the Middle Ages for its cutlery as Sheffield was later to become—reported that men and women were begging at the town's end, since "neither work nor victuals [were] provided for them unless they beg for it." In the same year the parish of West Ham, rapidly becoming a suburban slum of the expanding metropolis, claimed, no doubt with some rhetorical exaggeration, that the majority of its inhabitants were on relief.[80]

Table 6. Number of deceased described as poor in Chelmsford register, 1575–1599

Years	Total deceased	Number described as poor	Percent of total
1575–1579	240	6	2.5
1580–1584	261	19	7.3
1585–1589	314	20	6.4
1591–1594	363	25	6.9
1595–1599[a]	376	31	8.2

Source: Essex Record Office, Chelmsford, T/R 5/1/3.
[a] Three years only.

In Chelmsford the average annual number of deceased inhabitants described in the parish register as poor rose from one to ten between 1575 and 1599, as appears in Table 6. (*Poor,* of course, is a very relative term. The Chelmsford parish clerk seems to have reserved it for the utterly destitute.) By 1613 the hamlet of Moulsham in the parish of Chelmsford was "much surcharged with poor and impotent persons, and the rest of the inhabitants unable to sustain them." In 1618 the hamlet petitioned for a larger share of the relief funds collected in the parish.[81] Admittedly, these petitions come from only a handful of Essex's more than four hundred parishes, although they are geographically well distributed about the county. The petitioners, moreover, were interested parties, generally seeking to evade a fiscal responsibility imposed by the developing Poor Law. Where fuller evidence exists, however, it tends to confirm the impression of growing poverty.

Wrightson and Levine, in their work on the parish of Terling, have discovered that between 1570 and 1600 population growth "accentuated an existing tendency towards the social polarization of the village between prosperous market-oriented yeomen, farming substantial holdings, and landless cottagers and laborers, their numbers swelled by natural increase, by immigrants, and by the incorporation into the laboring population of declining small holders."[82] There is evidence of a similar process of polarization in the rural parish of Heydon, in the northwest of the county. Two informal censuses of the parish, taken in 1564 and 1625, suggest that between the two dates the number of families near or below the poverty level rose from thirteen to at least twenty-three, and probably to thirty, while the really secure households (defined as those who could be

relied on to contribute to the needs of their poorer neighbors) declined in number from nineteen to no more than twelve.[83]

Thus, in many areas at least, there was emerging a class of mar-
ginals, living at or below the level of subsistence, whose meager income had to be supplemented by private or public charity if they
were to be kept from starving and deterred from crime. This was a
proletariat in the Roman rather than the Marxist sense, superfluous
and dependent rather than productive. This dramatic expansion of
group IV was to have important consequences for groups I and II,
the local and national elites.

Landless or dwarf-holding families were unpopular with their
neighbors, since as real wages fell they were increasingly likely to
turn to crime or mendicancy. The cottager, wrote Harrison, "think-
eth himself very friendly dealt withal if he may have an acre of
ground assigned unto him whereupon to keep a cow, or wherein to
set cabbages, radishes, parsnips, carrots, melons, pompions [pump-
kins], by which he and his poor household liveth as by their principal food, sith they can do no better." Francis Bacon called cottagers
"housed beggars," and a century later—when wages had risen—
Gregory King still estimated that the expenses of the cottager's
household would regularly exceed income.[84]

Thomas Tusser gives us a vividly hostile picture of the archetypal
landless couple, Sir Hugh Make-Shift and his wife, Gillett, busily
making ends meet at their neighbors' expense:

> At noon if it bloweth, at night if it shine,
> Out trudgeth Hugh Make-Shift, with hook and with line,
> Whiles Gillett, his spouse, is a-milking thy cow,
> Sir Hugh is a rigging thy gate or thy plough . . .
>
> Some prowleth for fuel, and some away rig
> Fat goose, and the capon, duck, hen, and the pig.
> Some prowleth for acorns, to get up their swine,
> For corn and for apples, and all that is thine.

And Tusser adds, with a touch of detail too good to omit,

> Such walk with a black or a little red cur,
> That open will quickly, if anything stir;
> Then squalleth the master, or trudgeth away,
> And after dog runneth, as fast as he may.[85]

Tusser's description helps us understand why there was frequent conflict between cottagers and settled residents. "Divers quarrels and disorders" were recorded in Fordham in 1611, "great discord" in Bowers Gifford in 1617. There was similar friction reported in Tollesbury (1609), Wormingford (1612), South Ockenden (1616), Harlow (1619), and elsewhere.[86]

William Harrison described how enterprising farmers arranged for the lord of the manor to pull down the farmhouses attached to the land they had acquired, "saying that if they did let them stand, they should but toll beggars to the town, thereby to surcharge the rest of the parish."[87] Fifty years later the steward of Aveley warned manorial lords, "whatsoever they do else," to rid their lands of "inmates"—landless folk lodging with legitimate tenants. Aveley itself, he lamented, was swarming with them, "many of them being of lewd sort, as whores, scolds, lazy and idle people [who] have brought horrible and not to be named sins and wickedness into the town," along with "perpetual drunkenness, frays, and bloodsheds."[88] About the same time a royal proclamation authorized the eviction of cottagers on Tiptree Heath in the northeast of the county; they were alleged to "spend all their time in filching and stealing and other kinds of lewd and unlawful practices." In 1636 Earl Rivers was similarly vexed by the "ill-neighborhood" of cottagers who "having but small subsistence do continually commit spoils."[89]

Covenanted servants—men and women bound by yearly contracts and usually living in the home of their employers—were more comfortably housed and better fed than cottagers like Hugh and Gillett. But in most cases the price of security was celibacy, since few employers cared to retain married servants, especially with children.[90] As the labor surplus increased, moreover, servants were forced to move farther afield in search of employment, drifting on again after a few months or years when the master died or reduced his household, or when—for whatever reason—master and servant fell out. The life of semimigratory service became increasingly precarious as a man or woman's physical capacity declined. In nineteenth-century Dorset, where the old custom of hiring yearly servants at an annual fair still survived, Thomas Hardy watched an old shepherd staring vacantly at the ground, "having quite forgotten what he came for," and heard a farmer comment, "There's work in 'en still; but not so much as I want for my acreage." Hardy observed that "in youth and manhood this disappointment occurs but seldom, but at threescore and over it is frequently the lot of those who have no sons and daughters to fall back on."[91]

In Tudor-Stuart Essex men and women broke down long before threescore. The most common disability was lameness, a term that probably covered maladies as disparate as arthritis, rheumatism, rickets, and amputation. In 1575, for example, Reynold Green, "a poor fellow and very simple," was presented for living at home with his widowed mother, out of service. His neighbors testified that Green "would gladly serve others, but none will retain him because he is not able to do his work by reason of his lameness."[92] In 1601 Ann Brown of Great Burstead was "by God's visitation taken lame while in service." Since neither her master nor anyone else would retain her, she was "driven to want and misery, having no place to lodge in." In 1628 Margaret Lumley of Dengie fell "lame in her feet" while serving Goodman Acocke in the same parish. Acocke, no doubt with an eye on the rising parochial poor rates, convinced the local magistrates that Lumley had been born in Maldon, and she was accordingly whipped as a vagrant back to her supposed birthplace. On her arrival the authorities of Maldon demanded of the befuddled woman why she had falsely claimed to be a native of their town.[93]

Given the state of contemporary medical knowledge, the hostility of parish officials to infirm immigrants, and the growing competition for employment, the effects of disability, whether due to accident, disease, or simply advancing age, were devastating and irreversible. John Pirrye, for example, left his native parish of Lawford around the year 1606 "in good estate of health and body." He served in Great Bromley for five years and then in Foxall, Suffolk, for a little over two. After this he was hired, for a period of only six weeks, by a miller in Barkstead, Suffolk. When that job ended he found work building a wall for a relative in Walton, Essex, at a daily wage of 8d. By this time Pirrye was clearly having trouble finding work; his wages were 4d. a day below the statutory wage. After five weeks Pirrye broke his leg in a Sunday football game. Now "lame and impotent," he was relieved for a time by the parishioners of Walton, until they procured a warrant to return him to his birthplace.[94]

All of these cases—which could easily be multiplied—concern

agricultural workers. But journeymen in the cloth industry were exposed to similar hazards, as the trade became increasingly overcrowded and more vulnerable to fluctuations in overseas demand. John Greene was born in about 1598 at Hatfield Broad Oak and was bound apprentice to a weaver at the age of fourteen. After two years, however, his master went out of business, perhaps in consequence of the chaos caused in the cloth trade by the Cockayne project. Greene's friends apprenticed him to another weaver; he too became "poor and destitute." After a third apprenticeship Greene managed to serve out his term but lacked the capital to set up as a weaver. Instead, he became a covenanted servant with the minister of Rayleigh, where he stayed for three years. After marriage to a bricklayer's daughter, Greene moved from parish to parish for sixteen years as a journeyman weaver, during which time "he never had any settling, either by the hiring of any house or by being a covenanted servant for so much as one month together." (What became of Greene's wife during these years is unknown.) Finally, having become "utterly disenabled of . . . one of his legs," Greene petitioned the Quarter Sessions for relief, describing himself now as a simple "laborer."[95]

Tramping laborers and journeymen, living from hand to mouth, were naturally tempted to steal. Consider the case of a laborer named, aptly enough, John Bum. In 1636 Bum was working at odd jobs in Great Easton and the surrounding parishes, lodging with relatives and sleeping in employers' barns, until the day he spotted an apron lying out to dry in the sun, and made off with it. At his trial Bum could only maintain that "it was the first and should be the last that ever he did take in this kind."[96] There is no record of the judgement. One wishes him luck, belatedly.

As the researches of Joel Samaha and Jeremy Walker have abundantly shown, cases like John Bum's grew steadily more common during Elizabeth's reign. The enforced mobility of the lower classes combined with the fall in real wages to produce a stunning rise in crime, especially theft.[97] Table 7, derived from Jeremy Walker's data, reveals that felony indictments at the Essex Assizes and Quarter Sessions, even when adjusted for the erratic survival of court rolls, more than tripled between 1559 and 1603.[98] At the same time the proportion of these indictments accounted for by relatively minor economic crimes, such as larceny and the theft of small ani-

Table 7. Felony indictments at Essex Quarter Sessions and Assizes, 1559–1603

Years	Number of indictments	Number of surviving Assize files	Indictments per file	Minor crimes	
				Number	Percentage of indictments
1559–1567	272	12	23	115	42
1568–1576	398	14	28	200	50
1577–1585	594	16	37	330	56
1586–1594	827	17	49	478	58
1595–1603	829	11	75	563	68

Source: Jeremy C. M. Walker, "Crime and Capital Punishment in Elizabethan Essex" (B.A. thesis, University of Birmingham, 1971), p. 96.

mals such as sheep, pigs, and poultry, increased from 42 percent to 68 percent of the total. Table 8, from the same source, demonstrates that, as we might expect, the growth of criminality was disproportionately great at the bottom of the social scale, among those described as laborers. (The increasing percentage of laborers among the accused felons probably reflects as well the advancing proletarianization of the lower classes.)

Such an increase in criminality naturally upset the propertied and/or law-abiding members of the community. Their alarm is reflected in the increasing frequency with which juries returned verdicts of guilty. In the fifteenth century, according to M. Gollancz, suspects were acquitted "with an almost automatic regularity."[99] By the beginning of Elizabeth's reign, as appears from Table 9, the conviction rate had reached 47 percent; by the time of the queen's

Table 8. Felony suspects described as laborers, Essex Quarter Sessions, 1559–1603

Years	Total number of suspects	Laborers	
		Number	Percent
1559–1567	244	85	35
1568–1576	323	145	45
1577–1585	467	218	47
1586–1594	734	395	54
1595–1603	882	492	56

Source: Walker, "Crime and Capital Punishment in Elizabethan Essex," p. 76.

Table 9. Outcomes of felony trials (in percentages), Essex Quarter Sessions, 1559–1603

Years	Prisoners convicted	Convicted hanged	Convicted clergied	Prisoners hanged
1559–1567	47	45	32	22
1568–1576	59	52	34	31
1577–1585	61	31	47	19
1586–1594	60	33	49	20
1595–1603	68	29	55	20

Source: Walker, "Crime and Capital Punishment in Elizabethan Essex," p. 100.

death it had risen to 68 percent. Table 9 also shows, however, that while the rate of conviction rose significantly, the proportion of suspects who actually went to the gallows remained roughly constant, at about one-fifth, except during the years 1568–1576. In other words, more convicted felons were being granted clemency, usually by receiving benefit of clergy. Was this simply a legal anomaly resulting from the anachronistic survival of clerical privilege in an age of increasing lay literacy? Or was benefit of clergy merely a convenient fiction that enabled judges and justices to pardon offenders whose crimes had been motivated by genuine hardship? On the latter assumption, we might find in these figures some preliminary evidence for an ideological shift among members of the ruling class—a dawning sense that the social problems of the age required reform as well as repression.

The Elizabethan fear—and hatred—of vagabonds seems less paranoid in this context of increasing lower-class criminality. There seems no reason to challenge the contemporary perception that the number of vagrants was increasing in the sixteenth century. "So many beggars / Saw I never," lamented one poet (possibly John Skelton) as early as 1500.[100] A half-century later an Edwardian statute "Touching the Punishment of Vagabonds and Other Idle Persons" declared that beggars "do daily increase ... to very great numbers."[101] William Harrison, who claimed to base his observations on talks with the old men of his neighborhood, wrote in 1577 that the problem of vagrancy had grown more acute during the preceding thirty years. Things were now so bad, Harrison claimed, that "unless some better order is taken ... such as dwell in uplandish towns and little villages shall live in but small safety and rest."[102]

Certainly many vagabonds, especially disbanded soldiers, were desperate and often violent men, of whom peace-loving citizens were quite rightly afraid. In 1580 a band of vagrants terrorized a household in Ballingdon until the entire town, and several passing carters, were mustered to subdue them. One of the vagrants, placed in the stocks, was "very triumphant and full of mocks and lewd speeches unto every person"; another shammed madness by running naked through the town. Ten years later six vagrants claiming to be soldiers were taken in Navestock. They threatened to kill the constables who whipped them, and stole chickens under the noses of their guards. The constables reported that "the first night that they were committed, being watched all night, they would not rise in the morning until their breakfast was ready, which they had, and were conveyed to the next parish . . . from whence they would not depart until they had their dinners, unless the constables would have carried them in carts."[103] One thinks of Barnardine, the condemned prisoner in Shakespeare's *Measure for Measure*, obstinately refusing to be hanged: "I have been drinking hard all night . . . I swear I will not die today for any man's persuasion."[104]

Obviously not all vagrants were pathetic and passive victims of social change. The case of Elizabeth Mascall of West Bergholt provides a late but especially vivid illustration of flamboyant deviance. By the time her parish complained of her in 1666, Mascall had been a vagrant off and on for many years. She had lost one husband to the gallows for highway robbery but had somehow managed to find a respectable replacement, with whom, however, "she lived very lewdly and unpeaceably, often threatening to be the death of her said husband." This marital discord arose because her second husband "would not forsake his honest calling and . . . accompany her in the highway to take a purse." Since Mascall had "threatened in the night time to burn the house over his children's heads," the husband put them to board with neighbors, whereupon she threatened to burn down the neighbors' houses as well. She periodically ran off to London—especially during term time, when the law courts attracted well-heeled litigants from the provinces—and returned "with considerable sums of money, which she spent in a lewd manner." When the minister and parishioners threatened to prosecute her, she brought two of her illegitimate children into town and left them on the parish rates. "And in the meantime," the petitioners concluded, "she flourisheth in her silks and silver laces and vaunts over the said parish and threatens to burden the same with more children."[105]

The colorful literature of roguery demonstrates that respectable folk found vagabonds fascinating as well as frightening.[106] It was widely assumed that the sturdy beggars belonged to a countersociety with its own hierarchy, rituals, and argot. While authors like Robert Greene, Thomas Harman, and John Awdeley may have exaggerated the coherence of the underworld subculture, the Essex evidence suggests that something of the sort did exist. There are references to vagrants speaking "cant" or "peddlar's French," an argot that the magistrates found impenetrable.[107] The migratory underworld, moreover, had its own skilled craftsmen, who specialized in the production of counterfeit passes bearing the forged seals of local magistrates and certifying that the bearer had some legitimate reason to travel. Since discharged soldiers had a plausible excuse for being on the roads, traffic in these passes was especially brisk in Essex during the wars of the late sixteenth century. They were provided by men like Davy Bennet—a pockmarked young man who drifted about the county with a consort named Mary Phillips and their child, carrying a bag full of seals under his cloak. Bennet could forge a justice's signature and copy any seal that might be required. One satisfied customer testified that "if he but seeth it in wax, he will lay it afore him and carve it out in wood very perfectly." But Bennet had his competitors. Old Tom Whiting, for example, who was known for wearing a woolen nightcap with both flaps tied under the chin, perhaps because one of his ears had been bored for vagrancy. Wherever Whiting stopped for the night, he announced his presence to potential clients by chalking a fish (a whiting) on the outside wall.[108]

Prices for counterfeit seals varied. In 1590 a peddler named Kit Miller charged 12d. (Miller also loaned money to vagrants, who repaid him with interest "when they had gotten any cheat.") But Miller could be undersold. William Randall, the minister of Langdon Hills, forged passes in 1592 for 8d., and cheapest of all was a Dedham weaver named Thomas Elmes, whose passes could be had for a mere 2d. apiece.[109]

By the end of the sixteenth century a class of hereditary vagrants had come into being. A self-proclaimed former highwayman named Stanley observed early in James's reign that "there are thousands of these people that their place of birth is utterly unknown, and they had never any abiding place in their lives, or [were] ever retained in service, but were and are vagrants by descent."[110] Hence, thought Stanley, the statute requiring vagrants to "repair to the places where they were born or last settled" was totally unrealistic. Under the Commonwealth, R. Younge, minister of Roxwell in Essex, described this underclass as "an uncircumcised generation, unbaptized, out of the church . . . They have nothing in propriety but their licentious life and lawless condition . . . They have no particular wives, neither do they range themselves into families, but consort together as beasts."[111]

Indeed, there must have been a good deal of casual procreation along the roads, lanes, and pathways of Essex. Female vagrants were reasonably common. Of 124 vagrants presented to the Quarter Sessions between 1564 and 1572, more than a third (forty-six) were women.[112] We have already encountered Alice Thackwell, who enticed men's servants to wander with her; Elizabeth Mascall, who left her bastards to the charge of West Bergholt; and Mary Phillips, the mother of Tom Bennet's child. To these examples one might add Mary Anderson, alias "Fine Mary," apprehended in 1582 in the company of one Bartholomew Nowell (alias John Johnson); Mary, the wife of John Evans of Middlesex, who in 1616 was "taken vagrant and very suspicious with a great dog," traveling with a Surrey tinker; and the wife of John Mayfield of Marlborough, Wiltshire, who in the same year was found wandering with a petty chapman "as if she were his own wife." But these relationships were relatively conventional compared with the weird menage apprehended in 1590: a band of vagrants consisting of two men, four women, and twenty-six children. Their leader, James Simson, came from Wakefield in Yorkshire; other members of this strange family came from Lincolnshire, Cambridgeshire, and Norfolk.[113]

Most bands of vagrants were loose and impermanent alliances formed by social derelicts with virtually no prospect of rehabilitation, whose lives—as in Hobbes's state of nature—were nasty, poor, brutish, and short. These "sturdy beggars" could count themselves lucky to end in a wayside ditch rather than on the gallows. But not all wanderers were parasitic and demoralized. Occasionally one discovers apparently stable families, making their living in ways that, if not actually legal, seem to have been generally tolerated. There was the White family, for example: one man, three women, and two small children, taken as vagrants in 1639. They were allegedly from Yarmouth, but for the previous ten years had been traveling through England and Wales as "tellers of destinies." Twelve years earlier "seven lewd persons" had been apprehended for "cozening the country people of their money." The "lewd persons" were John Dawson; his wife, Frances, and sister, Ann; Robert Smith and his wife, Rose; and two apparently unrelated individuals named John Baker and Elizabeth Jackson.[114] It will be observed that these are all perfectly English names. Yet in the indictment they are described as "Egyptians"—that is, gypsies.

Families like the Whites, Dawsons, and Smiths were early representatives of a nomadic subculture that survives in the British Isles to this day.[115] Their descendants are known variously as gypsies, tinkers, or simply "the traveling people." The early evolution of this "traveling nation," as its members sometimes call it, remains obscure. What is certain is that several ethnic groups participated in its formation. This fact distinguishes the traveling people of Britain and Ireland from the more racially homogeneous gypsies of other lands.

The first gypsies arrived in England from the Continent no later than the fifteenth century, to carry on their traditional occupations of horse trading, fortunetelling, and petty theft. In 1563 they were commanded to leave the realm within six months on pain of death. But the gypsies survived in England because they performed useful services as middlemen (and magicians), and also because they looked after their own. They might steal chickens, but they did not leave bastards on the rates.

It has long been known that the gypsies in Britain, geographically cut off from their continental fellows, gradually absorbed dislocated families and individuals from the *giorgio* (nongypsy) society, such as the victims of the eighteenth-century enclosures, and members of the Scottish clans defeated in the Jacobite rebellions. The Essex materials reveal that this process of amalgamation that produced the traveling people began as early as the mid-sixteenth century. A number of native Essex men and women were indicted as "counterfeit Egyptians," for joining the gypsies and imitating them in "dress, tongue, and manner." Thus, in 1566 six Chelmsford men (designated, interestingly, as "yeomen"), together with others unknown, "feloniously consorted with forty people called Aegipciacos." There were similar cases in 1571 and 1578. In 1607 sixteen rogues in High Roothing "did counterfeit themselves, 'Jepsons.' " At Rochford four years later five laborers and five spinsters were taken "as vagabonds in the company of vagabonds called 'Egyptians' "; in the same year thefts were reported by "counterfeit Egyptians."[116] By this time it would appear that the distinction between counterfeit and authentic gypsies was becoming blurred in the minds of authorities, probably because the linguistic and racial identity of the gypsies themselves was becoming attenuated. In 1613 Joan Arrundall and Mary Lacie were arrested simply "for being gypsies," and in 1627, as noted above, seven "lewd persons" with English surnames were called Egyptians.[117]

I have found no references to Egyptians, real or bogus, after 1627. But since there are nearly fifty thousand gypsies and other travelers in the British Isles today,[118] and since they were especially numerous in Essex until well into the twentieth century,[119] they must have continued to travel the roads of the county throughout the seventeenth century, avoiding *giorgio* society except for brief business transactions, whether legal or otherwise, maintaining their own kinship ties, and occasionally incorporating a renegade from the growing class of landless poor. It is a satisfying irony, incidentally, that these despised outcasts, who seem doomed in our own time to cultural extinction, have preserved a heritage that the settled population of Britain has lost. Only among the traveling people are the ballads and folklore of preindustrial Britain still a living oral tradition. In 1964 Ewan MacColl, the great Scottish singer and folklorist, offered a Dorset gypsy called Queen Caroline Hughes £1 for each previously uncollected ballad she could sing him; by the next morning it had cost him £60.[120]

It was not only the mobile poor—the vagrants and sturdy beggars—who troubled the sleep of decent folk. The resident poor of the parish might also threaten their well-being. Hedgebreaking and petty theft were only minor irritants. The real nightmare was witchcraft. Far more disquieting than the thought of Hugh's wife, Gillett, "a-milking thy cow" was the sight of her mumbling what might be a disastrously effective curse in retaliation for a real or imagined grievance.

As Keith Thomas has shown, the persecution of alleged witches

Table 10. Indictments for witchcraft at Essex Assizes,
1560–1679

Years	Number of persons prosecuted	Number of indictments
1560–1579	52	82
1580–1599	111	195
1600–1619	44	78
1620–1639	25	35
1640–1659	63	83
1660–1679	12	14

Source: Alan Macfarlane, Witchcraft in Tudor and Stuart England: A Regional and Comparative Study (London: Routledge and Kegan Paul, 1970), p. 28.

was, in England at least, a novelty of the sixteenth century, virtually unknown in the Middle Ages.[121] (The first statute against witchcraft dates from 1542; successive acts were passed in 1563 and 1604.) Alan Macfarlane's valuable study of witchcraft in Essex, which provides the data for Table 10, has disclosed that prosecutions increased suddenly between 1580 and 1600 and gradually subsided thereafter, except for a brief but virulent outbreak of hysteria in 1645.[122]

Essex had a reputation for being especially witch ridden. In George Gifford's Dialogue Concerning Witches, published in 1593, a speaker representing popular opinion declares Essex to be "a bad county, I think one of the worst in England . . . There is scarce any town or village in all this shire but there is one or two witches at the least in it."[123] The statistical evidence would appear to bear him out. The researches of C. L. Ewen and Alan Macfarlane have disclosed 492 indictments for witchcraft in Essex between 1560 and 1680, involving 291 alleged witches. Apparently the rest of the counties on the Home Circuit—Hertfordshire, Kent, Surrey, and Sussex—managed to indict a mere 222 between them.[124]

The eruption of witch hunting in late sixteenth-century Essex must be set in the context of popular immiseration and of rising lower-class criminality in general. To be sure, the causes of what H. R. Trevor-Roper called "the European witch-craze of the sixteenth and seventeenth centuries" are complex and controversial.[125] Its intellectual and emotional basis was an intensified belief in the power and ubiquity of the Devil, a belief shared by Catholic and Protes-

tant alike. This obsession with Satan, already evident in the later
Middle Ages, was no doubt fostered by the decadence of the church
from the Great Schism down to the Reformation, and was nurtured
for another century or more by the wars of religion. The ideological
crisis, moreover, coincided with the collapse of the medieval social
order. The Prince of Darkness served as a metaphor for the destructive aspects of historical change. And if Satan was, as Luther proclaimed him, the lord of this world, then it seemed logical that he
must have servants and retainers, who had sworn him fealty in return for power. But the nature, chronology, and hence, one assumes,
the causality of witch hunting varied from country to country and
from region to region.

In England, and especially in Essex, there are strong reasons for
associating the fear of witches with the fate of Hugh and Gillet. Malevolent supernatural powers were sometimes thought to be part of
the Make-Shifts' inheritance. One of the most striking findings of
Macfarlane and Thomas is the fact that witches were almost invariably poorer than their supposed victims. Moreover, the supposed
witch was frequently thought to be retaliating for some "breach of
charity or neighborliness." The sceptic Reginald Scot described the
thought process that led to an accusation: "she was at my house of
late; she would have had a pot of milk; she departed in a chafe because she had it not; she railed; she cursed; she mumbled and whis-
pered; and finally she said she would be even with me; and soon
after my child, my cow, my sow, or my pullet died . . ."[126]

Once the belief in witchcraft had taken root, of course, accusations might arise from all sorts of interpersonal conflicts. But so far it
appears that the classic sequence was the one described by Scot. As
Thomas puts it: "the overwhelming majority of fully documented
witch cases fall into this simple pattern. The witch is sent away
empty-handed, perhaps mumbling a malediction; and in due course
something goes wrong with the household, for which she is immediately held responsible."[127]

The "bewitched," Thomas argues, were conscious of having violated traditional social obligations in denying food or drink. The accusations of witchcraft were thus provoked by their own guilty consciences. This was a period, he observes, during which the duties of
householders toward the poor were particularly ambiguous. The
poor were more numerous than ever before, yet the national Poor

Law was still in gestation. Indiscriminate begging was forbidden by the state, while the pulpit continued to urge charity toward the "deserving poor." Respectable householders resented the poor as parasites and feared them as deviants, but they also acknowledged a Christian obligation to bestow charity where the machinery of public relief was inadequate. Thomas believes that "the conflict between resentment and a sense of obligation produced the ambivalence which made it possible for men to turn begging women from the door and yet suffer torments of conscience for having done so."[128]

Thus, in 1578, when the inhabitants of Wimbish found their cows yielding blood instead of milk, their hogs, horses, and chickens dying, and their children and women growing ill, they naturally put the blame on Margery Stanton, whom they had repeatedly maltreated. Similarly, in 1582, Joan Robinson of St. Osyth, who had been denied charity, was held responsible when "a great wind nearly blew down a house, a cow could not calve, a goose deserted its nest, a mare died, a beast drowned in a ditch, a farrow of pigs died," and so forth.[129]

This combination of scapegoating and projection is psychologically plausible, and I find Thomas's argument both brilliant and, provisionally, convincing. What he understates, it seems to me, is the element of class aggression inherent in the English (or Essex) version of the witch hunt. It was generally acknowledged, as Thomas himself points out, that the poor, if unjustly treated, could call down divine wrath on their oppressors: this was the dreaded Beggar's Curse.[130] But the basis of the witch hunt was the assumption that it was not God but Satan who executed the curses of the poor. This was so even if the alleged witch had explicitly invoked the name of Jesus. Elizabeth Lewys of Waltham, for example, was accused in 1563 of saying "Christ, my Christ, if thou be a savior come down and avenge me of my enemies."[131] Thomas finds this "ironic," since, "if the curser was provoked by a genuine injury, it is hard to understand why contemporaries should have been so reluctant to see the outcome as a divine judgment."[132]

In fact, it is not hard at all, if we remember the hostility with which the growing class of landless poor was regarded. Crimes of all sorts were increasing. As the number of squatters, migrant day laborers, and petty thieves grew, indiscriminate neighborliness became obsolete. Old forms of charity were counterproductive, since, as many preachers observed, promiscuous alms giving tended to reward the shameless and aggressive rather than the docile and, hence, deserving poor. Under these circumstances, the notion that the poor could invoke divine sanctions in their defense became intolerable. If Gillett, in addition to stealing firewood and milking her neighbors' cows, was also casting spells, then she must be in league with Satan. The Beggar's Curse was diabolized; it became both a mortal sin and a capital crime to enlist supernatural aid against injustice or neglect.

The terror of witchcraft was perfectly genuine. Skepticism about the malign power of witches met ferocious resistance, as George Gifford discovered. He represents as typical the attitude of a woman who cried: "they that would not have [witches] hanged or burnt, I would they might even witch them unto Hell. If I had but one faggot in the world, I would carry it a mile upon my shoulders to burn a witch."[133] It was not, by and large, the rich who felt themselves the victims of witchcraft but rather men and women of limited means—principally yeomen, artisans, and their wives and children.[134] The economic position of such folk was often insecure during these decades of bad harvests, rising rents, falling wages, increasing crime, and recurrent plague, which is thought to have claimed over seventy thousand lives in London during Elizabeth's reign.[135] Fear of witches was a paranoid reaction to justified anxiety. Like all paranoid systems, it was an attempt to make sense of and ultimately to control a terrifying and chaotic world. Belief in witchcraft offered an explanation for unexpected calamity; witch hunting offered a means of wiping out ill luck altogether. As Gifford put it, harmless old women were put to death because the common people believed "that if there were no witches there should be no such plagues."[136]

In the late sixteenth century at least one Essex gentleman thought that the conditions described above amounted to a prerevolutionary situation. Writing to Lord Burghley, Sir John Smith argued that the growth of poverty, vagrancy, and crime "may turn this realm to great danger." As examples of the great danger he had in mind, Smith cited the slave rebellions of ancient Rome, the French Jacquerie, and the more recent peasant rebellions in Hungary and Spain.[137] It is easy enough to dismiss such fears as hysterical, since we know that even during the Civil War of the seventeenth century no English Jacquerie in fact occurred. But upper-class anxiety was justifiable, given the deterioration of popular living standards and the inadequacy of the available means of repression. In 1549 Robert Kett's rebels had seized Norwich, the nation's second city, a bare fifty miles from Colchester. As one contemporary chronicler wrote, "So hated at this time was the name of worship or gentleman, that the basest of people, burning with more than hostile hatred, desired to extinguish and utterly cut off" the aristocracy.[138]

The Norfolk Rebellion, which some Essex men were thought to have joined,[139] remained a living memory throughout the reign of Elizabeth, while rumors of insurrection and even a few abortive uprisings seemed to confirm Sir John Smith's fears. In 1566, during a period of depression in the clothing industry, one John Broke of Colchester concluded that "[the] weavers' occupation is a dead science nowadays, and it will never be better before we make a rising." A friend of Broke's named Edward White was heard to declare,

We can get no work, nor we have no money, and if we should steal we should be hanged, and if we should ask, no man would give us. But we will have a remedy one of these days, or else we will lose all, for the commons will rise: we know not how soon, for we look for it every hour. Then will up [sic] two or three thousand in Colchester and about . . . for ye shall see the hottest harvest that ever was in England.

The plan, as another Colchester weaver later confessed, was "to get a mad knave and set him on horseback, and to begin at Bocking town's end, and so to Braintree and Coggeshall, and through [Colchester] and to cry 'They are up! They are up!', and then people to get to the churches and ring awake." The rising was set for midsummer, "for that will be the best time," thought one conspirator, "for at that time began the last commotion."[140] (Was this a reference to the Norfolk Rebellion seventeen years earlier?)

The rising of 1566 was nipped in the bud, and thereafter the revival of the cloth industry, with the introduction of the New Draperies, temporarily alleviated the weavers' distress. But fears and fantasies of rebellion flared up again periodically. In the summer of 1576 rumors reached the Privy Council about plans for an insurrection in Essex by men who were in correspondence with conspirators in the north of England.[141] Seven years later an eccentric named John Tusser circulated "fanatical and false prophecies" of his own concoction, which darkly foretold that "the poor commonalty shall take the white horse for their captain and rejoice, because there shall come into England one that was dead . . . And then the laws shall turn, and then the people shall rejoice the dead man's coming, because sorrow and care shall be almost past."[142]

During the 1580s and 1590s, when bad harvests and heavy taxation produced near-famine conditions, embittered veterans and deserters brought back from the Low Countries the incendiary myth of an army of avengers. In 1581 David Brown, a husbandman of East Tilbury who thought that "it was a merry world when the service was in the Latin tongue," blamed England's international predicament on the social inequity of its legal code. The new vagrancy statutes were the reason, in Brown's view, that "we . . . have all nations in our necks, for there is no Christian prince that hath such cruel laws as to burn men through their ears as are used in this realm." Brown believed that the Earl of Westmorland, a leader of the Northern rising of 1569, was poised to invade England from Ireland with an army formed of "such men as have been burned through the ears already," and that the King of Spain had rewarded Westmorland "with a great dukedom for his good service." (Asked if he would join the invaders himself, Brown answered that "he would do the best he could.")[143]

This extraordinary fantasy of a vagrant army under Catholic commanders ready to liberate the poor of England persisted for at least a decade. In 1586 a Coggeshall laborer named William Metcalfe maintained that

the King of Spain, with the noble Earl of Westmorland, with Norton and six of his sons of noble birth, are come into England with others, and with fifteen or else twenty thousand Englishmen, whereof a great part are bored through the ears, of which the Queen hath a letter of their several names, which the King of Spain hath sent to her, and she may look on them to her shame . . . This world will be in a better case shortly.[144]

Such "revolutionary defeatism," as we should call it today, seems to have been fairly common in Essex during these years. In 1585 a Smithfield weaver declared in Pleshey that "King Philip was a father to England, and did better love an Englishman than the Queen's Majesty, for that he would give them drink and clothes."[145] The vagrants taken in Navestock in 1590 swore ("with most horrible oaths") that "if they were with the King of Spain, they should not be so used, with whom a great number of good fellows of their quality was."[146] As late as 1591 a laborer of Great Wendon named John Feltwell still hoped for a Spanish invasion to trigger a social revolution. Feltwell's analysis of the social structure was crude but forceful. He reasoned that "the Queen was but a woman, and ruled by noblemen, and the noblemen and gentlemen were all one, and the gentlemen and farmers would hold together one with another, so that poor men could get nothing among them." Hence, he was alleged to have said, "We shall never have a merry world while the Queen liveth; but [if] we had but one that would rise, I would be the next, or else I would that the Spaniards would come in that we may have some sport."[147]

The threat—or promise—of a Spanish invasion receded during the 1590s, and we hear no more expressions of revolutionary defeatism. But as the price of grain rose to unheard-of levels, there were some in Essex who were prepared to seek desperate remedies. In 1594 a Hatfield laborer named Peter Francis was heard to say, "Corn will be dear, and rather than I will starve I will be one of them that shall rise and gather a company of eight or nine score together and . . . go to fetch it out where it is to be had." When a neighbor sensibly asked what poor men could do against rich ones, Francis replied, "What can rich men do against poor men, if poor men rise and hold together?"[148] The next year, when grain prices rose even higher, a drunken smith wished to see speculating retailers "hanged at their gates." And in 1596 an Ardleigh weaver repeated the old argument that "it would never be better until men did rise and thereby seek an amendment," boasting that "he would be their captain to cut the throats of the rich churls and cornmongers, for he had served as a soldier divers times beyond the seas and could lead men." Prices abated somewhat around the turn of the century, but in 1605 the Earl of Dorset reported that once again "the poor people are ready to mutiny" over the high cost of corn.[149]

Grain riots, it has been argued, are essentially reformist rather than revolutionary (although we should not forget the role played by food prices in accelerating both the French and Russian revolutions).[150] It is true, too, that popular discontent in sixteenth-century Essex seldom led to more than a bit of seditious grumbling over a pot of "mad-dog," "dragon's milk," or some other consciousness-raising brew.[151] But the Elizabethan upper classes were edgily aware of their vulnerability, lacking both a professional police force and a standing army. And, as Sir John Smith observed of popular insurrections, "Commonly the beginnings are very small and therefore lightly regarded, but once begun, they suddenly grow great, and then they turn all to fire and blood."[152]

There was no fire and blood in Essex because no leadership was forthcoming from dissident elements in the upper class. Without such leadership no preindustrial popular movement could seriously threaten the social order. We have seen how the malcontents of the 1580s looked to King Philip of Spain and the northern earls. Ironically, the one gentleman who did try—half-heartedly—to launch a rebellion was Sir John Smith himself. Sir John had been a distinguished soldier and diplomat, but by the time he wrote his letter to Burleigh in 1589 he was ill, in debt, and emotionally unstable.[153] His private difficulties had aggravated his sensitivity to social injustice. Honest yeomen, he believed, were being sent off to be slaughtered in the Low Countries so that their landlords could jack up entry fines on their holdings.[154]

In 1588 Smith commanded the Essex troops at the Tilbury rendezvous, but his bizarre behavior on that occasion put an end to his military career. For the next six years he vegetated at his home in Little Baddow, writing eccentric pamphlets on military strategy (in which he defended the use of the longbow), begging permission to sell his manor to satisfy his creditors, and brooding on his grievances. One day in the summer of 1596, after an excess of sack had whetted his indignation, fired his public spirit, and addled his wits, he rode forth among the trained bands being mustered in the fields outside Colchester, shouting, "The common people have been oppressed and used as bondmen these thirty years; but if you will go with me I will see a reformation and you shall be used as freemen." There were traitors at court, he cried, and Burleigh himself was "a traitor of traitors." But not many were prepared to march on London behind an aging and impoverished squire, especially one who was certainly drunk and quite probably insane. A few men did step forward but withdrew when cooler heads asked them if they were eager to hang. Sir John, who had more of Don Quixote in him than of Wat Tyler or Robert Kett, was clapped briefly into the Tower but was released in less than two years. He lived on for another decade in the obscurity of Little Baddow.[155]

The leniency with which Smith was treated suggests that the council thought him a harmless crank. But as Sir John Neale observed, both the government and the aristocracy were seriously alarmed by popular disaffection during these years of conscription and near-famine.[156] Apart from the endemic nuisance of thieving cottagers and the more dangerous activities of witches and sturdy rogues, there was the frightening possibility that nostalgia for the Catholic past might induce the lower classes to remain neutral—or worse—in the event of a Spanish invasion. In this climate of unrest, men of substance came increasingly to believe that England's security and social stability required new institutions and a radical transformation of popular culture.

3 / The Crisis of Social Policy

> You have every saucy boy of ten, fourteen, or
> twenty years of age to catch up a woman and
> marry her . . . without any respect how they may
> hive together without sufficient maintenance . . .
> Then they build up a cottage, though but of
> elder poles, in the very lane end . . . , where they
> live as beggars all their life.
>
> —*Philip Stubbes, in* The Anatomy of Abuses, *1583*

Rhetorical promiscuity may have rendered the word *crisis* all but useless. Nevertheless, it is hard to describe English society in the 1590s without it. There was more to this crisis than inflation, bad harvests, war with Spain, and apprehensive impatience for the Queen's demise. I intend the word in a strict sense—not as a vague synonym for tension or hubbub but to denote a phase of uncertainty leading to a decisive change. The crisis that culminated in the 1590s, brought to a peak by the conjuncture of climatic disaster and military expenditure, left social perceptions and public policy decisively altered.

From the Black Death until well into the reign of Elizabeth, the English propertied classes felt vexed by the scarcity and high cost of labor. Much of the social legislation of the latter Middle Ages was designed to deal with the problem. The Statute of Artificers of 1563 was merely the latest and most comprehensive in a long series of statutes designed to maintain a cheap and abundant supply of labor.[1] It sought to repress insubordinate workers, like the two men of Barking who in 1556 refused to work "except at unreasonable wages," and who "attempted to persuade other men's servants to do the like."[2] The statute was also aimed against employers who broke ranks, ignoring the obligations of class solidarity, and paid wages in excess of the legally stipulated maxima. Twenty-seven such employers were presented at the Essex Quarter Sessions in 1572 alone.[3]

Early Elizabethan law did more than forbid idleness and fix

64

wages. It also required all unmarried individuals whose parents were worth less than £40 to enter convenanted service—that is, to bind themselves by contract to an employer for a fixed period, generally a year. In the language of the day, unmarried men and women were considered "masterless," and hence subject to the vagrancy laws if they worked "at their own hand," doing casual labor for various employers. They had to "get themselves a service" or risk prosecution under the vagrancy laws.

The multiplication of landless families solved the problem of labor shortage. As labor scarcity gave way to labor glut, it was no longer necessary to restrain employers from excessive generosity. I have found no prosecutions in Essex for giving excessive wages after 1580. As more and more families became dependent on wage earning, there was less need to force young men and women into yearly service in order to ensure a steady supply of labor. Between 1571 and 1580, 663 individuals were presented at the Quarter Sessions for living out of service, while in the following decade there were only 108. In the years of depression, from 1591 to 1600, there were a mere twenty-three. The number rose again to 124 in the prosperous 1600s but fell back to forty-seven between 1611 and 1620. Between 1621 and 1650 there were only twenty cases in all.[4]

Moreover, a new rationale began to be offered for such presentments as continued to be made for living out of service. It was alleged that unmarried folk who worked at their own hand in industry or agriculture competed unfairly for local jobs with married laborers who had dependents to maintain.[5] Thus, a measure designed originally to deal with the scarcity of labor became a means of fairly allocating scarce employment. In 1603 the vestry of Great Easton went so far as to forbid local employers to "set strangers on work in husbandry so long as any of the laborers of this parish can and will do the same work." Similarly, no one was to employ an unmarried tailor if a married one were available.[6]

The old social policy had been a response to the late medieval decline in population. But during the reign of Elizabeth the notion gained ground that England was becoming overpopulated. William Harrison still clung to the older view, but he was on the defensive. Most of his neighbors, he tells us, had already adopted what would later be called a Malthusian position, blaming "the great increase of poverty" on the "superfluous augmentation of mankind."[7] Thomas

Smith, another Essex man (and the son of Sir Thomas), used the argument that "England was never . . . fuller of people than it is at this day" in defense of his ill-fated colonizing venture in Ireland.[8] Upper-class indignation over the affluence of the lower orders gradually gave way to alarm at their poverty, and at the social unrest that poverty might produce.

The English Poor Law, which achieved maturity with the codifications of 1597 and 1601, was the great creative response of the Tudor upper classes to the problem. (One of its chief architects, Sir Robert Wroth, was an Essex man, though he sat for Middlesex. It is worth observing, without impugning Wroth's civic zeal, that his Great Bardfield estates had been heavily poached in the 1580s.)[9] The Poor Law prescribed a threefold strategy for alleviating distress and imposing labor discipline. The lazy and insubordinate were to be punished; the involuntarily idle were to be set to work on raw materials supplied by the parish; and the young and infirm were to be put on the dole.[10]

The system necessitated the reform and extension of local institutions. In April 1598 the Essex justices, meeting at Chelmsford, issued a series of orders for the relief of the poor. All parishes that had not already done so were instructed to choose overseers of the poor from among "the most discreet and principal persons" and to report on the stocks available for "setting the poor on work." A county House of Correction, for the rehabilitation through penal labor of vagabonds, idlers, and unwed mothers, was to be established at Coggeshall; twenty local Houses of Correction were to be distributed about the country. A county treasurer was appointed to collect 1½d. per week from each parish for the maintenance of these institutions. At the same time the justices enunciated the responsibility of the lineage for the relief of its own members: "the great-grandfathers, grandfathers, fathers [sic], and son upward and downward in lineal descent . . . shall relieve one another as occasion shall require." (Note that *fathers* appears in the plural. In contemporary usage *father* could mean "father-in-law.")[11]

The following year the justices amplified this order to require overseers to keep accurate records and to "set their hands to it, and the year and the day of the making of them."[12] Surviving documents give us only a glimpse of the development of the new institutions at the parish level, but they suggest that even before the order of

Table 11. Surviving accounts of Essex poor rates, 1560–1619

Decade	Number of parishes for which rates survived in that decade	Number of annual rates recorded	Average annual rates recorded per parish
1560–1569	1	4	4
1570–1579	2	5	2.5
1580–1589	7	15	2.1
1590–1599	8	23	2.9
1600–1609	8	31	3.9
1610–1619	12	31	4.3

Source: Transcripts, furnished by W. K. Jordan, of poor rate accounts in the Essex Record Office, Chelmsford.

1598–99, rates were being levied more frequently and were being more carefully recorded. Table 11 shows the density of parish poor rates—the average annual entries per parish—for the years 1560–1619. Arguments based on mere documentary survival are always dubious, but the table suggests that the implementation of the poor law was a very gradual process.[13] In 1606, for example, the town of Ashdon resolved to begin keeping full accounts of parochial expenditures, acknowledging that "heretofore great suspicion was grown among some of the parishioners . . . of the honest and just dealings of such officers as were chosen." Braintree made a similar decision in 1630, Woodford not until 1657.[14]

Sparse as they are, the records are sufficient to illustrate the complexity of the subject and to inhibit rash generalization. There was great variation between parishes, and from one year to the next within the same parish. The most informative early records—it is impossible to say how typical they may have been—come from the parishes of Latton, Royden, and Sheering in Harlow hundred, on the western border of the county. As may be seen from Table 12 the number of poor in 1598–1599 amounted to 20.4 percent of the population recorded in 1670.[15]

It is not very precise, however, simply to describe someone as receiving poor relief. An individual might receive anything from a few pence to several pounds in the course of a year. In Latton and Sheering weekly allowances ranged from 4d. to 3s. 4d., and people not in receipt of regular alms might receive casual disbursements in times of sickness or other emergency. In the rare cases where rates

Table 12. Number of poor in Harlow hundred, 1598-99, based on adjusted 1670 population

Parish	Aged and orphans	Laboring families	Total poor	Adjusted 1670 population[a]	Poor as percent of adjusted 1670 population
Latton	5	39	44	233	18.9
Royden	12	38	50	312	16.0
Sheering	10	50	60	211	28.4
Total	27	127	154	756	20.4

Source: Essex Record Offices, Chelmsford, D/DBa/08/1,2,4; Q/R Th 5.
[a] A multiplier of 4.4 was used to convert households to individuals.

survive from successive years, one finds startling fluctuations in the amounts assigned to the same individual from year to year. We are unlikely at this late date to learn the circumstances. Moreover, the poor of many parishes received alms from the endowed private charities, like those so carefully studied (though not, alas, for Essex) by W. K. Jordan.[16] In the more fortunate towns private charities afforded a significant supplement to public funds. The charities of Coggeshall yielded £43 during the 1630s, about one-third the average annual poor rate. The unusually well endowed town of Thaxted, with £25 annual income, seems to have been able to dispense with poor rates altogether in the 1620s, although there had been earlier complaints of public begging in the streets.[17]

Finally, not all relief was monetary. Parishes also provided the poor with firewood and, in times of dearth, purchased grain for sale to residents at controlled prices. From a modern point of view probably the most interesting aspect of the Elizabethan Poor Law is the requirement that parishes "set the poor on work" by supplying them with tools and stocks of raw material such as wool, flax, or hemp. The evidence is too skimpy to permit a determination of how widely this attractive policy was actually implemented, but a number of parishes at least made an effort. In 1598 Royden reported that it had raised a stock of £7 10s. with which to employ the poor. In the same year the parish of Harlow provided spinning wheels, as Braintree was to do during the 1620s. Often, however, it would appear that parishes found it simpler to arrange work for the able-bodied poor with private employers. Thus, in 1598 the overseers of Sheering reported that a stock of five or six pounds would be necessary to employ all their poor, but that they might equally well be "set awork by the parishioners as herebefore they have done."[18]

Merely "setting the poor on work," however, could not eradicate poverty. Even a fully employed laboring couple could not support two small children on their wages alone. According to the overseers of Latton and Sheering, the forty-five able-bodied adult paupers in these two parishes were all employed. Their problem was that they could earn too little by their labor to support, without alms, the fifty-four children with which they were collectively burdened.[19]

Thomas Tusser had warned his yeomen readers against immoderate procreation: "the child at nurse" would "rob the purse."[20] The danger increased as income fell. The London Puritan Philip Stubbes, quoted in the epigraph to this chapter, argued that the poor brought poverty on themselves by imprudent marriage. I myself have some doubts about those saucy boys of ten to whom he refers. But though Stubbes's demographics are a bit suspect, his general attitude was not eccentric.

As early as 1573 an anonymous commentator urged that apprenticeship regulations be more rigorously enforced so as to prevent the economic ruin of young men through early and improvident marriages.[21] Thirty years later a series of ordinances concerning the Wiltshire clothing industry included the provisions that "no apprentice shall come forth of his covenant of apprenticeship before he be four and twenty years of age, to avoid young marriages and the increase of poor people."[22] Enclosers of common lands, Harrison tells us, justified their behavior with the argument that "we have already too great store of people in England, and . . . youth by marrying too soon do nothing to profit the country but fill it full of beggars." Abundant common lands, it was widely agreed, encouraged the poor to multiply.[23]

In 1589 an act was passed forbidding the erection of cottages with less than four acres of associated land.[24] Some historians have seen in this act a paternalistic concern for the small farmer—an attempt to retard rural proletarianization—and some M.P.s may have supported the measure in this spirit. But the law made no alternative provision for those who lacked access to four or more acres, and indeed it explicitly forbade landless families to seek refuge with other families by stipulating that "there shall not be any inmate or more families or households than one, dwelling . . . in any one cottage."

This act of 1589, which remained on the statute books until the reign of George III, marked an important reversal of social policy. As late as 1550 an act facilitating the development of commons and wastes specifically provided for the preservation of cottages with less than three acres, on the grounds that they were both profitable to the landlord and socially harmless.[25] Because of its ultimate failure to check the growth of population, the act against cottages has received less attention than it deserves. Laws that cannot be enforced may reveal a dissonance between norms and realities: they may be symptoms of social disequilibrium. More to the immediate point, the law *was* enforced—selectively—for nearly a hundred years, which inflicted a great deal of hardship and anxiety on those whom their betters thought superfluous. Petitions to the Quarter Sessions during the first years of the law's existence give some idea of its impact. A petition of 1589, for example, states that Henry Witham of High Ongar "hath lived painfully many years together and by his painstaking in husbandry hath gotten a small sum of money to purchase for him and his poor wife . . . certain timber to build him a poor cottage upon an acre of freehold land in High Ongar, intending to leave it to his wife and daughter."[26] Witham had heard of the new law while putting up the frame of his cottage; so had Josias Protway of Rayne, who had bought a small plot of ground with the aid of his friends.[27] The next year Leonard Nightingale begged permission to remain in the cabin of "scratches" that he had built for himself, his wife, and five children. He had saved for years to buy the land and timber.[28] In 1592 John Weaver, a laborer of Danbury, who had hired an outbuilding on a farm and fitted it with a wooden chimney, sought to justify himself by "lamentably complaining that houses within the said parish are grown to such excessive rent that he, having a wife and poor children, is not able by his labor both to sustain them and also to pay such a rent."[29]

Between 1590 and 1601 petitions to erect cottages or convert barns into dwellings were frequently granted because there was either no housing at all in the parish or none that a poor man could afford.[30] In 1625 John Godfrey of Manudon declared that he had been "enforced, with the good help of his friends, to buy a little patch of ground whereupon stood an old piece of a small barn and to convert it into a cottage." He had been unable to remain in the house he had previously rented; there were no other houses vacant in Manudon; and Godfrey and his family had been refused admission into neighboring parishes. A group of Manudon residents, headed by the lord of the manor, supported Godfrey.[31] But such petitions are very rare after 1600: the case of John Godfrey is, so far as I know, the last of its kind. After 1601, as the following list demonstrates, presentments of cottagers and inmates at Essex Quarter Sessions rose sharply.[32]

Decade	Presentments
1581–1590	3
1591–1600	3
1601–1610	60
1611–1620	103
1621–1630	216

Hostility to undesirable immigrants was nothing new. The town of Aveley had been trying to get rid of troublesome inmates since the reign of Henry VIII.[33] With the growth of an unwanted proletariat and the development of parochial poor relief, local officials became increasingly anxious to exclude, or if necessary to expel, folk liable to be chargeable on the poor rates. Thus, in 1585 the "ancient inhabitants" of Dedham resolved that "none be suffered to remain in the town being neither a householder nor retained of any."[34] The law against cottages gave such policies additional legal sanction. The campaign against Hugh and Gillett was thus more intense than the Quarter Sessions records alone would suggest. Parish vestries were usually quite competent to get rid of cottagers and inmates on their own; only the most troublesome cases had to be brought before the justices of the peace. No doubt thousands of cottagers were tolerated, especially where their labor was in demand, but they lived in a state of suspended outlawry.

In Great Easton in 1603 the first of a series of orders "for the better relief of the poor" was that "no man shall receive into any tenement he hath to let any person out of another parish, without the consent of the overseers and four chief inhabitants" and that "none shall receive an inmate to dwell in one tenement with him."[35] In 1619 the Braintree vestry resolved that "no strangers nor outwellers" were to be admitted into the town without their approval, and one of their first acts was to petition the Quarter Sessions for the suppression of several "new erected houses in Coxall Lane," some of which had been inhabited for several years.[36] In November 1619 "the cottagers came to the townsmen to entreat favor of them": denied. The price of liberty, however, is eternal vigilance. In November of 1622 the vestry ordered a survey taken of journeymen living in Braintree without authorization. Sixteen were discovered and presumably expelled. Two years later another survey revealed still more illicit immigrants. Such matters occupied much of the vestry's time for the next thirty years.[37]

It was the same in Finchingfield. In 1626 the vestry's constitution declared that "for the preventing of more charges of poor no man shall let a cottage to any of another town's." The vestrymen inaugurated their new regime by delegating two of their number to "talk with Goodman How about security to the town to discharge the town of Francis Benson. If he will not, then they to deal with Nathaniel Waits [presumably an overseer or constable] about removing him."[38] Similar action was taken somewhat later in Woodford, where the chief inhabitants ruled in 1657 that "no owner shall admit any servant into any cottage till he give security to the parish that his tenant shall not by himself or his [dependents] bear any charges to the parish." The constables were to give "speedy notice to the vestry upon the entry of any new tenants into the parish."[39]

It was not only pauper families who encountered hostility but anyone who might become chargeable in the future. Given the physical and economic hazards of life in Tudor-Stuart England, this was a large category. In 1593 Henry White was evicted from a house in Stondon that he had occupied for two years. Before that he had lived for three years in Kelvedon, where his children had been born; yet neither parish would allow him to rent a house, though he had the money in hand. In the same year John Harrys complained that the parish of Fryerning, where he had spent the past year, would allow him to remain no longer because of the danger that his dependents might claim relief, even though Harrys had offered to post "sufficient bond for their security." Fryerning insisted that Harrys and his family return to their former residence of Little Baddow. But that parish rejected them as well, although once again Harrys offered to post bond against burdening the parish rates. Harrys was reduced to begging the Quarter Sessions "that I may have abiding or dwelling amongst them for my money, and if any of them can make objection against me for my evil behavior . . . I am content to yield to law if I have offended."[40]

When the Braintree vestry determined in 1619 that "John Haddaway, having left his wife and children in Sandwich, Kent, shall be sent home to his wife and children," they were undoubtedly less concerned with the integrity of the Haddaway family than with the danger that John's dependents might follow him to Braintree if he succeeded in establishing himself as a resident. In the same spirit three years later they expelled "one Richard, a married man coming from Chelmsford, that might prove chargeable." In 1626 Finchingfield denied settlement to any "new married couples not born in the town." Presumably this meant that both partners had to be natives—a means of enforcing parochial endogamy. The parish of Newport tried to maintain a similar policy. In 1613, Nicholas Haggas, a husbandman from Widdington, married a Newport girl. He was "admonished to depart . . . or else secure the town from future charges." Haggas prevaricated, promised to leave, but furtively erected a cottage in Newport. As luck would have it his wife—to the horror of the overseers—was delivered of twins, "very likely to surcharge the town." There is no suggestion that the Haggas family had yet required any relief.[41]

Settlement restrictions prevented friends and relatives from supporting each other in times of distress. In Langham in 1601 a poor man named William Profytt had obtained a license to keep an alehouse, with the support of "some of the meaner sort," but also of several parish notables. But when Profytt and his wife, enjoying their new economic security, took in his wife's son and his wife, "being a young woman" (that is, fertile), then the "chief and better-minded neighbors" had Profytt's license rescinded. At Wethersfield in 1631 Thomas Hills was prosecuted for lodging his brother and sister-in-law, natives of Ashen. At the same time there was a family of cottagers named Lacie in the town. Edward Lacie, senior, was cited for harboring his married daughter and, even worse, permitting her husband to visit her. Meanwhile, Edward Lacie, junior, had been allowed, because of his poverty, to build a cottage for himself and his wife. But he was presented before the Quarter Sessions when his wife's sister, "suspected to be with child," came from High Easter to stay with them. Lacie had refused to turn her out, "being thereof often admonished."[42]

Writing after the Restoration, Sir William Coventry observed that the laws against cottaging and inmates, and the exclusion of settlers likely to be chargeable to the parish, prevented many poor people from marrying at all.[43] This distressed him, since he believed that England was once again suffering from a shortage of labor. But it would not have distressed the men who framed and enforced that policy a half-century earlier; indeed, it was precisely their intent to keep the tribe of Sir Hugh Make-Shift from multiplying.

Those who were not deterred from marrying by the difficulty of finding a settlement might be subjected to more direct pressures. In the sixteenth and seventeenth centuries couples could marry only after purchasing a license or by publishing banns. Virtually none of the extant marriage licenses pertain to laborers, perhaps because even the modest fee imposed a hardship.[44] The reading of banns, however, gave parishioners a de facto veto power over the proposed union. In asking the banns of a poor couple in 1636, the rector of North Ockenden "signified to the parish that they would marry and go begging together," and invited objections. (This was a bit too clumsy, and it landed the Reverend William Jackson in the Archdeacon's Court.)[45]

Parishes sometimes prevented the marriage of poor couples even after a child had been conceived. In 1607 Robert Johnson confessed to having fathered a bastard by the woman with whom he had been living; in his defense he maintained that "he would have married her if the inhabitants would have suffered him." The Finchingfield vestry ruled in 1628 that "if William Byfleet shall marry Susan Crosley contrary to the mind of the townsmen . . . his collection shall be detained."[46] It is impossible to determine how often this sort of thing happened, but in 1674 in Carew Reynel, who agreed with Coventry that England needed more people, thought it "an ill custom in many country parishes, where they, as much as they can, hinder poor people from marrying."[47]

So one may well believe R. Younge of Roxwell when he tells us, in *The Poore's Advocate,* that the lower classes often married and divorced themselves "without minister or magistrate."[48] It is reasonable, too, to connect these new restrictions upon lower-class marriage with the sharp rise in illegitimacy discovered in late sixteenth-century Essex by Wrightson and Levine. They argue that economic hardship during these decades disrupted relationships that would normally have ended in marriage.[49] But parochial policy must have contributed to the same result. We have seen how the parish of Finchingfield sought to prevent William Byfleet from marrying Susan Crosley. Since the girl was sent to the House of Correction, there is a good chance that she was already pregnant, and that the action of the vestry prevented the couple from legitimizing their offspring.

Whatever the cause of the rise in illegitimacy, unwed mothers were exceedingly unpopular with parish officials, and no doubt with most rate payers as well. Parishes had the responsibility for rearing orphaned or abandoned children born within their boundaries and, in principle at least, for placing them out as apprentices when they became old enough to work. This could be expensive. In 1599 the parish of Sheering provided for the five orphaned children of Matthew Bennet, a native of the parish, as follows: 2s. per week and £5 2s. in clothing for George and Bridget Bennet; £3 apiece to bind Amy and Catherine Bennet as apprentices, probably as domestic servants; and £2, purpose unspecified, for William Bennet. The total expenditure on the Bennet children was thus £17 6s. It was bad enough when the children were legitimate offspring of parish residents. But in the same year Sheering had to lay out £2 16s. 8d. for "the setting forth of Anteny Say, born within this parish of a walking person and placed apprentice with a shoemaker."[50] Parish officials naturally did their best to see that such children were born elsewhere. In 1619 the Braintree vestry investigated rumors of "a wench entertained at John Beckwith's dwelling on Cursing Green that is supposed to have a great belly."[51] In 1629, when an unmarried pregnant girl took refuge with her mother in Paglesham, a local overseer threatened to "set the house on fire over her head." The threat worked: the girl bore her child in a barn in the neighboring parish of Great Stambridge. Ten years later a serving girl in Epping, dismissed because of her pregnancy, was forced to sleep in the streets because the authorities refused to let her lodge in the town.[52]

Given the hostility of rate payers to "great bellied wenches," it is

Table 13. Increase in baptisms and burials in Essex parishes, 1560–1639

Parish	Rural or urban	Surplus of baptisms over burials per decade 1560–1599	Increase of baptisms per decade 1600–1639, over 1560–1599	Increase of burials per decade 1600–1639, over 1560–1599	Surplus of baptisms over burials per decade 1600–1639
Doddinghurst	rural	+40.75	7.00	31.00	−24.75
Coggeshall	urban	+182.00	501.50	341.00	+160.50
Chelmsford	urban	−1.00	122.25	144.75	−22.25
Gt. Waltham	rural	+118.00	14.75	23.50	−8.75
Black Notley	rural	+36.70	26.50	36.70	−10.20
Ingatestone	rural	+7.50	22.00	48.50	−26.50
Dengie	rural	−6.50	−3.00	2.50	−5.50
Barnston	rural	+22.75	17.50	15.75	+2.75
Earls Colne	rural	+127.75	68.00	67.75	+0.25
Chigwell	rural	+40.00	12.50	0.75	−11.25
Lt. Chesterford	rural	+24.25	1.50	10.00	−8.50

Source: Essex Record Office, Chelmsford, parish registers.

not surprising to find the treatment of sexual offenders becoming more severe. Before 1580 the only punishment for offenders—at least if they were willing to support the child—was a few hours in the stocks.[53] Then, in 1588, the Quarter Sessions rolls record the first case of an unwed mother being whipped at the cart's tail, although the strokes were to be "moderately given."[54] After 1600 the sentences grew harsher: women were to be whipped until their backs were bloody.[55] After 1610 they were also sent to the House of Correction for a year.[56] It could have been worse: Philip Stubbes thought that capital punishment of fornicators would help rid the land of beggars.[57]

If the parishes that appear in Table 13 are at all representative, it would appear that the combination of economic and legal disadvantages imposed on the lower classes substantially retarded the growth of population in the smaller, more purely agricultural parishes, where the demand for labor was presumably lowest. The table gives the average surplus of baptisms over burials per decade between 1560 and 1599, the increase in the decennnial average of baptisms and burials between the periods 1560–1599 and 1600–1639. Had the individuals represented by the surplus of baptisms over burials between 1560 and 1599 succeeded in establishing households and reproducing themselves in their native parishes, we should expect to find an increase in the number of baptisms during the period 1600–1639 corresponding to the surplus surviving from the previous forty years. But as Table 13 demonstrates, this was not generally the case.

Like any figures derived from parochial records, these have to be handled very gingerly. Registers were erratically kept. The light they cast on past population trends is at-best an eerie flicker. The arrival or departure of an especially scrupulous clerk is apt to produce a mirage, vivid but insubstantial, of astounding demographic change. Some of the wild variations over time and between parishes in the table are baffling and suspect. But, such as they are, the figures suggest several observations. First, there is the overall impression of marked slowing of population growth. Not one of the nine parishes that produced a surplus of baptisms over burials between 1560 and 1599 maintained that surplus during the next forty years. (Of the two parishes with baptismal deficits in the earlier period, Chelmsford experienced a further decline of baptisms relative to burials, while in Dengie the deficit diminished slightly.) In fact, only three of these parishes seem to have experienced any natural growth at all in the early seventeenth century; and in two parishes, Barnston and Earls Colne, that growth was negligible.

The credibility of these figures is threatened by the possibility that burials were underregistered in the sixteenth century and more adequately recorded after 1600, though I have no reason to believe this was the case. But whatever their absolute value, the figures are surely indicative of differential population patterns. In seven of the eight rural parishes that produced a baptismal surplus in the sixteenth century, that surplus of survivors failed to reproduce itself fully in the next forty years. Unless these survivors emigrated, one would anticipate an increase in the number of burials in subsequent decades corresponding to the original baptismal surplus—although an increase in burials could also result from other causes, such as a higher mortality rate or net immigration. In Black Notley and Ingatestone, as it happens, the increase in burials did equal or surpass the number of surplus baptisms. But in Barnston, Little Chesterford, Chigwell, Doddinghurst, Earls Colne, and Great Waltham, the initial surplus failed to produce a corresponding increase in either baptisms or burials in the early seventeenth century. A dramatic extension of life expectancy might account for this phenomenon, but the scholarly consensus is that the average lifespan was, if anything, decreasing during the years in question. So we are left with the strong impression that many of these surplus survivors were moving elsewhere. Some emigrants were no doubt lured by brighter prospects from relatively comfortable homes. But one suspects the majority were people like Gillet and Hugh, driven out by economic necessity or the force of the law.

At the same time, it would appear that population continued to increase in urban areas, where there was greater demand for labor—notably in the cloth industry—and where laws against taking of inmates were harder to enforce. Thousands must have found their way southward to the metropolis, crowding into the shabbier back lanes of the City and into the liberties sprawling beyond the City walls. But our table of parish registers suggests that there were areas of net immigration within the county as well. One such region must have been the unhealthy but fertile and thinly settled marshlands along the North Sea coast. How else—assuming a rough stability of birth and death rates—can we account for the fact that burials in Dengie increased in the seventeenth century despite a negative balance of baptisms to burials in the sixteenth? As one might expect, however, it was the relatively urban parishes that were growing most rapidly. Inns and victualing houses proliferated in the expanding market town of Chelmsford, providing work for hostlers, tapsters, badgers, and petty thieves. The apparent growth of the smaller parish of Ingatestone is somewhat puzzling but may be due to its role as a minor marketing center astride the London-Chelmsford-Colchester road.

The figures from Coggeshall suggest that growth was most rapid in the clothing towns of the north. It seems reasonable to assume that Coggeshall was typical of nearby towns like Braintree, Bocking, Halsted, and Witham. Certainly, Colchester—by national standards the only real urban center in the county—was agreed to be expanding rapidly. In 1632 a witness in the Court of Exchequer testified that the population had tripled since the accession of James, while another, an alderman, maintained the number of inhabitants had increased by ten thousand.[58]

The alderman's estimate was almost certainly exaggerated, but there can be no doubt that Essex was experiencing considerable ur-

banization in the early seventeenth century, as rural immigrants
came to town in search of opportunity at best, or obscurity at worst.
In a preindustrial economy, however, the urban demand for labor
was relatively inelastic. As a result, the problem of poverty was displaced rather than resolved. We have noted the evidence of increasing destitution in and around Chelmsford, and while there was more
demand for labor in the clothing towns, they too were vexed by the
influx of potential paupers. In 1622 the town corporation of Colchester claimed that unregulated immigration from the surrounding
countryside was "the principal cause of the great poverty within this
town."[59] This transfer of population to the clothing areas was of
enormous consequence. The social stability of the county came increasingly to depend on the precarious and fluctuating fortunes of
the cloth trade.

Alarm at the growth of poverty was one cause of the movement
for moral reform that gained momentum in the late sixteenth century and that is generally associated with the religious tendency
known as puritanism. My own view of the meaning of puritanism
and of its relation to the social changes I have been describing will
become clear, I trust, in subsequent chapters. Here I wish to make
only two points: first, that there were compelling secular reasons for
regarding certain behaviors as vices and seeking to eradicate them;
and second, that any such campaign would necessarily have religious implications.

The vices that were most bitterly denounced from the pulpit and
on the floor of the House of Commons during the late sixteenth century were those that caused poverty: avarice and oppression on the
part of the propertied; envy, sloth, and sensuality on the part of the
poor. If poverty were to be abolished or sensibly reduced, what was
needed was what contemporaries called a "reformation of manners," and what I should term a culture of discipline.

This preoccupation with the moral causes of poverty helps explain the repeated efforts made in Parliament between 1576 and
1628 to outlaw drunkenness, illicit sexuality, blasphemy, and even
"excess in apparel."[60] Drunkenness, it was plausibly argued, led to
sloth and dishonesty; fornication left bastards on the poor rates.
Blasphemy brought bad luck—both to the blasphemer and the community that tolerated it—and one may assume it was highly corre-

lated with other undesirable social traits. Excess of apparel was a symptom of the competition for status. Conspicuous consumption depleted the charitable resources of the well-to-do and inspired humbler folk with self-destructive envy.[61]

Most of these bills failed to become law, perhaps, as Joan Kent has suggested in her valuable study, because members of Parliament feared that governmental interference with personal behavior might lead to restraints upon their own freedom.[62] But the flurry of private bills against immiserating vices reflected a strong current of propertied opinion, and one that was particularly strong in Essex. Among the most active supporters of the legislation were such Essex members as Sir Francis Barrington, Sir Robert Wroth, and Sir William Wiseman. These reformers did succeed in significantly tightening the legal restrictions on sex and alcohol. The new laws gave added impetus to the vigorous struggle for moral reform being waged at the local level, through the medium of the Quarter Sessions.

We have already noted the new severity with which fornication was treated. After sexual indulgence, and closely related to it, the most socially obnoxious vice was intoxication. The regulation or elimination of alehouses, those focal points of popular culture, was a central objective of reformers. Thus, in 1600 the Assize judges of the county urged the reduction of the "great number of alehouses, being the cause of great misdemeanours and outrages daily committed." Between 1590 and 1603 petitions for the suppression of alehouses reached the Quarter Sessions from at least nineteen parishes. The disorderly alehouse was a nuisance for several reasons. First, it was frequented by unsavory characters—rogues, cutpurses, fences, and killers. In 1586, for example, an alehouse was accused of entertaining a dozen vagabonds, "who being drunken fell together by the ears and brake the peace." Similar complaints were made about the inns along the approaches to London. The clientele of the Blue Bell Inn at Mile End was especially notorious.[63]

Alehouses undermined the social order in more subtle but more serious ways. They were a bad influence on the young, who learned to neglect their obligations to parents and masters and to waste time and money wenching, dancing, and gambling. In 1572 a Springfield tailor was accused of permitting the "common resorting of minstrels to his house where the youth of the parish do resort together on Sundays and holidays, rioting and reveling." (A major concern in this case, not found in later petitions, was the consequent "great decay of the use and exercise of artillery"—that is, archery.) In 1598 it was alleged that the alehouse of John Collyn in Barling was notorious throughout the hundred of Rochford for "dice-playing, cards, tables, shovegroat, scales, dancings, hobbyhorses, and such unreasonable dealing." When admonished by the constables, the unregenerate Collyns had succinctly replied, "Turd in all their teeth." A generation later the youth of Hadleigh were being corrupted by one Robert Prentis. In 1621 one of the constables of Hadleigh, "awaking out of his sleep . . . did call for some of his servants, and hearing no answer among them did rise, and going to Prentis's house . . . did find there at midnight his children and servants of the same parish."[64]

There was more than the selfish class interest of employers behind the assault on alehouses. It was sincerely believed that alehouses were bad for the poor themselves, and there can be no doubt that alcoholism, then as now, dragged many folk down from moderate hardship to utter destitution. So argued the inhabitants of Woodford, who spoke of alehouses "drawing away most part of the laborers' gains, so that many of their families are partly by necessity, partly by evil example, drawn to pilfering and stealing . . . to supply their wants." One laborer in Hadleigh confessed that at Robert Prentis's alehouse he had "spent and wasted £4 in the past twelve months, owing 20s. on the score for black pots of beer." That was a lot of money for a laborer; it would have fed a young child for nearly a year. One sees why in 1637 the town fathers of Bocking attributed their soaring poor rates to the "multitude" of alehouses, which were frequented by "journeymen and maids living out of service, by idle loitering people who break hedges and steal wood, [playing] unlawful games and neglecting their calling."[65]

The culture of discipline had important religious implications. In sixteenth-century England the ideas of social and spiritual reform were inseparable—indeed, they were virtually indistinguishable. Religious precept, purportedly backed by supernatural sanction, remained the most effective means of regulating behavior. More concretely, the widening competence of the parish in secular affairs promoted the confusion of church and state at the local level. With the decline of the manor and village court, the ecclesiastical parish became the principal institution of local governance; its powers and responsibilities were further enhanced by the elaboration of the national Poor Law.[66]

The assumption of these new responsibilities led to the reform of existing parochial procedures and the introduction of new ones. In Dedham in 1585 the two ministers agreed with the "ancient inhabitants" on a detailed set of principles for the "better ordering" of the town. In addition to excluding from the town anyone who was neither a householder nor a covenanted servant, the ministers and vestrymen agreed to meet each month and also to "visit the poor, and chiefly the suspected places, that understanding the miserable state of those that want, and the naughty disposition of disordered persons, they may provide for them accordingly."[67]

In 1619 the closed vestry of Braintree, known as the Company of Twenty-Four, drew up a new set of regulations concerning town government. The origins of the company are obscure, and I have found no evidence regarding its prior activities. According to the orders of 1619 it had been ineffective for "sundry years past" because it lacked clear procedural regulations. Henceforth, the Twenty-Four were to be chosen from the "chief inhabitants" of the town. Vacancies from death, disability, or expulsion were to be filled by cooptation; a fine of £3 6s. 8d. was to be levied on anyone refusing to serve. The company were to assemble "in their cloaks or gowns" after divine service on the first Sunday of each month and were to sit in the meeting in accordance with their order of precedence in church. The reform of the Braintree vestry was moral as well as administrative. The orders of 1619 specified that "none shall hereafter be admitted into the Company that shall be noted for any scandalous course of life, but rather supply shall be made of . . . those inhabitants that are unreproveable in their lives, though their ability [that is, wealth] be less." Members were also pledged not to "give scandal by haunting of taverns" on pain of expulsion and were to be fined 6d. for absence from divine service during prayers.[68]

The vestry of Finchingfield was similarly recast in 1626. Fines were imposed for refusing election, for absence from meetings, and for refusing a delegated task. The vestry agreed, as at Dedham, to keep a close eye on the poor: "some of us in our several ends of town shall go out in the nighttime and make search in such places which we shall suspect for disorderly persons in the manner of a privy watch, and this we agree to do once in a week, or once in a fortnight at the least."[69] Similar privy watches were carried out by the Twenty-Four of Braintree, who also, in 1623, appointed a beadle "to gather up about dinner and suppertime all that beg at men's doors, both of our town's and other towns', except such as the overseers think fit to permit."[70] In both towns the vestry's proceedings were to be kept strictly secret.

Perhaps only a few parish governments were as highly structured as those of Dedham, Braintree, and Finchingfield, but the steady increase in the survival of parochial records suggests a general tendency toward more formal organization. And it was the parish, backed, of course, by the justices of the peace, that imposed the culture of discipline. That is to say, it was the minister, churchwardens, overseers, and constables who evicted new settlers, petitioned for the suppression of alehouses, and generally attempted to elevate moral standards. The partnership between the minister and the chief inhabitants was the linchpin of the system. At Dedham the initiative for the reform of the local government seems to have come from the local clergy. During their incumbencies at Braintree and Finchingfield, respectively, Samuel Collins and Stephen Marshall were the most consistent participants in the monthly vestry meetings. It could scarcely be otherwise, given the unrivaled moral influence of the pulpit and the emotional and social centrality of the Sunday service in village life. When the Finchingfield vestry was concerned about unwanted immigrants, it decreed that "warning shall be given in the church the next Sabbath to the parish concerning inmates."[71]

In effecting a reformation of manners, the personal qualities of the minister counted for more than his institutional function as a performer of rituals. He should be distinguished by force of character, piety, and organizational ability. Above all, he must be a powerful preacher, capable of awakening the sense of sin and the longing for salvation. The sermon was the principal means by which new standards of self-restraint could be infused into the populace. The preacher's function was to link immiserating vice, especially drunkenness and lechery, with damnation, thereby enforcing the culture of discipline with the most frightful of sanctions.

Many of the most vigorous advocates of this culture of discipline, both clerical and lay, believed that a model of an ideally governed community already existed, a community that claimed, moreover, to have virtually eliminated the problem of poverty. This was Calvin's Geneva. But many Englishmen and -women found this ideal bitterly uncongenial. The culture of discipline was resisted by a large fraction of the populace, while the effort to reform the British church and state along Genevan lines encountered intransigent opposition from the Crown itself.

PART II

The Sword of God's Word: Puritanism to 1618

Think not that I am come to send peace on earth:
I came not to send peace, but a sword.

—Matthew 10:34

Enter ye in at the strait gate: for wide is the gate,
and broad is the way, that leadeth to destruction, and many there be which go in thereat: Because strait is the gate, and narrow is the way,
which leadeth unto life, and few there be that
find it.

—Matthew 7:13-14

4 / Preachers, Prelates, and Parliaments

> [Through] want of a sincere ministry of the
> Word . . . there is a flood of ignorance and dark-
> ness overflowing the most part of the land . . .
> Sins do undoubtedly with one voice cry aloud in
> the ears of the Lord, for vengeance upon the
> whole realm.
>
> —*George Gifford, in* The Country Divinity, *1582*

Essex was the most strongly Protestant county in England: so thought John Hampden in 1643 and the emigrant preacher Thomas Shepherd in 1625.[1] W. K. Jordan believes this was already true during the reign of Henry VIII.[2] In Essex, in fact, heresy of a proto-Protestant sort—demanding the vernacular Bible and a religion based on the preaching of the Word rather than on the ritual of the Mass—long antedated the Continental Reformation. The priority of Wycliffe and the Lollards in propagating doctrines later revived by Luther and Calvin was a source of pride to English Protestants, contributing to the identification of English nationalism with the Reformed faith, and this tradition of native heresy had been strong in Essex. John Ball had been a priest in Colchester; Lollards were burned there in 1402 and 1428, and another abjured in 1430.[3] Driven underground in the fifteenth century, Lollardy seems to have survived here and there in the villages of northern Essex, perhaps merging after 1520 with the movement inspired by Luther. In 1527 Bishop Tunstall's visitation identified more than eighty heretics in the county.[4]

During the reign of Mary at least twenty-two people in Essex were martyred for their beliefs, and another seven were awaiting execution in Colchester Castle at the time of Elizabeth's accession.[5] Colchester was regarded as the provincial capital of heresy. As William Wilkinson recalled, "This town, for the earnest profession of the gospel, became like unto the city upon a hill; and as a candle upon a candlestick gave light to all those who, for the comfort of their consciences, came to confer there, from divers places in the realm."[6]

The memory of the Marian persecutions, elevated to the status of a national mythology by John Foxe, remained a potent influence in the religious climate of Essex down through the Civil War. The steadfastness of the martyrs, most of them humble folk, became a touchstone by which to judge the authenticity of one's own faith. In the year of the Armada, a dying old woman told Richard Rogers, the famous preacher of Wethersfield, that "if she should be burned at a stake, she should set light by it, for the hope of the glory which was set before her." This testimony gave Rogers "good hopes" of her salvation.[7] Rogers's friend and colleague, Arthur Dent, declared on his deathbed that he had been prepared to suffer martyrdom for his beliefs.[8] In the summer of 1640, when the dissolution of the Short Parliament seemed to presage an intensified campaign against Protestant nonconformity, Matthew Newcomen, the lecturer of Dedham, urged his flock to fortify themselves against persecution by reading Foxe.[9]

As William Haller has brilliantly demonstrated, the great achievement of John Foxe was not merely to record the sufferings of the martyrs but to give them a cosmic meaning by relating them to the great battle between Christ and Antichrist.[10] That conflict had been raging since the beginning of time, but it had entered its climactic phase with the recovery of the true Gospel by the Reformation. It would end with the annihilation of Roman Catholicism, which most Protestants identified with the Whore of Babylon and the Beast of the Apocalypse.

Now this Protestant eschatology, which Foxe, so to speak, Anglicized, was a revolutionary creed in the strictest sense of the word: it prophesied the most radical subversion of the established order of things. But the order that it sought to destroy was the old regime of Antichrist, identified with the papacy. To borrow a phrase from Trotsky, this was a theory of permanent revolution against Satanic power. The final offensive, which had begun with Luther and the printing of the vernacular Bible (Foxe considered the invention of printing a miracle performed for the advancement of the Gospel), would sweep forward with ever-increasing momentum until the destruction of the adversary. The downfall of Rome would be the culminating and concluding event in secular history, to be followed by the Second Coming and the Last Judgment. This was a revolution far more radical than any of the secular versions envisioned by post-

Enlightenment theorists. Marx believed that the Communist revolution would initiate a qualitatively new stage of human history; the Protestants expected their revolution to abolish time itself.

These ideas were popularized in Essex by famous preachers like George Gifford and Arthur Dent. "Now, in this age," proclaimed Arther Dent, "shall be the very heat of the war, and brunt of the battle betwixt Papists and Protestants, betwixt God and Belial, betwixt the armies of Christ and ... Antichrist."[11] George Gifford identified Luther's ministry with the sounding of the sixth trumpet in Revelation; already, he maintained, "that bloody kingdom of Antichrist waxeth dark."[12] England's war with Spain and the confessional wars in France and Germany were swiftly building toward the final confrontation of Armageddon: "for assuredly and out of all doubt," said Arthur Dent, "they that live shall see the fulfilling of all this, and shall see the popish armies go down by heaps in all countries and kingdoms, and be made meat for the fowls of the air."[13] Such expectations were naturally most intense during periods of actual religious warfare. There was to be a revival of eschatological speculation after the outbreak in 1618 of the Thirty Years' War.

In this great conflict there were no neutrals, no noncombatants; all men and women were enrolled under the banner of Christ or Antichrist. It was, therefore, essential, Gifford and Dent agreed, that the nature of the struggle and its inevitable outcome be disclosed to all. "Every minister of the Gospel standeth bound," declared Arthur Dent, "to preach the doctrine of the Apocalypse to his particular charge and congregation ... both men and women, young and old, rich and poor." Both men acknowledged a common objection: that the Book of Revelation was too obscure and ambiguous for ordinary understanding. Their reply was that the Apocalypse was becoming steadily more intelligible, as one after another of its prophecies was fulfilled. Arthur Dent was quoting Gifford almost verbatim when he explained that "a man of mean learning ... may now in these days more easily understand and expound this work, than the learnedest Doctors and Fathers in ancient times."[14] The reason was that most of it had already come true. Half a century later, in a time of civil war, another famous Essex preacher, Stephen Marshall, told Parliament that "time (one of the best interpreters of prophecies) hath produced the events answering the types so full and clear that we have the whole army of Protestant interpreters agreeing on the general scope and meaning of it."[15] At the same time, Marshall's Essex neighbor and erstwhile friend, the Royalist minister Edward Symmons, quoted captured Parliamentary soldiers who had been influenced by Marshall as saying, " 'Tis prophesied in the Revelation, that the Whore of Babylon shall be destroyed with fire and sword, and what do you know, but this is the time of her ruin, and that we are the men that must help to pull her down?"[16]

The conviction that the Church of Rome was not merely degenerate but Satanic—literally Anti-Christian—prevented many of the more rigorous English Protestants from resting satisfied with the Elizabethan settlement. The populist element in Protestantism— the belief that ordinary men and women must labor to bring about the kingdom of Christ, and that "men and women, young and old, rich and poor" could all fathom the mysteries of the Apocalypse— inspired a significant minority to try to effect a more thorough reformation.

The great majority of those who sought a cleaner break with Rome were effusively loyal to the queen who had delivered them from the Catholic reign of terror. As William Lamont has demonstrated, the eschatology popularized by Foxe and his disciples was centripetal. It exalted the power of the temporal sovereign, at least if the sovereign was Protestant. The Godly Prince was to be the carnal instrument of Christ's victory on earth.[17] Protestants of this stripe accepted the Church of England, for all its deficiencies, as a true Reformed church capable of further amendment. To be sure, there were in Elizabethan Essex a few "hot gospellers," as they were called, of a more radical disposition. In 1574 a crowd of iconoclasts, led by the local vicar, did £100 worth of damage to the interior of Writtle church, much to the indignation of the churchwardens and the majority of the congregation of the parish, which was dominated by the recusant Petres.[18] In 1584 a Colchester woman "violently and without cause" ripped apart a stole in the parish church of St. Leonard's. The next year one of her fellow parishioners jeered at the minister for wearing the surplice, crying "that the fool had gotten on his fool's coat."[19] Even more radical was the Chelmsford shoemaker who in 1586 ripped the service of baptism from the prayer book, in the belief that if water washed away man's sins, then Christ had died in vain.[20] With the exception of a few extremists, however, all English Protestants were Anglicans. That is to say, they avowed themselves members of the national English church, whatever their private reservations about this or that rubric, ceremony, or ecclesiastical function.

The first concern of zealous Protestants, as of zealous Catholics, was for their own salvation. Since they assumed that only a small minority of mankind had been predestined to receive grace, and since godly behavior was the most reliable (though still not infallible) symptom of election, they strove to lead more pious and austere lives than the majority of their neighbors. But their aspirations were social, not to say pancosmic, as well as personal. They wished to play their part in the overthrow of Antichrist and in the creation of a social order acceptable to God. This vocation committed them to a reformation not only of religion but of manners and morals as well—a reformation that, as it happens, was strikingly relevant to the social problems I have analyzed heretofore. They were the most energetic proponents of what I have called the culture of discipline.

People who assumed this role for themselves in Elizabethan England were known by various names. The one to which they most readily answered was simply that of Christian. But, like fundamentalists in twentieth-century America, they used the word in a special and exclusive sense. It by no means implied a community of belief with all other *soi-disant* Christians. Everyone, after all, was Christian in sixteenth-century England, and advanced Protestants sought to distinguish themselves from the majority of their compatriots, even of those who had accepted the Reformation. An individual of this persuasion, referring to the collectivity with which he aspired to be identified, might speak of the *godly* or of the *Saints*—the latter term denoting, in Protestant usage, all those living and dead and unborn whom God had elected to salvation before all eternity. But since humility and self-criticism, tempered by ultimate confidence, were thought to characterize the truly godly, an aspirant Saint might hesitate to apply these terms reflexively. The more common term, at least for purposes of self-identification, was probably *professor,* a word that stressed the believer's commitment to godly values while avoiding hubristic claims of achieved sanctity.

Many professors had conscientious objections to what they regarded as vestiges of popery within the Anglican service, notably the use of the sign of the Cross in baptism, the wearing of the surplice, and the churching of women after childbirth. But they differed greatly in the degree of their hostility. The range of attitude ran

from grudging toleration to hysterical revulsion. Opposition to popish survivals was not the essence of godliness. What gave professors
their common religious identity was the emphasis they accorded to
Bible reading and especially to the preaching of the Word.

In 1584, for example, when William Negus was suspended for refusal to wear the surplice, his parishioners begged him to suppress
his scruples rather than deprive them of his preaching. "It [the sur-
plice] is a thing which we wish with all our hearts, if it pleased God
and our Prince, were removed," they wrote, "but yet we take it not
to be a matter of such weight, as that to the hazard of our souls and
loss of our spiritual comfort, the not wearing of it should deprive us
of your ministry."[21] For the godly, public worship centered around
the sermon. The "sword of God's Word" was the great weapon in
the battle against Antichrist. It was the mission of the preacher to
bring conviction of grace to the elect, to deprive the reprobate of the
excuse of ignorance, and to expose and excoriate sin. The immediate
objective was therefore to provide a godly preacher in every parish
in England. Professors held that the true minister must, of course, be
morally irreproachable and doctrinally sound, but these were necessary, not sufficient, qualifications. He must also be an inspiring ora-
tor who could terrorize the drunkard, the lecher, and the blasphemer and who could lead the future Saint from an agonized
consciousness of sin through the hope of regeneration to a final assurance—although always tempered by some lingering anxiety—of
salvation. Men who could do this were called "painful" preachers.
The pun is accidental but apposite.

Such preachers were in short supply in the Elizabethan church. A
survey of the Essex clergy compiled in 1584 by a group of reform-
minded ministers alleged that fewer than one incumbent in three
was an adequate preacher. Moreover, nearly half of the most diligent preachers were precisely those who objected most strongly to
this or that feature of the Anglican ritual. It was claimed that nearly
half of the "sufficient, painful, and careful" preachers in Essex had
been suspended or otherwise harassed for nonconformity.[22] Now,
whatever their personal views on the surplice or the sign of the
Cross, professors generally agreed that such practices were at best irrelevant to salvation and to the preacher's true function, which was
to preach the saving Word of God. And they further agreed that it
was outrageous that godly preachers should be silenced when

so many of their conforming colleagues were lazy, corrupt, and ignorant.

If the men and women who were called Puritans in prerevolutionary England shared any one distinguishing attitude it was surely
this emphasis on preaching as an instrument of personal and social
reform, together with a corollary depreciation of inherited ritual.
Here, then, is perhaps the best definition of puritanism, considered
as a broad current of lay and clerical opinion. And it is here, rather
than in any matters of church organization or theological dogma,
that we encounter the fundamental source of tension between puritanism, so defined, and the Crown.

Elizabeth, like her father, was at best suspicious of painful
preaching, because it provoked discord among her subjects. (Indeed,
it was intended to provoke discord, as Christ brought *gladium in
terris*.) She firmly rejected the priority accorded by professors to the
sermon over ritual; she categorically refused to promote preaching
at the price of ceremonial diversity. On this matter of ecclesiastical
priorities, James and Charles were to prove themselves good Eliza-
bethans (if not Henricians). But one should beware of establishing
too stark an opposition between the professors and the episcopal hierarchy on this point. Bishops disagreed as to the relative importance of painful preaching and ceremonial uniformity. Sermonism
always had its sympathizers on the episcopal bench. Even in the
reign of Charles there were bishops whose personal piety won the
respect of the most demanding professors. There is, indeed, no inherent contradiction in the idea of a Puritan bishop, once we reject the
misleadingly restrictive identification of puritanism with antiepisco-
pacy. In Essex, where episcopal policy wavered erratically between
repression and de facto toleration, there is little evidence—at least
before the rise of Laud—of any irreconcilable hostility to episcopacy
as such. George Gifford, one of the Essex leaders of the so-called
Presbyterian movement during the 1580s, explicitly stated that
"God hath ordained the office of Bishop in his Church for to govern
and feed his people."[23]

For nearly two decades after Elizabeth's accession, professors in
Essex had relatively little cause for complaint or alarm. If Crown
and hierarchy were sluggish in promoting a thorough reformation,
they did nothing to obstruct the voluntary initiatives of the godly. In

many parishes the godly met together with a respected minister for prayer, Bible study, and mutual exhortation.[24] As Patrick Collinson has observed, these voluntary "churches within the church" may be regarded as the seeds of later congregationalism; but very few of these Elizabethan professors regarded themselves as in any sense separatists. They participated in the official services of the Church of England, although their thirst for sermons might impel them to travel to another parish of a Sunday, if their local minister did not preach. This was called "gadding," after the wandering biblical tribe of Gad. Whereas separatists shunned contamination by the reprobate majority, these professors hoped by their example to awaken the consciences of their worldly neighbors: they sought to leaven the lump. The professors who met at Wethersfield in the 1580s with Richard Rogers blamed themselves for the "unprofitableness and coldness" of "other weak Christians" who looked to them for inspiration.[25]

The provision of more sermons was the key to reform. From at least the mid-1560s towns and individuals were endowing lectureships to support preachers. Some lectureships were provided to supplement a regular living judged insufficient to attract a learned divine; others provided maintenance for preachers unable to obtain a cure of souls. By the reign of Charles I there were at least twenty-six lectureships in Essex.[26]

Of greater immediate significance were the public assemblies called "prophesyings" that flourished from the early 1560s to the end of the following decade. Originally the prophesyings were exclusively clerical gatherings where ministers met to expound Scripture and to provide fraternal criticism of each other's preaching. The prophesyings, however, soon acquired an enthusiastic lay audience. "Such is the thirsty desire of people in these days to hear the Word of God," wrote William Harrison in 1577, "that they also have as it were with zealous violence intruded themselves."[27] At Maldon the town magistrates provided dinner (and claret) for the ministers after the exercise.[28] By 1564 there were regular prophesyings at Chelmsford, Brentwood, Maldon, Rochford, and Horndon, and by 1574 one had been established in Colchester as well.[29] "Prophesying," said Harrison, "is a notable spur unto all the ministers to apply their books, which otherwise (as in times past) would give themselves to hawking . . . cards . . . tippling at the alehouse."[30]

The prophesyings continued without official interference until the late 1570s. To be sure, the godly suffered setbacks during these years. There was the controversy over vestments, which led to Archbishop Matthew Parker's articles compelling ministers to wear the surplice, regarded by advanced Protestants as the "rag of Rome." But Edmund Grindal, the bishop of London, was not the man to conduct an inquisition over such an issue, and there is little evidence of preachers in Essex being molested. In 1573, after a lunatic of allegedly Puritan leanings assassinated the sea-dog John Hawkins (mistaking him for the markedly anti-Puritan favorite Sir Christopher Hatton), the Essex assize judges were instructed to deal more severely with clerical nonconformists. Nothing came of it.[31]

At the end of 1575 professors must have been relieved, even delighted, to learn of the elevation of Bishop Grindal to the see of Canterbury. Grindal was sympathetic to the advancement of preaching, the reform of the church courts, and a degree of administrative decentralization. A Grindalian episcopacy, as Patrick Collinson has suggested, would have posed no insuperable barriers to the cultural transformation that the godly were attempting to effect. Had Grindal's program prevailed, it is highly unlikely that any very significant group of professors would have come to regard episcopacy as Antichristian. But all this is to reckon without the queen. Whatever her positive views, Elizabeth was no Grindalian. The new archbishop and his godly supporters would receive no encouragement from a sovereign who believed three or four preachers quite adequate to a shire.[32] Grindal's effective tenure lasted barely a year. With the suspension of the archbishop, real episcopal power passed to the conservatives John Whitgift, Edmund Freake, and John Aylmer, Grindal's successor as bishop of London.

The immediate consequence of this shift in the balance of ecclesiastical power was the suppression of prophesyings. William Harrison, a serious Protestant but hardly a Puritan in any useful sense of the word, was dismayed. The attack on prophesying, he maintained, had been instigated by Satan through the malice of those who disliked hearing "the reprehension of sin."[33] Clerical resentment of the new breed of preachers certainly played a role in the reaction that followed Grindal's brief regime. The godly preachers antagonized their less energetic or talented colleagues by denouncing them as "dumb dogs" while poaching their flocks, and they offended theological conservatives with their insistence on the "dark and difficult" themes of election and reprobation. The conservatives and dumb dogs now took the offensive. Thus, Robert Wright, who as household chaplain to Lord Rich, the county's greatest landowner, had presided over the prophesyings in the great hall at Rochford, was imprisoned for nearly a year on charges that greatly exaggerated his radicalism and quite falsely impugned his loyalty to the queen. The testimony against Wright was supplied by a group of nearby ministers whose pastoral shortcomings had been "lovingly yet vehemently" reproved by Lord Rich himself.[34] Aylmer's aggressive new policy enabled them to gain revenge and curry official favor simultaneously.

The hierarchy could ban public prophesying and exclude the laity from overt participation, but it could not prevent godly preachers from conferring together in private, or secretly if need be.[35] There is, in fact, a continuous tradition of clerical conferences devoted to preaching and collective exegesis, a tradition extending from the public assemblies of the early 1560s down to the semiclandestine circle around Thomas Hooker in the late 1620s. It was largely through such conferences, and similar gatherings at the universities, that an aggressively Protestant homiletic tradition was sustained and elaborated through three generations.

The most famous—if only because the best documented—of these Elizabethan conferences met at Dedham from 1582 to 1589 under the leadership of Edmund Chapman. Twenty ministers from Essex and southern Suffolk belonged at one time or another, although its active membership never exceeded sixteen. The conference was exclusively clerical. The ministers met weekly to discuss points of doctrine, evaluate the moral and spiritual qualifications of the neighboring clergy, and resolve problems arising between themselves and their congregations. They also attempted to organize resistance to the conservative offensive, which gathered momentum with the appointment in 1583 of John Whitgift as archbishop.[36]

The Dedham conference maintained liaison with similar associations in other counties and with the group in London led by John Field. (In Essex there was also a small and not very vital conference around Richard Rogers in Wethersfield, and perhaps another around George Gifford in Maldon.) This network of conferences is generally described as a Presbyterian movement: an attempt to build, as it were from the ground up, the Calvinist structure of classes and synods within the Church of England. But as Collinson has shown, we must be cautious about words like *Presbyterian* or, for that matter, *movement*. The members of the Dedham conference may well have considered themselves a classis, but they were not all disciples of Beza or Thomas Cartwright, and they were not unanimously hostile to episcopacy. In fact, only one or two seem to have been dogmatic Presbyterians in this sense. The rest, whatever their animus against particular bishops like Aylmer, Freake, Whitgift, and Richard Bancroft, would probably have been reasonably content to acknowledge the authority of an Edmund Grindal, or in the next reign of George Abbot or James Ussher. In this respect the majority of members of the Dedham conference were far less radical than Cartwright or their colleagues in London. The Dedham conference never endorsed the Book of Discipline, and Edmund Chapman on several occasions expressed misgiving at the London conference's aggressiveness.[37]

But if such preachers were disposed to compromise, the hierarchy, as represented by men like Whitgift and Aylmer, was not. New articles issued by Whitgift required subscription to the Thirty-Nine Articles and assent to the entire contents of the book of Common Prayer. At least forty-three Essex ministers, including Richard Rogers and four members of the Dedham classis, were suspended for their refusal to comply.[38] These ministers and their sympathizers responded by appealing to the secular arm. Twenty-seven ministers, among them Rogers, George Gifford, and Arthur Dent, petitioned the Privy Council. They observed that it was not their theology that was being questioned. The petitioners took it for granted that Calvinism was the official doctrine of the Church of England. But they could not conscientiously profess that the book of Common Prayer contained nothing contrary to the Word of God. To accept the book without qualification, they argued, would place them at odds with the Reformed churches of the Continent.[39] This appeal to the unity of international Protestantism, even at the cost of discord within the Anglican communion, was to prove of great consequence.

Meanwhile, the godly laity were being stirred to action on behalf of the suspended preachers. In Colchester the backers of the silenced lecturer George Northey, including the town bailiffs, enlisted the aid of their recorder, Sir Francis Walsingham, and the Earls of Warwick and Leicester against the borough's patron, Sir Thomas Heneage, who was also a perennial knight of the shire.[40] From Maldon came a lengthy and melodramatic petition to the Privy Council on behalf of George Gifford, a man whom Bishop Aylmer regarded as the ringleader of the Essex Puritans. The petition merits attention, since it illustrates a rhetorical strategy that the godly were to pursue for the next sixty years. The petitioners first recalled the contributions of preachers like Gifford in promoting social discipline. Gifford, they declared, had "builded us up to obedience both towards God and towards her Majesty and towards all the ministers of justice under her." Preaching, then, was indispensable to political stability. And yet, it was precisely the godly ministers who had been suppressed. The conformists who remained were "for the most part utterly unfit." Some had been Catholic priests, others were "rioters, dicers, quarrellers, drunkards, and adulterers." It was these degenerates who were sapping the foundations of the church, persecuting Saints like Gifford with malicious accusations of sedition. The terrifying consequence was that all hell had broken loose: "the multitude of Papists, heretics, and other enemies to God and Her Royal Majesty are so increased and encouraged, that . . . they stick not openly to fill our bosoms with all contemptuous and bitter speeches, mocking and taunting us with our profession." The godly went in terror of their very lives.[41]

The strategy here was to shift the argument away from the technicalities of scholarly disputation over ceremonies and church polity and to stress instead the indispensability of these molested preachers to the defense of Protestantism and social order. It was an argument calculated to appeal to a far broader section of the upper class than would have endorsed a full-blooded Presbyterianism.

This was the rationale for the great survey of the ministry undertaken in mid-1584 at the instigation of the Dedham conference, the first, apparently, of seventeen such county surveys prepared during these years of crisis. The Essex survey, which must have required the collaboration of groups of professors scattered throughout the county, purported to show that fewer than one-third of the beneficed ministers were competent preachers of reputable morals. And of the painful preachers, nearly half had conscientious objections to

some aspect of the Anglican service, usually the wearing of the surplice and the use of the sign of the Cross in baptism. It was claimed
that in one area of the county, within a radius of sixteen miles, were
to be found thirty-two nonresidents, thirty "insufficient and de-
famed ministers," and nineteen silenced preachers—"and so the
people [are] suffered to perish for lack of due teaching." Under these
circumstances, the suppression of preachers for relatively minor ir-
regularities was an outrage against the Gospel.[42]

A majority of the Privy Council, including Burleigh as well as the
more predictably sympathetic Walsingham and Leicester, found
this argument persuasive. Having received an early version of the
Essex survey in September 1584, they protested to Whitgift against
the suspension of so many "zealous and learned preachers" while so
many incumbents were unlearned, and not a few were accused of
"filthiness of life." The intervention by the Privy Councillors was
successful. A face-saving compromise was arranged, and by the end
of 1584 all of the suspended ministers in Essex, with the exception of
George Gifford, were restored. Gifford himself remained in Maldon
as a lecturer for the next thirty-five years.[43]

The respite was only temporary, however. In the summer of 1586
Bishop Aylmer conducted a visitation of Essex, which resulted in the
renewed suspension of forty Essex ministers.[44] The bishop had a
close brush with ridicule when he reached Maldon, where George
Gifford enjoyed considerable popular support. According to Aylmer's report, a man had been hired to burst into the church dressed
as a fool, snatch off the bishop's cap, and toss it to the crowd,
"whereupon," declared the bishop, "it is not to be doubted but a
dangerous tumult would have arisen." The plot never came off. But
Aylmer took the opportunity to present the episode to Burleigh as
an example of "the sour fruits of these new reformers, and especially
such as be mercenary." It was a transparent reference to the salaried
lecturer George Gifford, whom Burleigh had already defended.[45]

Aylmer assured Burleigh that the authorities in Maldon were
"much dismayed" by the behavior of Gifford's supporters. Their
dismay did not, however, prevent two bailiffs, two justices of the
peace, four aldermen, fifteen burgesses, and twenty-four more of
the "best and substantialest" men of Maldon from presenting the
bishop with a very strong petition in the lecturer's favor. The Mal-

don petition sounded the familiar theme: Gifford had suppressed sin in the town and was now being slandered by the "profane and wicked."[46]

Aylmer received a similar petition from the supporters of Thomas Carew in Hatfield Peverel. There, too, it was alleged, libelous accusations had been directed against the minister by his enemies, who were suspected of popery. And there too "sin greatly increased in the town" after Carew's suspension. When the man Aylmer had appointed to succeed to the cure tried to enter the church, a "hurly-burly" erupted between Carew's faction and his opponents, which resulted in the temporary imprisonment of both Carew and his patron.[47]

The hopes of the godly lay not with the bishop of London but with the Parliament, which had been summoned in the fall of 1586. Edmund Chapman had suggested to John Field a national campaign on behalf of godly candidates. There is no other evidence of overt electioneering on the part of Essex preachers, although the canvasing of petitions on behalf of suspended ministers and the county-wide inquisition into the failings of the orthodox ministry must have had some influence on the electorate. The results were mixed. Colchester returned a godly lawyer named James Morrice, who later led the attack against the ex officio oath; Maldon elected Edward Lewkenor, a Suffolk gentleman who was one of the few really convinced Presbyterians in the House of Commons, and whose private papers include a rich collection of Puritan documents.[48] But the knights of the shire were the conservative courtier Sir Thomas Heneage, who was allied with Whitgift, and the secret papist Sir John (later Lord) Petre.[49] The godly party had no hold as yet upon the county electorate.

The Dedham ministers sought to exert pressure on the new Parliament by instigating more petitions from all over the county. The survey begun in 1584 was expanded to include Aylmer's latest victims. The inhabitants of Maldon and the surrounding countryside complained to their M.P.s, Edmund Lewkenor and John Butler, "not of the want of bread, or the scarcity of corn . . . but . . . the wrong done to our souls, and . . . the want of spiritual food." They warned of the Catholic menace at home and abroad. The preaching of the Gospel was especially needed "in these so dangerous days, and desperate practices of the common enemy." From Dunmow 236 professors begged of Lord Rich that the "traitorous brood and dangerous sect" of papists might be more tightly controlled. Petitioners from the hundreds of Hinckford, Freshwell, Uttlesford, and Clavering lamented the increase of "atheists, papists, and other heretics" owing to the silencing of the Word. Similar sentiments were voiced by one hundred men of Rochford, an area dominated by the county's preeminent lay professor, Lord Rich. Predictably, no petitions were addressed to Heneage and Petre as knights of the shire.[50]

This lobbying of Parliament was not without effect. Edmund Lewkenor of Maldon was committed to the Tower on February 27, 1587, for supporting Cope's Book and Bill, which would have replaced at a stroke all existing ecclesiastical legislation with a Genevan discipline. Significantly, Lewkenor's main argument in favor of Cope's proposal was the "necessity of preaching."[51] The effort was as futile as it was audacious. The bill was more than a half-century ahead of its time.

When a new Parliament was summoned in the fall of 1588, Lord Rich tried to contest the election of Sir Thomas Heneage, the vice chamberlain, and Sir Henry Gray, the Lieutenant of the Queen's Pensioners, by bringing crowds of freeholders to the election to support a candidate of his own—almost certainly Sir Francis Barrington. The plan was quickly squelched by the Privy Council, and Heneage and Gray were elected without incident.[52] In any case, this brief and obscure Parliament achieved nothing of importance. On March 8, 1589, the suspended ministers of Essex addressed yet another petition to Parliament. It was fruitless; Parliament was sent home three weeks later.[53]

The Elizabethan Puritan movement, as an organized campaign to effect reform through legislation, had now entered into decline, leaving conscientious preachers to make what peace they might with God and their ecclesiastical superiors. As a result the brethren were now plagued by internal dissension as well as governmental harassment. Most of the godly preachers were neither martyrs nor firebrands; they were prepared at times to resort to what may seem rather sordid equivocation. William Negus of Leigh, for example, when confronted with his failure to wear the surplice, disingenuously replied that there was none in the church. Asked if he would wear one were it provided, he evaded the question entirely, proposing instead that he be allowed to preach until such time as it was proven that there was a surplice and that he had refused to wear it. This is not exactly Luther at Worms. But Negus's own parishioners had urged him not to desert them "for such a trifle."[54]

Such ministers were under pressure from more radical associates as well. At Wethersfield, Richard Rogers gloomily observed the growth of separatism and the emigration of men like his friend Dudley Fenner to the Netherlands. Rogers felt trapped between conflicting pressures from the hierarchy and the maximalists of his own camp. On the one hand, he risked suspension for his omission of the surplice; on the other hand, some of his colleagues were demanding that the godly preachers hold no communication with members of the "dumb ministry." The agonizing question was also being raised "whether we may cease from preaching, being forbidden."[55]

The last meeting of the Dedham conference took place in June 1589. The next month Rogers wrote despondently, "There is little hope of any better state to the Church." George Gifford was equally pessimistic. In the preface to a collection of sermons published in 1589 he warned England of the fate of Sodom, observing that "men's hearts were never more . . . set upon riches and pleasures than now."[56]

The defeat seemed total. But the painful preachers had won, and were to retain, the support of a significant fraction of the local aristocracy. The support of the "noble professors," as the preachers called their gentle patrons, helped assure the survival of militant Protestantism during the dark years under Archbishops Whitgift and Bancroft.

Preeminent among the county's noble professors was the house of Rich. If Richard Rich, first Lord Rich of Leighs, had any religious convictions at all, they were admirably supple. He atoned for his perjured testimony against Sir Thomas More by his ferocious persecution of Protestants during the reign of Mary.[57] The second Lord Rich embraced the Reformed faith, however, as did his illegitimate brother, Richard Rich. This Richard Rich was imprisoned in the Fleet for defending John Stubbs and for possessing a copy of Stubbs's notorious tract against the queen's marriage with the Duke of Anjou. Richard Rich also patronized William Dyke, preacher at Coggeshall, who attracted official suspicion with his sermons against what were called "statute Protestants"—that is, time servers, who attended church merely from legal compulsion. Less is known about the activities of the second Lord Rich, but shortly after his death in 1581 Bishop Aylmer recalled having had "many storms" with him.[58]

Robert Rich, who became the third Lord Rich in 1581, enjoys the unenviable celebrity of having been cuckolded in print by Philip Sidney. Just after his accession Rich married Penelope Devereux, "Stella" to Sidney's "Astrophel." Thanks to Sidney's tedious and sarcastic punning on his surname, Rich has a modest and uncomfortable niche in English literature. After Sidney's death "Stella" transferred her affections to Charles Blount, later Earl of Mountjoy, with whom she lived in open adultery before finally obtaining a divorce from her husband in 1605. Rich was no luckier in war than in love. All we know of his military activities is that he sailed with his brother-in-law, the Earl of Essex, on the ill-fated Islands expedition and was sent home miserably seasick.[59]

So far he seems a thoroughly pathetic figure. But no layman did more to promote painful preaching in Essex than Lord Rich, whom the Earl of Leicester accurately described as "zealous in religion."[60] We should resist the psychohistorical temptation to derive his godliness from his marital difficulties. Rich inherited his religious orientation from his father and was to transmit it to his son, a man of very different temperament.

Rich retained his father's domestic chaplain, Robert Wright, who had been ordained at Antwerp and was regarded as a dangerous separatist. Wright's assistant for a time was the future martyr John Greenwood. Wright, as we have seen, took part in the prophesyings at Rich's Hall in Rochford, while Rich took it upon himself to reprove neighboring ministers ("lovingly" but "vehemently") for their shortcomings, while encouraging and defending godly preachers.[61] In 1582 he undertook to prosecute some rowdies who had disturbed a conference of ministers at Richard Rogers's home in Wethersfield. At the same Quarter Sessions one William Ruste, whom Lord Rich had just deprived of the vicarage of Felsted, was presented for slandering his former patron as well as for denouncing Rogers. "If the Lord Rich might have his will to put men out of their benefices," Ruste charged, "he would keep their livings and have some serve the cure for little or nothing." Lord Rich's neighbors, Ruste added, "would be glad if he were further from them."[62] To which one can almost hear a chorus of "amens" muttered by the old-fashioned ministers of the county.

The prophesyings at Rochford were discontinued, but despite the campaign of repression, Lord Rich continued to protect and promote godly preachers until his death in 1619, shortly after being created Earl of Warwick. Thereafter, the role of the county's premier noble professor was filled by Rich's son, the second Earl of Warwick, who inherited twenty-two advowsons along with his sixty-four Essex manors. So close was the association between the Rich family and the godly cause in Essex that local legend made Richard Rogers the son of the family steward. (Rogers's father was in fact a Chelmsford carpenter.)[63]

Closely allied with the Rich family were the Barringtons of Hatfield Broad Oak. Sir Francis Barrington, who according to tradition had converted his mother from Catholicism, succeeded his father in 1583 and became known as a "second Nehemiah" to the godly cause. In 1586 he headed the list of signatories to the petition from Dunmow in favor of the silenced ministers; in 1588 he was probably the man whom Lord Rich tried to elect as knight of the shire by mustering his legion of freeholders, although Rich could not seat Barrington in Parliament until 1601.[64]

In Colchester the godly had firm friends in James Morrice and Francis Harvey, both of whom were allied with the town's recorder, Sir Francis Walsingham. Harvey represented Colchester in the Parliaments of 1584 and 1586, while Morrice sat in those of 1588 and 1592 as well. The mayor and corporation of the town appointed Puritan preachers to their town lectureship: George Northey under Elizabeth, and in the next reign the great William Ames. In Maldon the godly were able to secure the return of the Suffolk Puritan Sir Edward Lewkenor in 1584, 1586, and 1592–93, and of John Butler, a local gentleman of similar views, in 1586 and 1588. Sir Robert Wroth of Great Bardfield, who in 1584 helped Richard Rogers regain his lectureship at Wethersfield, sat regularly for Middlesex from 1586 to 1601, when he helped draft the great Elizabethan Poor Law.[65]

Throughout the county the painful preachers enjoyed the support of a host of lesser patrons. At Dedham it was a clothier, William Cardinal, who in 1578 provided Edmund Chapman with his lectureship. Virtually unknown to us but of great collective significance were the ardent sermon goers among the parish gentry, men like William Massey of Springfield. "We should have had some . . . goodly sermon of you this day," Massey admonished his minister in 1598, and added contemptuously, "but belike you are not well-provided for the same."[66]

The preachers seem to have eschewed further political activity for the remainder of Elizabeth's reign, no doubt comforting themselves with the prospect of a more reliably Calvinist successor in King James VI of Scotland. In the Parliament of 1592–93 the Colchester burgess James Morrice denounced Whitgift's articles, and particularly the use of the oath ex officio to enforce them, as contrary to common law and subversive of the liberties of the realm. Morrice had the sympathy of Burleigh and the support of Sir Francis Knollys. But Whitgift convinced Elizabeth that Morrice sought to undermine her authority by introducing "a new kind of ecclesiastical government like unto that of Scotland," and Morrice was locked up, albeit comfortably, for two months.[67] In neither of Elizabeth's last two Parliaments (1597–98 and 1601) were there any further efforts on behalf of the preachers by the Essex delegation. Morrice was dead, and Lewkenor, for some reason, was not returned again by Maldon until 1604.

The accession of James occasioned a revival of godly agitation. The Millenary Petition, presented to James on his journey southward, enunciated the immediate program of the main body of Puritans. The preachers called for the abolition of some ceremonies, more sparing use of the oath ex officio, purification of the ministry, reform of the church courts. Above all, the petitioners sought official toleration for preachers with conscientious scruples about one or another feature of the Anglican service. Ministers were no longer to be required to wear the cap and surplice nor to subscribe to the entire contents of the Book of Common Prayer.[68] Here was the real heart of the matter, and the issue on which the petitioners could count on the broadest support amongst the godly laity. To point up the necessity for such toleration, the preachers revived their tactic of 1584-1586. Petitions were canvased among the laity, and surveys of the clergy were carried out in order to demonstrate the corruption of the conformist clergy. A summary of the Essex survey, which is to be found, significantly, among the papers of Sir Edward Lewkenor, records a total of only ninety-four "good and faithful" preachers out of 344 incumbents.[69] Once again there was a lurid catalogue of disreputable conformists—fornicators, gamblers, drunkards, papists, and the like, and even one abandoned wretch who gloried in his nickname of "the Vicar of Hell."[70]

There was some reason to believe that the king might grant the substance of the Millenary Petition. It was, after all, a fairly moderate document. Radical puritanism had been shattered. Moreover, the king's own chaplain, the Scot Patrick Galloway, was a leading organizer of the campaign. James was committed to episcopacy (which the petition did not, in any case, threaten), but he accepted that bishops might be fallible. He deplored pluralism; he was prepared to hear criticism of the ecclesiastical courts. Above all, he professed his devotion to a preaching ministry. According to Patrick Galloway, James wanted to plant "a resident Moses in every parish."[71] It was at least an open question whether he would compell Moses to don the surplice.

The king further quickened the hopes of the godly by agreeing to allow their representatives to debate the bishops at Hampton Court. It was an abrupt departure from Elizabethan precedent, at which the bishops were suitably alarmed, but these hopes were soon dashed. How soon remains a matter of some dispute. Mark Curtis has criticized the view that the conference was a complete fiasco. Noting that James agreed to some of the measures solicited by the Puritans, Curtis contends that the conference ended amicably and that the way seemed open to further reform. The real damage was done only after Hampton Court, as the bishops sabotaged the achievements of the conference and publicized their own distorted version of the proceedings as a Puritan rout.[72] At any rate, it was the bishops' version of the conference that reached Sir Edmund Lewkenor, sent to him from London by his wife. The account that he received concluded triumphantly that "Dr. Reynolds and his brethren [the Puritan delegation] are utterly condemned for silly men."[73] Lewkenor, who had regained his seat for Maldon in the 1604 election, can have had few illusions as he rode up to Westminster that further reformation could be effected without struggle.

The elections of 1604 went well for the godly. Colchester returned a Sussex lawyer named Edward Alford, whose zeal for God's Word was matched only by his aversion to new taxes. Lewkenor sat again for Maldon. Despite the bitter opposition of the Earl of Suffolk, Lord Rich managed to effect the choice of his friend Sir Francis Barrington as one of the knights of the shire.[74] Rich and Barrington were assisted in their campaign by the celebrated Lincolnshire preacher Arthur Hildersam, who is described during these months as Sir Francis's steward.[75]

Archbishop Whitgift, in the last weeks of his life, had dreaded the assembling of Parliament.[76] His fears were confirmed. The rumor went about that three-quarters of the House of Commons were Puritans. But the common denominator of Parliamentary puritanism remained what it had been in the 1580s: a desire to promote preaching as the essence of the national religion and, as a means to that end, a demand that the scruples of painful preachers be respected. Once again the great majority of the godly M.P.s demonstrated their acceptance, at least for the present, of episcopacy. A man rash enough to brand bishops with the sign of the Beast was clapped in the Tower by order of the House. But the Commons passed bills limiting the number of articles to which preachers must subscribe, reducing pluralism, and forbidding the harassment of preachers over the cap and surplice. None of the bills made it through the Lords, where the godly were always in the minority.[77]

It was 1586 all over again. Even had the Lords been amenable to the Commons' proposals, James would have had none of them. Calvinist theologian though he was, his position was not fundamentally different from that of Elizabeth. No more than she would he put the need for evangelical preaching above the requirements of ecclesiastical uniformity. The extirpation of evil, the regeneration of the believer, the terrorizing of sinners, the eradication of vice: these were not, for James, as they were for the godly, the ultimate priorities. Like Elizabeth, James demanded above all order and obedience, which clerical dissidence appeared to threaten. And it was an inescapable fact that many of England's most gifted preachers had embraced the ecclesiological tradition that did most to exalt their own function. James's desire to see a resident Moses in every parish gradually waned as it became apparent that Moses was all too likely to have an awkward conscience.

The machinery of repression was cranked up again in the summer of 1604 after the Parliament was prorogued. In July the king issued a proclamation requiring ministers to conform by November 30 or face deprivation; in September he approved new canons adopted by Convocation that required subscription to the entire Book of Common Prayer and endorsement of all Thirty-nine Articles.[78] These measures evoked a petition to the king by two hundred yeomen from the area of Hatfield Broad Oak. This was Barrington country, and in fact the petition was apparently instigated by Arthur Hildersam, still acting, or posing, as Sir Francis Barrington's steward. The petitioners complained of the silencing of preachers "through whose ministry we have been brought from . . . the power of Satan to God," and they begged not to be abandoned to "careless shepherds that aim wholly at the gain of the fleece." They would cheerfully lay their lives and property, so they claimed, at the king's feet. But the lack of preaching would expose "the souls of us and our posterity . . . to certain and inevitable ruin."[79] James was unmoved. He would not, in any case, have been favorably impressed by the petitioners' assurance that their preachers had taught them "to give to God the things that are God's and to give Caesar that which unto him belongeth." The question, of course, was which was which. Hildersam was summoned before the Privy Council, and a month later he was back in Lincolnshire and embroiled with the ecclesiastical authorities there.[80]

In principle the issue had been sharply defined. Puritans among the ministry faced the cruel alternative of conformity or deprivation. In practice, however, the situation was less dramatic. James had threatened to make the Puritans conform or to harry them from the land, but he lacked the spirit of the true inquisitor. While blustering at Hampton Court against nonconformity, he also warned the bishops not to treat their Puritan brethren too vindictively.[81] Moreover, the bishops were themselves divided. There were those, like Bancroft, who longed to translate James's petulant outburst directly into policy. But there were others, like Bancroft's successor, the careless and good-natured George Abbot, who either sympathized with the Puritans or merely hated fuss.

The church, in any case, disposed of a woefully ramshackle apparatus of coercion. The ecclesiastical courts were cumbersome and dilatory. The parish churchwardens, on whom the hierarchy relied to present nonconformists, were often unreliable, especially if they shared the views of the offending preacher. In a society where lay rights were jealously defended against prelatical intrusion, the bishops were often powerless to breach the shield of influence with which godly aristocrats surrounded their favorite preachers.[82] The careful research of Ogbu Kalu has demonstrated that even during Bancroft's primacy the persecution of Essex Puritans was sloppy and sporadic.

Richard Vaughan, bishop of London from 1604 to his death in 1607, was tolerant of Puritans, perhaps, as Professor Kalu suggests, because he had served in the "Papist-ridden" diocese of Chester. At any rate, Vaughan restored most of the ministers who had been suspended in 1604, and according to Richard Rogers, "permitted the godly ministers to live peaceably and to enjoy liberty." Only two Puritans were suspended. Professor Kalu believes that during Vaughan's tenure the number of Puritan clergymen—by which he appears to mean nonconformists—rose from fifty-five to seventy-five.[83]

Vaughan's successor, Thomas Ravis, however, was cast in the mold of Whitgift and Bancroft. "By the help of Jesu," he is said to have sworn, "I will leave not one preacher in my diocese that doth not subscribe and conform." Richard Rogers, who recorded Ravis's vow, was able to add with satisfaction that "Jesu helped him not." Ravis, however, made a good start. Forty-four clerics were prosecuted for nonconformity in 1607, of whom twenty-five were suspended and ten were deprived. But Ravis died in 1610, having failed, in Richard Rogers's words, "to root us all out." The new bishop of London was the permissive George Abbot. Rogers recorded Abbot's first visitation on September 8, 1610, with the words, "No hurt done. *Laus Deo.*"[84]

In the entire period from 1603 to 1610 sixteen clerics, including six lecturers, were deprived in Essex for nonconformity—hardly a reign of terror. Nor is there any reason to think that the preachers were cowed into submission. The sparsity of prosecutions, Professor Kalu has concluded, was the result of "administrative laxity" rather than "the conformity of a majority of Puritans."[85] The ecclesiastical history of Essex during the primacy of Archbishop Abbot awaits thorough scrutiny, but it would appear that the preachers enjoyed almost complete peace for at least a decade.

The most famous preachers in Elizabethan and Jacobean Essex were Arthur Dent, George Gifford, and Richard and John Rogers. Arthur Dent of South Shoebury, who dedicated his commentary on the Apocalypse to Lord Rich, barely survived into the reign of James I. But his works were regularly reprinted down to the Civil War, and his manual of piety, *The Plaine Man's Path-way to Heaven*, was one of John Bunyan's models for *Pilgrim's Progress*.[86] George Gifford, another prolific author, was a leader of the classis movement of the 1580s. He remained as lecturer of Maldon until his death in 1620.

More influential than either Dent or Gifford was Richard Rogers of Wethersfield, who lived until 1618. Rogers's *Seven Treatises,* the distillation of years of preaching, meditation, and conversation with neighboring ministers, first appeared in 1603 and went through seven editions before 1630. It was the first systematic presentation of the Puritan conception of godliness in its quotidian manifestations, and Rogers hoped that it would counteract the influence of the alarmingly successful manuals being disseminated by the Jesuits. The work went through seven editions by 1630, and excerpts achieved even wider circulation in *The Garden of Spiritual Flowers,* a pocket anthology of edifying Puritan prose.[87]

The greatest of Richard Rogers's many disciples was his nephew John, who as lecturer at Dedham from 1605 to 1637 achieved a popular reputation unsurpassed by any preacher of his generation. The power of his preaching drew the godly from miles around, including students from Cambridge who would ride down to Dedham, as Thomas Goodwin put it, "to get a little fire." After the Restoration, Giles Firmin wrote of Richard and John Rogers that "God honored none more in these parts of England with the conversion of souls than these men."[88]

Mention should be made of a number of other preachers who were active in Jacobean Essex, and whom later Puritans such as Giles Firmin and Cotton Mather associated with Richard and John Rogers in the evangelical tradition. Among Richard Rogers's students were his own sons, Daniel and Ezekiel, as well as Paul Baynes and the future emigrant John Wilson.[89] Samuel Collins was vicar of

Braintree from 1612 to 1658; at his funeral he was described by
Matthew Newcomen, John Rogers's successor at Dedham, as one of
those "whose names God had made precious among the Saints."
(Like Richard Rogers, Collins trained preachers in his own household and used his influence with godly patrons to procure livings for
them.)[90] John Smith, who preached at Clavering in the early years
of the seventeenth century, was celebrated as "the Essex Dove" for
his sanctity. At Great Stambridge, Ezekiel Culverwell, the friend
and editor of Richard Rogers, attracted gadders from neighboring
parishes to hear his sermons.[91] Richard Blackerby, renowned both
for his preaching and his Hebrew scholarship, settled at Ashdon on
the Suffolk border in 1609 and preached in the neighboring towns of
Castle Hedingham, Stoke, and Hundon for the next twenty years.
Blackerby too maintained a school in his home, which was attended
by the sons of "pious gentry, tradesmen, and yeomen." Several of
these pupils became distinguished divines themselves. Among them
was Samuel Fairclough, later the most famous of Suffolk Puritans,
who lived with Blackerby for several years prior to 1619 and
preached in the clothing towns of northern Essex.[92]

In all, Dr. Kalu has identified 167 clerics whom he considers Puritans and who were active in Essex between 1600 and 1628, serving as
incumbents, curates, or lecturers in a total of 118 Essex parishes.
Kalu's criterion of puritanism appears to be overt opposition to
some feature of the established ritual. By this definition Puritans
were active in fewer than one-third of Essex parishes. But they did
extraordinary work. The godly cause found new allies among the
gentry in families like the Mashams, Chekes, Mildmays, Waldegraves, Honeywoods, Grimstons, and Harlackendens, while retaining the patronage of the great families of Rich and Barrington. The
number of parishes experiencing cases of nonconformity among the
laity—opposition to the churching of women, gadding to sermons,
refusal to kneel at the sacrament, and the like—more than doubled
from thirty-four during 1602 to 1610 to seventy-one between 1611
and 1619. Perhaps most important of all was the increasing support
by the laity of Puritan lecturers. Dr. Kalu has discovered a total of
eighteen lecturers active between 1603 and 1609, of whom fourteen
were known Puritans. For the years 1623–1629, the number of lecturers rose to forty-four and that of known Puritans to forty-one. (In
all, according to Kalu, there were seventy-two lecturers active in

forty-three Essex parishes between 1603 and 1629. Fifty-nine can be securely identified as Puritans, while only three were certainly non-Puritans.)[93]

Thus, it would appear that under James I the work of the Gospel went forward in Essex with relatively little official opposition. But this de facto toleration was always precarious. The bad old days of Bancroft and Ravis, of Whitgift and Aylmer, might always recur. There was a worse prospect still. Within living memory there had been bishops named Gardiner, Bonner, and Pole. The nightmare of a Catholic restoration was never far from the godly mind—no farther, in fact, than the great folio of Foxe's *Book of Martyrs* chained to the lectern of the parish church.

5 / The Code of Redemption

He who is of God heareth God's Word.
—George Gifford, in *The Country Divinity*, 1582

In the long, bitter, and inconclusive controversy over the social effects of the Reformation, one obvious point has generally been overlooked. The social group whose interests were most directly advanced by the spread of Protestant doctrine was the rising new class of intellectuals who expounded it: the preachers themselves. The immediate beneficiaries of the Reformation were men to whom Protestantism opened the novel prospect of an intellectual career, attended with considerable prestige and reasonable economic security, without the need to practice (or feign) celibacy. One can easily imagine how the opportunity of combining service to God with a normal family life might have attracted a man like Thomas More, had he been reared in a Protestant environment; one knows how it attracted the young John Milton before he was "church-outed" by the Laudian reaction.

Like professionals in all ages, the preachers were eager to valorize their expertise. Their first task was to persuade a potential clientele that their services were indispensable. A good deal of their discourse, therefore, consisted of self-advertisement. Salvation for the Protestant is achieved *sola scriptura*—by the exclusive agency of the Word of God as revealed in the Bible. But the redeeming power of Scripture was not directly accessible, not even to those who were predestinate to salvation. The Word required translation into terms relevant to the sinful future Saint's personal condition. This task required learning, eloquence, piety, diligence, and divine inspiration: precisely the qualities that characterized the painful preacher.

Protestant "bibliocentricity" thus implied sermonism. Salvation, or so the godly assumed, would come through hearing words about the Word. "Preaching," said Arthur Dent, "is the food of our souls."[1] According to Richard Rogers, the man who seeks faith "must hear sermons often and diligently."[2] George Gifford agreed that "he who is of God heareth God's Word."[3] Dent warned that men who "esteem preachers but as prattlers, and sermons as good tales" are probably damned,[4] while Rogers, in a burst of promotional genius, asserted that "those who love preachers . . . can be assured against committing the sin against the Holy Ghost"—surely the most compelling advertising claim in history.[5]

This exaltation of preaching constituted an audacious bid for social prestige, and implicitly for power, by the preachers themselves. "No calling in the world" could be compared to theirs, wrote William Gouge. Sibbes called the ministry "Christ's mouth." William Perkins went furthest of all, and assigned to ministers the power of the keys to salvation that Catholics claimed for the Pope, although with a different theological interpretation.[6] The old cliché that Protestantism tends to level distinctions between clergy and laity clearly needs some modification in the face of these assertions.

The real difference between Protestant and Catholic doctrine lay in the nature rather than the scope of clerical power. The power of the Catholic priest to administer the sacraments derived from the institution of which he was a part. His personal intelligence and piety were irrelevant to the efficacy of his performance.[7] In contrast, it was precisely the individual qualities of the Protestant preacher—his sanctity as well as his homiletic talent and training—that enabled him to serve as an instrument of divine grace. The wicked man, even if learned, could never effect the conversion of sinners.[8]

This conception of the ministerial function entailed a violent intolerance of incompetence or moral laxity within the clergy. If preaching was essential to salvation, then the "dumb dog" was not merely a parasite. He was, in the words of George Gifford, a "murderer of souls."[9] Similarly, if preachers in their individual capacity were expected to wield the keys of heaven and hell, then the presence within the church of scandalous ministers was not merely a blemish but an abomination. It is completely beside the point to argue, as does J. P. Kenyon, that flagrantly immoral parsons cannot have been numerous.[10] What was at stake was the conception of the ministerial office, and the very basis of the clergy's claim to livelihood, power, and prestige. If the claims of the godly preachers were admitted, then the slightest leniency toward ignorant, lazy, or drunken clerics was sacrilege. As Charles and Katherine George have discovered, this intransigence toward corrupt or incompetent colleagues was a "relative monopoly" of preachers who were regarded as Puritans.[11] Here too, one may suggest, is part of the explanation for the seemingly disproportionate hostility of advanced Protestants to ceremonies, to the surplice, and to the sign of the Cross. To be sure, they were associated with popery, but so, for that matter, was the doctrine of the Trinity. These particular features of the old religion were obnoxious because they symbolized the institutional or corporate source of the minister's charisma, and hence distracted attention from the minister's personal qualities.

The sermonism espoused by the preachers was self-serving in that it constituted an unabashed claim to authority and prestige, but it was neither crudely nor naïvely so. Sermonism derived from a coherent theory of how the fundamental structures of human experience might be disclosed. To put it technically, the preachers based their claim to authority on their ability to manipulate a semiotic code. The term may be abrasively newfangled, but the concept is a useful one.

Semiotics, the science of signification, deals with the ways in which phenomena, forms, and relationships are endowed with meaning. These meanings are organized into systems that model the world, imparting a degree of intelligible structure to the chaotic flux of perceptions. Semiosis renders the word habitable, and, to some degree, tractable. Indeed, semiosis may be said to create the world as an object of human consciousness.[12]

Since natural language affords the most familiar example of a semiotic system, it is often fruitful to discuss other systems of organized meaning through analogies drawn from linguistics. It is still an open question whether apparent analogies between natural languages and other systems of behavior and belief are determined by the innate structure of the human mind, whether they are mere projections of the observers' own longing for order, or whether these two explanations may not be, at some deeper level, synonymous. It is a question we may safely leave for now to professionals in the field. My use of linguistic categories is primarily metaphorical. The Russian formalists believed that the purpose of literature was to make things strange (*ostranenie*), to freshen the world by disrupting habitual patterns of perception.[13] Familiar objects often reveal unsuspected qualities when placed in an unfamiliar light, affording what

Kenneth Burke calls "perspective by incongruity."[14] If I seem to be making the faith of the godly unnecessarily strange, I do so in order to loosen the grip of some anaesthetic conventions and to highlight certain aspects of godliness that are obscured by more orthodox treatments. Specifically, to consider religion as a kind of language is to insist that a religion cannot be reduced to a collection of propositions. Its meaning resides as much in the logic by which these propositions are connected as in the content of the individual elements taken by themselves. The linguistic analogy makes it immediately obvious that we must consider structure as well as content, just as in order to understand a sentence we must pay as much attention to its syntax as to the meanings of its individual words.

It would in any case be impossible to discuss the faith of the godly without linguistic imagery. Language is accorded a very high status in the Judaeo-Christian tradition, which conceives of God himself linguistically. The Old Testament treats the Creation as a speech act: "and God *said,* let there be light." Saint John, under the influence of Greek thought, goes further, treating the Word as both the primal fount of being and the Second Person of the Trinity. God does not merely speak, God *is* language: "the Word was with God and the Word *was* God." Creation is here identified with signification. The Incarnation is a unique semiotic act in which the signifier becomes the signified: "the Word was made flesh and dwelt among us." Nor is this linguistic conception of the divine energy merely metaphorical, for God discloses himself to humanity through the medium of language. The basis of the Judaeo-Christian tradition is a text purporting to be the Word of God: the Bible, the Book, wherein God "spake by the mouth of his prophets." The implication in this choice of medium would seem to be that speech is the human faculty best approximating the divine energy. God is the ultimate speech actor; for him act and speech are one. (Goethe's Faust missed the point: in the beginning word *was* deed.) This logocentrism is further enhanced in mainstream Protestantism by the emphasis placed on the Bible and the preaching of the Word. Salvation is *sola scriptura,* but even the Elect are normally dependent on sermons to gain full access to the saving doctrine that the Scripture affords. Sermonism stresses the hearing of words about the Word as the principle means (though not, of course, the cause) of salvation.

But the *Word of God* seems thus to have two quite distinct meanings. On the one hand it refers to God's power, on the other to a discrete product of that power—the corpus of divinely inspired texts represented by the Holy Scriptures. It is tempting to pun on Schopenhauer and distinguish these two senses as the Word as Will and Representation. Is this double use of the term mere equivocation? And if not, how are the two senses related? To put the question another way, so as to accentuate its urgency, how does what God has chosen to say in his Book relate to what he goes on saying in the created universe? How does the textual Word relate to the actual Word—that is, to the Word as act?

The answer given by Protestants to this question explains both their bibliolatry and their sermonism, and establishes the relationship between the two. The preachers held that the Scriptures, properly understood, contain not merely the record of what God has done and said but the code or program by which God operates. To revert to linguistic analogy, the bible discloses the syntax of God's will. The characters, events, and propositions contained in the Scriptures function as types, which serve to categorize all human experience, both personal and collective, historical and eschatological. The limited corpus of biblical texts enables us to decode the inner logic of an indeterminate sequence of events, in the same way that a very restricted number of propositions will suffice to state the grammatical rules that permit an endless sequence of propositions to be generated. Just as the rules of grammar remain constant no matter what is being said, provided one remains within the context of the given language, so the syntax of God's power remains constant throughout all its varied temporal manifestations, at least while the created world endures. To borrow the terms of Saussurean linguistics, the Bible yields the synchronic rules governing God's diachronic performance.[15]

The godly preachers, then, were structuralists *avant la lettre*. They believed that they could uncover, through the interpretation of the revealed Word, the deep structure of God's will, which is to say of ultimate reality. In one important respect, however, the linguistic analogy understates the informational capacity of the Bible. The grammar of a language is purely synchronic; it contains no provisions for its own evolution or supercession. But the Bible contains diachronic information as well. In addition to a syntax of recurrent types and functions it supplies, notably in the Books of Daniel and

of Revelation, a scenario according to which the whole system is un-
folding over time. The preachers claimed to possess what modern
linguistics has so far failed to achieve: a unified theory encompassing
the synchronic and diachronic planes.

The aspect of the divine grammar that interested preachers most
was what one may call the syntax of redemption. They seemed to
have assumed that God effected the regeneration of the elect sinner
by an invariant, tripartite operation. First came the traumatic conviction of sin, then the awakening hope of mercy, and finally the
transformation of behavior. As in linguistic syntax, the order of the
elements was as important as their specific content. Guilt at sin must
precede the hope of mercy and the reform of life. Only in this particular sequence did they constitute evidence of grace and election.
Preachers never tired of insisting that moral rectitude was worthless
without faith, which presupposed a shattering experience of sinful-
ness. However, the recurrence of excessive guilt and fear *after* conversion was a bad sign. It implied distrust of God's promise and perhaps called into question the authenticity of the original experience.
All Christians agreed that final despair of salvation was the uniquely
unforgivable sin against the Holy Ghost, yet Richard Rogers felt no
inconsistency in affirming that "despair of God's favor" in the initial
stages of regeneration was sign of grace.[16] When George Gifford
warned that the hope of God's mercy was "Satan's fortress," he was
referring not to the mature confidence of the regenerate Saint but to
the complacency of the sinner whose heart had not yet been broken
by contrition.[17] The scenario of salvation, as Arthur Dent wrote,
"hath in it not the nature of a tragedy, which is begun with joy and
endeth with sorrow, but of a comedy, which is begun with sorrow
and ended with joy."[18] Sequence determined significance.
    The first stage, then, was the recognition that we are all damned
by nature. We must experience, said Richard Rogers, "an holy despair of any remedy from ourselves, or any other creature"; we must
persuade ourselves that "many are damned for those sins which we
live in."[19] Godly preachers insisted that this recognition of sin must
be intensely traumatic. Thomas Hooker's collection of sermons, *The
Soules Preparation for Christ*, describes "how God breaks the heart and
wounds the soul in the conversion of the sinner."[20] Those who hope
to be saved, declared Rogers, "must sorrow and weep, turning their

laughter into wailing."[21] Hooker compared the sinner to "a man that hath a bone long out of joint, and it is now festered. It will make him cry many an 'Oh!' before it be brought into its right place again."[22]

The preacher's first duty was therefore to induce fear and remorse. "The words of a faithful minister," said Thomas Hooker, "are like arrows." George Gifford spoke of "the sword of the spirit" penetrating both body and soul.[23] Samuel Clarke recalled admiringly that "there was so much of God" in Richard Blackerby "that he left a perpetual dread upon many souls that would play with others' sermons." Daniel Rogers, Richard's son, and himself an eminent preacher, could never approach Blackerby "without some kind of trembling upon him."[24] Once, when John Rogers was preaching a marriage sermon, "God did so set in with the Word" that Rogers was enabled to turn this normally festive occasion into one of "bitter mourning."[25]

It was this emphasis on the trauma of regeneration that distinguished preachers known as Puritans from their more conservative or irenic colleagues. Godly preachers frequently complained of ministers who failed to denounce sin with sufficient fury. George Gifford went so far as to maintain that learned but nontraumatic ministers did more damage than popish or scandalous ones, since they seduced their auditors into a fatal complacency. It was the more necessary to denounce such pastors because most sinners, even churchgoing Protestants, naturally recoiled from the painful shock of conversion. Archbishop Ussher, a friend of the Barrington family and an admirer of Thomas Hooker, observed that "many men . . . desire a dead minister that would not rub up their conscience."[26] Common Protestants, or "carnal professors," said Richard Rogers, "make the assurance of salvation too common and easy a matter, and they count him little better than a mad man (or at least greatly troubled with some melancholy humor) that is perplexed and troubled in his mind, by doubting the favor of God."[27]

This general reluctance to submit to the trauma of conversion merely confirmed the orthodox Protestant assumption that the vast majority of mankind were damned. Conversion was painful because it involved a rupture with human nature, a rupture too drastic for more than a tiny handful of souls to achieve. Thus, the two doctrines—that true conversion must be painful and that the Saints were very few—were mutually supportive. After the Restoration, Giles Firmin came to believe that the earlier generation of godly preachers in Essex had unreasonably restricted the company of the saved. He thought men like Richard Rogers and his disciples had "cut off most of the sound with the unsound Christians." Yet, even the relatively optimistic Firmin, concerned to mitigate the rigor of his predecessors' teaching, held that "the number of real Christians, such as shall be saved, is very small."[28]

The universe, as depicted by the godly preachers, was not a cheerful place, and it is therefore not surprising that many professors suffered from chronic melancholia. The gloomy Puritan was a subject for hostile caricature, but a tendency toward morbid anxiety was acknowledged by many of the godly themselves. "Religious and zealous persons" admitted Richard Rogers, "are commonly more sad than any other," while Firmin spoke of the "sour, melancholy temper" of some professors, who found laughter offensive.[29] As Jeremy Dyke observed, however, in a sermon dedicated to Sir Francis Barrington, "there is no melancholy compared to the melancholy of Hell,"[30] and the true Christian must be willing to endure an eternity of torment if it should be God's will. The individual who sought Christ out of self-interest—that is, in hopes of being saved—was no better than the drunkard or swearer, said Richard Rogers's son Daniel. Daniel Rogers was admittedly notorious even among Jacobean Puritans for his gloomy disposition (Firmin attributes to him "a most woeful temper"), but Thomas Hooker also maintained that "the heart truly abased is content to bear the estate of damnation." Thomas Shepherd, Hooker's pupil, agreed. Hooker conceded, however, that " 'tis harsh, and tedious, and long ... ere the soul be thus framed."[31] One can readily imagine that it might be.

The preachers refrained, no doubt wisely, from insisting overmuch on this point. Instead they gave the penitent every reason to believe such resignation would remain purely hypothetical. Grief and guilt were, so to speak, self-negating; once they entered the soul they became symptoms of grace. It was only the elect who felt the burden of Original Sin. The reprobate, according to Arthur Dent, are guilt-free, "altogether blinded and hardened in it."[32] When a gentlewoman visited John Rogers with "long and sad stories of her bad heart, sad state, God's wrath due to her, danger of dropping into Hell," and so on, Rogers jumped up and "fetched a few frisks on the floor," crying "God be thanked, God be thanked!" The gentlewoman thought him insane, but Rogers had recognized in her anguish the first tokens of redemption; we are told, in fact, that she later became "an eminent Saint."[33]

Once the heart had been truly broken, and only then, the minister could console the penitent with the good news of unmerited redemption through Christ. When John Rogers had brought the wedding guests to the appropriate pitch of misery and panic, the rest of the ministers present took up the task of comforting these newly awakened consciences and advising them on their continuance in grace.[34] Preachers built reputations on this ability to alleviate spiritual suffering; they were called "physicians of the soul."[35] Thomas Hooker was especially celebrated for "the wise and fit management of wounded spirits." Hooker's prestige among the godly was first established by his success in curing the despondency of a wealthy merchant's wife.[36] Stephen Marshall also had a way with religious neurotics. His most famous patient was his patron William Kempe. Kempe had battered his wife in a jealous rage, whereupon he had been stricken with remorse and lapsed into a "melancholy frensie." He had not spoken for seven years when Marshall accepted the living at Finchingfield. Soon after his arrival Marshall had him talking again and attending church, to the admiring astonishment of the congregation.[37]

The "physician of the soul" had often experienced acute anxiety himself and understood it from within. At Cambridge, according to Cotton Mather, Thomas Hooker had undergone the agonies of self-disgust that were de rigueur for aspiring Saints, although his outward conduct, by all accounts, had been blameless. These inner storms, says Mather, gave Hooker "a most experimental acquaintance with the truths of the Gospel, and the way of employing and applying those truths." He conquered his insomnia by developing a technique of meditation upon "some certain promise of God." Later in his ministry he would recommend this technique to his auditors, assuring them that "the promise was the boat which was to carry a perishing sinner over to Jesus Christ."[38]

Gradually the penitent should acquire the assurance of election that was thought to characterize God's children. "The companion of faith is joy," declared Richard Rogers. The melancholy of the Saint was a sign that faith was still imperfect.[39] But the godly preachers were inconsistent on this question of assurance. They emphatically maintained that the Saints would achieve in this life certain knowledge of election; at the same time they warned against complacency and relaxation. In practice, therefore, chronic anxiety was regarded as a normal concommitant of regeneration. "Blessed is the man," said Richard Rogers, "that feareth always."[40]

Anxiety alone, however, was insufficient evidence of election. The behavioral transformation known as sanctification was expected as well. Godly behavior was a consequence rather than a cause of regeneration; it flowed from the Saint's gratitude at having been chosen by God "before so many thousands."[41] Preachers like Rogers, Dent, and Gifford took great pains to distinguish sanctification from conventional notions of virtue and morality. "Some think that courtesy, kindness, good nature . . . are regeneration," warned Arthur Dent, but "they are greatly deceived." Some of the reprobate might actually surpass some of the elect in the natural virtues like justice, temperance, and liberality. These natural virtues were admirable in themselves, but as Arthur Dent insisted, "many which in the world are counted good honest men . . . good neighbors and good townsmen" were doomed to perdition.[42]

The virtues that identified the Saint were religious, in the narrow sense, rather than ethical. Godly behavior consisted primarily of prayer, attendance at sermons, and association with other putative Saints. The "good honest man" who despised "zealous professors" and regarded preachers "but as prattlers" was likely to be damned, for all his natural virtue. When Arthur Dent enumerated the eight "infallible tokens of a regenerate mind," he placed "a love to the children of God" first, followed by "delight in his Word," and "often and fervent prayer." At the end of the list came "faithfulness in our calling," and last of all, "honest, just, and conscionable dealings in all our actions among men." These are the only two of Dent's eight signs of salvation with a clearly ethical significance.[43]

To be sure, the painful preachers commended charity and denounced covetousness. Moreover they promoted a comprehensive program of cultural reform. It would be wildly inaccurate to accuse them, as did Wallace Notestein, of "want of interest in social questions."[44] But in the final analysis these preachers thought it more important to be pious than good. Richard Rogers was explicit: the churchgoing Protestant who gave generously to the poor but lacked true zeal was "further off . . . from the Kingdom of Heaven" than the professor who neglected "duties of mercy" but who delighted in the Word.[45]

To put it more technically, these preachers laid greater stress on the first four of the Ten Commandments—the so-called First Table—than on the rest. The First Table states man's duties to God, while the remaining six—the Second Table—define the obligations of human beings toward each other. J. Sears McGee has persuasively argued that Puritans and Anglicans can be differentiated by their tendency to emphasize the First and Second Tables, respectively.[46]

The basic criterion of election was thus receptivity to the Word. The Bible, as interpreted by their preachers, afforded the godly a common sign system through which to interpret the world. The communion of Saints was established by a shared semiotic competence, analogous to the linguistic competence that unites speakers of a common natural language. Ability to hear and respond to true doctrine distinguished the Saint. But how, in an age of innovation and murderous controversy, was true doctrine to be identified? The answer was deceptively neat: a preacher's doctrine was validated by the approbation of the Saints. "My sheep hear my voice," said Christ, this time via George Gifford.[47] Once again the linguistic analogy is helpful: the elect could distinguish truth from error just as a native speaker discriminates intuitively between grammatical and nongrammatical utterance.

The Saint's election and the preacher's doctrine were thus reciprocally authenticating. But while the theology of this operation may have been sound, the logic was circular. The principle of reciprocal validation provided no means of deciding between the preachers of contradictory doctrines, each with his own flock of Saints. In the absence of institutional control, the semiotic community was fatally liable to fragmentation into all sorts of theological dialects, jargons, and creoles—the catastrophe of Babel on a higher semiotic plane. Here, of course, was the strongest argument against exclusive reliance on the Word: hierarchical authority was necessary to guarantee the stability of the code itself. This fear of semiotic catastrophe underlay the hostility that conservatives—from the sovereign down to the traditionalist parish rector—felt toward the painful preachers. The fear, as events would prove, was well founded.

* * *

Who were the godly? The traditional view that serious Protestants were most frequently found among the middle strata of society is both inherently plausible and consistent with the Essex evidence. Where else, after all, should the majority of the godly have come from? Despite the qualitative importance of noble professors, the aristocracy amounted to a scant 2 percent of the society. Nor were most gentlemen godly, even in Essex. Of 167 lay patrons during the reign of James, Ogbu Uke Kalu can conclusively identify only twenty-four professors.[48] As for the lower classes, they were virtually written off by the preachers themselves. Throughout history, complained Richard Rogers, the poor have suffered from "universal blindness," and Arthur Hildersam, the friend of Sir Francis Barrington, stated flatly that "the poor in all places are for the most part the most devoid of grace."[49] After five years of lecturing in Chelmsford, Thomas Hooker could "speak it by experience that the meaner sort of people, it is incredible what ignorance is among them."[50]

The preachers seem generally to be addressing an audience of respectable householders. As Charles and Katherine George have shown, preachers expected most Saints to be "of mean estate"—that is, middle class.[51] In a sermon dedicated to William Towse, an Essex justice of the peace and member of Parliament, Thomas Barnes assumed that his auditors were servants in their youth but that they now employed servants of their own.[52] In speaking of the problems and responsibilities of such men, Richard and John Rogers invariably say *we*, while the rich and poor alike are typically referred to in the third person. There are far more references in this literature to the "carking cares" that beset the small businessman than about the miseries of destitution or the obligations incumbent on great wealth. The very idiom of the sermons is revealing. The metaphors and exempla are drawn overwhelmingly from the world of trade; there is a striking absence of imagery drawn from rural or urban labor processes.

The community of Saints may have been drawn disproportionately from the middle strata, but this does not make the puritanism a middle-class ideology. For one thing, the godly did not constitute a majority of any social class. Only one town in six was "forward" in religion, said George Gifford, and he added that "even in the best and most religious towns the greater part have very little zeal."[53] On the other hand, true professors might be found in any social stratum. Even Arthur Hildersam asserted that some of the poor would be saved.[54]

To resist identifying godliness with a specific class is by no means to deny the interaction between religion and social life. On the contrary, I wish to argue that the godly found the preachers' discourse persuasive because it was consonant with their own perceptions of social change. Contemporaries were perplexed and alarmed by the growth of a "superfluous" population of marginal laborers, squatters, and drifters, and by the widening gap between rich and poor. John Winthrop, that patriarch among Saints, trembled to see "our shops full of rich wares, and under our stalls lie our own flesh in nakedness."[55] Accelerated social mobility, both upward and downward, generated considerable anxiety. There was money to be made by astute dealing, but there were also appalling dangers. A bit of bad luck or judgment and one might plummet down among the likes of Hugh Make-Shift. These conditions produced ethical anxiety as well. Old patterns of neighborliness were perforce dissolving, while the ethical code of the future, economic individualism, had yet to achieve social legitimacy. Both forms of anxiety, especially in combination, could gnaw away at an individual's sense of identity. The result, given the mental climate of the age, might be a morbid fear of damnation.

The doctrine of predestination, with its stark division of humanity into the irrevocably and inexplicably saved and damned, must have seemed congruent with the social conditions that the Saints saw around them. Many were called, few chosen, on earth as it was in heaven. It was not that the godly approved of the conditions they saw all around them. On the contrary, they were determined to eradicate whatever suffering and evil were due to human agency. But to men and women achieving a precarious prosperity in a world of spreading misery, the doctrine of double predestination must have seemed both more plausible and more insistently relevant than most people find it today.

Moreover, the preachers' scenario of regeneration provided a means of transforming anxiety from a liability into an asset. Since salvation was both traumatic and, to the elect, assured, fear and trembling could be welcomed as symptoms of grace. At the same

time, it was perversely reassuring, for the angst ridden, to learn that
their well-adjusted neighbor, the man of even temper, good humor,
and sound digestion, was not necessarily saved.

If spiritual anxiety was a sign of grace, however, mundane worry
was the sign of "an earthly slavish mind" and hence an obstacle to
regeneration.[56] Accordingly, preachers sought to distract the Saints'
attention from temporal cares to a fuller concentration on the state
of the soul. "When we are about a bargain," advised John Rogers,
"we should use the best and wisest lawful means we can, and then
commit [all] to God, and so be at rest." The faithful should not permit leases and contracts to disturb their sleep.[57]

Yet, the Saint was not urged to shun the temporal world and its
resources. The Reformed religion rejected asceticism, and found
nothing holy about destitution. "Riches and honors be good benefits," said George Gifford, because "by them men are the more enabled to good."[58] While intensely aware of the spiritual perils of superfluous wealth, the preachers emphasized the right, indeed the
duty, of professors to seek economic security. It was not covetousness, said Jeremy Dyke of Epping, to make "liberal provision" for
one's heirs.[59] In fact, parents who failed to leave "somewhat" to their
children, said George Gifford, were "worse than infidels."[60] Writing
after the Restoration, Giles Firmin warned against letting religion
interfere with secular responsibilities, and recalled "the old Essex
Christians" that would rise early so that "they might enjoy an opportunity for their souls without detriment to their families."[61]

Not only are the godly enjoined to maintain themselves and their
households in decent comfort; they are promised divine assistance in
doing so. The faithful, said Richard Rogers, are obliged to trust that
God will provide in this world as well as in the next, just as Noah
believed not only that he would be made an "heir of righteousness"
but also that he and his family would reach dry land. The godly
have a better chance of avoiding the "plagues and punishments"
that God inflicts on the sinful, such as "hunger, nakedness, diseases,
the pestilence, bondage to enemies and invasion of them, imprisonment, loss of goods, loss of life."[62] John Rogers urged his listeners to
charity by appealing to their material self-interest. By giving to the
poor, "we provide well for our outward estate." Charity is rent paid
to God for the loan of temporal prosperity, and God "will not put
him out of his farm that pays his rent so well."[63] Yet, the promise of

divine favor did not obviate the need for earthly prudence. Richard Rogers commended "skill and wisdom in men's trades" and advised caution in dealing with business associates, "the world being so full of deceit." He disapproved of standing security for another man's debts. While we should pity a man who has fallen prey to his creditors, we are not required to "meddle where we have nothing to do."[64]

By severing the link between salvation and moral virtue, while at the same time validating economic effort, it must be admitted that the preachers left the door ajar to a distinctively godly form of hypocrisy. To a farmer or merchant agonizing over a bit of sharp practice, it might come as a great comfort to learn, from Arthur Dent, that "some of God's dear children . . . are so troubled and encumbered with a crabbed and crooked nature that sins keep breaking out," but to the unregenerate this argument might seem disgustingly self-serving.[65] Some such perception may lie behind the claim made in 1598 by a Hempstead man that "men are the worse for hearing sermons" or this outburst in 1591 from an Elmstead woman: "a shame take all professors, for they are all dissemblers or liars."[66] Antilegon, the spokesman for the reprobate in Arthur Dent's *Plaine Man's Path-Way,* maintained the godly would "do their neighbors a shrewd turn as soon as anybody."[67] John Rogers records the common accusation that some "make a great show of religion, yet if they get money into their fingers one cannot tell how to get it again, for all their great preciseness and running to sermons."[68]

Any evaluation of a particular religion's social impact must take account of the perversions to which it is liable and the ways in which it may be exploited by its more cynical adherents. But the perversions must not be mistaken for the doctrine itself. None of these preachers denied that a certain number of hypocrites had insinuated themselves among the godly. Among other things, a reputation for godliness was a considerable advantage in business, as John Bunyan's Mr. Badman understood all too well. But it required great ingenuity, not to speak of colossal bad faith, to derive an acquisitive ethic from the sermons of these painful preachers. Thomas Aquinas himself could have endorsed most of what Dent, Gifford, and Richard and John Rogers have to say against usury, avarice, and exploitation. If the capitalist spirit consists of a relentless drive to accumulate wealth and a willingness to take risks in the pursuit of higher

profits, then these preachers did everything within their power to
stifle it. Richard Rogers condemned "the love of commodities of this
world" and "the desire of growing rich." Jeremy Dyke warned that
covetousness would bring temporal disaster as well as spiritual peril.
The examples could be multiplied forever.[69] After all, what possible
relevance would a capitalist ethic have had for the farmers, small
merchants, and artisans of Jacobean Essex? We are not dealing with
Victorian Lancashire. In early Stuart England an ethic of unbridled
acquisitiveness would have brought ruin to most of those foolish
enough to adopt it.

The vast majority of the preachers' auditors could hope, at best,
for a modest prosperity and the chance to pass along a suitable inheritance to the next generation. These were the aspirations that the
preachers encouraged and assisted their followers to achieve. They
were almost certainly right in claiming that sanctification was con-
ducive to a modest material success, quite apart from direct supernatural aid. The ethic of godliness, by harmonizing the requirements of economic survival and eternal salvation, may well have
saved many of the middling sort from ruinous self-indulgence.

Sanctification, insofar as it affected secular behavior, amounted to
an elaborate program of detoxification. The Saints were enjoined to
rid themselves of debilitating addictions—to luxury, prestige, sex,
and alcohol. All of these vices led to catastrophe in this world as well
as the next. Avarice and vanity drove people to live fatally beyond
their means in a world without guaranteed loans or bankruptcy
clauses, a world in which usurers foreclosed and debtors went to
prison. "Debt and poverty," warned Richard Rogers, "arise of
needless and excessive spendings, going above our ability in diet,
apparel, purchasing, and building."[70] It was not the whole explanation, but it was what small property owners needed most to hear and
heed.

Lust, even within the bonds of matrimony, distracted folk from
their calling. (The group of professors who met in Wethersfield with
Richard Rogers acknowledged their fault in making excessive "use
of marriage."[71]) Illicit sex undermined the family unit and filled the
parish with bastards to be reared at public expense. But contrary to
the modern stereotype of the Puritan, the godly preachers were not
especially preoccupied with sexual transgressions. They reserved
their heaviest fire for the sin of drunkenness, which was assigned,

with revealing monotony, pride of place among the vices.

Drunkenness, whose prominence in these sermons is at first somewhat startling, represented the victory of carnal appetite over man's higher faculties. As such, it was the emblem of Original Sin; each drunkard was reenacting the fall of Adam. The conversion of a drunkard was therefore the paradigmatic case of regeneration. Drunkard and Saint represented the poles of human potentiality. But drunkenness was a terrible scourge quite apart from its theological implications. Then as now, alcoholism caused physical debility, clouded the judgement, eroded the will, and cost a great deal of money. Even a mild drinking problem could prove ruinous to the farmer or tradesmen whose position was precarious to start with, and who relied on hard work and clear thinking to get by. For the cottager and the poorer artisan, drinking habits could mean the difference between bearable hardship and destitution. Historians who reconstruct the curve of the standard of living often overlook this crucial variable. The painful preachers never forgot it. They knew that the quickest and surest way for a man to improve his economic, as well as spiritual, condition was to stay out of Mother Tibbald's alehouse.

To establish a connection between religion and material life it is not necessary, and it is often ill-advised, to identify specific classes as the natural carriers of specific doctrines. Although Saints seem to have been most numerous among the middle strata, no one social group had an exclusive franchise on godliness. It was not only the middling sort who found that sanctification brought practical as well as spiritual benefits. Diligence, thrift, and sobriety might enable the yeoman to buy up his leasehold and the clothier to increase his stock, but the same virtues could save the debt-ridden gentleman from his creditors, and the weaver or husbandman from a pauper's grave.

Godliness worked. As Christopher Hill has said, it seemed to point the way to heaven because it helped the faithful live on earth.[72] But it was not enough for the Saints to cultivate these virtues in their private lives. One of Arthur Dent's eight signs of salvation was "zeal for God's glory,"[73] and God's glory required that godliness be imposed, as far as might be possible in a fallen world, upon society at large.

6 / Society and Puritanism

> When some would . . . bring in the Ministry of
> the Word, and others oppose it, how must not
> the Devil have his throne in such a place?
>   —John Rogers, in *A Treatise of Love*, 1637

Today the word *neighborhood* has lost much of its former resonance. In the sixteenth century (and, in British usage, down to recent times) the word meant not merely "vicinity" or "a number of persons living near one another" but also the ties of reciprocity that supposedly bind the spatial community together. The clumsier modern synonym would be "neighborliness."[1] It was in this sense that contemporary moralists lamented the demise of "good neighborhood" in Elizabethan England. A culture based on mutual aid, so it was claimed, was being eroded by predatory individualism. "Neighborhood nor love is none," runs the refrain of a popular ballad, "true dealing now is fled and gone."[2] According to George Gifford this attitude was widespread in Essex. The common folk, he tells us, believed that former generations had "lived in friendship and made merry," but "now there is no love [or] good neighborhood . . . Now is every man for himself, and [all] are ready to pull one another by the throat."[3] The preacher Richard Rogers agreed that nowadays "the mighty devise to pill and make bare the meaner sort . . . whereas the predecessors of them both lived together before them in love and good will."[4]

The loss of community is, of course, one of the timeless myths of Western culture. Stable, cozy social units have been disintegrating ever since Lucifer, alienated from the predominant social norms, destroyed the harmony of the cosmos and touched off history. The first human community included those prototypical deviants, Eve and Cain. (Like the community, the family has been falling apart for some time—even longer than the middle class has been rising.)

The more that historians and anthropologists examine the traditional community, the harder it becomes to sentimentalize it, or even to generalize about it at all. Spite, envy, gossip, and enforced conformity are at least as characteristic of small, close-knit social settings as good neighborhood. Certainly no one familiar with the Paston Letters will be tempted to idealize social relations in fifteenth-century England. Despite the relative paucity of information, it is likely that life in the villages and towns of pre-Reformation Europe was at least as risky and stressful as we imagine ours to be. The community was threatened from without by environmental aggression—plague, fire, flood, famine—and from within by all manner of social, generational, and sexual conflicts.[5] Poor old John Worme, for example, who assaulted his neighbor's wife because, as he complained, "he could make as good a cunt of a lathe and two coney skins" as his own wife possessed, is a lamentably universal human type.[6]

And yet, and yet . . . The cliché of the moribund *Gemeinschaft* denotes, while distorting, an important and recurrent process: the destruction or transformation of existing forms of human solidarity and the elaboration of new ones. The concept of community becomes uselessly metaphysical only when the process is presented as a linear sequence, without loops or switchbacks, and when the loss of community is imagined as a uniquely decisive event, like the Fall or the Incarnation.

In the fallen world, communities (patterns of interaction) are endlessly dying and being born. The historian's job is to specify what, at a given moment, is changing into or being annihilated by what. The pre-Reformation parish possessed an elaborately articulated culture, a webbing of traditions, rituals, and institutions that served to sustain solidarity against internal tensions and external threats. Above all, there were the collective rituals of the church. In addition to the regular weekly services there were prayers and processions to avert episodic disaster, festivals to mark the phases of the agricultural cycle, church-ales to commemorate the dedication of the parish church and raise funds for its maintenance, wakes to honor the local patron saint, "help-ales" to provide for the relief of distressed parishioners. William Harrison recalled that under the Pope nearly half the days of the year were in some sense holy: in addition to the Sabbath there were ninety-five feast days and thirty *profesti*, or saints' eves.[7] In addition, there were celebrations to mark the great transitions of personal life—christenings, bride-ales, and soul- or dirge-ales for the departed.[8]

The quotidian routine of parish life was liberally punctuated with dances and booze-ups. In the fifteenth century Saffron Walden had its May revels on the eve of Pentecostal Sunday, its Corpus Christi procession, and its midsummer fair, all under church auspices. In 1538, F. G. Emmison tells us, "players and minstrels, as well as cooks figured in the expenses of the Gt. Dunmow May Feast." Some parishes constructed special buildings for social activities, such as the Church House in Romford or the Marriage Feast House in Matching, both of which survive from the fifteenth century.[9]

The most elaborate and sophisticated products of this culture were the miracle and mystery plays that flourished in Essex from the mid-fifteenth century until the middle of Elizabeth's reign. Thirty towns and villages in Essex produced liturgical plays during this period, among them Colchester, Saffron Walden, Maldon, Chelmsford, Heybridge, Dunmow, Great Baddow, Boreham, and Billericay. Many productions involved the participation of neighboring parishes as well. Twenty-five communities joined in the Dunmow festivities at Corpus Christi during the early sixteenth century.[10]

The festive calendar varied from parish to parish, but processions, feasts, ales, and morris dances seem to have been as ubiquitous as collective worship; all were affirmations of solidarity. As a sympathetic Caroline bishop put it, wakes were useful "for composing differences by meeting of friends, for increase of love and amity," while the church-ales, which celebrated the anniversary of the parish church's original consecration, served to link the living community with its ancestors.[11]

It has been observed that these jollifications were often rowdy affairs, which produced a regular crop of hangovers, broken skulls, and bastards.[12] Moreover, ritual can express conflict as well as harmony. The annual perambulation of the parish boundaries at Rogationtide, which Keith Thomas has described as "the corporate manifestation of the village community, an occasion for eating and drinking, and the reconciliation of disputes," could also be the occasion for a rousing brawl with the lads of the adjacent parish.[13] Thus, in 1578 the parishioners of Runwell and Rettendon fell out during Rogation week over possession of a stretch of common between the two settlements. Similar clashes over common rights, also provoked by Rogation perambulations, occurred in 1564 between High Ongar, Greensted, and Stanford Rivers, and in 1580 between Stock and South Hanningfield.[14] Within the parish even ostensibly religious practices could be used to express hostility. In Hornchurch, for example, in 1566 the parish play served as a vehicle for a satire on the local ministers.[15] Even here, though, ritual may have performed a stabilizing role. One function of what Keith Wrightson has called "festive sociability"[16] is to provide a relatively controlled outlet for aggression and sexual energy, in such a way as to affirm the unity and permanence of the community as a whole.

These religiously sanctioned festivals also contributed to social stability by effecting a limited redistribution of economic resources. They provided opportunities for the more prosperous parishioners to exercise hospitality by donating food and drink, while the lord of the manor would be expected to keep open house on major holidays—especially Christmas. The ritual redistribution effected by these events was largely symbolic, but symbols matter. Moreover, the clerical doctrine of good works must have encouraged the better-off to regard the poor as, in some sense, a spiritual resource. They were the essential raw material upon which charity could be exercised, for the external profit of the donor. This positive inducement to generosity was reinforced by a negative ideological sanction as well—the belief that the beggar's curse in response to ill-usage would be ratified by divine retribution.

This integrative ritual culture, rooted in the Catholic (or pre-Christian) past, was drastically weakened by the religious revolution of the sixteenth century. Among the parochial institutions effaced by the Reformation were the religious guilds and chantries that in some parishes served as rudimentary mutual aid societies. It is true that the guild, whether trade association or religious confraternity, seems to have been relatively weak in Essex. There is little evidence, even in Colchester, that guilds played a significant social role in the later Middle Ages. But this impression may be due simply to shortage of evidence. In any case, we know that in 1473 the statutes of the Guild of All Saints at Moreton provided for the maintenance of a stock to relieve the older "brothers and sisters" and included a mutual undertaking not to engage in litigation with fellow members.[17] In 1527 there is a reference to similar guilds in Braintree and to the Jesus Guild House, owned by the Plough Wardens; there are records from the early sixteenth century of guilds in Great Horkesley, Takely, and Chelmsford.[18] But it is impossible to know how common these rural guilds were. A royal commission listed a mere twenty-four at the time of the Reformation, but it may well be that only the richest guilds received royal notice.[19] In any event, such guilds as existed were abolished, their property confiscated by the Crown and frequently transferred thence into private hands. Thus, in Chelmsford the chapel of the Corpus Christi Guild became the private chapel of the locally dominant Mildmay family.[20]

The Reformed religion, moreover, was hostile to the entire culture of festive sociability, both because of its idolatrous and cryptopagan associations and because of the promiscuous attitude toward charity that the culture endorsed. The Royal Injunctions of 1547 forbade religious processions to invoke divine aid in times of emergency, allegedly because of "the strife for precedence and general disorder which marked these occasions." The Plough Monday processions were banned, the parish church-ale moved compulsorily from the local date to October 1, and all other wakes were banished. Rogation survived, but the ceremony was drastically curtailed. By the Injunctions of 1559 no bells or banners were to be carried, and only the curate and the leading property owners of the parish were to participate in the perambulation, to confirm the parish boundaries.[21] A jubilant popular festival had become a sober assertion of property rights.

The extinction of the old culture proceeded unevenly. But by 1576 William Harrison could write with satisfaction of the "saints' days, superfluous numbers of idle wakes, guilds, fraternities, church ales, help-ales and soul-ales . . . with the heathenish rioting at bride-ales" that had been "well diminished and set aside." Many staunch Protestants, however, wished to go further. Harrison himself hoped to see the abolition of "the feasts of all our apostles, evangelists, and martyrs, with that of All Saints . . . and those of the Virgin Mary" as well as the holy days after Christmas, Easter, and Whitsuntide.[22] Others objected to the survival, even in attenuated form, of old customs like perambulation. In 1565 an unlicensed preacher in Essex named John Goose "spoke certain words against the going about in Rogation weeks to see the limits of the parish, saying 'is there an idol to be worshipped that you have a drinking?' "[23] The previous year the conservative rector of Stisted (rumored to be unsound on the doctrine of predestination) drew the fire of his more radical colleagues for blessing the parish boundaries.[24]

Among the casualties of this religious revolution was the Essex drama. Interestingly enough, the drama enjoyed a brief but spectacular revival after the accession of Elizabeth. The most lavish performances in the county's history occurred in 1562, when the towns of Chelmsford, Maldon, and Braintree joined forces to present a cycle of mystery plays in all three towns.[25] The productions were a financial failure, John Christopher Coldeway tells us, but a popular success. They inspired a flurry of dramatic activity throughout the county for the next decade, as costumes from the original plays were rented out to more than twenty parishes. This attempt to revive the dramatic tradition in a Protestant county and under a Protestant queen—there was no such revival under May—is intriguing. In theory, of course, there was no reason why dramatic forms could not have been adapted to Protestant, or at least Anglican, purposes. Bishop John Bale had attempted to do so during the Henrician reformation. Bale's creative abilities were hardly up to the task of founding a Protestant drama, but dramatic talent was not scarce in Elizabethan England. The lavish productions of 1562 seem to represent an effort on the part of at least some leading townsmen to assimilate the legacy of the past to the new order. There is no suggestion that these productions were regarded as in any way irregular or subversive. They seem rather to represent a reassertion of local harmony after the murderously divisive years of the Marian persecutions.

Yet, the drama in Essex was extinct by 1579. The immediate causes of its demise remain obscure, and I do not find Dr. Coldeway's attempt to relate it to the vestiarian controversy very convincing.[26] There was no official repression through the secular courts, and only sporadic harassment by the church courts, when the actual church fabric was put to unseemly uses. But the whole spirit of Protestantism was hostile to the drama. Even ostensibly religious plays were obnoxious to stern Protestants. They dealt with saints and miracles, they distracted folk from hearing sermons and reading Scripture, and they were accompanied by what William Harrison would no doubt have considered "heathenish rioting." (Charles Phythian-Adams has described in detail how the communal drama, and festive ceremony in general, died out in the town of Coventry during this same period; R. C. Richardson has done the same for Chester.)[27]

To the extent that the old ritual culture preserved at least the illusion of social harmony, the destruction of that culture by Protestantism must have contributed to the notion that "now there is no love nor good neighborhood." But Protestantism can also be seen as a creative response to social changes that, quite independently, had doomed the old culture. One reason for the appeal of Protestantism, especially in its more rigorous forms, may have been the fact that the symbols of collective identity had been rendered dysfunctional by widening ethical and economic divisions. Keith Thomas, for example, attributes the decline of Rogation ceremonies to "the increasing reluctance of wealthy householders to pay for the riff-raff of the village to drink themselves into a frenzy."[28]

The proliferating tribe of Make-Shift was regarded with alarm instead of complacent pity. The decline of collective festivity coincides with the rise of witch-hunting, which had the effect of outlawing the pauper's most effective weapon of self-defense, the invocation of divine vengeance. The beggar's curse was diabolized. Only the devil, it was assumed, would answer the prayers of an indignant and insubordinate beggar; God would aid only the submissive poor.

Attitudes toward charity were changing. Individual acts of benevolence, performed in the context of festive sociability and ritual redistribution, were attacked on both social and theological grounds. First, such acts rested on the (recently) fallacious doctrine of salvation by works. Second, they failed to differentiate between the deserving poor and the indolent or wicked. The two arguments were complementary; sound theology made practical sense. "The wicked will be most clamorous," John Rogers told the people of Dedham, "and if we go by that, oft times the better-minded poor, which be more bashful and slow to speak for themselves shall have wrong." For this reason Rogers deplored the "great disorder in some great men's keeping open house at Christmas." Traditional displays of hospitality attracted only the "rude, idle, and profane," since the truly poor could not brave the "dirt and cold and crowd."[29]

This distinction between the deserving and undeserving poor was embodied in the Elizabethan Poor Law, which William Perkins considered "in substance the very law of God." When John Rogers declared, "for those that can work and will not, let them starve," he was merely articulating one of the central premises of the existing law.[30] With the institution of the compulsory poor rate, the parish assumed the basic responsibility for keeping the poor alive. But neither the Poor Law nor the doctrine of salvation *sola fidei* extinguished the obligation to exercise charity. Good works were the expected fruits of regeneration, and the Protestant ethic required that surplus wealth (beyond what was required for the maintenance of an appropriate standard of living) be devoted to socially benevolent purposes. In a sermon against covetousness Jeremy Dyke of Epping rejected the idea that "men having enough should give up their honest calling and receive in no more." They should continue to accumulate wealth, and "make the overflow of their cup serviceable." On this occasion Dyke had in mind primarily "the maintenance of God's worship," but the injunction applied to temporal purposes as well.[31]

Richard Rogers divides society into three broad classes: the "merely poor" who depend on alms; the intermediate households, who can "in some sort partly maintain themselves," but only by borrowing from their neighbors; and finally those truly competent households that dispose of a surplus above their basic needs and can thus come to the aid of poorer families. Like many of his contemporaries, Rogers seems to have assumed that wage labor alone could not support a viable household. The loss of economic independence for a householder meant pauperization. Families headed by the likes of Hugh and Gillet would inevitably need relief. As Rogers puts it, men who because of "want of stock" are compelled to "give over occupying"—or who, in modern terminology, are forced out of business by lack of capital—"may with the peace of their conscience receive alms," because they have no alternative.[32]

The possibility never occurred to Rogers—nor, so far as I am aware, to any of his contemporaries—that a rise in real wages might lift Hugh and Gillet out of destitution. The spread of poverty could be checked only by slowing the growth of the class of laborers. Therefore, the duty of the prosperous householder, as Rogers saw it, was not to pay out higher wages. There were laws, in any case, against exceeding the rates fixed by the justices, and there was limited demand for the sort of labor, outside the household, that Hugh and Gillet could provide. Rather, those who "are able to lend or to

give" must try to prevent those who "can in some sort partly maintain themselves" from sliding down into the "merely poor," and
must "help them up when they are decayed." Rogers believed that
the ruin of these intermediate households was due largely to "the
hardness of their hearts who will forgo nothing to the relief and setting up of such." The prosperous householder, Rogers argued, was
obliged to extend interest-free loans to neighbors whose farms or
trades were failing, to grant the debtor as much time as might be required for repayment, and even to remit the principle altogether if
the debtor, after trying in good faith, proved unable to repay.[33]

Richard Rogers, in fact, had more to say about lending than
about alms giving. He was more concerned with shoring up the de-
caying household through easy credit—that panacea of the small
commodity producer—than with relieving the already impoverished. His nephew John took the same line. "Help them 'ere it be too
late," he pleaded with his Dedham parishioners; "we must not tarry
till they have sold their cupboard, bed, their best coat." A timely
loan, he observed, might preserve the independence of a household
that would otherwise need alms. John Rogers further argues that we
are "as much bound in conscience" to make loans to honest and
competent artisans who "want stock to employ themselves" as we
are "to give a piece of bread or a penny to a poor miserable creature."[34] Richard Rogers even claims that, in times of general hardship, the man of means must lend his entire surplus, without asking
interest, to those in need. Only in prosperous times may the well-to-
do "continue their patrimony and inheritance to their prosperity."[35]

The implications of this social ethic are thoroughly conservative.
Certainly the utopia one might extrapolate from these sermons
would not look much like capitalism. Insofar as capitalism required
for its growth a large class of families dependent on wage labor,
these men stood squarely against it. Their social ideal is far closer to
that of Thomas Jefferson than Alexander Hamilton. A godly commonwealth would be a society of independent producers—like that
of early Massachusetts. Diligent labor would assure a moderate
prosperity to most households, since God looks after his own. To be
sure, even the elect suffer temporal afflictions; none are free from sin.
But a godly commonwealth would provide safeguards against misfortune. Inequality would not be cumulative, as in the fallen world.
There would be no exploitation since, in the words of Richard

Rogers, "usury and oppression, like witchcraft and idolatry, have no place among God's people."[36] Moreover, there would be a continual redistribution of wealth from the godly rich to the godly poor. Decayed householders would be helped back on their feet by free loans and outright subsidies. Only the aged and infirm would need regular alms, which would be given without stigma. There would be no vagabonds, beggars, or able-bodied paupers.

Seventeenth-century Essex, alas, did not much resemble the commonwealth we have imagined. This utopian projection is useful merely as a way of disclosing some of the implications of the godly ethic for social policy in a world that fell far short of the ideal. In the real world most of the poor were vicious and irreverent, a menace to themselves and to their neighbors, "and not so miserable in their corporal as in their spiritual state."[37] We have noted Richard Rogers's assumption that most of the poor were damned; his nephew went so far as to suggest a direct correlation between poverty of goods and grace: "they that be most poor that crave alms," he affirmed, "are very graceless."[38]

These preachers—as well as, one suspects, most of their respectable parishioners—assumed an explanation of poverty that has been revived in our own day. Put baldly, the theory attributes most poverty to the moral failings of the poor themselves. In his 1970 study of the North American urban crisis, Edward Banfield gives us the theory in modern dress. The real cause of poverty, says Banfield, is the character structure of what he calls the "lower class individual," who "lives from moment to moment": "impulse governs his behavior, either because he cannot discipline himself to sacrifice a present for a future satisfaction, or because he has no sense of the future. He is therefore radically improvident . . . His bodily needs (especially for sex) and his taste for 'action' take precedence over everything else—and certainly over any work routine. He works only as he must to stay alive."[39]

Allowing for the difference in jargon, Banfield's attitude is very close to that of preachers like Richard and John Rogers. The godly, as we have seen, were assured of a modest prosperity. Hence, poverty was, in most cases, *prima facie* evidence of sin, if not of ultimate reprobation. Richard Rogers taught that poverty "might well be avoided, if sin were taken heed of and resisted, and by labor and watchfulness the unruly heart subdued."[40] If we substitute *bodily needs* for *sin* and *radical improvidence* for the *unruly heart,* we have arrived at Banfield's *Unheavenly City.* The preachers, moreover, would certainly have appreciated the Augustinian allusion in Banfield's title.

This theory of poverty is neither as heartless nor as crude as it might appear. John Rogers, for instance, urges the prosperous to observe the sufferings of the poor at first hand, "their ruinous and cold houses, poor fire, empty cupboards, thin clothing." The preachers recognized that some of the poor belonged to the "Household of Faith," just as Banfield concedes that what he calls a "middle-class personality" may be trapped, by ill-luck, inside the skin of a slum dweller. But the deserving poor are clearly a small minority, and they are by definition the least demanding and the most submissive. It is only the "very graceless" who clamor for relief, just as none but witches seek supernatural revenge on their betters.[41]

The consequences of this theory for social policy were obvious. The way to reduce poverty, or perhaps more realistically to check its growth, was to reform the outlook and behavior of the poor, and of those whose characterological flaws were likely to impoverish them. The preachers thus provided a theological legitimation for the cultural revolution that contemporaries called the "reformation of manners." It entailed a massive assault not only on behaviors that were generally stigmatized, such as fornication and outright drunkenness, but upon the whole context of popular sociability, which was assumed to foster impulsiveness and self-indulgence. The preachers proposed to substitute for the culture of neighborhood and good-fellowship a new culture of discipline. Richard Rogers promised that the imposition of godliness would "break off ill customs ... which bad meetings the foolish and ignorant world calleth good fellowship." The "ungodly fellowships" that Rogers wished to extirpate included "dissolute merry-makings . . . stage plays, May games, lords of misrule, morris dancing, stockings, and meetings together at victualling houses."[42]

The war against popular culture consisted of innumerable minor battles and skirmishes. Richard Blackerby achieved a small but exemplary victory for the culture of discipline at Castle Hedingham by transforming a frivolous group of young friends, who met together to "dance and frolic it in their youthful sports, sins and vanities," into a prayer group of "gracious Christians."[43] In Maldon, George Gifford was "much valued . . . for the good reformation he had made in that market town by his preaching, where very notorious sins reigned before his coming."[44] Before Thomas Hooker arrived in Chelmsford in 1626 "there was more profaneness than devotion in the town," but during the few years of his lectureship "the Sabbath came to be very visibly sanctified among the people," thanks to "the power of his ministry in public, and . . . the prudence of his carriage in private."[45]

Preachers like Blackerby, Gifford, and Hooker were the indispensable allies of local elites grappling with the problems of overcrowding, unemployment, and disorder. As we already know, there were compelling secular reasons for attempting to regulate the morals of the poor and for promoting self-restraint among potential welfare cases. The psychological sanctions afforded by religion were essential to a campaign of moral reform, since vast tracts of the popular culture had to be, so to speak, infernalized.

The laymen who were most active in promoting the reformation of manners were very likely to be earnest Protestants, committed to the institution of a painful preaching ministry.[46] In Parliament, Sir Francis Barrington, Sir Robert Wroth, and Sir William Wiseman promoted godly legislation directed against drunkenness, fornication, blasphemy, and extravagance in apparel; such men also opposed the suppression of painful preachers for nonconformity. At the local level it was generally the godly members of the parish who sought to suppress superfluous or disorderly alehouses. A petition of 1602 from East Tilbury captures the crusading fervor of the town's "principal and chiefest inhabitants." According to the petitioners an alehouse keeper named John Nicolson had "of his own evil mind procured and by force compelled divers to commit that horrible vice of drunkenness, whereby his good neighbors are greatly grieved, the Sabbath day profaned, God dishonored, and the Kingdom of Satan erected."[47] (One wonders exactly what sort of force Nicolson employed to compel his clients to besot themselves.) Keith Wrightson has studied ten petitions against alehouses presented to the Essex Quarter Sessions between 1617 and 1629. In four cases the list of signatories was headed by a man Wrightson considers a "known Puritan," in two more cases by a "probable Puritan." Two more

petitions came from parishes with Puritan ministers, while the remaining two show "marked adherence to 'godly' rhetoric in the language."[48]

A reformation of manners might help to save souls; it would certainly bring relief to taxpayers by eliminating immiserating vices. At
the same time, charity and poor relief could serve as agents of behavioral and moral reform. In Chelmsford in 1622 the parishioners decreed that before the poor received any relief from the town, they
were to be interrogated by the pastor in the fundamentals of Christianity, so that "some restraints may be made to those which shall be
found most negligent and ignorant." In Braintree during the following decade the vestry denied alms to paupers who failed to attend
church. There was a similar ordinance passed in Royden after the
Restoration.[49] Private charity, said John Rogers, should be accompanied by exhortations to the poor to attend church regularly and to
"bring up their children to work, not to pilfering, idleness, or begging."[50]

There were obviously sound economic reasons for wishing to see
the morals of the poor reformed. But we must not be anachronisti-
cally secular in explaining the reformation of manners. We shall not
understand the godly unless we take their fundamental assumptions
as seriously as they themselves did, and they took their theology very
seriously indeed. Godly preachers and their supporters were concerned about the social consequences of vice, but they were also
concerned about the wrath of God. Blasphemy, for example, was regarded with almost as much horror as drunkenness, although the
deleterious practical effects of swearing are less clear to the modern
mind. In part, no doubt, blasphemy suffered from associative guilt,
habitual swearers were likely to be disreputable in other ways as
well. In particular blasphemy was probably quite closely correlated
with alcohol intake. But the real objection to blasphemy was that it
offended God and might bring down divine punishment upon the
community that tolerated it. Similarly, drunkenness and fornication
were abominable not only because they caused distress and conflict
but because, as a clerical cliché expressed it, they "stank in the nostrils of the Most High." Jeremy Dyke's strongest objection to alehouses was that by profaning the Sabbath they invited disaster in
the form of divine "judgments."[51] The reformation of manners was
intended to do more than foster the patterns of behavior necessary

for social harmony, it was also designed to avert plagues, invasions, bad harvests, and other judgments inflicted by an angry God. The same considerations applied to the countenancing of popish survivals or idolatrous innovations.

At the local level the reformation of manners could be accomplished only through close cooperation between the minister and the chief inhabitants of the parish. "In a town, when chief men hold together," asked John Rogers, "what evil can stand against them? What good may they not effect?"[52] The widening competence of the parish in secular affairs promoted the confusion of church and state at the local level, and enhanced the administrative responsibilities of the minister, the parochial officials, and the vestrymen. In Dedham in 1585 the rules for the "better ordering of the town" resulted from consultation between the "ancient inhabitants" and the town's two ministers, both leaders of the classis movement.[53] At Braintree the incumbent, Samuel Collins, presided over the reconstitution of the select vestry, the Company of Twenty-Four. At Collins's funeral Matthew Newcomen reminded the parishioners of Braintree that their late pastor had been "the means of directing you into some kind of order and form ... of civil government in this town, and thereby into a way of more vigorous suppressing disorders, and more comfortable providing for your poor, than is almost to be found again in any town in the country."[54]

Stephen Marshall played a similar role in reforming the government of Finchingfield. In Terling, Keith Wrightson and David Levine have documented a reformation of manners coinciding with the growth of godly attitudes among prominent local laymen during the reign of James. Alehouses were suppressed, the bastardy rates reduced, and men of dubious morals expelled from the village government.[55] In 1625 Thomas Shepherd, later a famous Puritan preacher in Massachusetts, was living in Terling with the incumbent, Thomas Weld, another future emigrant. Shepherd found himself surrounded by "the best ministers ... in the best county in England."[56] But this association of godliness with repressive social reform was not peculiar to Essex; the same connection has been discovered in Kent by Peter Clark and in Lancashire by R. C. Richardson.[57]

There is a further point to be made about the connection between religion and local government. Effective parochial administration, as we have seen, required close cooperation between the local lay authorities and a preaching minister who enjoyed their confidence. Together they could exercise social control, and perhaps effect a reformation of manners, through a combination of temporal and spiritual sanctions. But what else was presbyterianism, at the level of the parish? From one point of view presbyterian ecclesiology can be seen as the projection of a tendency inherent in the elementary facts of village life after the decline of feudalism and serfdom. One might almost say, parodying R. H. Tawney, "manorialism ends, presbyterianism begins." If a parish were to cope with the crisis in social policy, some sort of functional presbyterianism was imperative, regardless of the doctrinal preferences of parson and vestry.

It was particularly desirable that parochial officials be godly because they were unpaid. In his study of Somerset T. G. Barnes has observed a striking contrast in efficiency between the salaried officials of the county and the unpaid constables, overseers, and churchwardens. The latter, he suggests, sought to evade office if possible and to shirk their duties when chosen.[58] But the religious convictions of professors inspired them to seek civic responsibility. Men who believed themselves elect required no earthly wage to perform their duties with diligence.[59] Power tends to flow toward people who are willing to work hard for nothing. In many parishes the indifferent majority—folk who were neither especially godly nor especially profane—must have been quite content, at least at first, to allow their more zealous neighbors to assume burdens that they themselves shunned. Peter Clark has observed that in Dorchester, Exeter, Manchester, and Salisbury, godly ministers and magistrates "earned approval not merely for their theological superiority but for their greater sense of civic service and responsibility."[60]

It would, however, be a serious mistake to exaggerate the popularity of the godly and their program of cultural reform, even in "the best county in England," before the accession of Charles. The zealous professors arrogated to themselves a vanguard role in the struggle with Satan, and aspired as predestinate Saints to live visibly holier lives than the great mass of their neighbors. Such people were not universally esteemed. The professors, both lay and clerical, had enemies who found their style abrasive and their pretensions insufferable. Those who dismissed the godly as prigs, fanatics, or mere hypocrites had different names for them, the most familiar of which was Puritan. It is a word I have hitherto used sparingly. Historians have grown increasingly uncertain about how to identify Puritans. Distressed by inconsistent usage in the seventeenth century, and despairing of any unequivocal definition, some historians prefer to drop *Puritan* from the historiographical lexicon altogether. To do so would, I believe, be a serious error.

Part of the problem comes from trying to assign a clear denotative significance to a supremely emotive and judgmental term. Wittgenstein's observation, that to understand the meaning of a word one must know its use in particular "language games" applies with particular force to the word *Puritan,* whether as adjective or noun. In the later sixteenth and early seventeenth century the word was always in play. It was constantly being hurled, deflected, or defused. However uncertain we may feel about the exact coloration and distinctive markings of a typical Puritan, there can be no ignoring the empirical fact of conflict between people who were called Puritans and the people who did the name calling.

The word *Puritan* encoded a specific indictment. It associated the avowed elitism of the godly with the schismatic arrogance of the medieval Cathars. Moreover, it implied that the profession of the godly was spurious, since it was believed that the sanctimonious Cathars, especially their Perfecti, had in fact been hideously depraved.[61] For the godly themselves, however, the word had not merely a different meaning but an entirely different function. As Wittgenstein might say, they used it in a different language game. The godly, of course, rejected the accusation of schism and hypocrisy, but more important they maintained that the very use of the word *Puritan* served to identify the speaker as an enemy of God and godliness. In semiotic terms, anti-Puritans used the word as a sign denoting the people I have referred to as professors. For the professors, the targets of this pejorative designation, the word was an index—its use was a symptom of depravity.[62] As Timothy Rogers, the minister of Steeple Bumstead, put it, "Not to be a loose and dissolute liver is to be a Puritan, in common conversation." It was the "lewd and profane of life" who used this "odious name" to denigrate their spiritual betters.[63] John Rogers also waxed indignant over the way the godly were slandered as Puritans and "Precise fellows."[64]

Properly understood, then, the term *Puritan* refers not merely to the godly and their beliefs but to the hostility that godly behavior aroused in their less austere neighbors. The conflict between Puritans and "honest good fellows"—or, from the Puritan point of view, between the godly and the profane—divided virtually every parish in southern England. In Wiltshire and Dorsetshire in the 1630s it was the custom in many parishes to balance the factions by choosing one Puritan and one "honest man" as churchwardens.[65] This conflict was far more ubiquitous and intense, I would argue, than antagonisms based explicitly on social class or even economic interest.

I believe that the word *Puritan* remains indispensable to the description and analysis of this state of affairs, and I shall no longer attempt to avoid it. I shall use *Puritan* and (less frequently) *puritanism* in subsequent pages to denote the aggressive, reformative, and hence socially disruptive aspects of zealous Protestantism. *Puritan,* as I understand the term, implies a will to impose certain standards upon society as a whole. *Puritanism* entails hostility to the traditional culture as well as enthusiasm for sermons and predestinarian theology. A man of irreproachable personal piety who nevertheless has no objection to his neighbors' boozing on the Sabbath or fornicating in haylofts is not a Puritan. A Puritan who minds his own business is a contradiction in terms.

John Bastwick, the celebrated victim of Laudian repression in the 1630s, was born in Writtle in 1593. In his youth, as he later recalled, he had been "bred in as great a hatred of Puritans, as any tender years were capable of . . ." On the rare occasions when a sermon was preached in the neighborhood, "half of it commonly was railing against Puritans."[66] Writtle, it is true, was a nest of recusancy. But things were scarcely better in Maldon, nine years before Bastwick's birth, where the godly, by their own account, went in fear of open violence from a "multitude of papists, heretics, and other enemies to God and her Royal Majesty."[67] In 1598 George Gifford complained of a "flood of ignorance and darkness overflowing the most part of the land."[68] Thirty years later John Rogers claimed that "it is more safe from the hatred and ill-tongues of most to be anything rather than to be zealous and godly." Most people loved the Saints "as a dog loves a pitchfork."[69] The redoubtable Richard Blackerby had to contend with "many profane persons" that would "curse ministers bitterly," although Blackerby himself was able to terrorize them into silence.[70] At Wethersfield there were "envious persons" who tried to get Richard Rogers silenced and who slandered his patron, Lord Rich.[71]

As Patrick Collinson has noted, the papers of the Dedham classis show that "unruly and unresponsive elements" were to be found in nearly every parish in the conference, and that "these were not necessarily confined to the dregs of the community."[72] In some parishes—Coggeshall and Stratford among them—the ministers dared not prosecute disruptive parishioners for fear of making themselves even more unpopular. Even at Dedham, the center of the conference, the vicar Richard Parker wondered what to do "when disorders be risen up in a church, and [are] publicly reproved, and the chief of the parish and the officers dealt withal . . . and yet nothing is done."[73]

Between 1582 and 1591 there were well-documented clashes between Puritans and their opponents at Hatfield Peverel, Wethersfield, Felsted, Aldham, East Hanningfield, Halstead, Goldhanger, Finchingfield, and many other parishes.[74] At Stanford-le-Hope in 1591 the congregation was split between the supporters of the Puritan lecturer Tristram Blaby and those of the rector Martin Clipsam, who administered communion in bread alone, "after the Popish manner." Near-riots erupted when Blaby denounced Clipsam from the pulpit as a "dumb dog" and a "murderer of their souls," and again a week later when Clipsam riposted by shouting during Blaby's lecture, "Come down thou prating Jack, thou foamest out thine own poison."[75]

The godly regarded papists, both foreign and domestic, as their most dangerous and implacable foes. The approach of the Spanish Armada brought Richard Rogers to the verge of panic. "We are now in peril of goods, liberty, and life by our enemies the Spaniards," he confided to his diary, "and at home Papists in multitudes ready to come upon us unawares."[76] The papist rising never materialized; even as Rogers wrote these lines, the Spanish fleet had been shattered off Gravelines. But Rogers's fears were not utterly groundless. Even in Essex the old faith retained its adherents. Among the gentry the families of Audley, Capel, Petre, and Waldegrave, as well as branches of the Wiseman and Mildmay clans, were reputed Catholics; so were a host of lesser families. There was a current of popular Catholicism as well, typified by George Binks, a tailor of Finchingfield, who persisted in the belief that "the Mass is good, and *confiteor* is good" and approved of wayside crosses and the images of saints. George Binks and his brother William had corrupted an illiterate husbandman named Brown by reading him "certain books." Brown ceased to attend sermons and forbade his wife to go, "to her great grief."[77]

George Gifford thought conversions like that of Brown were distressingly common. He blamed the ignorance and immorality of the official clergy, which contrasted unfavorably with the courage and learning of the Jesuits. But he also believed that religious nostalgia might be caused by economic distress. "The simple sort, which cannot skill of doctrine," he noticed, "speak of the merry world when there was less preaching, and when all things were so cheap, that they might have twenty eggs for a penny."[78]

Thus, as the Catholic past receded into the mists of folk memory, it became possible to associate the disruptive social trends of the age with the change in religion. "Now favor hindreth equity," wrote a Catholic gentleman of Walthamstowe,

> And riches rule the roost.
> In vain the poor cry "Charity,"
> "God help you," say the most.[79]

As we have seen, at least a few Essex laborers looked for a Spanish invasion to install an egalitarian and orthodox utopia.

The godly, however, almost certainly exaggerated the danger of Catholic recidivism. (The menace of popery was, after all, their strong suit in the face of episcopal repression.) Bishop Fletcher of London concluded after his visitation of 1595 that there were few recusants in the county.[80] At about the same time the Jesuit missionary John Gerard reached a similar conclusion. If there were many like George Binks, Gerard failed to make contact with them. In Essex, unlike Lancashire, he found himself in constant peril of detection, because the people were all "fierce Protestants."[81]

One did not need to be a Catholic, however, to dislike Puritans. Many loyal members of the Church of England found the emphasis on preaching and biblical exegesis both arid and divisive. "If the preacher do pass his hour but a little," complained George Gifford to his auditors, "your buttocks begin for to ache and ye wish in your heart that the pulpit would fall." Gifford's character Atheos, who "did never put any trust in images," wished the Pope "in a dung-hill," and believed that preaching was "good now and then," but disliked truly painful preachers. "They be over-hot and severe," he protested, "and preach damnation to the people." Public discussion of matters such as election and predestination, he argued, "make men worse."[82]

If Atheos' attitude was as widespread as Gifford claims, then William Clybury, vicar of Halsted, probably scored a telling point when he declared, "My fine fellows and my jolly fellows can suck out their doctrines out of their fingers' ends, but I preach my doctrine out of ancient doctors and writers of these three hundredth [sic] years old." One reason why William Binks clung to the old religion was that "the preachers now do preach their own inventions and fantasies, and therefore I will not believe any of them."[83]

The insistence that the laity must study, and argue over, the Scriptures also appeared unreasonably demanding to many. In 1577 a Bury petticoat maker told a group of servants at the house of John Wentworth, a Puritan gentleman of Bocking, "It was never merry in England sithence the Scriptures were so commonly preached and talked upon among such persons as they were."[84] Similar views were voiced from the pulpit. An unnamed minister cited in the "View of the Clargie" denounced as Puritans those who demanded that artisans read the Bible.[85] A fair number of people agreed, like the Sabbath-breaking shopkeeper who reviled his godly neighbors by "wishing them and their Bibles hanged one against the other."[86]

Resistance to the Puritan program was naturally strongest in what Keith Wrightson has called the "dark parish"—the disreputable subculture of drunkards, fornicators, drifters, ballad singers, and criminals. In most parishes there would appear to have been a few really hopeless cases, men and women completely insensitive to threats of hellfire. The records of the church courts are full of examples. In 1607 James Bottell of Colchester proclaimed defiantly that "he careth no more to go to church than the church cares to go to him." Similarly, Averius Blacks of Chissell Parva refused to attend church "so long as he lives or breathes." John Prentice of Fryerning in 1613 "disgracefully misused and abused" his minister, who admonished him for "playing on instruments in assemblies" during serice time. In 1620 five Great Burstead men incited their children and servants to ridicule the minister while he was catechizing them.

In 1606 the parson of North Ockenden was vexed by servants "laughing, jeering, and jesting" during his sermons.[87] In Chelmsford, where paupers were regularly examined in the articles of Christian religion, respectable parishioners were distressed by the presence of "tippling poor people, and houses of profanation" at the very foot of the church. In 1623 it was resolved to nail shut the gates in the fence that segregated the dark parish from the Children of Light, lest the congregation be disturbed during divine services.[88]

The profane had their spiritual leaders, just as the godly had their preachers. At West Ham one William Ford led a group of townsmen who devoted their Sundays to "drinking, swearing, and singing ribald songs, and abusing Mr. Holbrook." Mr. Holbrook was the local vicar. When he reproved Ford for his disgraceful behavior, Ford "bid him kiss his tail."[89] In Rayleigh at the time of the Armada the antipastor was named John Radcocke. He and his cronies staged an impromptu Feast of Fools in Mother Larkinge's alehouse, impersonating the parson, churchwardens, and "honest men" of the parish while "sitting upon their alebench and greatly amusing themselves . . . like drunken sots." Twelve years later a rather charming ceremony was enacted at Corringham. Three friends, much the worse for drink, took several pots of beer out into the fields and "humbly kneeling down and kissing the pots and drinking to one another, prayed for the health of all true and faithful drunkards." They especially remembered in their devotions one Mr. Andrew Broughton, whom they called "the maintainer and upholder of all true and faithful drunkards." At the conclusion of the rite they kissed each other, and "for a memorial of their worthy act" each made his mark on an ash tree.[90]

As the reference to Mr. Andrew Broughton, a local gentleman, suggests, opposition to godliness was not limited to the lower classes. At Rainham in 1601 the vicar accused a gentleman name John Frith of supporting "all the rogues and knaves and whores and thieves and a murderer" against him.[91] John Walford, a substantial yeoman of Wethersfield, was "a common ringleader . . . of evil rule and disorder."[92] John Rogers denounced "the wicked magistrate, that is very friendly to all the country and keeps a good house all the year, and yet suffers sin to reign, and houses of disorder to abound in his circuit."[93] It was worst of all when the parson himself was in league with the dark parish. In 1586 the Puritan "Survey of the Unpreaching Ministers in Essex" denounced the parson of Widford, Mr. Palmer, as a "gamester and pot companion," and a former soldier to boot, who had "received into his house a strumpet who was brought to bed there, which was to save her from punishment." It was also alleged that "he usually marrieth unknown persons without any banns." There were good social as well as theological reasons to purge the church of ministers like Palmer; there would be little hope of reform in Widford while such a man held the pulpit.[94] In North Ockenden in 1611 the minister was accused of being "a maintainer of drunkards and whoremasters" who would "sooner bear with them than with good Christians."[95]

It was not only degenerates who opposed the reformation of manners. Many who hated the Puritans were simply attached to traditional forms of sociability. They agreed with the anonymous minister cited in the "Viewe of the Clargie," who said that

> Those who are so precise
> That they will have no Christmas pies
> It were good the crows
> Should pick out their eyes.[96]

Preachers like Dent, Gifford, and Hooker often attributed to their enemies some pretty persuasive arguments. Gifford's Atheos, for example, prasies his local curate as "a very good fellow" who composes neighborhood quarrels by inviting the parties to "play a game or two at bowls or cards, and to drink together at the alehouse." He is, says Atheos, "none of these busy controllers." From Gifford's point of view this amiable curate is a murderer of souls because he does not denounce vice or "preach damnation to the people." For Gifford a minister must be a "busy controller." But it is not easy to share Gifford's outrage, or to disagree with Atheos when he says, "I think it a godly way, to make charity."[97]

Folk like Atheos, whom Gifford acknowledges to have been in the majority, were deeply affronted by the Puritan attack on tradition. As Atheos tells Zelotes, Gifford's mouthpiece, the popular pastimes that the "busy controllers" condemn "were used before you were born, and will be when you are gone, so long as men think no hurt when they play and be merry." In a predominantly rural and only semiliterate society, it was hard to expect people to break so radically with the ways of their forebears. Atheos insists that "there were as wise men, and wiser than be now among our forefathers, and they would not have used nor allowed such things, if they had not been good . . . I pray God I may follow our forefathers and do no worse than they did . . . I would we could do but as well."[98]

Despite the tendentious name Gifford gives him, Atheos considers himself a religious man, and most modern readers would accept him as such. His objection is that the Puritans have made Christianity unreasonably complicated. "I mean well," he declares, "I hurt no man, nor I think no man any hurt. I love God above all and put my whole trust in him: what would ye have me more?"[99] Arthur Dent's Asunetus elaborates on this theme: "If a man say his Lord's Prayer, his Ten Commandments, and his Belief, and keep them, and say nobody no harm, nor do nobody no harm, and do as he would be done to, have a good faith to God-ward, and be a man of God's belief, no doubt he shall be saved, without all this running to sermons and prattling of the Scripture . . . God who made me must save me. It is not you who can save me, for all your learning and all your Scripture."[100]

Above all, the "cavillers" rejected the malevolent and capricious God of Calvin. "God is merciful," declared Gifford's Atheos, "he is not so severe as you would make him to be."[101] Thomas Hooker reported that unregenerate neighbors would attempt to undo a preacher's good work by assuring the guilt-stricken sinner that "the Lord is more merciful than men are, ministers must say something."[102]

On the whole, men like Asunetus and Atheos strike one as considerably more healthy minded, in William James's sense, than their Puritan opponents. They certainly seem to have been more comfortably integrated into their social milieu. That God was merciful meant that conviviality (or social conformity) availed of salvation. An essentially benign conception of the Almighty was linked to the affirmation of social norms. Hooker quotes a caviller as telling the preacher, "Good sir, spare your pains. We are sinners, and if we be damned, then every tub must stand upon his own bottom. We will bear it as well as we can."[103] Such a reply was a sign of impending damnation to Hooker; we are more likely to be impressed by its sanity and good humor.

Gifford's Atheos maintains that his dislike of puritanism is shared not only by the poor but by some of the "best in the parish."[104] In

towns where Atheos did possess allies among the local elite, the reformation of manners encountered fierce resistance. As John Rogers
observed, "When some would pull down houses of mis-rule, and
others, to cross them, and out of spleen to them, shall strive to up-
hold them; when some would bring in the Ministry of the Word and
others oppose it, how must not the Devil have his throne in such a
place?"[105] One such town was Gifford's Maldon, where the struggle
between his partisans and antagonists was intertwined with disputes
over the powers and policy of the governing corporation. In 1595
Richard Fletcher, bishop of London, found in both Maldon and
Colchester "great quarrels and contentions, both in their civil bodies
and among their ministers, the people divided and the priests taking
part on both sides and at war with themselves, as well in matter of
popular quarrels as points of doctrine."[106]

At issue in Maldon, and in a number of other parishes as well, was
the attempt of a local elite, centered around a Puritan minister, to
impose the culture of discipline upon a refractory majority. In 1582
George Gifford found Maldon one of the "desolate places . . . where
it appeareth by the abundance of iniquity that of long time Satan
hath had his throne." And Satan was naturally resisting deposition:
["he] stirreth up his warriors, which like wild boars root up all that
may be planted." Gifford expressed his thanks to the Earl of Sussex,
whose seat at Boreham lay ten miles from Maldon, for having
helped suppress Satan's warriors. Such aid from the civil arm was
needed to preserve the "little flock" of the godly, which was "always
compassed about with so many enemies, that they are able to devour
and eat it up, and yet their bellies no whit the fuller."[107]

Gifford also had the support of the town corporation. Upon his
suspension by Whitgift in 1584, a petition was presented on his behalf by fifty-two residents, including "many . . . of good rank in the
town": two justices, two bailiffs, fifteen burgesses, and Gifford's replacement as vicar, Mark Wiersdale. They defended Gifford as "a
great and diligent preacher" who had wrought a great reformation
in the town; the charges against him resulted only from the malice of
the "profane."[108] (Gifford's supporters, it will be recalled, had laid a
plot to humiliate Bishop Aylmer in 1586.)

God's little flock in Maldon continued to battle Satan's warriors
through the 1590s. While Gifford continued in the town as lecturer,
his supporter Mark Wiersdale was replaced as vicar by Robert

Palmer, formerly chaplain to the bishop of London, and perhaps the "Mr. Palmer" previously complained of in Widford. In 1592 Palmer imported the vicar of Hawkwell, a man named Frith, to disrupt Gifford's lecture. Palmer's accusers claimed that while the nightly prayer assemblies that Gifford conducted were subjected to official harassment, Palmer spent his days bowling, and his nights tippling. In return, Palmer attacked the town's bailiffs, saying that they favored artisans over gentlemen. He also complained that "there was a universal dumbness in the church at the time of common prayers, and that none in the church answered 'amen' when the prayers were read."

Palmer's supporters, it would appear, included many who for one reason or another resisted the "great reformation" effected by Gifford and his allies in the town government. A clothier and former bailiff named John Morris, for example, called the corporation a pack of "Precisians and Brownists," but also berated them for stinginess toward visiting actors. Actors were the servants of noblemen, he observed, and in former times they "had such entertainment when they came to the town that the town had the favor of noblemen, but now . . . the town was brought into contempt." Another of Palmer's faction, Edward Hunt, haberdasher, declared that "the cheer of the town was lost." Thomas Spigurnell, described as "sometime apprentice with a book-binder, after a vagrant peddler, then a ballad singer and teller, and now a minister [sic] and alehousekeeper in Maldon," complained that "there is no penal statute but the same is executed . . . to the uttermost." Spigurnell was also accused of trying "to stir up the commons of the town to oppose themselves against the . . . governors, and to cause a tumult and uproar within the same town," specifically by attacking the enclosure of the town's common pastures.[109]

Puritans not only accepted conflict, they welcomed it. Like Calvin himself they were fond of quoting Jesus Christ's chilling declaration, "I came not to send peace, but a sword."[110] John Rogers set no great value upon "good fellowship" or the "civil love that is between ordinary people in the world," because "our savior . . . comes not to bring such friendship but rather debate"—and this from *A Treatise on Love*.[111] "There was stir and hurly-burly wherever Paul came," said George Gifford. In fact the absence of strife was a very bad sign.

If a preacher set forth the Word truly, the wicked would always "storm and fret against him."[112]

Conflict was inevitable because there were only two sides in the cosmic antagonism between God and Satan. "Can ye put fire and water together but they will rumble"? asked George Gifford. "Would ye have God and the Devil agree together?" There were no neutrals, no spectators. "All whoremasters, drunkards, dicers, railers, swearers, and such like are the Devil's army, as, on the other side, such as profess God's word and live godly are His soldiers."[113] The battle between the two sides would endure, as Richard Sibbes later expressed it, "till all the one be in Hell . . . and the other be in Heaven."[114]

Thomas Hooker was especially eloquent on the antagonism between the Saints and the reprobate. Addressing himself to the latter, he warned them with obvious relish of the coming day of retribution: "though you make nothing of your swearing, and idle thoughts, and reviling of God's people, yet the God of Heaven will require them at your hands . . . For the Lord cometh with thousands of his Saints in flaming fire to punish . . . [T]he Lord will call thee to an account for all thy abominations, nay for all thy speeches against the people of God, upon thy ale-bench when thou didst toss them to and fro."[115]

One consequence of this metaphysic of strife was the conflation of the most disparate attitudes, beliefs, and behaviors into one great hypostasis of evil. Puritans saw the hand of Satan (not to speak of his horns and tail) in virtually everything of which they disapproved, from the Spanish Inquisition to the dirty joke. They envisioned all their opponents enlisted under a single banner. It was a motley crew: drunkards, morris dancers, great-bellied wenches, good-humored curates, murderers, sodomites, ribald minstrels, lenient magistrates, witches, epicurean bishops, Jesuit martyrs, Spanish dons. Satan's legions on the march must have been quite a sight, even in the mind's eye.

PART III

---·◆·---

Crown, County, and Antichrist
1618–1642

A great many behavioral phenomena become intelligible according to the hypothesis that man elaborates every sequence of signals received by his sense organs as if it were a meaningful message.

—V. V. Ivanov, in *Soviet Semiotics,* 1977

Time (one of the best interpreters of prophecies) hath produced the events answering the types so full and clear that we have the whole army of Protestant interpreters agreeing in the general scope and meaning of it.

—Stephen Marshall, in *The Song of Moses,* 1643

7 / Faction and Policy in Jacobean Essex

> This business in the Palatinate is but a thread in the texture . . . We declared our resolution for religion and all the Protestant part of the world . . . The cause of religion hath been opposed, and therein we have engaged ourselves.
>
> —Sir Nathaniel Rich, in *Commons Debates of 1621*

Recent scholarship has shaken or demolished a number of familiar notions about the coming of the English Revolution. Historians have tended to see Parliament steadily and purposefully encroaching upon royal power from the reign of Elizabeth to the outbreak of civil war. The decisive phase in this campaign of aggression occurred during the constitutional struggles of the 1620s, when, it has been argued, the parliamentary opposition succeeded in wresting the initiative in legislative matters from the Crown and its servants. The Civil War was thus the culmination of a struggle for sovereignty between two clearly defined antagonists: the Court and the Country.[1]

This teleological interpretation, or at least the simplified version presented above, can no longer be sustained. Its foundations have been fatally undermined by a whole squad of saboteurs, among them T. G. Barnes, Alan Everitt, Derek Hirst, J. S. Morrill, and above all Conrad Russell.[2] Their researches have exploded the myth of a coherent Country party in opposition to the Crown in the 1620s. It has been demonstrated that not only were most M.P.s fundamentally conservative; they were intensely localist in their concerns. *Country* in their usage meant "county" more often than "nation." Thus, when members spoke of the "liberties of the country," they were frequently referring to the special interests of their neighbors.

Derek Hirst, it is true, has demonstrated that the House of Commons was more representative of public opinion than we had imagined. Under the early Stuarts the franchise was being widened, until in 1640 it may have included as much as one-third of the adult male population.[3] Moreover, members took seriously their responsibility to articulate the concerns of their constituency. But the public opinion thus represented was radically parochial. The parliamentary electorate was expanding, but it was not acquiring a vocation for political sovereignty.

The effect of this revisionism has been to diminish the autonomy of parliamentary history. As Conrad Russell elegantly puts it, "stories flit through the parliamentary debates as, in Bede's story, the sparrow flitted through the hall of King Edwin."[4] One need not entirely accept Russell's reinterpretation to applaud his emphasis on the extraparliamentary context of the political crisis. Twenty years ago Christopher Hill observed that the English Civil War was not fought by a handful of M.P.s at Westminster.[5] Now, the work of a new generation of historians has demonstrated that a narrowly political approach is inadequate even to the study of Parliament itself. The implication of this new research is that the problems, values, and interests of the constituents deserve as much attention as those of the members.

This perspective would assign a new significance to the social and economic context of political crisis. The first two decades of the seventeenth century were, generally speaking, years of prosperity and peace. They were followed by three decades that Peter Bowden has described as "probably among the most terrible years through which the country has ever passed." Repeated harvest failure combined with persistent depression in the cloth trade to produce frightful hardship. Under James and Charles real wages stood at their lowest recorded point in English history; poor rates rose steeply; there were cases of outright starvation. In 1625 and 1636–37 there were serious outbreaks of plague.[6] At the same time the Crown was attempting to exact higher taxes with which to pursue unpopular policies in church and state. While Protestantism was fighting for its life on the Continent, a Counter Reformation seemed to have begun in the Church of England. Preachers interpreted all the country's varied misfortunes as divine punishment for apostasy. These circumstances provide the essential background of the constitutional catastrophe.

Any account of politics in prerevolutionary Essex must begin with Robert Rich, the second Earl of Warwick. One of the solid achievements of recent historiography has been the rediscovery of the House of Lords.[7] The nobility as a class may have been in crisis in the early seventeenth century, but individual nobles still possessed enormous clout, and the Earl of Warwick was among them. In 1619 he inherited, along with his title, at least sixty-four manors in the county of Essex alone and the advowsons of twenty-two Essex livings.[8] The estate has yet to be studied in detail, but it was certainly one of the largest in England. Lawrence Stone puts the gross rental in 1602 of Warwick's father, the third Lord Rich and first Earl of Warwick, at between £3,600 and £5,399. Ten years later the Venetian ambassador to the Savoy reported—on what authority I have no idea—that Rich had an income of £15,000. In 1618 he was able to purchase the earldom of Warwick for £10,000 in ready cash.[9]

Nor was the family's wealth confined to real estate. The third Lord Rich had invested heavily in the most lucrative business venture of the age: robbing Spain. From at least 1600 he financed a private fleet that preyed on Spanish shipping in the Caribbean. The peace concluded between England and Spain in 1604 was a minor embarrassment. Rich simply moved his base of operations from London to Middleburg and Flushing in the Low Countries and sent his privateers out under Dutch rather than English letters of marque. When the Dutch made peace five years later, Rich obtained a commission from the Duke of Savoy. Spain never lacked for enemies.[10] As we have already seen, Rich supported painful preachers whose integral Protestantism brought them into difficulties with the hierarchy—preachers whom Archbishop Bancroft, less inhibited than modern historians by the problems of precise definition, did not hesitate to call Puritans.[11] William Pemberton in 1613 addressed his patron as "a faithful doorkeeper in the house of God" and commended his "saving knowledge in the mystery of godliness" and his "zeal for God's glory." Rich was acutely sensitive to the menace of international Catholicism. He received the dedication of Arthur Dent's apocalyptic commentary *The Ruine of Rome*, which foretold the imminent overthrow of Antichrist, embodied in the papacy and the Spanish Empire. Pemberton could be sure of striking a responsive chord when he warned Rich against "the soul-killing poison of the Romish strumpet," which was gnawing at the vitals of England.[12]

Rich's militant Protestantism was perfectly consonant with his business interests. For Rich, as for Sir Francis Drake, plundering Antichrist was a work of righteousness. (Drake, we may recall, carried Foxe's *Book of Martyrs* aboard ship.) Religion gave moral sanction to a profitable but ethically dubious enterprise at a time when aristocrats, like everyone else, were struggling to keep abreast of inflation. From another angle, godly preachers and Caribbean privateers were complementary weapons in the defense of the Reformed faith. There is no reason to regard this tidy synthesis of piety and self-interest as hypocritical; it is precisely the force of conviction that makes ideology effective.

Neither Rich's religious views nor his privateering was likely to endear him to King James. Not that he was consciously in opposition to the Crown. Like most militant Protestants he looked to the sovereign for national leadership against the legions of Antichrist. In 1598 he accompanied his brother-in-law the Earl of Essex in the attack on Cadiz, although his participation was cut short by violent seasickness.[13] In 1612 it was rumored that Rich was to be given command of ten thousand infantry in the service of the King of Denmark; two years later his eldest son, the future second earl, raised four thousand troops for the Duke of Savoy. But nothing came of either of these ventures.[14] King James did not share the Riches' view of his divinely appointed mission. The king aimed to preserve ecclesiastical uniformity, if need be by silencing refractory preachers, and to pacify Christendom through an alliance with Spain. The elder Rich, by supporting intransigent clerics and dispatching privateers to prey on Spanish trade, jeopardized both objectives. In 1617, when Lord Rich sent out three ships under Savoyard letters of marque, he did so without his sovereign's knowledge. If the secret got out, warned the Venetian ambassador, "various heads would fall." In 1618 two vessels that Rich had dispatched to the Indian Ocean—at a cost, it was alleged, of £19,-466—were forced to take refuge in the Savoyard port of Villafranca because the Spanish ambassador had demanded their seizure.[15]

It is true that these considerations did not prevent James from granting Rich an earldom in 1618. But the timing is significant. It was not just that the king was increasingly short of funds and that Rich was prepared to pay £10,000 for the title. Rich's elevation coincided with a temporary breach in relations with Spain, in the aftermath of the Overbury scandal and the momentary eclipse of the Howards at court. This state of affairs did not last. Within the year Sir Walter Raleigh had been executed to appease the Spanish, and negotiations for a marriage alliance were resumed.[16]

Thus, despite his preeminence among the landowners of Essex, Rich never enjoyed royal confidence. Instead, James supported the claims of the Howard family to dominance in Essex. In 1604 the Privy Council intervened on behalf of the Howards' client against Rich's candidate, Sir Francis Barrington, and the Howard Earls of Suffolk held the prestigious office of *custos rotulorum* down to the summoning of the Long Parliament. Yet, as B. W. Quintrell has observed, the Howards' interest in the county was confined to the building of their great mansion at Audley End, on the Cambridgeshire border. After 1611 Thomas Howard, Earl of Suffolk, did not even bother to attend the Essex Quarter Sessions over which he nominally presided; nor did his son Theophilus, who succeeded to the title in 1624. The lord lieutenancy, meanwhile, was conferred upon the Radcliffe Earls of Sussex, another declining family with only tenuous ties to the county. For twenty-four years the lieutenancy was exercised, if that is the right word, by the unstable and incompetent fifth earl, whose performance was hampered by his debts, his apathy, and his weird marital troubles.[17]

Royal mistrust of the Rich family thus drove a wedge between economic and political power in the county. Essex was subjected to political absentee lordship during the reign of James and well into that of his son. Since neither the Howards nor the Radcliffes took much interest in Essex, or enjoyed, as far as one can tell, any great local influence, the official representatives of royal authority were unable to provide the county community with coherent leadership. It was an unstable and potentially dangerous situation.

The first Earl of Warwick enjoyed his title for barely half a year; he was succeeded in 1619 by Robert, his eldest son, born in 1587.[18] During his school days at Eton College Robert Rich had befriended the young William Gouge, who was destined to become one of the leading Puritan preachers and theologians of Charles's reign. Gouge later recalled the "continual favors" that Rich had shown him from his youth.[19] At the age of sixteen Rich entered Emmanuel College, Cambridge, which had been established by another Essex man, Sir Walter Mildmay, and which Queen Elizabeth had correctly feared would become a Puritan seminary. Rich spent no more than a year at Cambridge, but he must have met some of the divines with whom he would later be associated. We know that he continued his friendship with Gouge at Cambridge, and it is tempting to assume that he met John Preston and Thomas Hooker, who were nearly his exact contemporaries. In 1604 he was admitted to the Inner Temple, and he appears to have taken his legal studies more seriously than most. In 1621 he was one of the few members of the House of Lords who could read law French with facility.[20] In 1610 Rich left England to travel for several years on the Continent.[21]

As a young man Rich enjoyed considerable social success at court. He was darkly handsome and was an excellent jouster; he took part in at least one of Ben Jonson's court masques. But unlike his younger brother, Henry, Robert Rich seems never to have contemplated a career at court. As his steward, Arthur Wilson, wrote many years later, "He would not stoop to observances." Wilson added that "his spirit aimed at more public adventures."[22]

Did he in fact have much choice, one wonders? It is true that Warwick's younger brother succeeded brilliantly at court. But Henry Rich had, to put it charitably, a more pliable character than Warwick, who inherited both his father's Protestant zeal and his predatory hostility to Spain.[23] As Arthur Wilson remarked, he was more concerned with "planting colonies in the New World rather than himself in the king's favor," and Wilson was correct in implying that the two objectives were not altogether compatible.[24]

Like his father before him, Warwick patronized godly and "painful" ministers, which is to say effective, and aggressively Protestant, preachers. He presented some to livings in his gift, and extended informal protection to many more. In the words of Edmund Calamy, he became "a great patron and Maecenas to the pious and religious ministry." Clarendon made the same point, from the opposite perspective, claiming, with some exaggeration, that Warwick spent "a good part of his estate" supporting those preachers "who caused all the trouble." Warwick was closely associated with the careers of William Gouge, John Preston, Thomas Hooker, Stephen Marshall, Richard Sibbes, Jeremiah Burroughs, Hugh Peter, and Edmund Calamy, to name just a few.[25]

Yet, Warwick, as his youthful activities at court might suggest, was scarcely a stereotypical Puritan. To be sure, Edmund Calamy eulogized him as "very zealous and devout." A more disinterested modern historian has observed that "Warwick's appetite for sermons was exceptional, even among sermon-loving Puritans." His will expresses an intense Calvinist piety. But Warwick seems to have been a remarkably amiable man. His daughter-in-law remembered him as "one of the best-natured and cheerfullest persons I have in my time met with," while Clarendon, who hated him, acknowledged him to have been "a man of pleasant and companionable wit and conversation, of a universal jollity." Clarendon, indeed, could not resist adding, with partisan malice, that "a man of less virtue could not be found out"; it was only by bribing preachers that he "got the style of a godly man."[26]

Robert Rich's involvement with the colonization of America began before he turned twenty years old. He was a member of the Virginia Company as early as 1612, and two years later he helped to found the Somers Islands Company for the settlement of Bermuda. In 1618 he became a charter member of the reconstituted Guinea Company, which trafficked in African slaves; in fact the godly and good-natured Rich financed the first shipment of blacks to be sold in Virginia. In 1620 he joined the council of the New England Company.[27]

Like his father, however, the future Earl of Warwick was already engaged in activities less legitimate than planting colonies and trading slaves. In 1616 he sent out two vessels to privateer in the East Indies. It was a profitable venture, but it brought Rich into a prolonged conflict with the East India Company, which was anxious to remain on good terms with local potentates. Agents of the company only narrowly prevented Rich's men from seizing a ship belonging to the mother of the Great Mogul of India. Years later Warwick was still trying to win damages for this frustration.[28] In 1618 he sent a vessel named the *Treasurer* to prey on Spanish shipping in the Caribbean. This voyage, conducted like the East Indian venture under a commission from the Duke of Savoy, embroiled Rich in a conflict with his more scrupulous associates in the Virginia company, particularly Sir Edwin Sandys. The disclosure of *Treasurer*'s illicit activities placed the younger Rich in some personal danger. (This was the year in which Sir Walter Raleigh went to the block on behalf of Anglo-Spanish amity.) As Nathaniel Rich, Warwick's cousin and business agent, wrote at the time, if the full truth had come to light, Warwick would have been "brought under the clutches of the king of Spain," who might very well have "crushed him to pieces." And yet, Warwick immediately took up Raleigh's project to establish an English foothold on the continent of Latin America. He reorganized the Guiana Company in the wake of the Orinoco disaster, and in 1620 sent out an expedition of 120 men under the command of Sir Roger North. The project aborted. Negotiations for a Spanish marriage were reopened, and North's license was revoked, at Gondomar's insistence.[29]

For both the first and second Earls of Warwick, confrontation with Spain was the essence of the colonial enterprise. To that extent, therefore, the second earl was already in opposition to the policy of James I. But James's own government was divided. There was a strong anti-Spanish faction, led by Pembroke and Southampton, within the Privy Council itself. Hostility toward Spain did not imply dissatisfaction with the constitutional structure or with the economy of power between Crown and Parliament. Policy might change; James was mortal; Warwick might reasonably hope to be called to the council board himself one day. There is no reason to think him a born *frondeur*.

Warwick inherited from his father a close alliance with the Barringtons of Hatfield Broad Oak. Sir Francis Barrington served Essex as knight of the shire in every Parliament from 1601 to his death in 1628, with the possible exception of the Addled Parliament of 1614, for which no returns survive. He was a zealous Puritan, maintaining a lectureship at Hatfield Broad Oak, where John Preston and Bishop James Ussher preached during the 1620s. He was also a firm believer in the culture of discipline. In his will, which contains an elaborately Calvinistic preamble, he left £10 to set the poor on work, "thereby to keep them from haunting alehouses, breaking hedges, and lopping trees."[30]

It would be wrong to treat the Rich-Barrington nexus as a simple relationship of patron to client. The connection dated from at least 1564, when the Barringtons purchased Hatfield Priory from Richard Rich. The Barringtons were the older of the two families, and the Riches acknowledged it. In endorsing Sir Francis for Parliament in 1604, the elder Rich spoke of "the ancient name of Barrington . . .

whose ancestors I can aver to be knights before English was in England."[31] Whatever that obscure remark may mean, it was more than could be said of the name of Rich, unknown before the Reformation.

During the reigns of James and Charles a relatively small group of men represented the county and boroughs of Essex in Parliament. As B. W. Quintrell has shown, twelve men, drawn from seven families, sat forty-one times out of a possible total of sixty-four.[32] One of these men was the Earl of Warwick himself, who represented Maldon before being elevated to the peerage; five more were closely associated with him. These were Sir Francis Barrington, his son, Sir Thomas, and his son-in-law Sir William Masham; Sir Thomas Cheke, Warwick's brother-in-law and partner in the Virginia Company; and Sir Nathaniel Rich, Warwick's cousin and business agent. Yet, it would be misleading to regard Warwick as the deus ex machina of Essex politics. The story is both more complicated and more interesting.

The Parliament of 1621 was deeply distressed by the economic condition of the land. Sir Edwin Sandys even raised the specter of social revolution. Looms were idle, the poor were unemployed, farmers lacked money to pay their rents. These had been the causes of the terrible Peasants' War in Germany a hundred years earlier.[33] The causes of the economic depression of the 1620s are in dispute today, as they were at the time. The cloth industry had prospered for a decade following the conclusion of peace with Spain in 1604, during which time it may have expanded in an ultimately unhealthy way. By extending further into the countryside and involving more agricultural households in the spinning of yarn, the clothiers may have increased output at the expense of quality. At the same time the expansion of the industry ensured that any depression would affect a broader section of the population than the slumps of the preceding century.

From 1615 to 1618 the trade was crippled by the fiasco of the Cockayne project, that ill-conceived and ill-fated attempt to assert royal control of the cloth industry and to promote the production of fully finished and dyed textiles. Sir Francis Barrington, who sat for Essex in 1621, had six years earlier received a petition from the clothiers of the county warning that this scheme would ruin the local industry.[34] The cloth trade had no sooner recovered from the Cockaigne project than the Thirty Years' War broke out in Germany, severely curtailing the Continental demand for English goods. Currency manipulations in Europe caused the overvaluation of sterling, and a consequent shortage of bullion in England. To make matters worse, the king sought to recoup his losses on the Cockaigne project by laying new impositions, the so-called pretermitted customs, on exports of English cloths.[35] On December 1, 1619, eighty clothiers and "many thousand" workmen of Essex and Suffolk proclaimed themselves ruined by the bankruptcy of a London merchant to whom they had entrusted £20,000 worth of cloth.[36]

In 1621 the most articulate member of the Essex parliamentary delegation was Edward Alford, a gentleman lawyer seated in Sussex, who repeatedly represented the borough of Colchester.[37] Alford was fully aware of the concerns of his constituents in that major clothing center. He attributed the depression to increased taxation and the corruption of government officials, and demanded that these grievances be redressed before new taxes were voted: "we cannot (with grief I speak it) do anything. Traffic is gone, imposition undoes us, all people live upon hopes, and that of this Parliament. We must not carry them home rattles."[38] Alford blamed the decay of trade on high taxation and the corruption of government officials. He attacked domestic monopolies while demanding protection against foreign competition for Bermuda and Virginia tobacco; he proposed a bill requiring the wearing of woolen cloth.[39]

The Earl of Warwick probably agreed with Alford on all these issues—especially, no doubt, on the need to protect the Bermuda tobacco trade. Warwick's agent, Sir Nathaniel Rich, now sitting for Tewksbury, attacked "the great impositions laid on cloth, as the pretermitted customs and the like" in terms almost identical to those used by Alford.[40] And yet, Alford's preeminence within the Essex delegation to this and subsequent Parliaments illustrates the limits of Warwick's hegemony over the county; for not only was Alford independent of Warwick and his friends, but his political philosophy was opposed to theirs on some fundamental points.

We have virtually no record of Warwick's activities in the Parliament of 1621 beyond Arthur Wilson's assurance that he was one of the seven "gallant spirits" in the House of Lords who "aimed at the public liberty more than their own interest," and who "supported the old English honor and would not let it fall to the ground."[41] But it is probably safe to assume that his views were consistent with those expressed by Sir Nathaniel Rich in the House of Commons.

Historians have only recently begun to accord Rich the attention and respect he received from contemporaries. He was an aggressive Protestant, whose "sincerety, wisdom, and right judgement" in religious matters were commended by no less an authroity than Archbishop James Ussher, in a letter to the great Puritan preacher Richard Sibbes. Rich was at least as distressed by the Catholic victories in Germany as by the domestic economic crisis. He believed that all temporal misfortunes, from the cloth depression to the fall of the Palatinate, had a common cause in God's wrath. "His arrows light on us round about," he declared in 1621, "either in ourselves or our neighbors."[42]

Rich supported, and may have drafted, a resolution declaring the Parliament's willingness "to spend our lives and estates in the service of God's glory, the safety of religion, and defense of the patrimony of the King's children." The immediate reference here was to the restoration of Frederick and Elizabeth to their territory. But Rich insisted that "we declared our resolution for religion and all the Protestant part of the world, not the Palatinate only." He called for a general league of all Protestant nations, to be confirmed by Parliament. Meanwhile, war must be waged against Antichrist on the domestic front as well. Rich deplored "the lamentable state of religion at home" and called for a day of humiliation to seek God's mercy. England could never prosper while popery was tolerated.[43]

The Earl of Warwick agreed that England should go to war on behalf of the Protestant cause. Like Sir Nathaniel Rich, Warwick equated Protestantism with national prosperity; he was to express this conviction in his last will and testament.[44] Warwick was, after all, waging a private war against Spain already. In 1620 he executed a royal commission to impress sixty seamen to defend the Essex coast; he also contributed £500 to Frederick's cause and encouraged others to do likewise. He was ready, as he told the king, "to sacrifice not only my poor fortune but my life also at his Majesty's command." True, this was by way of refusing a royal request for even more money. But Warwick could reasonably claim that he was already doing his bit, and that it was up to Parliament to commit the resources of the nation as a whole to the struggle. His response contrasts with that of Thomas Lord Howard, the Essex *custos rotulorum*, who declared himself well-disposed to the Palatinate but refrained from contributing until he saw what his "betters" would give.[45]

Warwick and his friends were imperialists who believed that England's imperial vocation was divinely mandated. From their point of view the one great political issue was the defense and expansion, under English leadership, of the Kingdom of Grace. Concretely this meant suppression of domestic popery, intervention in Europe on behalf of the Protestants, aggression against the Spanish Empire, and the planting of colonies in North and Central America. The realization of these interlocked objectives, it was assumed, would resolve the domestic social crisis brought on by population growth and hasten the fulfillment of God's plan. It would also bring honor, power, and wealth to the imperialists themselves.

Now, Edward Alford had no sympathy for this grand design. It is true that he deplored the imperfections of the English church; he was suspicious of the pretensions of hierarchy, warning that "the Bishops, if we look not to them, will encroach upon all men's rights and lands in England."[46] But he was consistently opposed to the aggressive imperialism advocated by Warwick and Rich. War with Spain, as he rightly perceived, would be a very expensive proposition, and the righteousness of the cause did not justify the cost to his Sussex neighbors and Colchester constituents. Alford therefore opposed the House of Commons' offer to "spend our lives and estates in the service of God's glory," on the grounds that this would "lay upon us too great an engagement."[47]

Conrad Russell has described Edward Alford as the quintessential champion of the Country interest. Alford was a localist, instinctively obstructive of proposals to extend the powers of the state. He was an articulate spokesman for the majority of M.P.s, who, in Russell's words, "almost always put concern for their own counties above any concept of the national interest." Alford objected to Giles Mompesson's patent for the licensing of alehouses, in part because it undermined the power of local justices; he was hostile to the Court of High Commission because of the expense imposed on the counties by the centralization of ecclesiastical authority in London. He resisted proposals for the reform of the militia for fear of the "charge to the county."[48]

Men like Alford, it must be frankly stated, were largely responsible for the political and military paralysis of the early Stuart monarchy. They refused to recognize the fiscal crisis that a century of inflation had produced, and they obstructed every proposal for reform that might have remedied the situation. At the heart of the Crown's financial difficulties was the steady decline in the yield of the subsidy, which resulted both from the general price inflation and from the absurd underassessment of taxpayers by the local gentry themselves. In Essex, according to Lord Keeper John Williams, the yield of the subsidy had fallen by one-half owing to the laxity of the local commissioners.[49] In Alford's home county of Sussex the subsidy fell even more sharply. The average assessment of seventy leading families dropped from £61 to £14 between the Reformation and the death of Henry VIII and that of James.[50] And yet, Alford fought to maintain the system of assessment by neighbors that had caused this "fiscal catastrophe." Conrad Russell has correctly observed that in supporting Alford on this issue, the House of Commons displayed an "adamantine resistance to the principle of honest assessment for taxation."[51]

"Countrymen" like Edward Alford were resolute "little Englanders." Their obstructive localism rendered the English state impotent to intervene in Continental affairs, let alone to challenge Spain in the New World. Antichrist would have little to fear from England so long as Alford's views prevailed. At the same time, there would be no hope of alleviating domestic social pressures through colonial expansion. An impotent England could not retain an overseas empire.

Sir Nathaniel Rich, in contrast, did not believe that a commitment "to the service of God's glory" was "too great an engagement." Throughout the 1620s Rich was one of a very few members—including John Pym, Benjamin Rudyerd, and Dudley Digges—who were genuinely concerned with restoring the Crown's financial solvency in return for a degree of parliamentary influence in shaping foreign policy. Rich was thus a notable exception to Russell's generalization that M.P.s sought to avoid both fiscal burdens and political responsibility.[52]

If we wish to make sense of the conflicts of the 1620s and 1630s, we must distinguish between two forms of opposition to the Crown—two constellations of resistance that might often overlap on particular issues but that were governed by quite different values. No simple labels are likely to be completely satisfactory, but for convenience I will call these groups—represented by Alford and Rich, respectively—the Countrymen and the imperialists. The program of the Countrymen was almost entirely negative and localist. The imperialist program was animated by a vision of global scope.

The great merit of Conrad Russell's work, and that of his fellow revisionists, is to have revealed the nature and limitations of the Country ideology. The great weakness of the new interpretation is its neglect of the imperialist tradition, which was of far greater importance in bringing about the overthrow of the Crown. As the following pages will show, the members of the Warwick group, including Sir Francis Barrington, Sir Thomas Cheke, and Sir William Masham, as well as Sir Nathaniel Rich, evinced no hostility to the state or to centralized authority as such.

It is true that in 1621, as again in 1626, Sir Francis Barrington, together with his son-in-law Sir William Masham, refused to contribute to a Forced Loan levied by the king. But in 1628 he willingly cast his vote for the grant of six subsidies, since the tax was being sought in "the Parliamentary way."[53] It was not the power of the Crown to which they objected but the way that power was being exercised. Above all, they disapproved of the Crown's failure to defend the Protestant cause at home and abroad. Their Protestant zeal was undoubtedly suffused with self-interest. But Warwick and his friends, who included John Pym, Lord Saye and Seale, and Oliver St. John, as well as his Essex associates, had a clear sense of national vocation—a concept that was wholly foreign to the County mentality.

If, as Edward Alford claimed, the people of Essex had looked to Parliament for relief from their economic distress, their hopes were frustrated. Had the 1620s been a decade of bountiful harvests and vigorous trade, the political history of the period might have been considerably more tranquil. But the economic crisis worsened. Bad harvests produced near-famine in Lancashire and outright starvation in Cumberland. The situation was less desperate in southern England, but T. G. Barnes speaks of the "terrible corn scarcity" in Somerset. The judgment would apply to Essex as well.[54] "Our corn grows dear," complained the preacher of Great Waltham, "markets bad; the earth denies her foison." In 1622 Lord Keeper Williams warned the deputy lieutenants that grain prices in the county were unconscionably high; the Privy Council ordered superfluous ale-houses suppressed and the strength of beer reduced so as to conserve grain for food.[55]

Meanwhile, the effects of dearth were aggravated, in Essex as in Somerset, by increasing unemployment among cloth workers. By the early autumn of 1622, weavers had begun to riot in the West Country. The disturbances, in the view of the Privy Council, were caused in part by the distress attendant on the "decay of clothing," but had been fomented by "lewd and vagrant persons that omit no opportunity of raising tumults and disorders for their own private ends."[56] (We shall encounter again this belief that vagrants—the outside agitators of their day—were behind all expressions of social unrest.)

The disorders spread to Essex and Suffolk in December. The Privy Council wrote to Sir John Deane, the high sheriff and a member of the Parliament of 1621, that the unemployed cloth workers were threatening "unlawful and disorderly courses to get relief." The sheriff and deputy lieutenants were instructed to take measures for "preventing and appeasing of all tumultuous assemblies." The danger was enhanced by the return, during this same winter, of men conscripted for Sir Horace Vere's luckless expedition to the Palati-nate. The Privy Council reminded the justices of Essex and Kent "how evil consequence it is, especially at this time, that persons of their condition continue together in one body." The justices' task was complicated in March by the council's order to impress another one hundred men for service in Germany—men who would have learned what to expect from the tales of Vere's returning veterans. Moreover, Essex in 1622 was swarming with vagabonds, beggars, and gypsies.[57]

The council's promises to provide "speedy relief and employment" for the cloth workers proved hollow. The Crown had no policy for reviving the cloth trade, nor did it develop one in the subsequent decades. The Essex justices managed to restore order, and attempted to shift the blame for the riots to the weavers of Suffolk, who were safely across the Stour and out of their jurisdiction. The council summoned a delegation of afflicted clothiers to London to explain their difficulties. There is no record of any result.[58]

In fact, such measures as the government took to regulate the cloth trade only made matters worse. In 1623 the council issued an order forbidding the transport of fuller's earth by water, in order to prevent it being smuggled to the Continent. This measure greatly increased the cost of transporting the earth from Kent, where it was produced in abundance, to the clothing districts in Suffolk and northern Essex. The episode was trivial in itself, but it exemplified the general ineptitude of the government's economic policies.[59] In the summer of 1623 distress in the county once again reached flash point. The deputy lieutenants were ordered to prepare the trained bands for the "speedy suppression of tumultuous assemblies."[60]

It will readily be appreciated that these conditions did nothing to foster sympathy for the Crown's fiscal plight among the taxpayers of Essex. On the contrary, they sought, wherever possible, to lighten the burdens placed upon them. They apparently reneged on their commitments to the great Dutch engineer Vermuyden, who was engaged in draining marshes along the Thames terrace. On December 26, 1622, "many poor men" employed in the work protested that Vermuyden withheld their wages; the Dutchman maintained that the county had failed to repay the £3,600 he had already expended.[61]

So far as we know there was no overt resistance to the collection of the two subsidies that had been voted by the Parliament of 1621, a tax that would have cost Essex just under £5,000.[62] But we have seen that at least three Essex gentlemen refused to contribute to the royal loan in 1621. The following year the justices of the county complained to the council of the extortionate behavior of the royally appointed clerk of the market, and the Essex grand jury quarreled with the king's commissioners over the amount to be paid in composition for the right of purveyance. The Crown claimed £3,566, while the county was prepared to offer only £2,303.[63] The sum in dispute amounted to nearly half a subsidy.

As the economic situation deteriorated, the arguments of the Virginia Company appeared steadily more persuasive. The only realistic solution to England's social crisis was colonial expansion, and the transfer of the surplus population to the wilderness of the New World. Yet, during these very months the Virginia settlement was threatened with extinction. On March 22, 1622, some three hundred settlers were massacred in a surprise Indian attack; in the following winter five hundred more died of disease and malnutrition. In the spring of 1623 a flood of letters reached England from Virginia describing the plight of the colonies. The Warwick faction placed the blame for these disasters on Sir Edward Sandys, who was accused of having recklessly enlarged the settler population while concealing the precarious state of the colony even from his own council. The breach between the two factions was now irreparable and led to the dissolution of the Virginia Company in the following year.[64] The Earl of Warwick had already turned his attentions further north, having joined the New England Company in 1620.

Meanwhile, Englishmen who shared Warwick's dream of a Protestant empire had cause for alarm closer to home. The dissolution of the angry Parliament of 1621 was a victory for Spain and for the Spanish interest at court. The Duke of Buckingham personally congratulated the Spanish ambassador, who described the dissolution as "the best thing that has happened in the interests of Spain and the Catholic religion since Luther began to preach heresy."[65] As James pressed forward with negotiations for the Spanish match, the persecution of English recusants was relaxed. Rumors of an impending declaration of indulgence swept the land. Buckingham and Prince Charles left for Spain on their *opéra bouffe* expedition to woo the Infanta.

Modern historians, persuaded that James never really wavered in his allegiance to the Protestant faith, are inclined to dismiss these fears as mere paranoia. But consider the following episodes, in which sane observers might well discern a sinister pattern. In 1618 James issued the Book of Sports, granting official sanction to traditional Sunday games and festivities. James argued that the Puritan war on traditional culture was causing many of his subjects to relapse into popery, particularly in backward areas like rural Lancashire, where the Reformation had never taken deep root. To the godly, however, James's policy of accommodation meant surrender to Antichrist. James forbade the Parliament of 1621 to discuss the Book of Sports. In the summer of 1622 he struck another blow at the Puritans by issuing a set of Directions for Preachers, which prohibited the discussion of the "deep points" of predestination and reprobation before popular audiences. These themes were, of course, the very heart of Puritan evangelism.[66]

It was probably the new Directions that occasioned the first clash between the corporation of Colchester and the Bishop of London's commissary, Robert Aylett, later a vigorous executor of the Laudian program. In May 1623 Aylett wrote to the corporation to denounce Colchester's "factious multitude, who will allow no minister but of their own calling." While professing his respect for the town's governors, he reproached them for their "neglect of the more learned clergy"—no doubt a reference to the Colchester corporation's habit of appointing Puritan divines to the town lectureship. Aylett offered to cooperate with the town, but he added truculently, "Whether you affect war or peace I am indifferent, in so good a cause." Aylett made it clear that he was on the side of the conforming Anglican clergy, "with whom I hold it no discredit to suffer." Aylett had been a student at Trinity College of Dr. John Cowell, whose book *The Interpreter* was condemned by the House of Commons as an apology for absolutism. From 1629 throughout the Personal Rule, Aylett sat on the Court of High Commission.[67]

Given the assumptions of the age, it was not eccentric to posit a direct connection between the temporal disasters befalling the realm and what was beginning to look like apostasy on the part of the country's rulers. Thomas Barnes, lecturer in the Earl of Warwick's parish of Great Waltham, reminded his congregation in 1623 that "afflictions are the fruit of sin."[68] The general principle was universally acknowledged, however fiercely people might differ over specific applications. The Virginia massacre of 1622, as the Virginia Company admonished the survivors, had been brought on by "enormous excesses of apparel and drinking, the cry whereof cannot be have gone up to heaven."[69] The same logic could easily be directed against royal policy—against the Spanish match, the desecration of the Sabbath, and the suppression of the "deep points" of predestination. Among the sins for which England was being punished Barnes included Sabbath breaking and disrespect for painful preachers and professors, as well as failure to come to the aid of "God's people" in Germany.

Moreover, these afflictions were but "tragical prologues"; there might be worse to follow. Barnes feared that the Lord would permit "those hellish fire-brands, the Jesuitical faction" to kindle a religious civil war in England, as they had done in France, or that He would "send a fierce nation against us." Barnes denounced the "abominations of the land" and the indifference of the English to "the great affliction of the Lord's heritage in our neighbor nations." There was biblical precedent for this state of affairs, as there was for everything. Barnes cited from 2 Chronicles 1-14 the story of Manasseh, the king whose relapse into idolatry brought ruin to Judah. This reference to the "sins of Manasseh" was an ominous motif, and one that would sound with growing insistence in succeeding years. Barnes was precocious in announcing it as early as 1623. But he was no sectarian tub thumper, preaching to a lunatic fringe. He dedicated this sermon to his "very much respected friends" William and Katherine Towse, with the added comment that "if I were not confident of acceptation I should not presume to present you with it."[70] William Towse represented Colchester in every Parliament from 1621 through 1626.

In the autumn of 1623 the political situation was abruptly transformed. Charles and Buckingham, angered and humiliated by their reception in Madrid, returned home amid scenes of popular glee, determined upon war with Spain. Thomas Barnes's congregation in Great Waltham must have thought that their prayers had been answered. The confrontation between the Crown and "God's little flock" had been averted, for the moment.

Throughout England the elections to the Parliament of 1624 were dominated by the issues of war and the threat of popery. In his election address the sheriff of Cheshire, Sir Richard Grosvenor, denounced the toleration of recusants and "dependency upon foreign princes." In phrases that anticipated the rhetoric of 1642 (although Grosvenor was himself to be a Royalist), he spoke darkly of "busy-headed working politicians" seeking to "bring in bondage both church and commonwealth." Derek Hirst has found candidates being accused of popish leanings in the elections for the counties of Kent, Norfolk, and Yorkshire, and the boroughs of Canterbury, Ludlow, Winchelsea, and Pontefract. According to Hirst there were more contested elections in 1624 than for any other Parliament of the 1620s.[71]

The events in Essex are less clear than one might wish, but it appears that there were disputed elections for Harwich, Maldon, and the county. (No contests at all are recorded for either 1614 or 1621.)[72] The details are unfortunately sparse. But in Maldon the election resulted in the displacement of the courtiers Sir Julius Caesar and Sir Henry Mildmay by Sir William Masham, Francis Barrington's son-in-law, and Arthur Herris, another associate of the Earl of Warwick.[73] Both men had been granted the freedom of the borough on the very day of the election. The bailiffs apologized to Sir Julius Caesar, who had supported the candidacy of Mildmay and may have sought to retain his own seat as well. They explained that the franchise was exercised by the entire body of free burgesses and that a majority of the electors were "now affected to men of quality near to our township." This explanation may have been disingenuous, since the unusual number of five freemen were created just before the election, four of whom voted with the corporation. There were protests that the freedom of the town was being politically manipulated. (Masham won by a margin of five votes, forty-seven to forty-two.)[74]

It seems evident that this election substantially enhanced the power of Warwick and his friends. The knights of the shire were his allies Sir Francis Barrington and Sir Thomas Cheke. Sir Nathaniel Rich sat for Harwich, along with Christopher Herris, the son of Sir Arthur. One of the members from Colchester was William Towse, a man who, to judge from the sermon Thomas Barnes dedicated to him, shared Warwick's vision of a Protestant empire. The other Colchester representative was Edward Alford, the only member of the Essex delegation who was definitely out of sympathy with Warwick's views. Nor was the influence of the Warwick-Barrington group confined to Essex. Sir Francis's son, Sir Thomas, sat again for Newport on the Isle of Wight; his son-in-law Gilbert Gerard sat for Middlesex.

The Parliament of 1624 was the most harmonious of the early Stuart age. Buckingham had determined on war with Spain and had entered into an alliance of expediency with the Protestant imperialists. Warwick himself was regarded by the Spanish ambassador as one of the duke's closest advisers. The great Puritan preacher John Preston, Warwick's friend and the tutor of his children, enjoyed favor at court. Preston had been denouncing the Spanish match for several years.[75]

Hence, there was apparent unanimity between the dominant faction at court and the Protestant imperialists in Parliament, who on this occasion could carry with them the majority of both houses. The only opposition came from Countrymen like Edward Alford, who predictably balked at the expense of the projected *jihad*.[76] But this appearance of harmony was deceptive. First of all, there was a fundamental disagreement over the nature of the war to be fought. Buckingham, supported in this matter by James himself, envisioned a land war in Germany, while Parliament favored a diversionary naval campaign in alliance with the United Provinces. Parliamentary treasurers were appointed to see to it that the £300,000 voted for the war effort was expanded for the strategy that Parliament favored. Buckingham had no intention of allowing Parliament to dictate his foreign policy or military strategy. As things turned out, he had no difficulty in eluding these constraints.[77]

This Parliament was also concerned with the purification of morals and religion at home. Puritans had always argued that the suppression of popery and the reformation of manners was necessary to secure divine favor, and in times of crisis even moderate Protestants in the Parliament found these arguments persuasive. The Parliament of 1624 passed bills against drunkenness, blasphemy, and the profanation of the Sabbath. James was presented with what he called a "stinging" petition, probably the work of John Preston, calling for the stricter enforcement of recusancy laws.[78]

This same Parliament saw the beginnings of the conflict between the House of Commons and the rising Arminian faction within the church. Under the leadership of Pym, the Commons accused Richard Montague, the king's chaplain-in-ordinary, of subverting the Reformed faith by adulterating the doctrine of predestination. Warwick and his Essex associates may have played a role in bringing Montague to the attention of the House. In addition to his royal chaplaincy, Richard Montague held the living of Stanford Rivers in Essex. One of his two main accusers before the House of Commons was Nathaniel Ward, whom Sir Nathaniel Rich later presented to the Essex parish of Stondon Massey.[79]

King James had little sympathy with the hopes and fears of the godly members of Parliament. He derisively vetoed their bill against Sunday amusements. He did nothing to suppress papists. He took no action against Montague. He commended Bishop Harsnett of Norwich—an Essex man and tutor of the future Royalist leader Sir John Lucas—for suppressing "popular lectures." Harsnett had been attacked for introducing religious images into the churches in his diocese. James commended the practice, pointedly observing that the pictures of apostles adorned his own chapel, and commanded the other bishops to follow Harsnett's example. The "beauty of holiness" did not originate with Charles and Laud. James charged his bishops to be as "careful to sweep out the Puritans" as to suppress papists.[80] James's declaration would have strengthened the hand of Robert Aylett in his struggle against lecturers favored by the "factious multitude" of Colchester.

Despite their alliance of convenience with the parliamentary Puritans, neither Buckingham nor Charles was any closer than James to sharing their fundamental values. James had abandoned the view that the Pope was Antichrist, and there is no evidence that Buckingham or Charles ever held it. Without this doctrine the whole metahistorical basis of Protestant imperialism collapsed.

The tactical unity of court and Country in 1624 thus concealed a more profound conflict. What was at stake was the eschatological vocation of England. The Protestant imperialists, who included not only men like Warwick and Rich but Archbishop Abbot as well, held that the children of light were engaged in the climactic battle against Antichrist. James, Buckingham, and Prince Charles, who were responsible for leading the nation in that struggle, denied it. This disagreement over the nation's divine mission was to have serious consequences.[81]

There are signs that even in 1624, when they were in tactical alliance with the favorite and the heir to the throne, the godly leaders of Parliament were developing into something like a party. A Royalist tract of 1647 alleges that even before James's death, Warwick, Saye, and Pym were meeting frequently at the house of "a great mistress of the Faction." This can only refer to Lucy, Countess of Bedford, who administered the affairs of her invalid husband. The former Lucy Harrington had been the girlhood friend of Elizabeth, the Princess Palatine. She was closely associated with the Earl of Pembroke, who exercised her husband's proxy in the House of Lords. It is at least highly likely that in addition to Pembroke, Warwick, Saye, and Pym, her guests included Sir Nathaniel Rich, Sir Francis Barrington, and Sir William Masham, and perhaps John Preston as well. By the end of 1624 this group was clearly regarded as a coherent and independent faction to be reckoned with. Sir George Goring warned Buckingham to beware of the "ill counsels of Bedford House."[82]

According to the anonymous Royalist historian, the countess of Bedford declared during James's lifetime that "their party was then strong enough to pull the king's crown from his head, but the Gospel would not suffer them." Whether or not anyone at Bedford House was yet speaking in those tones, a sense of crisis prevailed among the godly during 1624. On May 18 a divine named John Wing preached a sermon at the Hague before the exiled Princess Palatine, Lady Bedford's old friend, which he dedicated in its printed version to Sir Francis Barrington, Sir Thomas Barrington, Sir William Masham, and their wives—all of whom he addressed as Saints. The text of his sermon was, "Esteeming the reproach of Christ greater riches than the treasures of Egypt." Wing sought to alleviate the despondency and self-doubt that descended even upon Saints "if outward things go hard with them," and sought to persuade his auditors and readers of the final irrelevance of poverty, imprisonment, slavery, persecution, and death.[83]

Wing's subtitle was, "The welfare of the faithful in the worst times." He was thinking primarily of the disasters that had befallen the Protestants of Germany. But of more immediate concern to the neighbors of the Barringtons and Mashams was the persistence of the economic depression. During the bitter month of February, as Parliament was assembling in London to clamor against Catholic aggression, the Braintree minute book recorded that "Shreeve, complaining for want of work and . . . sending his boy a-begging, had now 2s. given him and was warned not to send his child a-begging anymore." Whatever Shreeve may have thought of about the plight of the Elector Palatine, he had more pressing needs. At the same meeting of the Braintree vestry, the overseers were voted an additional nine months' rate "in regards of the great wants of the poor." The next month the vestry arranged a conference between the chief clothiers and the local justices to discuss "the raising of means for the maintenance of the poor." In the summer and fall more houses were provided for the poor in Coggeshall Lane, and a survey was taken to eject strangers who had settled in the town during the past ten years. The town had enough trouble maintaining its own. The clothiers on the vestry did their best to take on unemployed weavers, but it became necessary to give them work spinning or picking stones from the fields instead of weaving. By the end of 1624 it was evident that more strenuous measures were necessary, and plans were set afoot to provide work for the poor at the "hospital," which was to be converted into a House of Correction.[84] Such was the state of affairs in one Essex town as the nation prepared to go to war with Spain.

8 / The War Years

Faithful ministers are the defenders of states, churches, and commonwealths ... It is wonderful to see what a good minister can do in a good war, how he can fight against principalities and powers, and spiritual wickedness in high places.

—*Thomas Hooker, "Spiritual Munitions," in* Thomas Hooker: Writings in England and Holland, 1626–1633

Most articulate contemporaries saw only two solutions to the problem of overpopulation in early Stuart England. One was colonial expansion; the other was war.[1] An imperialist war might thus appear doubly beneficial to the commonwealth. War was a means of setting the poor on work. A successful campaign might pay for itself through plunder, while a military disaster would at least reduce the number of sturdy beggars in the land. On June 23, 1624, the Privy Council urged the lord lieutenant of Essex and his deputies to enlist men for service with the Dutch, pointing out "the ease and benefit the county will find in being disburdened of many unnecessary persons, that want employment and live lewdly or unprofitably."[2] The volunteers should be given press money and be imprisoned if they deserted.

Thomas Barnes, the preacher of Great Waltham, hoped that conscription might "rid the country ... of those straggling vagrants ... which do swarm amongst us." It was both pious and prudent, he argued, "to spend the worst first, and spare the best to the last extremity." War, for Thomas Barnes, was a reformation of manners by other means. It would be better for "loitering fellows and lewd livers" to be "fighting in field" than "tippling in our tap-houses" and "pulling down with both hands as fast as they can [God's] heavy judgments upon the whole nation." Barnes believed that the terrors of battle might even provoke a few sinners to repent, although most of them were past hope. "And is it not pity," he asked suavely, "that one soul should be lost for lack of any means which may do it good?"[3] It is one of the odder excuses for mass butchery on record. The sermon from which these quotations are taken was dedicated to Sir Horace Vere, Baron of Tilbury, an Essex man and commander of the unsuccessful expedition of 1623.

In the spring and summer of 1624 the prospect of war stimulated the old dread of domestic Catholic subversion. A papist husbandman of South Ockenden, described as "a poaching fellow" who filched his neighbors' fowl, fish, and bees, was accused of harboring "strange popish recusants" from London. The vicar of West Mersea was found to possess a rosary and an English missal, which he had been seen reading "in the church priviliy upon his knees, and many other times in his hands as he walked in the fields." These were the first such cases to reach the Quarter Sessions during James's reign.[4] Moreover, there were no more reports of "railing" against Puritans; significantly, the last of these had occurred in 1618, the year Frederick seized the Bohemian throne.

So there was presumably some sympathy in Essex for a Protestant crusade. Actually putting an army in the field, however, was a different matter. The musters in Essex had been neglected during the long years of peace. In 1623 the rolls, although fuller than for twenty years past, still fell short of the four thousand foot soldiers required of the county, and many of the four hundred light cavalry failed to appear. In November of that year the boroughs of Colchester and Harwich refused outright to provide the funds levied upon them for ammunition. The following June the deputy lieutenants reported an improvement in the condition of the foot companies, but the cavalry remained "very defective, some of the better classes setting a very ill example."[5]

Preparations for war placed new administrative burdens on the county's leaders and exposed with painful clarity the shortcomings of its lord lieutenant. Thomas Radcliffe, the Earl of Sussex, had made an unfortunate marriage many years before, which had recently ended in an unusually sordid divorce case, involving allegations of brutality, attempted murder, and witchcraft. An Elizabethan portrait, attributing to the earl a countenance utterly devoid of expression or intelligence, bears the legend *par amando troppo son rovinato*. Whether or not his grace had indeed been "ruined by too much loving," he was a wretched lord lieutenant.[6] In June of 1623

Sussex had complained of his deputies' failure to obey him. A year later three deputy lieutenants—Sir Francis Barrington, Lord Maynard, and Sir John Deane—blamed Sussex for the disgraceful condition of the county's mounted militia. The favoritism Sussex showed to the wealthier taxpayers was causing lesser men to default. At the end of 1624 Sussex was charged by the Privy Council with levying 750 men for service with Count Mansfeld. Rather than bestir himself, he "wholly referred" the matter to his deputies.[7] It is a telling comment on the Jacobean regime that a character like Sussex was allowed to remain for decades in a position of high responsibility, when thoroughly competent noblemen like the first and second Earls of Warwick were shunted aside.

Parliament had voted £300,000 with the express provision that it not be used to finance a land war in Germany. The money was to be dispensed by parliamentary commissioners solely for the defense of the realm, for assistance to the United Provinces and other allies, and for naval operations against Spain. Parliament was to be recalled in the autumn of 1624 to discuss further measures. Buckingham ignored these engagements. He dissuaded James from reconvening Parliament, and with the funds Parliament had already granted began to raise twelve thousand men for the relief of Breda *x* under Count Mansfeld.[8] In October the Essex justices were ordered to press 750 men for Mansfeld's expedition. The commander of the Essex contingent was Warwick's younger brother, Sir Charles Rich.[9]

The deputy lieutenants were aware that zeal for the Protestant cause might not be universal among the lower orders. Anticipating that "likely people for the service will, when it is known, absent themselves," the deputy lieutenants ordered the justices to search the alehouses the night before the musters. They also specified that "men of able and lusty bodies" be chosen to conduct the recruits to their places of rendezvous.[10] These fears were justified. In December the Privy Council wrote to Lord Maynard—significantly bypassing Sussex—that the soldiers in Essex were committing "divers insolencies to the great wrong of the inhabitants, which your watches . . . are not able to withstand." In January 1625 orders were issued at the Chelmsford Quarter Sessions to carry out privy searches for deserters throughout the county. Those apprehended were to be tried as felons. Another two hundred men were to be pressed to replace the deserters and the conscripts who had died awaiting embarkation at Dover. A month later the Privy Council complained that the "runagates" from Mansfeld's army were still returning to Essex and Suffolk.[11]

In Colchester a group of separatists protested that they were being unfairly singled out for conscription. Addressing John Marshall, one of the bailiffs, the separatists' spokesman argued that Marshall especially had no right to persecute them, since he himself had conscientious objections to the Anglican settlement. Why should men "of a godly life" be treated more harshly than those of "rude behavior" who had been excused from service because of their family obligations? Moreover, the Saints would experience "great misery" by being exposed to the evil company of other conscripts.[12] Meanwhile, another five hundred men were conscripted from Essex for the navy. Essex, along with Suffolk, Cornwall, and (oddly enough) Hertfordshire, had the highest quota in the country. The parishes on which these troops were billeted naturally resented the expense. Brightlingsea, for example, petitioned directly to Buckingham against the Essex deputy lieutenants, who had charged them with the quartering of one hundred soldiers, in violation of the parish's alleged liberties.[13]

James I died on March 27, 1625, while Mansfeld's troops, cast ashore in Holland without food or ammunition, deserted or died. Despite the catastrophe, the alliance between Buckingham and Warwick's group held firm through the elections to the new Parliament in April. Warwick supported the duke's policy of alliance with France. Indeed, his brother, Henry, now Viscount Kensington, over whom Warwick exercised exercised considerable influence, was conducting the preliminary negotiations for a marriage alliance.[14] Whether Warwick would have approved of the terms Charles and Buckingham were prepared to offer for the hand of Henrietta Maria is quite another matter; but these terms were not yet known. James had in fact promised that he would not concede toleration to England's Roman Catholics.

In 1625 there was an electoral contest in Maldon; the elections for Colchester and the shire may have been disputed as well.[15] Once again Sir Julius Caesar failed to persuade the Maldon corporation to elect a client of his. Sir Arthur Herris was again elected to the first borough seat, but Sir William Masham was replaced by Sir Henry

Mildmay of Wanstead.[16] Mildmay was Buckingham's man, but he had probably already formed connections with the Warwick group. He was a shameless opportunist, but he was also known to be a vehement opponent of Arminianism. As early as 1621 a translation of Pierre du Moulin's tract against Arminius had been dedicated to him. Mildmay was also an intimate friend of the great Puritan preacher John Preston. Mildmay was not, however, otherwise remarkable for his piety. If I read her will correctly, Mildmay's intensely—indeed, pathologically—Puritan wife was resigned to seeing him damned.[17] During the Parliament of 1624 he somehow incurred James's displeasure, apparently in his eagerness to curry favor with the militant Protestants in the House.[18] The combined backing of Buckingham and Warwick would explain why Mildmay was able to supplant Sir William Masham. In any case, Masham assumed the first borough seat when Sir Arthur Herris chose to serve for the county instead. Significantly, Mildmay won because he had the support of the majority of common freemen of Maldon; the corporation supported Sir Julius Caesar's candidate. Warwick's group was acquiring a popular base.[19] Herris's son Christopher sat once again for Harwich, along with Sir Edward Sawyer; Towse and Alford were returned for Colchester. The county members were Sir Francis Barrington and Sir Arthur Herris. These were Warwick's candidates, whom he personally recommended to his "friends and neighbors," the freeholders of Colchester. Warwick's choice was endorsed by Thomas D'Arcy, Viscount Colchester, acting "at the request of my Lord of Buckingham."[20]

Despite the continuing alliance between Buckingham and the imperialists, the new Parliament of 1625 was far more restive than its predecessor. The commitments of the preceding year had been broken. The subsidies that Parliament had voted for a diversionary campaign at sea were squandered on Mansfeld's disastrous expedition. More seriously, the French match was concluded in May upon terms that serious Protestants found repellent and that James himself had vowed never to accept. The price of Henrietta Maria's hand was the toleration of her coreligionists in England and English aid in suppressing the rebellious Huguenots of La Rochelle.[21]

To men accustomed to seeing the hand of God in the most trivial occasions, it could hardly seem accidental that the relaxation of the penal laws coincided not only with military disaster but with the worst outbreak of plague in living memory. One of the new Parliament's first actions was to petition the king for a public fast to entreat divine mercy. They appointed a private fast day for themselves on July 2, at which they invited John Preston to preach. Preston told them, "It is not our army by land, nor our navy at sea . . . nor our policy, counsel, and strength that will secure and defend us, but it is turning to the Lord, and cleansing the land from the sins wherewith he is provoked that will do the deed."[22] Sir Henry Mildmay echoed Preston in August, when the Parliament had moved to Oxford to escape the pestilence. Mildmay told the House "that their coldness in religion was one of the principle causes of the grievous visitation then upon them."[23]

Parliament's first concern was to inform the king "of the late great increase of Papists in this realm, and of the dangerous consequences thereof, unless timely remedy be provided." An elaborate petition to this effect was prepared under the direction of Pym and Sandys.[24] But it was also necessary to defend the Calvinist identity of the Church of England itself. "For the Church at home," warned John Preston, "you see the Lord hath begun to make a breach upon us . . . Why do wicked men cry down all religion and zeal under the name of preciseness?"[25] Once again there were bills introduced for the sanctification of the Sabbath. Sir Nathaniel Rich proposed adding to the petition against papists the provision that silenced Puritans be allowed to preach so long as their doctrine conformed to the Thirty-Nine Articles. The most pressing issue, however, was the case of Richard Montague, who since the previous Parliament had made himself even more offensive to strict Calvinists with the publication of his *Appello Caesaram*. In appealing to the Crown against parliamentary censure, Montague had exalted the royal prerogative while denouncing Puritan lectureships as seditious, as James's defense of Bishop Harsnett invited him to do. Instead of punishment he had received promotion. Sir Henry Mildmay argued that Arminians, no less than papists, were agents of the King of Spain, and hence, "little less dangerous than a foreign invasion."[26]

The majority in the House of Commons felt that these religious grievances must be resolved before the Crown could be entrusted with more money. This was the position of Sir Nathaniel Rich, who told the House on August 6 that "the Israelites could not prosper, so long as the execrable thing was among them; we have as little hope of success as long as idolatry is so common." Furthermore, Rich insisted that the king declare exactly who the enemy was to be, and employ "grave counsellors in the government of these affairs," perhaps a veiled demand for the summoning of Warwick to the council board. But Rich was a moderate, and his position was by no means wholly negative. He had promised a temporary compromise in the Montague case: that Montague should be set free on bail. He was also concerned with placing the king's finances on a sound footing. He wished Parliament to "look into the king's estate, that so he might be enabled to subsist of himself."[27] Rich may have had in mind the scheme that he had formulated in 1623 to grant the Crown a franchise on pepper and tobacco from the New World.[28] Like the Earl of Warwick (but unlike Edward Alford), Rich wanted a strong state, capable of realizing England's imperial vocation. The colonies might not only absorb the surplus population but solve the Crown's fiscal problems as well.

Gradually the members of the House of Commons were coming to believe that England would never thrive with Buckingham in power. Sir Henry Mildmay defended his patron on August 6, reminding the House of the duke's responsibility for breaking off the Spanish match, but even Mildmay conceded that Buckingham might be "faulty in some things." Warwick and Rich, however, remained on good terms with the favorite throughout the summer, hoping that Buckingham and Charles might yet espouse the complementary policies of naval warfare and Calvinist repression. But the duke remained bewitched by the prospect of victories on the Continent. Charles was already testifying his devotion to the High Church of Montague and Laud. Parliament was dissolved on August 12 without having voted supplies.[29]

Throughout England 1625 was a vintage year for popish plots, comparable to the legendary *vendanges* of 1588 and 1605. Almost all of them were either imaginary or wildly exaggerated.[30] But the people of Essex had real cause for anxiety. There were plausible rumors of an impending invasion from Dunkirk by the fleet under the great Spanish commander Spinola. The Essex coast, and particularly the port of Harwich, would be the natural target of such an invasion. On August 26, just two weeks after the dissolution of Parliament, the Essex trained bands—some three thousand strong—were mustered for the defense of Harwich. The deputy lieutenants found the scene disquieting. They feared the men would either mutiny or desert. The sight of large numbers of their inferiors in arms always disturbed the gentry.[31] Worse yet, their commander, one Benjamin Moore, proved corrupt and unreliable. The fortifications of Harwich were ruinously decayed. Sir Harbottle Grimston described the town as totally unfit to repel a serious attack. Sussex found the troops without ammunition or pay. The commanders who had conducted them thither begged leave to go home. The Privy Council ordered the fortifications to be immediately repaired and promised reimbursement from the royal treasury.[32]

At this moment of crisis the Earl of Warwick, who had not yet broken with Buckingham, was joined with Sussex in the lord lieutenancy to conduct the defense of the Essex coast. Sussex was intensely vexed at this slight to his honor. He vapored to the council about his ancestors' long and loyal service, and complained of being regarded as "a cipher rather than an assistant." He refused to be mollified by the council's assurance that he would be restored to full authority once the crisis had ended. "What a disparagement it will be unto me," he exclaimed, "to be a lieutenant in time of peace, and in time of supposed employment to be held incapable of it!" To Warwick's brother, the newly created Earl of Holland, Sussex expressed a wish to be relieved of the lieutenancy altogether, preferring to be "quite forgotten in Essex, rather than to be remembered to my dishonor."[33]

Warwick, meanwhile, set about the business. In the first week of September he rode 120 miles back and forth across the county, rallying the trained bands. In his first letter to the Privy Council as joint lieutenant, he acknowledged Sussex's resentment, but added drily that his appointment was "very well relished both by the gentlemen and the generality," and there is no reason to doubt him. He demanded, however, that Sussex cease communicating with the council behind his back. He requested a commission of martial law and announced that he was sending to the Low Countries for military engineers and experienced commanders. Only one of the trained band captains, whom Warwick promptly promoted to sergeant-major general, had the faintest idea what war was about. Warwick described the troops themselves with good-humored irony: "we do daily cause our men . . . to be exercised, and find in them a great alacrity and courage to be dealing with their enemy, but I believe as yet we must expect better service from them with the great end of their muskets than the small, that course of fight coming nearest the flail and mattock to which they have been most accustomed."[34]

Warwick made a rapid assessment of the strategic situation. The greatest threat would be troop-carrying frigates from Dunkirk. Newcastle colliers would afford the best defense for the harbor until the fortifications were repaired. Ipswich was even more vulnerable than Harwich; Suffolk must raise one thousand troops for its defense immediately. Then there was the danger of the Catholic fifth column. The people of Essex were greatly upset by reports of "a very dangerous and secret conference of recusants and popish affected persons in multitudes together both in Suffolk and in Norfolk." Warwick suggested that the papists be disarmed, especially since some of them possessed whole stables full of war horses, "wherein the want of this county is lamentable." Like Richard Rogers in 1588 and Sir Henry Mildmay in the preceding parliament, Warwick feared equally "the enemy's designs both abroad and at home."[35]

Essex was in a state of panic. Tales flew about that the king had been struck down by plague, that Spinola's frigates had appeared off the coast. As folk fled inland from the seaboard, the theologian Joseph Mede—England's greatest living authority on the Apocalypse—wrote of "women crying and howling, as if Tilbury fort were come again."[36] Sir Francis Barrington reported more papist plots. The county was abuzz with rumors of "a great concourse to the Papists' houses, and of their preparations." He enclosed the examination of a tailor named Burling, who had denounced the recent proclamation against Jesuits and had warned his neighbors to "beware of their own back wing" when Spinola came. Burling said he would "hold with the queen, but not with the king"—exactly as opponents of a Catholic match had feared. Barrington also urged that papists be disarmed, a precaution that Warwick carried out a month later.[37] Warwick himself, meanwhile, had discovered that a recusant named Sheldon had established an intelligence network between Dunkirk and the Essex coast. Viscount Colchester, a deputy lieutenant whose family was justly suspected of Catholic leanings, found himself the object of "vile and scandalous" reports that left him powerless to contribute to the defense of the coast.[38]

Secretary Conway promised money, ammunition, and ships. But, as Warwick explained on September 18, Essex had already spent more than £4,000 and refused to pay more. The taxpayers recalled that Queen Elizabeth had borne the expenses of mustering the trained bands in 1588 and 1599. The inhabitants wanted the trained bands returned to their own parishes and hundreds, to defend them against the expected papist insurrection. Furthermore, the county was simply unable to pay. Trade and agriculture were paralyzed. "Scarce any man has half an ordinary crop of corn," Barrington and Maynard informed the council, "clothiers complain of want of vent of their wares and so forebear to set the poor on work." The plague in London had ruined business for graziers, hopmasters, and grain dealers. Michaelmas rents were coming due; the subsidy was being assessed; and above all, plague and depression had driven the poor rates to unheard-of heights. Many farmers were on the point of abandoning their holdings. All in all, it was a bad time to impose new and inequitable burdens on the county.[39]

The Braintree vestry book confirms the grim story told by the deputy lieutenants. The clothing industry had sunk to a new low in the late summer. Adrian Mott, the leading spirit among the lay members of the vestry, was delegated in July to meet with the other clothiers about finding work for the unemployed. In September the leading inhabitants assembled in the church to consider the same problem. Two months later an extraordinary levy of £50 was raised to provide a stock to "set the poor on work."[40]

Warwick and his deputies were forced to borrow money on their own account, at interest, in order to pay the troops. (There is no evidence that Sussex, still sulking, did anything whatever.) But the county was "bare of money." Warwick found that even "the richest men in the shire," such as the great merchant Sir Paul Bayning and the clothiers of Colchester, were short of cash because of the interruption of commerce with London. Warwick was growing angry. He complained that the council ignored his dispatches and that his reputation in Essex was being undermined.[41]

Very belatedly, some of the money promised to Essex for the defense of Harwich came in. At the end of October the Earl of Suffolk finally submitted a list of persons in his county fit to contribute, although there is no record of any money actually being collected; this was left to Warwick. In November, Essex received £658 from the Exchequer to defray the cost of repairing the fortifications, but there seems to have been no reimbursement for the billeting of troops. A year and a half later, the county was still trying to secure payment of the funds it had been promised by the Crown.[42]

Yet, Warwick had performed effectively. So far from blasting his reputation, his service in the fortification of Harwich enhanced his prestige sufficiently to provoke the jealousy of the Duke of Buckingham. The garrison was disbanded on October 8, the immediate threat to the Essex coast having passed. But in the same month occurred the catastrophe at Cadiz. Four hundred Essex conscripts had sailed with the duke on that ill-fated adventure. Those who survived malnutrition, disease, and Spanish shot straggled home during the winter of 1625–26. The events since the dissolution of Parliament must have raised grave doubts in Warwick's mind whether the Crown could be trusted to defend its own subjects, let alone assail the Whore of Babylon.

By the end of 1625 Warwick and his friends had probably decided to force Buckingham to take sides in the struggle between Calvinists and Arminians within the Church of England. In December, John Preston and Bishop James Ussher both preached at Barrington Hall in Hatfield Broad Oak. It was a day of public thanksgiving, perhaps for the end of the plague. Preston sounded his favorite theme: England must repent her sins to avoid further calamities. It is highly tempting to assume that Preston and Ussher were preaching to more than just the Barrington household on this occasion, that in fact there was a sort of regional synod of the godly assembled at Hatfield during the closing days of 1625, and that plans were made for the confrontation with Buckingham and the Arminians.[43] Buckingham did not yet regard the Warwick group as his enemies, however. None of Warwick's allies was excluded from the Parliament of 1626 by being chosen sheriff, like Sir Edward Coke and Sir Robert Phelips; it was Edward Alford who was thus disqualified. Barrington, Towse, Rich, Cheke, Masham, and Christopher Herris were all returned to the Commons.

As Parliament was about to assemble, Warwick, together with Lord Saye and Sir John Coke, arranged for a debate between John

Preston and Richard Montague and their respective adherents, to be presided over at York House by the Duke of Buckingham. It has been suggested that Warwick forced this confrontation on Preston and the duke, both of whom would have preferred to avoid it. Preston's performance apparently disappointed his supporters, but the conference had the effect of forcing the duke to side openly with the Arminians. As one of Joseph Mede's correspondents put it shortly after the debate at York House, "The business of religion is like to follow [the duke's] standing or downfall."[44]

In Essex, meanwhile, although the immediate threat of invasion had receded, fears and rumors persisted. The Protestant stronghold of La Rochelle remained under siege by Louis XIII. There were confused reports of gunpowder being smuggled from Colchester to Dunkirk, and the Earl of Warwick rode down from Westminster to look to the defenses of Harwich. The servant of an Essex justice found a letter concealed in a glove lying on the road outside Colchester; it was from an English priest in Dunkirk, describing the hopes of the exile community for an imminent Spanish invasion of England.[45]

Against this background the Commons pressed the attack against Buckingham and the Arminians. When a resolution condemning Montague passed the lower house, it was Nathaniel Rich who proposed that John Pym carry it up to the Lords. The prosecution of Montague was said to be "the greatest business that hath come into the House since *primo* Elizabeth." Rich had now clearly broken with Buckingham. He served as one of Pym's two assistants in the impeachment proceedings against the duke.[46]

With the government effectively paralyzed, Rich supported an astonishing proposal from Dudley Digges to carry on the war with Spain by private enterprise. A council of war would be organized as a joint-stock company to prey on Spanish shipping—a syndicate in piracy. Rich added the suggestion that the new corporation be exempt from the tax levied by the Lord High Admiral on prizes taken at sea, and that its seamen be immune from conscription.[47] Nothing came of the scheme for the moment, but the idea forms an interesting link between the activities of the Warwick faction in Virginia and Bermuda before 1624 and the policy that Warwick, Rich, Pym, and their associates pursued through the Province Island Company

in the 1630s. Warwick himself, meanwhile, was sending out privateers on his own account during these very months.[48]

The Commons' resolution against Montague passed on April 17,
the articles of impeachment against the Duke of Buckingham on
May 13. To save the duke, Charles dissolved his second Parliament
on June 15 and began to cast about for ways of raising money without the nuisance of recalling it. Writs were issued for the collection
of a Forced Loan, amounting in value to five subsidies. This would
mean a figure for Essex of rather more than £10,000 which squares
with the surviving assessments from fourteen of the twenty hundreds
of Essex, which record a total of £7,214 levied on roughly two-thirds
of the county's population.[49]

Assessment, however, was easier than collection. On August 30
the Essex justices protested. They were willing, so they said, to contribute to their country's defense, but they insisted that funds be
raised "in a Parliamentary way."[50] Furthermore, they reminded the
council that they had yet to be reimbursed for their expenses in the
defense of Harwich. At the end of October, Sir Francis Barrington
and Sir William Masham refused to serve as collectors of the loan.
Barrington was committed to the Marshalsea and Masham to the
Fleet.[51] In November, after some of the royal judges had voiced misgivings about the loan's legality, Warwick joined Saye and some fifteen other peers in refusing to pay.[52] More loan commissioners in
Essex defaulted, including the great gentleman clothier Sir Paul
Bayning and Warwick's ally Sir Harbottle Grimston, who was imprisoned.[53] Moreover, the example of the dissident gentlemen spread
downward. More than three hundred individuals in Essex were reported to the Privy Council for resisting or evading the loan. On the
evidence of the State Papers for 1627–28, £2,462 remained uncollected out of a total of £7,214 levied on fourteen Essex hundreds.
Conrad Russell believes that Essex was unique in the extent of resistance from taxpayers below the rank of the gentry.[54]

Warwick, Barrington, and Masham were put out of the Commission of the Peace. Warwick had already lost his lord lieutenantcy
because, according to Joseph Mede, "the Duke would not have him
joy and glory too much in his service of overseeing the work at Harwich." Since his command was to be assumed by the feckless Sussex,
Warwick prudently requested that "gentlemen of quality and skill"

be appointed to inspect the work he had performed, lest he be blamed for anything that went wrong later.[55] For the first time Warwick and his friends had been driven into explicit opposition to the Crown.

The same can be said of puritanism in general. From 1626 it is possible to detect a new radicalism among painful preachers, particularly of the younger generation. The profession of Christ seemed more and more to entail resistance to the drift (the term is exact) of royal policy. The breach with Buckingham prompted John Preston to consider emigration, but only a few days after the York House debate a group of his colleagues and disciples went on the offensive. They founded the Feoffees for Impropriations to advance the godly ministry, especially in parliamentary boroughs.[56]

In Essex there was a resurgence of activity comparable to that of the 1580s. Samuel Collins, the "painful" but politically cautious rector of Braintree, recalled that about 1624 "certain refractory ministers of the county" began encouraging nonconformity among his flock "by private meetings and leaving schismatical books among them."[57] Collins does not name these refractory ministers, but he was almost certainly referring to Thomas Hooker and his circle.

Thomas Hooker, the future founder of Connecticut, was John Rogers's most famous protegé. At Cambridge, according to Cotton Mather, he had already undergone the agonies of self-disgust that were de rigueur for aspiring Saints, although his external conduct, by all accounts, had been blameless. Indeed, one suspects that the power of his later preaching derived in part from his inability to rid himself completely of his youthful anxiety. In New England he once told a young divinity student who was terrified by the prospect of damnation that he, Hooker, could "compare with any man living for fears." Hooker settled in the Stour valley in order to study with Rogers. Rogers tried unsuccessfully to find Hooker a benefice at Colchester, and the young man spent the first half of the 1620s as an itinerant preacher in Essex and London. In 1626, however, the county town of Chelmsford, "hearing the fame of his powerful ministry," invited Hooker to become their lecturer and "break the bread of life to them." His career in Chelmsford was to be brief but spectacular.[58]

Men and women flocked to Hooker's lecture from all parts of

Essex. Like his teacher, John Rogers, he was a vehement and over-powering preacher. "Let there be fire in it," he once advised a younger colleague. We have already sampled the violence of his imagery and heard him compare the Word of God to a sharp sword. According to a man who had heard him in Chelmsford, Hooker had a "choleric disposition" and a "mighty fervor of spirit," which he handled like a mastiff on a chain. During his three years in Chelmsford, Hooker built up a popular following unrivaled by any other preacher in the county's history. "Our people's palates," wrote Samuel Collins, "grow so out of taste that no food contents them but of Mr. Hooker's dressing." Among his auditors at Chelmsford was the Earl of Warwick.[59]

Hooker attracted a distinguished group of younger ministers to Essex, and became "their oracle in cases of conscience and points of divinity, and their principle library." He presided over monthly fasts and conferences, which were modeled on the old Elizabethan prophesyings.[60] One of these young ministers was probably Hugh Peter, whose stormy career led him to a regicide's death in 1660. Around 1622, while still a schoolmaster in Laindon, Essex, Peter had been inspired by Hooker with a sense of election and a vocation for the ministry. After taking orders in 1623 Peter had been presented to the living of Rayleigh by the Earl of Warwick, who would prove a steady friend to Hooker and his disciples.[61] Another of Hooker's proteges was the future emigrant Thomas Shepherd. In 1625 Shepherd entered the household of Thomas Weld, the minister of Terling (another future emigrant), and met Hooker shortly thereafter. He found himself among the "best ministers" in the "best county" in England. On Hooker's advice, Shepherd accepted a lectureship at Earls Colne. His initial reception was frosty; apart from the schoolmaster, with whom he lodged, there was not a godly man in town. But after a time the Lord blessed his labors, and he made converts among the Harlackendens, the leading family of Earls Colne. Richard Harlackenden, upon whom "the Lord wrought mightily," became one of the principal Parliamentary commanders in the Civil War, while his young brother, Roger, emigrated to New England.[62]

Puritan preachers like Hooker and Shepherd were invaluable to local elites during the crisis of the 1620s and 1630s. For one thing, they were good for business. Hooker's preaching brought "flocks and tumults" to the Chelmsford market—no small achievement during a severe depression.[63] (Recall that in September of 1625 the deputy lieutenants reported that commerce in Essex was virtually dead.) According to Matthew Newcomen, Samuel Collins's ministry brought a similar prosperity to Braintree by attracting "some whole streets" of new inhabitants. The stricken cloth town of Earls Colne applied to Hooker's circle for a lecturer in hopes "that the lecture might enrich that poor town."[64]

More important, the Puritan preachers were the prophets of the culture of discipline, at a time when the economic crisis made a reformation of manners more than ever imperative. When Coggeshall invited Thomas Shepherd to become their lecturer in 1626, they hoped he could work the kind of reformation his mentor was effecting in Chelmsford. In the same year the town petitioned the Quarter Sessions for an order to prevent the breaking of the Sabbath.[65] Secular policy was impotent to resolve the economic crisis, but a reformation of manners could both strengthen social order and recapture God's favor. This argument was later made explicitly by Sir William Masham, who blamed drunkenness for bad harvests and asserted that "justice against this sin is the best expiation."[66]

But the argument that plagues and punishments were caused by sin was potentially subversive. If there was a special providence in the fall of a sparrow, it could hardly be coincidental that the king's marriage to a Catholic, his countenancing of idolatry, and his betrayal of the Huguenots of La Rochelle should be attended by military disaster, economic depression, and pestilence. It was for this reason that the hierarchy and the Crown were suspicious of that favorite Puritan institution, the public fast for collective prayer and repentence. In July 1626 James Harrison, the Barringtons' private chaplain, preached in Hatfield that a fast should be held when there was sin in the land and "when affliction is upon the Church."[67] Thus, a fast implied that the official magic of the church was failing, which in turn might suggest that the government had lost (to borrow a phrase from a different culture) the mandate of heaven. These considerations help explain why Laud was insistent that the dearth of 1629–30 was caused not by God but by grain speculators.[68]

Puritan preachers were assuming the mantle of the Old Testament prophets, who had also been notoriously troublesome citizens. Upon their ability to decode God's messages they based a claim to define national purposes, to prescribe the broad outlines of policy, and to castigate any backsliding or deviance on the part of the rulers. "God reveals his mind to his ministers," said William Gouge, the schoolmate and friend of Warwick and Sir Nathaniel Rich. Godly ministers equaled the Hebrew prophets in their ability to "foretell judgments," not so much because they were directly inspired as their predecessors had been, but because their mastery of scriptural interpretation enabled them to identify and predict the consequences of sin. Gouge claimed the preachers had predicted the outbreak of plague in 1625.[69]

"Faithful ministers," asserted Thomas Hooker in 1626, "are the defenders of states, churches, and commonwealth." By their prayers they could avert the wrath of the Lord, as William Gouge claimed the public fast of August 2, 1626, had lifted the shadow of famine from the land.[70] But the preacher could also serve as the instrument of divine vengeance. Thomas Barnes of Great Waltham cited the Book of Revelation to prove that the ministers of the Gospel had God's commission to pour forth his curses upon "earthly-minded men." Preachers, said Barnes, must sometimes be "sons of thunder." Hooker also stressed the power of a godly preacher to divert calamity from the righteous to the wicked. "Take heed," he warned, "of wronging a praying minister."[71] It is frankly difficult to see on what anthropological grounds these asserted powers are to be distinguished from sorcery, despite the Puritan hostility to the magical aspects of Catholicism.

In 1626 the Puritan preachers were ferocious proponents of the war that Charles was supposed to be fighting. Thomas Barnes's *Vox Belli,* dedicated in 1626 to Sir Horace Vere, is an excellent illustration of their militarism. "Cursed be he that withholdeth his hand from blood," cried Barnes, quoting Judges 5:23. His text was drawn from the story of Meroz, the tribe that was accursed of God because it had remained neutral in the conflict between the Lord and his enemies. Years later a more famous Essex Puritan, Stephen Marshall, won lasting notoriety for his use of the same text to justify armed resistance to the king.[72] But Marshall was neither original nor exceptionally bloodthirsty in citing this rather obscure biblical episode. Nor was it a discovery of Barnes's; the example of Meroz cursed seems to have been a commonplace of Protestant rhetoric during the 1620s. It was, in fact, cited by the Speaker of the House of Commons at the opening of the Parliament of 1625, to encourage the voting of supply for Charles's military operations. (The Speaker, Sir Thomas Crews, was something of a Puritan, but he was also a royal appointee.)[73]

Barnes found the curse of Meroz "a text so terrible that at the first it made me fearful to meddle with it." But he soon recovered his nerve. Christian pacifism Barnes rejected out of hand as "that fantastical conceit of the Anabaptistical sect." Christ's commandment to love our enemies did not forbid our killing them in a worthy cause. Moreover, the war in which England was currently engaged must be waged to total victory. Barnes looked for the day when the "Romish beast" should be "trodden down as straw for the dunghill," and the scattered stones of Sion, the Protestant churches of the world, be gathered together again.[74]

In this great conflict the Puritan preachers saw themselves as front-line commanders. "It is wonderful," said Hooker, "to see what a good minister can do in a good war, how he can fight against principalities and powers." Hooker's earliest surviving sermon, preached on June 22, 1626, was entitled *Spiritual Munitions*. Faithful ministers, said Hooker, were the surest defense of the realm. Those who opposed them were traitors to king and country, as surely as if they had transported to Spain all the powder and shot in England. The war must be waged on the spiritual as well as the physical plane. In phrases that closely parallel those of John Preston, Hooker insisted that neither "the weakness of our land" nor Spain's might was as much to be feared as "our treacherous hearts at home."[75]

Preaching on Guy Fawkes Day, 1626, Hooker reminded the people of Chelmsford how God had miraculously delivered England from Bloody Mary, from the Armada, from the Gunpowder Plot. He had thus far spared her the horrors that convulsed Bohemia and the Platinate. England was the "mirror of mercies." But these very mercies imposed special obligations. England would be held to higher standards and a stricter account than less favored nations. Hooker now feared that the nation's sins were about to cause God to withdraw his protection. Drunkenness was spreading like the pestilence; once regarded as the sin only of beggars, it had now infected the aristocracy. There was "wickedness in high places." Idolatry was countenanced, and the godly were reviled. If neither plague nor famine brought the English to repentence, God would loose the third of his arrows: war. The Spanish *tercios* would execute upon the apostate English a vengeance proportionate to the mercies they had spurned.[76]

The moral reformation that Hooker considered essential to military success required the close cooperation of minister and magistrate. Yet the magistrate was profaning the Sabbath and conniving at the spread of popery while "drunkards and belly-gods" were promoted in the church. Among the national sins that William Gouge believed were most likely to provoke God's wrath were "magistrates' abuse of authority" and "ministers perverting their function . . . emboldening the wicked and . . . discountenancing the upright."[77] Both sins, he warned, were rampant in England.

Hooker did not flinch from affixing ultimate responsibility for England's woes. In a sermon at the Essex Assizes, preached before a "vast congregation," which included the justices of the peace and the circuit judges, Hooker once more "declared freely the sins of England and the plagues that would come for such sins." But this time he went further. He prayed that God would "set on the heart of the King" the eleventh and twelfth verses of the second chapter of the Book of Malachi. Hooker did not quote the passage, but the judges and justices riffled through their Bibles until they came to "an abomination is committed: Judah hath married the daughter of a strange god. The Lord will cut off the man that doth this." The audacity is breathtaking. Royal policy might be altered; prelates and councillors could be replaced; but was Charles really supposed to repudiate his wedded queen? No wonder it was said that Hooker, when doing the work of the Lord, would "put a king in his pocket."[78]

Hooker was not, however, alone. In November of 1626 John Preston warned Charles that God would destroy him and his dynasty if he did not exert himself to the utmost on behalf of the Kingdom of Grace. This sermon was later dedicated by Preston's editors to Sir Nathaniel Rich. In the same month Hugh Peter, whom Warwick had presented to the vicarage of Rayleigh, also blamed the plague and the loss of the Palatinate on England's backsliding. He prayed that God would enlighten the king in the art of government and convert the queen from "the idols of her father's house." After this sermon Warwick had to intercede with Bishop Mountaigne to shield Peter from prosecution.[79]

Sermons such as these obviously discouraged cooperation with Charles's fiscal experiments, which would have earned resentment in the best of times as an encroachment upon traditional liberties. In Protestant thought, popery and despotism were very closely associated. Describing the horrors to be expected from a Catholic victory, Thomas Hooker stressed the total loss of personal rights. Had the Gunpowder Plot succeeded, "a man's goods should have been taken from him, and no law to help him, nay his liberty should have been despaired of, and his blood shed, and no man to relieve him." Lawless oppression was "the fruit of popery and the practice of papists."[80]

It was difficult for a Protestant gentleman of the day to conceive of a threat to his liberties that did not in some way emanate from the Romish Beast. As late as 1689 William III thought it sufficient to remind the Commons of his Protestantism to allay their concern for judiciary independence.[81] There was consensus that the Englishman's rights were adequately protected under the Ancient Constitution. On this point Conrad Russell is quite right to say that the nation was not ideologically divided. Hence, the perceived threat must originate from an external source, and where else but from the throne of Antichrist? At a deep level, liberty, property, and religion were not just intimately associated; they were aspects of the same thing.

In this connection it is instructive to examine the geographical incidence of resistance to the Forced Loan. There was very little opposition in most of the purely rural hundreds in the west and along the south and east coasts, with the significant exception of Rochford. In March 1627 the Privy Council ordered fifty men conscripted from the most refractory hundreds, *pour encourager les autres;* the hundreds were Rochford, Becontree, Chelmsford, and Hinckford. The later reports of the loan commissioners suggest that we should add Lexden to the list. Braintree, Witham, and Maldon were cited as particularly obstinate towns, and hence suitable targets of the forced billeting of troops.[82]

We may leave aside the half-hundred of Becontree, which was virtually a suburb of the capital. The remaining hundreds were precisely the areas where Puritan preachers were most active. Rochford was the territorial base of Warwick's power in Essex. In addition to his dairy ranches, he held a number of advowsons there, including that of Rayleigh, to which he had presented Hugh Peter. John Rogers, Thomas Hooker, Thomas Barnes, Thomas Shepherd, and Stephen Marshall were all preaching in the contiguous hundreds of Chelmsford, Hinckford, and Lexden. Thomas Weld at Terling was barely a mile across the border of Witham hundred. At Leighs Priory, on the Chelmsford-Hinckford border, the Earl of Warwick maintained a veritable seminary of unbeneficed divines, just a mile from the famous Puritan grammar school of Felsted, which his great-grandfather had founded.[83]

As Table 14 shows, the greatest resistance of all was encountered in the clothing districts of Hinckford and Lexden, where the growth of Puritanism coincided—not accidentally—with severe economic distress. Braintree, where schismatical books were circulating among Samuel Collins's congregation, twenty-four failed to pay their assessment, including most of the leading members of the vestry. Several of these men were among the tiny minority of Essex testators who referred explicitly to the doctrine of predestination in their wills. Nineteen failed to pay in the adjoining village of Bocking. John Rogers's parish of Dedham produced thirty-four defaulters, including Rogers himself. The only other clergyman who is known to have refused payment, however, was the otherwise obscure William Allison of Sturmer, in Hinckford hundred, who defied the commissioners to their faces. The Crown's harassment of defaulting clothiers aggravated the economic crisis. In March 1627 "hundreds of poor men" begged for the release of their imprisoned employers.[84]

The attempt to intimidate resisters with the threat of conscription proved to be a serious blunder. The loan was demanded of subsidy men, who might be called upon to serve in the trained bands, but virtually never in conscripted levies. Most of them simply ignored the deputy lieutenants' summons to appear in Chelmsford. The seven Chelmsford men who did show up refused to accept the press money.[85] Meanwhile, handbills abusing Lord Maynard, who was in charge of the attempted conscription of loan resisters, began to appear on trees along the highways. They were, as Joseph Mede remarked, "ill symptoms."[86] The government backed down, still uttering vague threats of some "exemplary prosecutions" yet to come.

Table 14. Resistance to Forced Loan in selected Essex hundreds as of September 1627

Hundred	Total assessment (£)	Amount unpaid (£)	Percent of assessment unpaid
Hinckford	1,292	436	33.7
Lexden	647	139	21.4
Tendring	424	36	8.4
Winstree	307	5	1.6
Witham	215	20	9.3
Thurstable	122	2	1.6
Total	3,007	638	21.2

Source: Public Record Office, London, SP 16/76/13 I, 22 III.

The Privy Council had displayed the classic combination of brutality and weakness that so often characterizes an *ancien régime* in crisis.[87]

In April the Crown encountered a more organized display of resistance. A levy of £1,605 in Ship Money, the estimated cost of outfitting a vessel of two hundred tons for four months, had been imposed upon Colchester. The townsmen alleged the calamities that had recently befallen them—the loss of six vessels to pirates, the embargo on cloth exports to Spain, the "lamentable visitation" of the plague—and professed their inability to pay.[88] Since these complaints were substantially true, the Privy Council was behaving reasonably when it ordered that the burden of Ship Money be shared by the entire county. But here the Crown ran up against the legalism and sheer selfishness of the county community. As in Kent, Cheshire, and Somerset, the corporate identity of the county community, of the county as a country, was expressed at the Quarter Sessions, and was especially embodied in the grand jury. It is not too much to say that the Quarter Sessions could serve as a sort of provincial parliament for the articulation of the essentially local concerns of the lesser gentry and substantial householders.[89]

The government's attempt to extend Ship Money to the county at large, and the resistance it evoked, reveals the vitality of provincial political life in early Stuart England. In 1627 the Crown should have been able to rely upon the leading magistrates of the county. Troublemakers like Warwick, Masham, Barrington, and Grimston had been purged from the commission, and Warwick was actually setting out to sea. Yet, the justices felt they must refer the matter to the deliberations of the county as a whole, which was a virtual invitation, from the duly constituted authorities of the county, to obstruct the Crown's will. The justices, finding no precedent for the imposition of Ship Money on the entire county, felt obliged to seek the "general and unanimous consent of the whole county" before proceeding with the collection. What is most interesting is the assertion that there was an established procedure in such cases; normal practice would have been "purposely to assemble the county together to receive their resolutions." Since time did not permit this general assembly, the letter of the Privy Council was presented to the grand jury, which was explicitly identified as "the representative body of this county." The grand jury in turn consulted with all the petty juries at the Quarter Sessions, and with "any other freeholders" in attendance. The unanimous answer was no. Citing the county's expenses in the defense of Harwich, and the wealth of the town of Colchester, with its income of £500 from its commons, the county community "did all with one consent desire to be excused."[90]

The justices forwarded the grand jury's answer to the Privy Council, which was understandably shocked at this "confronting of the counsels and directions of His Majesty and this board with the counsels and directions of a grand jury of Essex."[91] But that was just the trouble with the Ancient Constitution. The unpaid justices and deputy lieutenants who were charged with exercising royal authority in the provinces found themselves whipsawed between the demands of the Crown and the obdurate self-interest of their countrymen. The government had the same problem everywhere—in Somerset and Sussex as well as Essex. This explains why the military preparations of 1626–1628, undertaken, as Conrad Russell remarks, "on a greater scale (and at greater cost) than anything since 1588," produced such pathetic results.[92]

Meanwhile, the troops being embarked at Harwich for service under King Christian of Denmark were deserting in droves. On April 3 their commander, Richard Saltonstall, wrote that he had seized a waterman who had been slipping up to the camp at night and ferrying deserters to freedom. Saltonstall now lacked 150 of the five hundred men he was supposed to embark, and more men scampered off at each nightfall. To prevent further desertions, the conscripts were placed on board a pair of ships moored out in the harbor. The result was mutiny. Some rowed ashore and vanished into Essex and Suffolk; the others seized Saltonstall and his lieutenant as hostages.[93] The Earl of Sussex did nothing, as was his wont. Once again the Privy Council was forced to call on the Earl of Warwick. Warwick ordered Robert Gosnold, who had served him well at Harwich in 1625, to raise the trained bands.[94] But before Gosnold arrived, the justices had worked out a sensible compromise with the mutineers. "After long discourse and much debate," they reported, "we first showed them the danger they were fallen into, and then promised them redress in any injury." The captain and the lieutenant were released, the ringleaders were taken into custody. The rest of the mutineers promised to go off docilely to the wars, if only they could be billeted on land in the meantime.[95]

Before the leaders could be sent up to London, their fellow conscripts tried to rescue them from prison, vowing to defend them to the death. Their resolve was not equal to their generosity of spirit. These weavers and farmers were not soldiers; Saltonstall and Gosnold were. Swinging their pikes, the two officers waded among the rioters, dealt out a few cuts and bruises, and dispersed the crowd. The seven leaders were brought up to London in the latter part of April. The council wanted them hanged; the London jurors were more sympathetic. On May 25 the ringleader, a Colchester man of Dutch parentage named John Toner, was tried and acquitted.[96] These events, on the eve of Buckingham's expedition to La Rochelle, boded ill for the Crown's war effort. Throughout the summer of 1627, as the bad news from the Isle of Rhé filtered back home, there were more complaints in Essex about the pressing of troops, the cost of maintaining them, and the hardship to farmers of being drawn from their fields at harvest time to serve in the trained bands.[97]

In June, Sir Francis Barrington and Sir Harbottle Grimston were finally released from prison. Both were in poor health. Barrington, indeed, was thought to be dying. "His stomach is almost lost . . . his flesh is greatly wasted," wrote Barrington's physician, who blamed the "ill and close air of the prison." Barrington was subsisting on a diet of mother's milk. In fact, he had a little over a year to live—long enough to serve his county one last time at Westminster.[98]

The Earl of Warwick, meanwhile, had renewed his private war against the Spanish Empire. On the ninth of March, two of his vessels sailed into Plymouth harbor with a prize in tow: a Portuguese vessel bound for Brazil with a humble cargo of salt, iron, and meal. Ship and cargo were worth a paltry £1,500. On April 17 Charles enlarged Warwick's commission, giving him leave to plunder or colonize as he saw fit any possessions of the King of Spain in Europe, Africa, or the Americas. Warwick had earned Buckingham's hostility, however, and the duke's secretary wrote that Warwick's commission would never have been approved had Buckingham not been distracted by his preparations for the La Rochelle campaign.[99] In April and May, as Warwick was preparing to set sail from Plymouth with a fleet of seven ships, he was spied upon by Sir James Bagg, a Buckingham creature who had succeeded Warwick's friend Sir John Eliot as vice-admiral of Devon. Bagg reported to his master that Warwick was constantly to be seen in the company of Sir John Eliot, "that pattern of ingratitude," as Bagg termed him. Warwick was also observed conferring with Sir Fernando Gorges and one Corrington. Such companions, said Bagg, were enough to identify Warwick as an enemy to both Buckingham and the king.[100] Bagg, acting on the duke's authority as High Admiral, tried to hold Warwick and his ships in Plymouth. Warwick, referring to his direct commission from the king, disregarded Bagg and Buckingham and set sail in late May.[101]

As Warwick's ships drove out into the Atlantic, Buckingham found a way to avenge the slight to his authority. The City of London had failed to contribute enough pistols for the cavalry that he proposed to take to the Isle of Rhé. Warwick's armory was reputed to contain six or seven score pistols, which his countess was forthwith instructed to sell to the Crown. When she refused to do so without her husband's permission, Buckingham sent a party of men to break into the armory and seize the pistols without compensation.[102]

Warwick' objective was to capture the Spanish treasure fleet off the coast of Brazil. Instead, he was set upon by a superior Spanish force in the Azores, and was hard pressed to break through their line and return safely to England. Militarily the expedition was a total failure, but it nevertheless enhanced Warwick's popular prestige. His admiring seamen spread tales of his daring. It was reported that, unlike his father on the first Cadiz expedition, Warwick was "never sick one hour at sea." Despite his forty years, he could "as nimbly climb up to top and yard as any common mariner in the ship." During the desperate encounter with the Spanish, he had been "as active and as open to danger as any man there."[103]

While Warwick was at sea, there were more rumors of Catholic plots in his county. The son of Lord Petre of Ingatestone was apprehended with the son of Lord Herbert while embarking for Flanders with "many letters, and two barrels of treasure." Worse, it was said that for a fortnight "divers great Papists" had been meeting at Lord Petre's house.[104] In this climate of suspicion, it is no wonder that the Catholic Lord Rivers had difficulty levying fifty men from the Essex trained band for the garrison at Harwich. The men told him that if conscripted, they would emigrate to the New World.[105]

The government's reputation sank to a new low in November, when Buckingham's forces were ignominiously routed from the Isle of Rhé. Two days before the disaster, John Preston preached his last sermon before the court. "God is angry," he declared, "and He is never angry but for sin." Once again he blamed the enemy within the gates, who was "striking at the root of this Church and Commonwealth." After this sermon Laud forbade Preston to preach again in London. In the following month Hugh Peter's license to preach was revoked. Even the venerable John Rogers feared, during 1627, that he might be silenced. He jotted down a resolution to give up his lectureship sooner than violate his conscience, a resolution he was called upon to keep two years later.[106]

In the aftermath of the Rhé disaster the Privy Council ordered the regiments under the command of Sir Ralph Bingley and Sir Piers Crosby to be billeted, and the deputy lieutenants levied a rate of £1,000 on the county for this purpose.[107] The troops were not well received by their reluctant hosts. The inhabitants refused to receive even well-behaved soldiers, as the deputy lieutenants reported to the council. Given their recent performance, the troops could not have seemed a very sound investment. But what made the situation intolerable was the fact that the troops of Crosby's regiment were Irish papists. Even worse they were billeted on the towns of Maldon and Witham, as punishment for having resisted the Forced Loan.[108]

It was a prescription for disaster. Two of the most disaffected communities in the most Protestant county in England were invited to entertain armed men whom they believed to be devotees of Satan. The results were predictable. Captain Rossecarne was soon complaining of the insults his men received in Maldon, while the towns-folk accused the soldiers of all manner of "insolencies and outrages." They brawled drunkenly in the streets, they smashed furniture, they flung food that displeased them about their hosts' kitchens. "They command in our houses as if they were lords and we their slaves," complained one group of citizens. Householders were compelled to stay home from church to guard their goods, wives, and servants. Fear of the Irish had driven the country folk from the Maldon market, causing great poverty. A general exodus of the better sort was said to have begun.[109] These lurid tales apparently induced the Privy Council to order the troops transferred to Witham, despite the latter town's vehement protestations of poverty. The results at Witham were to be even worse.[110]

In the meantime, however, fiscal necessity had forced Charles, against the clairvoyant advice of Laud and the Arminians, to summon another Parliament.[111] The attempt to raise an additional £605 in Ship Money and to extract another Forced Loan were abandoned.[112] The elections of 1628 consolidated the dominance of the Warwick-Barrington constellation in Essex politics. Sir Henry Mildmay and Sir Arthur Herris sat for Maldon, Sir Nathaniel Rich and Christopher Herris for Harwich. At Colchester there was a dispute over the franchise between the corporation and the generality of free burgesses. On January 25, meeting in the upper chamber of the Moot Hall, the forty-two members of the corporation chose Warwick's brother-in-law, Sir Thomas Cheke, and paired him with their old friend Sir Edward Alford, who had done them "long and loving service" since the days of Elizabeth. Meanwhile, the free burgesses, who rejected the exclusive claim of the corporation to the town's franchise, assembled in the room below. They also endorsed Sir Thomas Cheke, but they replaced Alford with Barrington's son-in-law, Sir William Masham.[113] On March 28, the House of Commons ruled in favor of the broader franchise and admitted Masham to the seat.[114]

The Colchester free burgesses had been at odds with the governing corporation for some time, although the details are shadowy. The corporation was attempting to exclude ordinary freemen from participation in the election of aldermen and other officials.[115] There was also conflict over the oligarchy's administration of the town's common pastures. Some of the land had already been enclosed and was being leased out at the corporation's discretion. During the previous summer the oligarchy had claimed for themselves the exclusive right to pasture cattle in one of the fields that remained. Masham had apparently identified himself with the aspirations of the larger body of free burgesses, and he seems later to have mediated a settlement of the dispute remarkably favorable to their interests.[116] During the 1620s, as Derek Hirst has observed, there were similar conflicts, and similar exploitation of popular grievances to electoral advantage, in Coventry, Warwick, Chippenham, and no doubt elsewhere.[117]

The episode makes it clear that the Earl of Warwick did not, in any simple sense, control the corporation of Colchester. The aldermen and common council were cooperative enough in returning Warwick's brother-in-law, but in order to unseat Alford in favor of Masham it was necessary to appeal beyond the charmed circle of the oligarchy to the free burgesses at large. The year before, the corporation had rejected Warwick's nomination for the position of town preacher.[118] And yet, the corporation's obvious independence of spirit did not deter Warwick from addressing them courteously in February 1628 to recommend his choice of candidates for knights of shire.[119] The whole question of patronage and influence has often been treated much too simplistically, as if the only alternatives open to a borough in its relations with a local magnate were defiance or servility. Like the force of gravitation, influence in seventeenth-century politics admitted of subtle gradations.[120]

Warwick's candidates in the county election were Sir Francis Barrington and Sir Harbottle Grimston, both of whom had been imprisoned, like Sir William Masham, for their opposition to the Forced Loan. The Duke of Buckingham sought to secure the return of more pliant candidates. Earl Rivers wrote to the Colchester bailiffs on February 9, at Buckingham's behest, to recommend Sir Richard Weston, the Essex-born Chancellor of the Exchequer. Rivers added, with just a hint of menace, "I would wish you well advised before you deny him." The Earl of Warwick countered with a letter of his own, which showed a more tactful regard for the corporation's dignity. He was eager not to irritate their prickly sense of independence while the controversy over the borough election was still in progress. Warwick assured the bailiffs that he had perfect confidence in their good sense and would never have intervened, "were it not that some of my neighbors of good quality have used means to procure some friends of theirs to be chosen." But since Rivers had sought to exert his influence, Warwick was obliged by his love for the county to declare himself for Barrington and Grimston, and he delicately requested the Colchester bailiffs to "acquaint as many of your neighbors as conscientiously you may with the purport of this my letter."[121]

On or about February 17 there was an attempt, presumably initiated by Buckingham, to outmaneuver Warwick's party by conducting a snap election of court supporters at Stratford Langthorne, near London. Sir Thomas Fanshawe and Sir Thomas Edmunds had secretly procured writs of election and summoned the sheriff to Stratford Langthorne, where it was intended to convene a suitably docile electorate and to return candidates supportive of the duke— perhaps Weston and Sir William Wiseman, or Fanshawe himself.[122] Word of the secret election leaked out, and one thousand freeholders appeared in Stratford to support Barrington and Grimston. Fanshawe and Edmunds withdrew in confusion. According to the Venetian ambassador, it was this incident that encouraged other counties to reject the duke's candidates and return men who had refused the Forced Loan.[123]

What happened next is somewhat obscure. Apparently, Sir William Wiseman, Sir William Maxey, and Sir Thomas Fanshawe, acting on orders from Buckingham, sent a letter to the high constable of Tendring hundred. He was to round up and bring all the freeholders in his district to Chelmsford, where they were to cast their votes with the majority of the justices of the peace. The electoral strategy of Buckingham's party is revealing. Tendring was a thinly populated, economically backward, and politically conservative region. It contained no clothing towns and harbored, so far as I am aware, no Puritan preachers. More to the point, it had been probably the most cooperative hundred in Essex in paying the Forced Loan. So it was a natural area whence to draw pliant and not very well informed electors. It is perhaps more surprising that Buckingham's friends thought they could count on support from a majority of the county's magistrates. But it must be recalled that Warwick, Barrington, Masham, and Grimston had been purged from the commission over the Forced Loan. The Tendring constable, however, showed the letter to Barrington and Grimston, who alerted their supporters.

One observer claimed that between ten and fifteen thousand men flocked to Chelmsford to elect Barrington and Grimston.[124] Such accounts are notoriously unreliable, but it is worth noting that this is the largest contemporary estimate for any prerevolutionary election.[125] The duke's secretary charged that many of the voters had been enfranchised on the spot by receiving freehold tenements, which they surrendered back again immediately after the election. As far as the House of Commons was concerned, however, it was Buckingham's clique who had attempted to rig the election. The letter to the Tendring constable was exhibited as "an unparalleled violation of the subject's liberties," and Sir William Wiseman was committed to the Fleet by the council to forestall his prosecution by the House of Commons.[126]

What seems clear is that in both these elections Warwick's friends were able to muster considerable popular support—against the corporation in Colchester and against the majority of the county's justices at Chelmsford. Once again, the influence of the network extended beyond Essex. Sir Francis Barrington's two sons, Robert and Sir Thomas, represented the borough of Newport on the Isle of Wight, and his son-in-law, Richard Knightley, sat for Northamptonshire.

This election of 1628 may have been the first in which godly preachers played an active political role. We know that Stephen Marshall, Nathaniel Ward, and several other Puritans were preaching in Maldon during the campaign, and it is not at all unlikely that they were rebutting the absolutist arguments of Arminians like Montague and Manwaring, who succeeded Montague to the rectory of Stanford Rivers later in the year.[127] The Warwick faction would make very effective use of Marshall and his colleagues in the elections to the Short Parliament.

On March 17, the day Parliament assembled, the hostility between the Irish troops billeted in Witham and the local inhabitants flared into open violence. It was the feast of St. Patrick, and Captain Carew's men were performing sword dances in the streets of the town. The soldiers wore red crucifixes in their hats in honor of their national patron. A mischievous lad, apprentice to a local cobbler, tied two of these crosses to the tail of a dog; ten other boys hung a cross on the town whipping post. The troops, who had already drunk themselves into an appropriately devotional frame of mind, broke into a riot. Captain Carew was quietly drinking in the George Inn with William and Ralph Wiseman, members of a prominent local recusant family, when he heard that his men were on the rampage. He raced out of the tavern, screaming orders in Irish. Muskets went off. Carew fell with a head wound, which was not as serious as it looked. Several soldiers and townsmen were wounded, and a rumor went about that thirty people had been killed. It was a wild exaggeration; there is no hard evidence of any fatalities at all. But the rumor itself, which anticipates the more substantial atrocity stories of 1641, is evidence of the hatred and fear evoked by the presence on English soil of armed Irish papists.[128]

This, then, was the local background to the critical Parliament of 1628. The Essex delegation was alarmed; they perceived a combined threat to property and religion. On March 26 Nathaniel Rich attacked the Forced Loan, arguing that security of property was essential to both the prosperity and the safety of the realm. "If no propriety, there will be no industry," he declared, "and then nothing will follow but beggary, and if no propriety there will follow no valor. What shall be fought for?"[129] Meanwhile, the Earl of Warwick, in one of his very few recorded speeches, eloquently argued that the imprisonment of his friends for resisting the loan had been in violation of the liberties of the subject as guaranteed by Magna Carta. The survival of this speech in at least six manuscript copies suggests that it was widely circulated.[130]

At the same time, these men were not unwilling to contribute to the war effort, provided that constitutional forms were observed. "I denied the loan," Sir Francis Barrington acknowledged; but in April 1628 he voted a full five subsidies, because it was being done "the parliamentary way."[131] Later in the summer another loan resister, John Rogers of Dedham, urged his congregation to pay their taxes cheerfully.[132]

The billeting of troops, however, was an intolerable imposition. On April 9 Sir Nathaniel Rich brought in a petition against the troops. Like the citizens of Maldon, Rich accused the soldiers of ruining the economy and terrorizing honest folk, but he also expressed the fear that "the meaner sort of people" would join with the troops and so "fall into mutiny and rebellion."[133] This was a peculiar apprehension in the aftermath of the riot at Witham, which revealed ferocious popular hostility toward the troops, but we have to remember that Calvinists like Rich assumed that the majority of the poor were enrolled, like the papists, under Satan's banner. If the Jesuits were the Devil's commandos, and rank-and-file Catholics his front-line troops, then the unregenerate poor were his irregular reserves. Given a suitable opportunity, they might be ready at any time to open the gates to Antichrist.

More serious was the fear that Catholic troops would defect to an invading enemy or even participate in a coup d'état by domestic papists. The growing hostility to Buckingham fed this latter fear. Rich had probably heard how an Irish lieutenant in Witham, when challenged by the town constable, had replied that "he neither cared for the king nor his watchman" but only "for our good lord and duke."[134] It was madness, said Rich, "that in these times of common calamity, when our religion is almost extirpate, we should here lodge an army in our bowels of papists."[135]

As Conrad Russell has observed, it was Rich, Pym, and Richard Knightley who, on June 5 and 6, wove the fear of the Irish troops, Arminianism, and absolute monarchy into a "coherent fabric of terror."[136] The heart of the matter was religion. Knightley asserted that "our miseries come from decay of religion," and he contrasted the flourishing state of England under Queen Elizabeth with its incipient decline under King James. Knightley put the blame squarely on Buckingham, whom he denounced as an enemy not only of England but of all Christendom. Rich agreed, although his language was less histrionic. On June 6 Rich denounced the harassment of Calvinist ministers and lecturers, the neglect of preaching, and the efforts of some, "unknown to his Majesty," to undermine religion "and so ruin the state." In a list of grievances drawn up at the same time, Rich condemned "the often abortions of Parliament" and the removal from office of magistrates who, like Warwick, Barrington, and Grimston, would not execute unconstitutional commands. All of these "innovations in government," Rich implied, sprang from "this doctrine of absolute sovereignty," which was being promulgated by the Arminians.[137]

On June 7 Charles gave his assent to the Petition of Right and accepted the grant of five subsidies. Bonfires were lit to celebrate the apparent reconciliation of Crown and Parliament; the jubilation was heightened by the belief that Buckingham had been sent to the

Tower. Copies of the petition, now a statute of the realm, were distributed throughout the country.[138] The people of Essex, who had resented with particular acuity the abuses it denounced, must have listened with corresponding relish to the terms of the petition as they were read out by the parson from his pulpit or the scrivener from the ale bench. But on the very day the Petition of Right was enacted into law, Sir Nathaniel Rich and Sir Edward Coke introduced a remonstrance that laid all of the country's grievances—innovations in government and religion, military defeat, the decay of trade—to the charge of the Duke of Buckingham. The remonstrance against the duke passed the House on June 11. Charles, who had reached the limit of his forebearance with the Petition of Right, prorogued Parliament on June 26.

In the summer of 1628 King Charles showered favor on the men whom the godly had most cause to fear. Buckingham was given charge of another expedition to La Rochelle. Bishops Neile and Laud were raised to the council. Richard Montague was made bishop of Chichester; Roger Manwaring, condemned by the House of Commons for his sermons in support of the Forced Loan, was made a royal chaplain and succeeded Montague in the Essex rectory of Stanford Rivers.[139] Warwick and his friends were learning, in Conrad Russell's words, "that for a clergyman to be complained of by the Parliament was probably the shortest road to preferment."[140] And not only for clergymen. In July the king granted a baronetcy to Sir William Wiseman, who had been denounced by Parliament for his attempt to manipulate the Essex county election in Buckingham's interest. A few months later Charles frustrated the prosecution for recusancy of Lord Petre, whose mansion at Ingatestone was thought to have been the scene of papist conferences.[141]

Sir Francis Barrington, the lay patriarch of the godly party in Essex, whose battle with Antichrist went back to the days of the Armada, died on July 3. His death released a blizzard of elegies from prominent Puritans, both lay and clerical, celebrating his piety and political courage.[142] Barrington's coreligionists no doubt remarked bitterly on the contrast between the favor being shown to the Arminians and Charles's treatment of Barrington, whose imprisonment had hastened his death.

Very different was the county's reaction to the assassination, on August 22, of the Duke of Buckingham. Rumors connecting the Earl

of Warwick and other opposition peers with the murder were, of
course, unfounded. Sir Francis Barrington's heir, Sir Thomas, noted
with approval that John Felton had died penitently, disclaiming on
the gallows any justification for his deed. Barrington described the
whole episode as a "strange tragedy."[143] Yet, it is hard to believe
that professors in Essex were exactly prostrate with grief. While the
Earl of Sussex wept for the death of his friend and protector, Warwick and his friends may have hoped that the duke's passing would
bring Charles to his senses.[144] Indeed, there were some encouraging
signs of a shift in policy. Only five days after Felton struck down the
favorite, Warwick was entrusted by Secretary Conway, himself a
Puritan sympathizer, with the security of the Essex ports. By November, Warwick had recovered the effective command of the fort
at Harwich and was attempting to buy the Earl of Sussex out of his
share of the lord lieutenantship.[145] A commission of members of the
Privy Council, the House of Lords, and the House of Commons was
appointed to review the condition of the church. Sir Thomas Barrington informed his mother that "divers of the council have spoken
well in the cause of religion."[146]

Barrington's remark is another reminder that the court was not
monolithic. The godly had sympathizers on the council, although
not always very vocal ones. The most eminent was the Earl of Holland, Warwick's younger brother. Holland had already won the
favor of Queen Henrietta Maria, whose marriage with Charles he
had helped to negotiate and whom he had escorted to England. In
December, Sir William Masham was encouraged by the prospect of
Holland's being named Buckingham's successor as Lord Admiral.
Masham would have preferred Warwick himself, but he believed
that Holland would follow his elder brother's counsel. Other signs
were less heartening. The notorious Hispanophile Sir Francis Cot-
tington was elevated to the Privy Council. Sir Thomas Barrington
was disgusted by the sycophantic congratulations tendered to Cot-
tington by the University of Cambridge, Barrington's alma mater.
There were rumors that Bishop Montague had converted to Catholicism, although Barrington believed them at least premature. But,
in December, Barrington himself felt the political situation sufficiently bleak to contemplate going off to the wars. With Warwick's
help, he was trying to get command of a regiment bound for service
with the Venetian republic.[147]

The hopes of the godly rose again, however, when Parliament was recalled on January 20. The most urgent concern of the House of Commons was the threat to England's Protestantism. "I pray God direct us in this most weighty business," Robert Barrington wrote to his mother, "the success whereof is and will be the foundation of our happiness or misery to come." He was thrilled by the great speeches being made against popery and Arminianism by men like Pym, Rous, Sherland, and Erle. Robert Barrington was outraged at a remark attributed to Dr. John Cosins, to the effect that "the king had no more to do in matters ecclesiastical than his horse-keeper."[148] Barrington's indignation reminds us that orthodox Protestants among the English laity considered themselves, and not their Arminian opponents, to be the true defenders of the royal supremacy. They dreaded clerical domination even more than royal absolutism, although they tended to conflate the two. Barrington was shocked that Manwaring, Sibthorpe, and Montague had received royal pardons, and he hoped that those responsible would be identified and punished. He could not yet bring himself to admit that it was the king himself who was shielding the Arminians from parliamentary wrath.

The hopes of the godly were soon dashed. Charles intended no further concessions. As the dissolution of Parliament loomed, Sir Thomas Barrington described the despondency of "all men that wish well to church or commonwealth." The only cheerful faces in London belonged to papists and Arminians. In 1642 Sir Thomas would organize the county of Essex to wage war against the king. But his attitude in early 1629 was anything but revolutionary. On the contrary, he was seriously worried by the rashness of some of his parliamentary colleagues. He made the trite but sensible reflection that it is easier to steer clear of the rocks than to escape from a shipwreck. Barrington felt that the attack on Charles's government should be moderated. "Princes," he observed, "should in policy have some time and way left to evade, when point of honor is in competition."[149] (As Conrad Russell has recently shown, the position of Sir Nathaniel Rich and John Pym was quite similar.)[150]

Sir Thomas found the stormy session of March 2, when Speaker Finch was forcibly restrained while the Three Resolutions were voted through, dreadfully upsetting. His dominant impression of that great historical moment, like Fabrizio's impression of Waterloo, was one of confusion: "no man almost knowing what to do, the distraction was so sudden." He thanked God the tumult had not ended in bloodshed. Barrington could not know that the scene he had just experienced marked the beginning of eleven years without a Parliament, but he was filled with apprehension. "Well, God of his mercy look upon us," he wrote his mother as the late winter dusk thickened around him, " 'tis far more easy to speak bravely, than to be magnanimous in suffering, yet he whose heart bleeds not at the threats of these times, is too stupid. I pray God send us better grounds of comfort, and withal to be armed for the worst that can befall us. I pray God give us faith and judgment to carry us through this storm."[151] The Personal Rule had begun.

9 / Noble Professors

> Where birth is greater, maintenance more
> ample, time longer, means of grace more plenti-
> ful, there a great account is of the Lord expected.
>
> —*Roger Williams to Lady Joan Barrington, 1629*

We know too little about the Puritan gentry. I have given some of
the reasons why the doctrine of the painful preachers might have
appealed to members of the middle classes, from which I have argued, the majority of the godly were drawn. But while gentle professors necessarily composed only a small minority of the preachers'
audience, their power and wealth made them disproportionately
vital to the movement. The Puritan gentry, bound together by an
elaborate webbing of blood ties and business connections, was unquestionably the social group most responsible for carrying resistance to Crown policy to the point of armed rebellion, and later for
carrying rebellion through to victory and revolution. Yet, we still
lack an adequate treatment of this group and its internal articulation. The greatest authority on lay Puritanism has been more concerned with the "industrious sort of people" than with the aristocracy; the leading expert on the aristocracy devotes only a few pages
of his great work to religious attitudes.[1]

To focus on a single county necessarily precludes any attempt at
such a comprehensive analysis. But it is possible to indicate a few
lines of inquiry suggested by the Essex evidence, which in itself con-
stitutes a fairly substantial chunk of the mosaic. The principal
source for the study of aristocratic puritanism in Essex is the Barrington correspondence among the Egerton manuscripts in the British Museum. More than one thousand letters survive for the reign of
Charles I alone. A systematic and exhaustive study of this correspondence, such as I have not attempted, would yield material for a
richly textured account of the mentality and behavior of a major
Puritan clan. Even a fairly cursory sampling, such I have performed,

conveys a vivid sense of the constant interweaving of secular and religious motifs in the lives of these aristocrats. The perspective is always abruptly shifting from the mundane to the divine and back
again. References to rents, weather, serious and trivial maladies, sex
scandals, dowries, court gossip, and foreign wars intermingle with
prayers, outbursts of religious terror, speculations about Antichrist,
and gruesome stories of divine vengeance. Sir William Masham, a
sensible and hard-working justice of the peace, writes of prosecuting
drunkards as the surest way to avert crop failure. In another letter
he pokes fun at Catholic superstition, and in the very next para-
graph described how a gentleman of Grey's Inn, a notorious blasphemer, was mauled to death in his chambers by the Devil, who had
assumed for the occasion the form of a great black dog.[2]

The bulk of these letters were addressed to the matriarch of the
clan, Lady Joan Barrington, née Cromwell, the widow of Sir Francis
Barrington, the mother of Sir Thomas, the mother-in-law of Sir
William Masham, Sir Gilbert Gerrard, and Sir Richard Knightley,
the aunt of Oliver Cromwell, and so and on and on. A full account
of Lady Joan's genealogical connections with the parliamentary opposition would tax the powers of recall of Claude Lévy-Strauss himself.

Lady Joan was a complex and formidable character. The patriar-
chal rhetoric of the age notwithstanding, she became the unchal-
lenged head of the clan upon the death of Sir Francis in July 1628.
Her eldest son, Sir Thomas, conspicuously deferred to her. Her
daughter and son-in-law, Elizabeth and Sir William Masham, gave
her the final say in the choice of a husband for Elizabeth's daughter
"Jug." When the Earl of Warwick wanted Sir Thomas to stand as
surety for him, Warwick asked Lady Joan's permission. Warwick
also had the greatest respect for her judgment of clerics. He would
sooner take her recommendation, he said, than that of "all the bishops in the kingdom." The Earl of Bedford described himself as her
"affectionate servant and friend."[3]

She was capable of warmth and good will. She gave effective spiritual comfort to her son and other members of the family; her son's
two little children, Lucy and Oliver, adored her.[4] James Harrison,
the lecturer at Hatfield Broad Oak, wrote to her with affection as
well as respect, and she stood godmother to his son. When Harrison
appealed to her for money to relieve some impoverished Saints in

Ipswich who were being neglected by their wealthy townsmen, he expressed confidence in her habitual generosity, and he was not disappointed.[5] (It is true that Ezekiel Rogers, who had served a decade earlier at Hatfield, felt that in his day the Barringtons had been rather niggardly toward the godly poor.[6] But Ezekiel Rogers was often censorious of her ladyship.)

Lady Joan was subject to attacks of melancholy that alarmed her family and friends. Since she was a Calvinist, these bad spells gave rise to fears of damnation, which of course deepened her depression. She read William Perkins, she corresponded with Arthur Hildersam and Roger Williams, she held "serious and solemn converse" with Ezekiel Rogers about the workings of grace, she entertained John Preston and Bishop Ussher at Hatfield; but none of them could give her firm assurance that she was saved. Ezekiel Rogers described her as "oft in doubtings and tears." In these moods she could turn very nasty. She accused her son, to his great consternation, of cheating her. An admonishing letter from Roger Williams, the Mashams' chaplain, threw her into a black rage. Months later Sir William Masham warned her that her enmity toward Williams had become a scandal that was bringing the whole community of the godly into derision.[7]

We can learn a good deal about the relationship between preachers and gentle professors by considering how different ministers tried to handle Lady Joan's "old disease of melancholy." Ministers, after all, were supposed to be "physicians of the soul"; they were paid to help people achieve saving faith. Lady Joan's chaplain and lecturer, James Harrison, urged her not to worry overmuch about being in a state of grace. Her very sufferings were a good sign, and a strenuous desire to be saved would always be gratified. Ezekiel Rogers assured her from his personal experience that "the Lord so sought will sooner or later be found." Sounding a theme particularly dear to John Preston and Thomas Hooker, Rogers reminded her that God's covenant was unbreakable. If she had ever felt the merest breath of divine love, then her faith was secure: "when the Lord hath once given you a promise it shall be always as true as ever it was."[8] If we try to imagine what this argument might have meant to a morose character like Lady Joan, we shall better appreciate the horror that Puritans felt for the doctrines of Arminius. Predestination was the foundation stone of the covenant. Not many sane individuals, however gloomily disposed, would cling to Calvinism for any length of time without some divine encouragement, some twinges, however feeble and intermittent, of grace. Relatively few, on the other hand, were granted an absolutely unwavering assurance.

Lady Joan's nephew Sir Thomas Bourchier, a member of the same family as Oliver Cromwell's wife, is a case in point. "In the beginning of my conversion," he recalled, "my soul was so abundantly ravished with the beauty of the Lamb that truly I was scarce well when my tongue was not speaking of the infiniteness of that mercy to me so unworthy a wretch." Yet, on other occasions he suffered from "such infinite sadness springing from fears of my union with Christ that I have scarce been able to subsist."[9]

It was greatly comforting, therefore, to be told that election was immutable, that grace once known might be mislaid but never lost. If it were once admitted that grace might be permanently withdrawn, then people like Lady Joan Barrington would become liable to soul-killing despair. What was hateful about the Arminians was not so much their high opinion of the human will as the way they seemed to deny the Lord's fidelity. For a troubled soul who doubted his or her own election, such doctrine was an invitation to spiritual suicide. Yet, if the believer put too much trust in the covenant, it might lead to a damnable complacency—even to an ability to dispense with the services of preachers altogether: the heresy of antinomianism. It was sometimes necessary, therefore, to induce terror rather than to allay it. Ezekiel Rogers felt compelled to remind Lady Joan that many professors would not reach heaven, and to warn her, rather superfluously in her case, against the perils of overconfidence. He also chided her lack of generosity to the Saints and complained of her diminished appetite for his own company.[10]

Ezekiel Rogers was a more captious divine than the bland James Harrison, which is probably why Harrison was preaching at Hatfield while Rogers was dispensing his improving counsel from Rowley in Yorkshire. But Rogers retained her ladyship's favor and some measure of influence over her conscience. Not so Roger Williams, who won her implacable hostility by an ill-timed resort to godly terrorism. Some eight months after Sir Francis Barrington's death, when Lady Joan was especially depressed, she had summarily rejected Williams's suit for the hand of her grandniece Jane Whalley.

Williams purported to accept her decision with good grace, but at the same time found himself divinely charged to declare that her soul was in grave danger. Her recent sufferings were tokens of God's anger against her; the godly were beginning to entertain serious doubts whether she were one of them after all.[11] Now, the power of the Puritan preacher depended, as we have seen, upon his ability to manipulate anxiety. But terrorizing aristocrats was a dangerous operation and required a very sure touch. Williams was hoist with his own petard. When Williams fell ill of a fever that all believed would kill him, he begged Lady Joan's forgiveness. There is no sign that she ever relented.[12] From the way he handled this wealthy, influential, and morose old lady, still suffering from the shock of widowhood, one can already see why Roger Williams was destined to found a colony of his very own on the shores of the Narragansett.

Lady Joan's encounter with Roger Williams dramatically illustrates the potential conflict between the material power of the aristocracy and the ideological pretensions of the clergy. Even in godly circles there was always tension between these two claims to social hegemony. Cotton Mather tells us that when John Wilson reproved the guests at Lady Scudamore's table for their irreverent conversation, he was sharply advised to keep a civil tongue in his head.[13] Giles Firmin remarked that even sympathetic gentlemen found the gravity of Richard Rogers forbidding, and Richard's nephew John Rogers once told a colleague that while grim austerity might overawe the common folk, it was necessary to be more affable and good-humored in order to win the gentry—an idea he might have picked up from the Jesuits.[14] The Earl of Warwick, Clarendon tells us, was fond of teasing his Puritan preachers, who did not dare alienate him by fighting back.[15] Clarendon is never very trustworthy on the subject of puritanism, but it is amusing to imagine Thomas Hooker, Stephen Marshall, and Edmund Calamy forcing appreciative chuckles through clenched teeth at the earl's banter. Sir Thomas Barrington was easier to bully. On at least one occasion the hectoring of Puritan divines drove him to flee his own home in fear for his very wits.[16] Before 1640, however, most preachers were suitably docile, and such episodes were correspondingly rare. Even Williams, after all, made abject apologies. After the Laudian hierarchy had been swept away, men of God would be less deferential to their so-

cial superiors, and the latent conflict between aristocratic and clerical pretensions would burst into the open.

Sir Thomas Barrington, who in the summer of 1628 succeeded his
father as the county's leading commoner, and as the Earl of Warwick's chief local ally, was a less masterful character than either Sir
Francis or Lady Joan. Yet, he was destined, rather despite himself,
to play a larger historical role than his father had done. He was also
a considerably more appealing man. Sir Thomas was born no later
than 1589. He inherited (or more probably he acquired through
early modeling) his mother's disposition to melancholy—though
not, it would appear, the more neurotic aspects of her piety. In his
youth he suffered from chronic depression, insomnia, and violent
nightmares. Ezekiel Rogers, who served at Hatfield as domestic
chaplain during these years, later claimed to have permanently im-
paired his own health by rising so often in the middle of the night to
"cherish and comfort" the young squire.[17]

These fits of depression continued to plague him as an adult,
especially during periods of ill health (and his constitution was not
robust). Once, while suffering from some "strange throws of the
spleen," he expressed to his mother the opinion that "if there be any
ill spirit that is no devil, it is Melancholy." Unlike the case of his
mother, to whom the distinction between melancholy and diabolic
possession was probably less clear, there is no evidence that depression caused Sir Thomas to fear for his salvation. Melancholy, Sir
Thomas believed, was not itself a sin, although the Devil enjoyed
watching the godly writhe in it. Commiserating with his mother on
their common affliction, he expressed the hope "that you and I shall
be ever careful not to give way to outward griefs, by God's blessing."[18] "Be comfortable unto yourself," he begged his mother on another occasion. He advised her to keep "some cheerful body" with
her at all times. For his own part, he professed his willingness to experience the sanctifying grief of repentence, those "private and in-
ward sorrows which end in joys inexpressive." But he prayed to be
delivered from "those unnecessary sadnesses" that made him "unfit
for all duties to God, man, and myself."[19]

Despite his episodic melancholy and his Puritan upbringing, Sir
Thomas Barrington could appreciate earthly pleasures. He patronized preachers and took dutiful notes at their sermons, to be sure.

But he attended plays as well.[20] The Barrington account books for the 1630s also record payments to fiddlers, harpers, morris dancers, and a Welsh conjuror; there is even a purchase of a shipment of Irish whiskey.[21] Sir Thomas's library contained a manual of falconry and volumes of Shakespeare, Petronius, Ovid, and Aesop, as well as the works of Erasmus, John Preston, and Edward Coke.[22] Above all, Sir Thomas could value, accept, and express affection. "Next under God's love to me," he wrote, "nothing doth so much affect me as the view of friends' respect toward me and mine, and the nearer the relations are, the more comfort to me, I thank my God." His mother was often cranky, but she evidently provided him with what modern jargon would term adequate mothering. He was already past forty when, embroiled in a conflict with the Crown over his property rights, he wrote her that "the affectionate expressions in your letters do much animate me in my sufferings, and put a stronger armor upon me."[23]

In personal relationships Barrington was a romantic rather than a classicist. "My dearest," he wrote to his second wife, when he was having difficulties with his mother, "in obedience, in love, in all virtue, there is no mean to be held, nor can there be excess."[24] Of his first wife we know nothing, except that she was another Puritan of melancholy disposition, that she bore him two sons and a daughter, and that she was dead by 1621.[25] In that year Sir Thomas fell deeply and rather hysterically in love with a widow named Judith Smith, a cousin of the great diplomat Dudley Carleton, later Viscount Dorchester. To judge from the correspondence generated by this courtship, Sir Thomas Barrington was still remarkably immature, for all his thirty-two years, his three children, his knighthood, and his seat in Parliament. The gossipy John Chamberlain congratulated Carleton on his cousin's having made "a very fit match for years, blood, estate, conformity of studies (somewhat poetical)." Most important of all, Judith had found a suitor "so much enamored of her and her virtues that she may make her own conditions."[26]

Perhaps for this very reason, and perhaps also because, as Sir Thomas acknowledged, there were some "false scandals" circulating about the lady, his father at first opposed the match. Thomas went into a dither, as he was wont to do under pressure. "My heart is so full of perplexities," he wrote to his mother, "as that I have written to my father I know not what, and now I am writing to you I know

not how. I beseech you pray for me, and favor me, help me and excuse me now in my abruptness. The God of Heaven send me an issue
of occasion granting me marriage."[27]

Lady Judith's first husband, Sir George Smith, had died fighting
for the Protestant cause in the Palatinate, but Barrington took heart
from the reflection that "he was not a fit half for her, the world
knows well." Sir Thomas considered it "a great advantage to a man
to be a successor to a husband not superlatively good."[28] Sir Thomas
did not overflow with self-confidence. He was attracted to strong
women, even if he found them a little frightening. He was overawed
by his mother, but his letters reveal genuine love and concern as well
as filial respect. He was capable of feeling sympathy for a woman
who had poisoned her drunken husband, and of expressing outrage
when she was burned at the stake.[29] And in his second wife he had
found a woman who was more than his equal in force of character
and business sense.

Judith was aggressive and self-possessed. Sir John Bramston
called her "that ever-lasting impertinent talker."[30] She was also a
militant Protestant. She was outraged at Laud's suppression of a
conventicle in Blackfriars, which she preferred to regard as a prayer
meeting of "honest people." She followed the desperate struggle in
Germany with keen attention and consoled herself for Protestant re-
versals by recalling the tribulations of Israel. She sent vivid and
richly textured accounts of the latest battles to her mother-in-law.
Even if she lifted the details from newsletters and corrantos, Lady
Judith displays a somewhat alarming and decidedly unladylike fas-
cination with the craft and science of war. (Her letters contain far
more military details than those of her husband, for example.)[31]

Sir Francis's reservations about the marriage were perhaps not
unreasonable. Chamberlain was right to predict that Judith could
get her own way with Sir Thomas. His father was angered by the
marriage settlement, which he considered prejudicial to the children
of his son's first marriage; and indeed Judith and her eldest stepson
were to quarrel shabbily after Sir Thomas's death. She herself bore
no children, and in her will she elected not to be buried with her second husband but rather "to lie beside her dear father" back in
Hertfordshire.[32]

Nevertheless, there is no reason to doubt that the marriage was a
happy one. Judith Barrington provided her husband with much-

needed advice and supervision. She took a hand in managing his financial affairs. She used her connections at court to help him evade the burdensome office of sheriff.[33] When a conflict with the Crown over his parklands on the Isle of Wight plunged Sir Thomas into irritable lethargy, Judith told their Puritan steward, John Kendall, that he must rouse her husband to action: "though your master chides us all," she wrote, "yet his good and credit lies so much at stake, that those that love him must not care for his anger." If Kendall's efforts were unavailing, he was to arrange for their kinsman Sir John Bowers to call on Barrington. Lady Judith knew how to manipulate her husband for his own good. She also took good care of her stepchildren. She fretted when it appeared that little Lucy's fever might turn to smallpox; she insisted that when the two boys visited Hatfield, they should not be allowed to go fishing so often that their studies suffered.[34] She got along splendidly with her mother-in-law, which is further evidence that she combined strength of character with diplomatic finesse.

Sir Thomas, for his part, adored her. When his niece, Jane Took (née Whalley), who had been a servant at Hatfield, wished to describe her own husband's tenderness during her sickness, she said, "He reminds me of Mr. Barrington, that was so careful over his wife when she lay very weak, I thought that I should never see the like." Although there is no evidence that young Thomas Barrington ever received much emotional warmth from Sir Francis, he became a fond, even indulgent father himself. Shortly before Christmas, 1629, he sent his mother the presents his children had made for her, "even to my son Oliver, who would not so much as have it looked on till he had finished." Perhaps, with the stern visage of Sir Francis in his mind's eye, he felt a little embarrassed by his own affection. "I would not persuade them so much to trouble you," he assured his mother, "but I was unwilling to discourage them in that loving endeavor, which was so merely from out their own good natures."[35]

Just as art historians would gladly trade acres of Rubens for a few more square feet of Vermeer, so a good many historians today would exchange bundles of manorial accounts for more details of domestic life. "I am called to dinner," Sir Thomas writes at the foot of a letter to his mother, "and my paper put off the table to give place to meat. I thereupon commit us all to God with my blessing."[36] This trivial scene of a Puritan gentleman scribbling away at his dinner table

and holding up the evening meal gives us only a fleeting and perhaps deceptive glimpse of Sir Thomas Barrington *en famille*. But the
impression is unmistakable: it is the picture of a happy man.

Sir Thomas was far less comfortable, however, in his public role.
Indeed, the whole purpose of this biographical excursus is to demonstrate that some rebels are not only made rather than born but are
made entirely against their will. Sir Thomas Barrington would
much have preferred it if history had left him alone. Not that he
lacked a sense of social responsibility. He was concerned about the
problem of poverty and instructed his wife to find work for the unemployed laborers of Hatfield. (He also remarked that this would be
the cheapest time to put in a new fishpond.)[37] Cruelty and injustice
made him indignant, sometimes to the point of incoherence. He was
deeply shocked by the "unheard of ferity" of Sir Robert Howard,
who slashed the face of his long-time mistress, Lady Purbeck,
"which though to her is justice from God, yet from him, the cause of
all her shame and sufferings, most unmanly and savage."[38] The mis-
treatment, by a mercenary captain named Todd, of English and
Scots volunteers serving with the Protestant forces in Germany
roused him to a paroxysm of rage. He called Todd "that careless and
bestial man ... who cared not for men's lives." Todd had apparently permitted the needless slaughter of more than a thousand
English and Scottish troops at the siege of Stade. "My very bowels
yearn against him for such inhumanity," Sir Thomas cried, "he
hath made me so passionate I have almost forgot to write sense."
(One of Todd's crimes was to have permitted his Scottish soldiers to
fight duels in front of the rest of the troops, saying that "the Scottish
men must let out one another's hot blood."[39] Barrington's revulsion
against this racial slur on the Scots is worth noting; it anticipates the
alliance between the Scots and the parliamentary opposition in
1640, and helps explain the failure among the godly of Charles's appeal to English chauvinism against the northern invaders.)

Barrington shared the Puritan commitment to moral reform. He
subscribed to a strict sexual code (seen in his belief that the disfig-
uring of Lady Purbeck was "justice from God" for her fornication).
Like his father, who left strict instructions that hedge breakers be
excluded from his bequests to the poor, Sir Thomas wished to see the
culture of discipline imposed upon the common people. He was

especially concerned with the suppression of drunkenness. He believed that the guilt of the woman who poisoned her husband with melted lead was mitigated by the man's drunkenness, and with rather tasteless gallows humor he remarked that whole story might have a salutary effect on the tipplers of Hatfield, especially since plumbers were then at work restoring the Barringtons' lead roofs.[40] He understood the need for a painful preaching ministry to spearhead the reformation of manners. In 1627, during his father's imprisonment, we find him reviewing testimonials to the moral character of a candidate for one of the Barrington livings. The man had already been invited to demonstrate his preaching ability at Hatfield.[41]

The effective exercise of power, however, requires more than generous impulses, high morals, and a sense of responsibility. It also requires clear judgment and steady nerves—qualities that Sir Thomas was slow to acquire. He was excitable and easily befuddled. The syntax of his letters, which is tortuous even by the standards of the period, seems a fair reflection of his cast of mind.

Sir Thomas sat in every Parliament from 1621 until his death in 1644. He made no speeches until 1641, but then only a handful of members ever took the floor of the Commons. Even Sir Francis spoke very rarely. Sir Thomas attended diligently and left behind valuable diaries of the proceedings in 1621 and 1625. Indeed, his journal for 1621 has been called the most comprehensive parliamentary account before the advent of modern reporting.[42] Yet, this diary, while bearing witness to Barrington's assiduity, also displays his intellectual limitations. Barrington, as Conrad Russell has said, is "the Nennius of diarists, [who] gives a peculiarly full list of colorful words, phrases, and incidents, but is correspondingly bad at discovering the logical structure of a speech."[43] The cognitive style reflected in the Barrington diary—compulsive attention to detail combined with a failure to perceive overall form—would be labeled hysterical by a modern clinician. And indeed a number of Barrington's character traits—his impulsiveness and his tendency to dither and lose heart, for instance—also belong to the hysterical syndrome.

It is easy to see why Sir Thomas might not have welcomed the political responsibility that devolved upon him at his father's death. He had never taken an active role in the affairs of the county.

Throughout the 1620s he sat in Parliament for the family's pocket borough of Newport on the Isle of Wight. Moreover, it was not the easiest moment in English history to come politically of age, and to assume the mantle of a courageous and venerated father. We have seen how alarmed he was by the breach between king and parliament.

Whatever the reason, Sir Thomas hesitated to assert his hereditary claim to leadership in county society. The godly were frankly disappointed in him. In July 1629 William Masham told Lady Joan that "Essex longs for that happy day of settling which I hope will produce another patriot for them out of that noble family which hath been honored so long by them." The obvious implication was that Sir Thomas did not yet fill the bill. The family lecturer, James Harrison, had serious doubts about Barrington's zeal for godliness. In September 1629, when Lady Joan was staying with her kinfolk at Harrow in Middlesex, Harrison wrote that her presence would be necessary to revive "the ancient honor" of the family as a truly religious household.[44]

The godly brethren gave Sir Thomas, on at least one occasion, a thorough working over. Mutual admonition was a central feature of Puritan religiosity. Barrington himself averred that he was eager for friends to reveal to him his failings. But at one period, probably in the early autumn of 1631, the censoriousness of the Saints around Hatfield reached such a pitch that he found the place uninhabitable. "In truth, in truth," he wailed, "somewhat must be done to alter the miserable condition of distraction that we are falling into." Barrington thought himself the victim of "an envious aspect and desire to deprave, that nothing but reproach can satisfy." His position was "worse than the poorest servant," since his every act was more captiously scrutinized. Barrington does not identify his persecutors, but we can guess that the inquisition, to use his word, was organized by the more radical preachers of northern and central Essex, and included members of Hooker's circle. (Sir Thomas implies that both Harrison and Sir William Masham stood by him during this onslaught, even though they had their own reservations about his character.) Finally, things got so bad that he was forced to flee from Hatfield to the family estate on the Isle of Wight. "Had I not taken my journey when I did," he told his mother, by way of explaining his abrupt departure, "I was in a fair (or foul) way to a dangerous fever."[45] Sir Thomas believed firmly, and in his own case probably correctly, in the psychosomatic origin of disease.

We know that he read Shakespeare, and he was fond of theatrical analogies. As he rode from Hatfield down toward the Isle of Wight, one wonders if he thought of another son and heir, also afflicted with melancholy, whose father had also entrusted him with a fearful responsibility. One wonders if he murmured the lines, "The time is out of joint. Oh cursed spite / That ever I was born to set it right." If he did, then he would have cast Sir William Masham as his Horatio. Sir William was older and more experienced than Barrington, but he accepted the fact that it was up to a Barrington rather than a Masham to lead the Essex gentry. It is clear from the Barrington correspondence that he wished to counsel and encourage Sir Thomas rather than join in the general chorus of denigration. And his efforts bore fruit. By the midsummer of 1629 he was able to tell Lady Joan that her son was at last beginning to play his proper role in county politics. The disciplining pressures of social rank, religious training, and family tradition were beginning to impose themselves. There was hope, Masham assured Lady Joan, that Sir Thomas would *patrizare* after all: he would take after his father.[46]

Social identity is governed by a number of factors, in varying proportions and combinations: gender, class, ethnicity, religion, lineage, and so on. The godly in early Stuart England regarded themselves, and were perceived by their opponents, as in some sense a people apart, a nation unto themselves. They spoke of themselves as a tribe, or a family, as "God's children" and the "Household of Faith." They addressed each other as "Brother." John Pym called Sir Thomas Barrington "Brother," although they were not related.[47] Sir Thomas Wentworth referred to John Hampden in 1637 as "a great Brother," adding that "the very genius of that nation of people leads them always to oppose . . . authority."[48]

Sermon notes taken at Hatfield in the 1630s, perhaps by Sir Thomas himself, refer to "the hatred of the World"—here meaning the majority of mankind—for the "People of God." Yet, the hostility of the world is to be welcomed, since it unifies the community of the saved: "for God is a good shepherd [who], when he sees that we scatter from each other sends his dog out to force us to join together in one flock."[49] The godly formed a mutual aid society, sharing both material and spiritual resources. Wealthy professors had a special obligation to exercise charity toward impoverished Saints.[50] In times of crisis the professor could appeal for the prayers of the godly. "I had never more need of the prayers of God's Saints than now," wrote Jane Took, when she feared that her faith was insufficient for the ordeal of childbearing. Association with other Saints was itself a token of election. Ezekiel Rogers told Lady Joan that she need not doubt her salvation because "you delight in [God's] Saints because of His stamp upon them, though their disposition natural be not so suitable to yours."[51] However, the godly were expected to shun, as far as possible, the company of the people of the world—"not only the grossly profane," according to the same sermon notes, "but even the hypocrites and formalists who want the organs of discerning the mysteries of godliness."[52]

Such advice fostered a strong tendency toward endogamy among the godly. The Saints naturally hoped to reproduce their kind. Thomas Bourchier wrote to Lady Joan that he hoped his pregnant wife would be a means to enlarge God's kingdom. Godliness was not strictly hereditary, but one's chances were better with a sanctified spouse. In seeking a match for her daughter, Elizabeth Masham sought to advance God's glory. She was skeptical of potential suitors from the nobility because she feared that "few lords have the ... true fear of God, which I prefer before all the honor in the world." And yet material considerations were by no means disregarded. Elizabeth Masham hesitated to consent to the match, arranged by Sir Nathaniel Rich, between her daughter and the young lawyer Oliver St. John. She was impressed with his piety and good character, "but God commands us ... to have a care of outward conveniences," and St. John's means were slender. The match was at length concluded, but not before St. John's patron, the Earl of Bedford, had been pressured to augment the estate he had offered to provide for the young man.[53]

The sense of membership in the household of faith tempered, though it did not efface, the class consciousness of the godly aristocrats. In 1642 this dual identity would enable them to break with the majority of their class and assume the leadership of a popular rebellion. Oliver Cromwell would apply the same calculus in the choice of his officers that Elizabeth Masham applied to her daughter's suitors, preferring "true fear of God" above "all the honor in the world."

The godly aristocrats were a long way from rebellion in 1629, however. It would be a mistake to regard the dissolution of Parliament as opening an unbridgeable rift between Court and Country, or between Crown and Opposition. As recent research has shown, the court of Charles I was far from monolithic. The Country—or one segment of it—occupied a salient within the court itself. Warwick and his friends in the opposition were closely linked to a faction at Whitehall that was working for an anti-Spanish, pro-French foreign policy and a reconciliation between Crown and Parliament. The leading members of this group, which benefited from the favor of Queen Henrietta Maria, were the Earls of Pembroke and Holland, and Dudley Carleton, later Viscount Dorchester. Holland was, of course, Warwick's brother; Dorchester was Judith Barrington's cousin. Pembroke and Warwick had been political associates since the reign of James, when they met together at Bedford House, along with Pym, Saye and Seale, and other political Puritans.[54]

The Earl of Holland was scarcely a Puritan in his personal life, nor did he evince any great interest in theology until almost the very eve of his execution by Parliament in 1649. He was venal and vacillating. Yet, he was linked to the godly party by upbringing, political culture, and religious prejudice. He believed, insofar as he was capable of principled conviction, in parliamentary monarchy, and he felt an instinctive Elizabethan hostility toward Spain and popery.[55]

Holland's usefulness to the godly derived from his influence over the queen, whose affection he had captured with his courtesy, charm, and good looks while participating in the marriage negotiations. A papist queen might seem an unlikely focus for a faction of Protestant imperialists, and indeed the unpopularity of Charles's marriage contributed largely to the alienation of public opinion. But from a pragmatic point of view, Henrietta Maria's religion was of less moment than her nationality. Belligerence with Spain, in any sane foreign policy, implied alignment with France. The French, after all, were the main opponents of Hapsburg domination of Europe; and French Protestants, despite the obliteration of most of their political privileges at the hands of Richelieu, still enjoyed liberty of worship. Since Charles had fallen deeply in love with his French queen after the death of Buckingham, it was not absurd to suppose that she might win him to the anti-Spanish policies favored by the Protestant imperialists, and that this shift in policy would restore harmony between king and Parliament. We know that this strategy failed. Henrietta Maria was far more interested in securing toleration for English Catholics, and ultimately the conversion of the realm, than in promoting a war with Spain. The king found the pro-Spanish orientation of Weston and the neutralism of Laud and Strafford far more congenial than the Protestant imperialism of Holland, Pembroke, and their Country allies.

The strategy failed, but only hindsight makes it seem ridiculous. At times, Holland and the "Whitehall Puritans" seemed on the point of success. Holland nearly achieved the Lord Admiralship in 1632. There were rumors of a recall of Parliament in 1631 and 1635.[56] Even as late as 1637 Charles flirted with the idea of an anti-Spanish alliance and encouraged English privateering against the Spanish in the Caribbean.[57] In the meantime the Puritan faction at court was in a position to perform useful favors for Warwick and his friends. Holland managed to maintain royal toleration of the Providence Island Company, through which Warwick and Pym were attempting to carry out a virtually independent foreign policy.[58] Holland intervened on behalf of Sir Thomas Barrington in his troubles with the Crown over his forest rights. Holland and Viscount Dorchester blocked an effort by Barrington's enemies to have him pricked as sheriff in 1632.[59] These continuing links with the court help explain why Warwick, Barrington, and Masham continued to serve the Crown loyally and efficiently in county government after the dissolution of Parliament.

10 / The Sins of Manasseh

> So if thou has set thyself to oppose and secretly
> undermine any that is a true faithful minister of
> Jesus Christ, know thou art a traitor to thy king
> and country, because thou persecutest him who
> labors in his place to keep back wrath from seiz-
> ing upon the land.
>
> —*Thomas Hooker, in "Spiritual Munitions," 1626*

English history might have been very different if Charles's eleven
years of Personal Rule had been a period of sustained prosperity. A
long run of abundant harvests and a renewed expansion of the cloth
trade would have rendered the government's fiscal expedients less
burdensome, and might have muted opposition to the policies of
Archbishop Laud, since good times could be interpreted as a sign of
divine favor. But except for a brief recovery from 1632 to 1635,
England suffered from inferior harvests and industrial stagnation
down to the outbreak of the Civil War. The coincidence of economic
hardship, intensified after 1636 by a recurrence of plague, with the
Laudian repression of painful preachers enabled the beleaguered
Puritans to argue that England was being chastised for her apostasy,
as the kingdom of Judah had been punished for the idolatry of King
Manasseh.

Before turning to the narrative of these years, it is useful to establish some trends for the period as a whole. The campaign against
Hugh and Gillett continued in the 1630s; if anything, it was intensified. In the 1620s there had been more presentments for cottaging
(182) than in the entire previous thirty-six years of the statute. In the
1630s there were 178, although only thirty-nine Quarter Sessions
rolls survive for that decade, as against forty-two for the 1620s.[1] But
in spite of this vigilance, poor rates continued to climb, especially in
clothing towns. Unfortunately, the data are sparse. Few usable series
of accounts survive for individual parishes, and even where the

Table 15. Braintree poor rates, 1610–1639

Decade	Number of recorded annual rates	Total sum recorded (to nearest £)	Average annual rate (to nearest £)
1610–1619	3	157	52
1620–1629	3	295	98
1630–1639	7	1,051	150

Source: Essex Record Office, Chelmsford, D/P 264/8/2.

records are fairly ample, we have no way of knowing whether the extant entries record all the rates that were actually levied. The fluctuation in annual rates is sometimes so large that one suspects they may have been levied irregularly, to cover disbursements over preceding years, but there is no way to be sure. Nevertheless, the steep upward trend is clear enough for Braintree (see Table 15), where both the average yearly rates and the total known expenditure more than doubled. The increase was also substantial in Finchingfield (see Table 16), though somewhat less dramatic. (Finchingfield was less heavily dependent on the cloth trade.)

As Tables 17 and 18 suggest, purely agricultural parishes like Royden and Great Easton may have held their rates stable for most of this period, although the total known expenditure rose in Royden; and even Great Easton, in the open-field district, was sharply affected by the dearth of 1631, when the poor rate rose to nearly £18, triple the previous average sum. Yet, the situation in Boreham and Great Burstead, both primarily agricultural parishes, was more like that in the cloth towns. The fragmentary records for Boreham show a total of £35 disbursed between 1580 and 1609, with an average

Table 16. Finchingfield poor rates, 1610–1639

Decade	Number of recorded annual rates	Total sum recorded (to nearest £)	Average annual rate (to nearest £)
1610–1619	1	30	30
1620–1629	5	211	42
1630–1639	9	470	52

Source: Essex Record Office, Chelmsford, D/P 14/8/la.

Table 17. Royden poor rates, 1600–1639

Decade	Number of recorded annual rates	Total sum recorded (to nearest £)	Average annual rate (to nearest £)
1600–1609	4	40	10
1610–1619	9	77	9
1620–1629	10	106	11
1630–1639	10	117	12

Source: Abstracts supplied by W. K. Jordan.

entry of £15; between 1621 and 1630 alone (ten years as opposed to thirty) the known total reached £155, and the average entry rose to £17.[2] No rates survive from Great Burstead, but we have the word of the overseers and town fathers that by 1639 the annual rate had risen to £54 from a level "in former times" of £36.[3]

As might be expected, the rising poor rates were not popular with those called upon to pay them. In 1629 John Rogers acknowledged that many prosperous householders considered the poor "ill-tongued" and "thievish," inclined to break hedges and pluck up stiles for firewood. Why should decent parishioners support them?[4] Then there were disputes over the social distribution of the tax burden. In Great Burstead, Great Waltham, West Ham, Great Oakley, and Great Horkesley, conflict arose over the differential rates to be paid by tenants and landlords.[5] In Chelmsford the vestry was engaged in litigation throughout much of the 1630s to force Sir Henry Mildmay of Moulsham to pay his fair share.[6] In Bocking the conflict was between farmers and clothiers. The latter resented paying taxes

Table 18. Great Easton poor rates, 1600–1639

Decade	Number of recorded annual rates	Total sum recorded (to nearest £)	Average annual rate (to nearest £)
1600–1609	4	22	6
1610–1619	—	—	—
1620–1629	2	11	6
1630–1639	1	18	18

Source: Essex Record Office, Chelmsford, D/P 232/8/1.

on the capital that they employed "in setting the poor on work," while the idle surplus capital of the wealthy farmer was exempt.[7] "In most parishes," wrote John Rogers, it was "a great fault . . . that the meaner sort bear the chiefest burden and not the richest."[8] These disputes could bring a parish's whole system to a halt. It happened in Epping in 1627, where the poor were "many times not relieved" because of the "many and great contentions incident to the business of common rates."[9] In 1629 John Rogers attributed the following jeremiad to his parishioners: "there be such a number of charges every way, to the king, and for soldiers, to the ministers, to the repairing of the church, to bread and wine for Communion, and briefs, and one collection or other, that I can never a Sunday be quiet: and now you come for the poor. I think you will have all."[10]

Against this background the outrage and self-pity provoked by Charles's fiscal experiments becomes more comprehensible. Still, the English were not very heavily taxed by European standards, even in the 1630s. What made the impositions intolerable was the prevalent belief that the government was at best inept and at worst malevolent. It was under these circumstances that puritanism became, in effect if not yet in intention, a truly subversive force. With the lucidity common to prophets and paranoids, the dissident preachers persuasively linked England's misfortunes to the rise of the Arminian faction, the toleration of Catholics, the king's own marriage to "the daughter of a strange God," and, naturally enough, to the persecution of Puritans.[11] By the end of the 1630s many men and women in Essex had come to regard puritanism (or at least Protestant intolerance) as synonymous with religion, love of country, and common sense.

The suffering caused by the cloth depression had been alleviated in 1627 and 1628 by relatively abundant harvests. But the harvest of 1628 was mediocre, and those of 1629 and 1630 were disastrous.[12] This combination of trade depression and dearth produced the most serious popular disturbances between the Reformation and the Civil War, at a time when public opinion was already alienated, especially in the clothing districts, by Laud's offensive against Puritan preachers.

In January 1629 there were riots in the south of the county, as men and women brandishing pitchforks, and rumored to be acquir-

ing muskets, hijacked cartloads of grain headed for the Thames.
Two months later the purchase of grain by Dutch factors provoked a
more substantial dispute near Maldon. More than a hundred
women and children from Maldon, the clothing town of Witham,
and the squatters' colonies on Totham Heath boarded a ship that
was taking on grain and forced the crew to fill their aprons and caps
with rye.[13]

Meanwhile, the situation in the clothing district was nothing
short of catastrophic. A report prepared for the Privy Council by the
Essex deputy lieutenants revealed the depth of the crisis. In Braintree the weekly production of bays had fallen from one hundred to
forty, and 1,500 remained in stock unsold. It was feared that many
Braintree clothiers would "forsake their dwelling suddenly and give
over their trade." (The fear was justified; the town of Braintree,
Massachusetts, was founded in 1634.) Production had declined from
four hundred to forty bays in Bocking, from forty to ten in Witham.
There were 2,500 unsold bays in the warehouses of the Bocking
clothiers and three thousand in the towns of Dedham and Langham,
which had sold fewer than one hundred bays in the preceding eighteen months.[14]

The cloth workers had reached the point of desperation. Their
wages, which they complained were "but small in the best of times"
had been cut by seven shillings in the pound; many had been forced
to sell their beds to buy food. The poor of Bocking were "very unruly." The depression was making the town "very hazardous for
men of better rank to live." The clothiers of Witham were afraid to
face their workmen, whom they could not pay.[15] In April the Essex
justices were accosted by a delegation of some two hundred weavers
complaining "of extreme necessity and disability to maintain . . .
themselves and their families." The rattled justices informed the
Privy Council that the petition was proffered "with too many words
and outcries, following us from place to place, and moving us for
commiseration, and urging present answer, being unwilling almost
to give any space of time to consider what was to be done for them."
At the same sessions the Bocking clothiers presented a petition de-
tailing their own desperate and unavailing efforts over the previous
year to keep their weavers employed, and pleaded for government
action to revive their trade.[16]

The Privy Council replied to these reports with bland assurances and irrelevant proposals, which demonstrated that the Crown was completely out of touch with economic realities. The ministers of Braintree and Bocking were to assure their congregations that peace with Spain would restore the cloth trade. The justices were advised to force neighboring parishes to contribute to the relief of the clothing towns. But the Privy Councillors also expressed a suspicion that much of the agitation was being fomented by mere vagrants who had no desire to work at weaving or any other trade. It is not known how the artisans of Braintree and Bocking reacted to the council's promises. The justices, however, replied that the taxation of adjoining parishes would be extremely unpopular, and that in any case all parishes in the clothing hundred were equally distressed. As for the order to suppress those troublemaking vagrants, the justices promised to do so—as soon as they could find any.[17]

The clothiers and cloth workers had looked to the Parliament of 1628–29 for some legislative solution to their problems.[18] Not only were these hopes frustrated by the dissolution of Parliament, but the industry was further crippled by the subsequent refusal of merchants in Colchester as well as London to pay tonnage and poundage without parliamentary authorization.[19] Tonnage and poundage were not mentioned directly in the weavers' petitions, but it would be surprising if the Essex clothiers passed up this opportunity to shift the blame for unemployment from themselves to the Crown. Royal taxation was blamed for the difficulties of the trade in 1621 and again in 1640. Moreover, the people of Essex were further antagonized by Laud's harassment of popular lecturers like Thomas Hooker. Samuel Collins warned that "all men's ears are filled by the obstreperous clamors of [Hooker's] followers against my Lord of London as a man endeavoring to suppress good preaching and advance popery." Collins observed that the economic depression had already provoked "many clamors and commotions" in the county, and he feared that continued repression of preachers would "enrage ... our tumultuous vulgar." Should that occur, Collins feared that "the rout may prove dangerous."[20] Collins's fears were shared by some at court. Sir Henry Vane's chaplain, William Lake, thought a general insurrection was possible if Warwick and Maynard failed to pacify the weavers.[21]

The danger was exaggerated, but it was not entirely imaginary. A few weeks later the weavers themselves informed the council that if the Earl of Warwick and Lord Maynard had not pacified them with "mild persuasions," then "many wretched people would have gathered together in a mutiny and have been with your Majesty before this time to have made their miseries known . . . for they said words will not fill the belly nor clothe the back."[22]

On May 22 a mutiny of sorts did in fact occur, although it was not directed against the Crown. A crowd of some three hundred, many of them weavers from Bocking, Braintree, and Witham, descended on Maldon and looted fifteen quarters of rye from ships bound for Europe. The riot had been organized by a woman named Ann Carter, who had also played a prominent role in the disturbance at Maldon two months earlier. She had allegedly visited the clothing towns to stir up discontent, and sent out letters—written for her by a Maldon baker, since she was illiterate—describing herself as "the Captain of the ——" (something or other—the report is unfortunately mutilated—doubtless one of those pseudomilitary titles so often adopted by the leaders of preindustrial crowd actions, like Captain Pouch, Captain Swing, and General Ludd). Carter rallied her local followers with the cry, "Come, my brave boys of Maldon. I will be your leader, for we shall not starve."[23]

John Walter, who has studied this entire episode in great detail, has stressed the contrast between the authorities' response to this riot and the earlier one. He has suggested that popular action against speculators and corn exporters enjoyed a measure of official tolerance, provided it did not exceed a fairly low threshold of violence. Female rioters were likely to be treated with particular indulgence. The May riot was regarded as a more serious affair than the one in March because it was considerably larger, with perhaps three times the number of participants, and because a majority of the rioters in May seem to have been male.[24] The men of property, however, proved to be more violent than their inferiors. Ann Carter and three other leaders were hanged at Witham. After the trial at least one man was heard to mutter that the jury were "bloodsuckers." But "the better sort of people," according to Sir Thomas Fanshawe, "were much pleased . . . being before much dismayed with the insolency of these people."[25]

The Maldon grain riot was hardly the conflagration Collins and Lake feared; there was no loss of life or limb. But it seemed to show that the danger of rebellion was genuine. Justices Mildmay and

Herris, the members for Maldon in the previous Parliament, reported that "rumors are so much spread of an intention to assemble in far greater numbers speedily that the country beginneth to be in great fears." Sir Thomas Fanshawe recalled that at this time there had been "a general inclination for all who pretended poverty to rise and do mischief."[26] A month or so later, during a grain riot in Colchester, a man tried to incite a crowd of more than one hundred to plunder the mansion of the Catholic Lord Rivers, promising that they would find there "gold and silver enough."[27] No one heeded him. But anti-Catholic riots swept through the Stour Valley at the outbreak of the Civil War, and Rivers's estate was among the first to be looted.

Fanshawe admitted to the council, without evident embarrassment, that the work of repression had "for the present . . . laid asleep all other business for the provision of the poor," but he seemed to believe that mere repression would suffice to keep the poor in line. "This justice hath so terrified them," he informed the council, "that . . . we are satisfied they will find work enough rather than run to outrage again."[28] But the problem of unemployment remained. The wardens of the cloth trade in Bocking and Braintree deplored the resort to violence by the Maldon rioters but alleged that the majority of cloth workers had no way to pay their rents "without using unlawful courses."[29] The clothiers were increasing the length of the bays without raising wages, and taking on additional apprentices, thereby worsening the unemployment among adult weavers.

On July 17 the Earl of Warwick took up the weavers' case before the council, and recommended that wages be fixed and the length of bays regulated. But a conference at Braintree failed to produce agreement. "We could effect nothing for the help of the poor weavers," the justices confessed, "which gave them much discontent."[30] In October the justices fell back on the old expedient of cutting down the number of apprentices and journeymen in the trade. An order was made at the Quarter Sessions requiring the immediate discharge of unlawful apprentices and reinforcing the provision that no weaver might keep more than three narrow looms or employ more than three journeymen. But apprenticeship to the cloth trade was a traditional manner of providing for the children of indigent parents. When two clothiers of Coggeshall brought this consideration to the attention of the Assize judges, the order was suspended.[31] Nothing seemed to work; every remedy had intolerable side effects.

The cloth trade remained severely depressed for the next two years, which were also years of dearth. The bad harvests created splendid opportunities for speculators in grain, like "one Archer" of Southchurch, who was brought before the Star Chamber for hoarding corn and raising prices, "to the undoing of the poor."[32] By December 1630 the normally corn-rich hundred of Dunmow was short of barley, peas, and corn. A few weeks later the overseers of Little Braxted, in Witham hundred, were presented at the Quarter Sessions "for neglecting the poor so much that divers children there are almost famished and one already dead for want of relief."[33] In February 1631 the bailiff of Colchester wrote that "the poor people are almost ready to famish and to commit outrages for want of corn." A month later Sir Thomas Barrington warned that "if there be not some speedy course taken for prevention, extreme scarcity and want are likely to fall upon the kingdom, and this county especially." Few in Essex could now afford wheat. Barley, "the chief sustenance of the general body of the kingdom," had now reached 4s. 4d a bushel.[34]

The food shortage was bad enough, but as the Privy Council observed in April of 1631, "the poor suffer as much in want of work as in the price of corn."[35] It was the combination of harvest failure with the ongoing cloth depression that was truly calamitous. As the Essex justices exlained the situation, "The clothiers forbear to set the weavers on work, alleging that they have already disbursed more than they are able, and that their cloths lie upon their hands, which has occasioned many complaints of the poor weavers, and a more than usual resort of them unto the justices at their present sessions."[36]

Moreover, there were more complaints of wage cutting. In February 1631 the council received a petition from one "Sylvia Herbert, spinster, a poor distressed widow," on behalf of herself and a "multitude of others"—spinsters, weavers, and combers in the Stour Valley. Herbert charged that, "of late years most of the clothiers, who by the labors of such poor artisans have gotten great estates, out of a covetous disposition have abridged their wages by detaining from the poor spinsters out of every nine pence, which with great pains they have labored for, one penny; from the poor weaver out of every

20s formerly paid, four shillings." As a result, workers in the trade had recently been forced "to sell their beds, wheels, looms, and other working tools to buy bread for their wives and children . . . many of them ready to perish for want of food." In May of the same year, three hundred "poor men" of Colchester also proclaimed themselves "much distressed by the abatement of their usual wages in these times of scarcity and dearth."[37]

The fine harvest of 1631 brought prices down to reasonable levels again. According to Peter Bowden's index of prices, the average level for all grains during the 1620s had been 594 (taking the average price for 1450 to 1499 as 100). In the harvest year 1630 the index shot up to 880; in 1631 it fell back to 602. The cloth trade too may have picked up a bit during these years; at least, there is no evidence of distress. But the economic recovery was feeble and short-lived. The grain price index soon began rising again: to 698 in 1632, 711 in 1633, and 824 in 1634.[38] There was a relapse in the cloth trade as well. By December 1634 the clothiers of Essex and Suffolk claimed to have £100,000 worth of unsold cloth in stock.[39] By the summer of 1636 unemployment and its attendant social tensions had again reached critical proportions.

According to the Bocking clothiers the decay of trade was forcing them to sell their wares below cost, and in recent months there had been no sale at all. The smaller clothiers were being driven out of business. There were at least two hundred "combers, spinners, weavers, and rowers" unemployed. Two London merchants went bankrupt, owing the clothiers of Braintree, Bocking, Coggeshall, and Witham a total of £3,944. In Colchester the clothiers had been ordered by the Privy Council to raise wages by one-sixth, which they protested was impossible. In any case, they insisted, the poor suffered more from unemployment than low wages. The clothiers were unable to provide work even if wages were cut by one-sixth.[40] Three Colchester weavers, meanwhile, claimed that they and two thousand of their fellows, all employees of one Thomas Reynolds, had been "reduced to exceeding misery by the smallness of wages and the troublesomeness of their work." Reynolds was also accused of paying his employees in truck—unsalable bays or other "dead commodities"—instead of cash.[41]

Another grievance was the cheap competition afforded by unapprenticed newcomers, who could be used to further undercut wages. In Bocking the combers protested against the "multitude of apprentices and . . . foreigners [who] do inhabit and marry, which makes so many poor men." In Colchester the free burgesses were outraged that "many of the poorer sort of weavers . . . do daily take journeymen, boys, women, wenches, and girls and employ them . . . and thereby bring great poverty upon themselves and . . . the inhabitants of this borough."[42]

It was natural, particularly in a time of severe depression that established artisans should wish to bar new entrants from their craft. But there was another side to it. The raising of barriers to the cloth industry robbed many young men (and women as well, to judge from the complaint above) of their only chance to escape agricultural wage labor. Richard Vaughan, for example, had bound his son out as an apprentice weaver. But Vaughan failed to meet the property qualification established by the Statute of Artificers. When this came to light, the son was discharged, and then—against the father's will—bound out by the town authorities as a servant in husbandry, although Vaughan protested that he had never received poor relief. Since then, as he deposed in 1637, Vaughan had prospered and now possessed "a competent estate . . . to the yearly value in and by the statute required." Once again, Vaughan bound the boy out to a weaver, "out of his fatherly care for the good of his child for time to come." The indentures had been entered and enrolled by the warden of the trade in Bocking, but now this same warden had presented the boy as an unlawful apprentice. The weavers of Bocking could not afford generosity in 1637.[43]

As if this were not enough, the harvest of 1637 was catastrophic. The Bowden index number for all grains rises to 969 for the following year, nearly one hundred points higher than for the disastrous year of 1630.[44] And plague had returned to the county. In the summer of 1637 Chelmsford and Moulsham reported that "being heavily afflicted with the plague" for the past thirteen weeks, they had been forced to spend £104 to relieve the sick alone, "besides the ordinary collection, which is very great, and is like to increase exceeding much," since not even healthy inhabitants could find work.[45]

The Quarter Sessions Bundles for these years are filled with personal accounts that provide vivid glimpses of lower-class experience during these terrible times. John Harvey of Halsted, for example, was a collier—probably a carrier and seller of hearth coal rather than a miner; his wife Susan was a hat dresser. In 1637 neither could find work in Halsted and so were forced "to travel forth the country." While passing the house of John Argur, the Puritan minister of Layer de la Haye, Susan "espied certain night caps and other small linen which she . . . took up, intending to sell them to buy therewith some small relief for herself and the little one she carried with her." She was soon apprehended; there is no record of her fate.[46]

Henry March also came to grief in Layer de la Haye, though for different reasons. He fell lame in 1636 while working for a yeoman named Bridge. His employer kept him on until his covenant expired, but there was no question of engaging him for the following year. So March was reduced to seeking casual daily labor in the surrounding parishes, lodging in the home of poor neighbors, until "it pleased God to visit the poor man's house with an infectious disease." The plague claimed most of the family, but March concealed the fact of his exposure, until he collapsed during harvest work at Stanway and was carried back to Layer de la Haye to his old master. March recovered from the plague, but could no longer work. Bridge petitioned the parish to be rid of him.[47]

Folk like Henry March and John and Susan Harvey were passive victims. But the case of Robert Hamond is different, and more revealing. Hamond was a comber from Bocking, who declared in the summer of 1636, "[I] have not had half work enough since Whitsuntide, and my charge is so great that I can make shift no longer, for I have five children to keep and had much ado to keep them when I had work enough, and I have made all the shifts that I can." Hamond insisted that he wanted work, not charity, but he was tired of being fobbed off with hollow promises. Alluding the riots of 1629, Hamond insisted, "I never took no lewd course for to wrong any man nor yet run about the country as others have done, as it is well known that some went for corn to the seaside and took it by violence, some again ran up to London begging. I never stirred, but kept my work, and it is nothing else which now I crave: to maintain my charge, that I may not take no unlawful course." But Hamond's patience was running thin, "for it is hard to starve. Job saith, 'skin for skin, and all that a man hath he will give for his life.' "[48] The desperation, the veiled threat, and the scriptural justification were all portents of the coming decade.

Despite unquestionably worthy intentions, the Crown proved helpless to deal with the economic depression of the 1620s and 1630s. This inability fatally undermined Charles's program of fiscal and religious reform. The Privy Council was, of course, aware of the circumstances I have outlined, but its efforts at intervention were futile or redundant. In fact, the Crown had no economic policy worthy of the name. It relied very largely on homily, exhortation, and false promises. In 1622 the council's instinctive response to the riots in the cloth district was to blame outside agitators: "lewd and vagrant persons that omit no opportunity of raising tumults and disorders for their own private ends." The council ordered the justices to put down all "tumultuous assemblies" and to assure the cloth workers "that we have had special considerations of their wants and with extraordinary care have taken course (as by the effects they shall shortly find) for their speedy relief and employment." It was pure waffle. The council had no scheme for the "speedy relief and employment" of the weavers, nor did it develop one in the subsequent decade. In 1629 we find the council repeating the same empty reassurances.[49]

True, it is hard even in retrospect to imagine what the government might have done. The root of the county's problems was the continuing "lack of vent" for English textiles on the Continent. Some members of Parliament felt that the solution to England's difficulties lay through imperial expansion at the expense of Spain, and it is true that the Spanish-backed Catholic offensive in Germany was partly to blame for the loss of English markets. But the aggressive mercantilism that some members advocated was not only uncongenial to Charles, it was utterly beyond his means—a fact he understood more clearly than his critics. But in 1629 Charles dissolved a Parliament to which Essex clothiers and weavers were looking anxiously for some unspecified relief.[50] The king thereby made himself politically liable for an economic situation that was largely beyond his control.

Moreover, Crown policy tended to make things worse. From the producer's point of view, the task was to increase demand. The

Crown, in contrast, sought to maintain wage levels in a time of growing unemployment, and to cut back supply. Thus, in February 1630, we find the council granting a petition from the Eastland Company to bar interlopers from trade with the Continent, thus further restricting the outlets available to the clothier. In 1631 and again in 1636 the council attempted to force clothiers to raise wages, which can hardly have helped the problem of unemployment.[51] In the winter of 1634–35 the council ordered the suppression of independent cloth dealers in London, restricting wholesale and retail trade in the capital to members of the Merchant Adventurers and Drapers' Shopkeepers, despite the protests of the clothiers of Essex and Suffolk. In the following year the rights of Colchester clothiers to trade directly with the Continent were further curtailed by the Crown. Finally, in 1637 the council instructed the Essex justices to begin to phase out the manufacture of bays, "since that commodity is not now so vendible as heretofore."[52] To the clothing interest in Essex—which directly or indirectly included most of the population—such a cure was worse than the disease. Essex folk would find more persuasive the argument of Harbottle Grimston, who in 1642 blamed the industry's troubles on "the many taxations and oppressions" imposed on cloth by "divers ill instruments of state."[53] The Crown itself was held to blame.

It has been asserted that a vigorous royal paternalism at least alleviated the hardship of these years, particularly during the dearth of 1629–1631.[54] It is true that the Privy Council received reports and issued instructions, which culminated in January 1631 with the famous Book of Orders, requiring justices to regulate the price of grain, suppress hoarding and speculation, and enforce the Poor Law. John Walter and Keith Wrightson have argued that this intervention produced "a remarkable vitalizing of the efficiency of administrative control in Essex."[55] But there are two points that need to be made here. First, there is no evidence that the Book of Orders had any dramatic effect on the county's apparatus of poor relief. As Table 19 demonstrates, the development of parochial institutions, at least as reflected in the survival of poor rates, proceeded slowly and steadily from 1570 down to the Civil War. The table shows the number of parishes for which any records of poor rates survive for the decade in question, the number of annual recorded rates for all these parishes, and the density of parish poor rates, expressed in average

Table 19. Surviving accounts of Essex poor rates, 1560–1659

Decade	Number of parishes for which rates survived in that decade	Total number of annual rates recorded	Average annual rates recorded per parish
1560–1569	1	4	4.0
1570–1579	2	5	2.5
1580–1589	7	15	2.1
1590–1599	8	23	2.9
1600–1609	8	31	3.9
1610–1619	12	52	4.3
1620–1629	15	68	4.5
1630–1639	18	78	4.3
1640–1649	17	90	4.2
1650–1659	19	100	5.2

Source: Transcripts of Essex poor rates supplied by W. K. Jordan.

annual rates recorded per parish. There was no unusually great increase in the 1630s, either in the quantity or the density of surviving rates. The implication would seem to be that the system of poor relief was gradually elaborated on the local level, quite independently of the central government.

The second point is that the magistrates who most vigorously enforced the policy embodied in the Book of Orders were the Earl of Warwick, Sir Thomas Barrington, and Sir William Masham, all of whom were to take up arms against the king in the Civil War. Among future Royalists only William Lord Maynard, now yoked with Warwick in the lord lieutenancy, was conspicuously energetic. It was Warwick who repeatedly tried to mediate between cloth workers and their employers; it was Warwick who in 1630 commanded Archer, the grain speculator, of Southchurch to bring his hoard of corn to the Rochford market after the local justices had failed to intervene—even though, as Sir Thomas Richardson commented in the Star Chamber, Warwick was exempt, as a peer, from the burden of enforcing the Book of Orders.[56] Barrington and Masham were perhaps the most diligent of all the county's justices in regulating grain prices, suppressing alehouses, and securing adequate provision for the poor. They not only implemented the Book of Orders, they anticipated it. Indeed, Barrington's reports to his kinsman, Viscount Dorchester, may have helped to shape royal policy.[57] In 1634 Barrington and Masham informed the council of their efforts to punish vagabonds and suppress alehouses, "finding by good experience that this doth both prevent the impoverishing of the inferior sort and much further the peaceable government of His Majesty's subjects." They had also discovered that the binding of poor children as apprentices "doth exceedingly prevent both disorders and poverty."[58]

It is hard to believe that such men needed much advice from the central government, especially one with which they were in so many ways at odds. Their puritanism provided them with a perfectly adequate ideology of social reform: they labored to institute the culture of discipline. The behavior of Warwick, Barrington, and Masham during the early years of the Personal Rule does suggest that there was no fundamental conflict between the social welfare objectives proclaimed by the Crown and the aspirations of the godly. The paternalism embodied in the Book of Orders cannot plausibly be listed among the causes of the Civil War in Essex. The Privy Council merely generalized the techniques that had been implemented over the previous half-century by parochial, municipal, and county elites, especially by those of a godly persuasion. The godly were, in fact, the logical and indispensable allies of the Crown in any attempt at paternalistic reform.

But this consensus between the Crown and the godly was superficial. For the latter, social welfare entailed more than the regulation of grain prices and the relief of the poor; it required the spiritual and moral regeneration of society as a whole. This perspective was vividly expressed by Sir William Masham in a letter to Lady Joan Barrington. Commenting on the bad harvest of 1629, Masham observed that

the best cure rests in a consideration of the cause of this evil, which is our sins. And this hand of God upon the creature (the materials of drink) doth point out as it were with his finger the special sin of our nation, which is drunkenness. We have great cause to be humbled for this, and to be earnest for reconciliation and reformation, lest the hand cast us forth with the drunkards. Justice against this sin is the best expiation, according to that of Phineas, Psalm 106:30. ["Then stood up Phineas and executed judgment: and so the plague was stayed."] Whereof a precedent I made this day in punishing four drunkards, four drinkers, and two alehousekeepers in one town. I could wish the like were practiced in other places: we should have less drunkenness and less judgments.[59]

Moreover, the imposition of a culture of discipline was intimately connected with the propagation of the Gospel by painful preachers. This program could never be implemented under the regime of William Laud. Laud's ecclesiastical policies alienated those very social groups whose cooperation was essential to the success of Stuart paternalism: ministers, vestrymen, and noble professors.

In the spring of 1629, when the two grain riots at Maldon seemed to presage a general uprising of the poor, the Privy Council ordered the Essex justices to "understand the true state of your [county] from the ministers, churchwardens, and overseers of the several parishes" and take appropriate measures.[60] Had Charles's government fully grasped the implications of their own instructions, the Puritan Moment might never have occurred, for this directive acknowledged the essential fact about local government: social order required close and effective cooperation between ministers, parish officials, and local elites. To recapitulate the argument advanced earlier, the parish had replaced the manor as the elemental administrative unit. It was the minister and his lay associates who constituted (outside the household, of course) the first line of political authority. The tendency in the sixteenth and early seventeenth centuries was for these men to form themselves into vestries—elected or (increasingly) self-coopting bodies that met regularly to address all manner of secular and spiritual problems.

For a vestry (or a less formal vestrylike body) to work effectively, it needed a minister with moral stature and administrative ability. The minister was the linchpin of the whole system. Since his role was to maintain the ideological consensus and to legitimate social norms, he had to be able to manipulate symbols and emotions. In the seventeenth century this meant that he must be an effective preacher. The laymen, for their part, needed to be men of some public spirit. And if parish government were to seem legitimate to the subordinate parishioners, they had to be of good moral repute. In the seventeenth century this meant they had to be or to appear godly. And finally, for the parish to function optimally the minister and vestrymen must be compatible—must share, in other words, the same broad social and religious values. It would help, therefore, if the leading laymen had some influence over the selection of the incumbent.

Given its new centrality and the responsibilities imposed by the Poor Law, the parish needed, ideally, the following features: a preaching minister enjoying the confidence and support of (perhaps even chosen by) the leading laymen, and a body of public-spirited and pious laymen concerned with both the temporal and spiritual well-being of the community. In times of overpopulation and economic crisis, both minister and laymen would need, in the interest of social stability, to effect a reformation of manners, and to establish what I have called a culture of discipline.

The presbyterian system associated with Calvin's Geneva seemed to many magistrates and local worthies ideally appropriate to this state of affairs. As I have suggested, a tendency toward de facto presbyterianism was inscribed in the very structure and function of parish government, as it had evolved by the seventeenth century. Predestinarian theology provided an appropriate ideology for the parish elite, and painful preaching afforded the principal agency of cultural reform. This social puritanism, if I may be permitted the term, had taken root during the reign of Elizabeth, and it was strengthened by the evangelical activities of the preachers who poured forth from Cambridge after 1580. But its appeal to local elites was also intensified by the economic hardships of the 1620s and 1630s. The spread of poverty, and the attendant heightening of social tensions, was closely related to the growth of Puritan attitudes among the laity, especially those in a position of responsibility at the local and regional level. In the years before the Civil War, as Lucy Hutchinson later recalled, concern with the problem of poverty was regarded in itself as a token of puritanism.

Social puritanism did not necessarily imply hostility to the Church of England, still less to the Crown itself. The social Puritan might not even object to the governance of the church by bishops, provided that they refrained from meddling destructively in parochial affairs and from hounding effective and godly preachers about ritualistic trivia. Warwick, Barrington, and Masham, for example, seem not to have opposed episcopacy as such during the 1630s. Barrington occasionally referred to prelates with jocular irreverence, but he greatly admired Bishop Ussher. The family followed episcopal promotions closely. They distinguished between prelates and knew that these differences mattered.[61] Before 1641, according to

Clarendon, Warwick "never discovered any aversion to episcopacy, and much professed the contrary."[62]

The credit for transforming social puritanism into a revolutionary force belongs very largely to William Laud. As Dr. Kalu has demonstrated, there was no really serious campaign of repression against Puritan preachers in Essex before Laud's elevation in 1628 to the see of London.[63] But Laud was nearly as hostile to social puritanism as he was to the clerical nonconformity with which it was often associated. Laud disliked the very institution of the vestry, with its mutual dependence of minister and governing laity. Vestry doctrine became a Laudian code word for puritanism. How Laud imagined the English countryside could be governed without something like a parish vestry is unclear. In any case, he was unable to launch a frontal assault on the institution itself. But his policy subverted the culture of discipline in other ways. Valuable preachers were silenced for resisting the apparent Catholicization of the church. The Book of Sports, reissued in 1633, the year Laud became primate, encouraged the profanation of the Sabbath and undercut the authority of householders, who could no longer prevent their servants from engaging in "profane sports and pastimes."[64] Meanwhile, divine wrath was being stoked ever higher by popish innovations in the liturgy and in the physical fabric of the churches. Taken as a whole, this program appeared quite literally satanic to many sane and responsible English Protestants, especially when it coincided with such obvious tokens of God's displeasure.

After the dissolution of Parliament, Charles gave the Laudians a free hand in silencing Puritan lecturers—among them John Rogers of Dedham, his son Daniel of Wethersfield, and above all Thomas Hooker of Chelmsford. We have already noted Samuel Collins's warning that the suppression of Hooker would "enrage . . . the tumultuous vulgar" at a time when the economic depression had already provoked "many clamors and commotions." Collins himself is a complex and interesting character, whose predicament tells us much about the way the middle ground between revolution and reaction was being eroded. Collins can be reasonably described as a moderate Puritan. He was eulogized at his death by Matthew Newcomen, one of the Smectymnuuans. He signed petitions in favor of Daniel Rogers. He exerted his influence on behalf of John Bedle.

But in 1629 he was still hoping to remain on good terms with both
Laud and the "bold and fiery spirits," as he termed them, around
Thomas Hooker.[65]

Collins professed, with what sincerity we cannot know, that he
deplored the spread of nonconformity and was doing what little he
could to suppress it. "It is the greatest grief of my soul," he sighed,
"to see how full of whirligigs the heads of our people begin to grow."
Collins urged that Hooker be persuaded to leave the diocese quietly.
If he were forcibly silenced, he would remain in Essex and continue
his private conferences. Should that happen, Collins predicted that
"his genius will haunt all the pulpits where any of his scholars may
be permitted to preach," and the disciples were even more radical
than their master. These younger preachers would inspire contempt
for the conforming ministry among the people, especially in the
larger towns. The situation of the conformists—bad enough already—would become intolerable.[66]

Collins was thus playing a double game. He acknowledged as
much by begging Arthur Duck, Laud's chancellor, to keep his letter
secret, since "if some in the world should have the least inkling
thereof," Collins's reputation and career would be ruined. He must
have been thinking of the Earl of Warwick, who was lord of the
manor of Braintree and the patron of both Collins and Thomas
Hooker. But before we accuse Collins of lack of moral fiber, we
should note that bolder Puritans than he were equivocating with the
Laudian regime during these years. Samuel Ward at Cambridge
confided to his diary his fears that Holland, Warwick, and Nathaniel Rich would despise him for seeking to compromise with the new
regime. William Gouge, the schoolmate of Warwick and Rich at
Eton, wrote a letter to Laud in 1631 that may strike us—at a safe
distance of three hundred years—as both shifty and obsequious.[67]
We have to remember that these men saw themselves as above all
preachers of the Word, whose first responsibility was to minister to
their congregations. Deprivation would not only impoverish the
preacher but also endanger the souls of his flock. It was not a risk to
be taken lightly.

Collins wrote this letter on May 20, two days before the weavers of
Bocking and Braintree rioted at Maldon. On the third of June, after
Hooker had been summoned to appear before the bishop, Collins
wrote again, warning that Laud was holding a wolf by the ears.

Collins reported that "all men's heads, tongues, eyes are in London," and that the debate over Hooker's case "drowns out the great question of tonnage and poundage." Collins was more uncomfortable than ever in the role of mediator. "I dare not say half of that I hear," he confessed, since "paper walls are easily broken open." Prudence might yet save the situation. Hooker's graceful withdrawal from Essex would benefit not only the church but Hooker himself. "For let him be as cautelous [cautious, circumspect] as he will, yet in his present course the humors of our people will quite undo him."[68] The implication of this interesting remark is that the rank and file of the godly were driving Hooker into open confrontation with the hierarchy. Certainly it would have been neither the first nor the last time that a radical leader was swept farther and faster than he intended by the enthusiasm of his own followers.

Nevertheless, Hooker did his best to stay out ahead of the pack. It was probably at about this time that he preached in Dedham, in the place of the suspended lecturer John Rogers, Hooker's own mentor. The theme of the sermon entitled, "The Faithful Covenantor," was the sin of backsliding from the profession of the Gospel. "What means the fierce anger of the Lord against this nation?" Hooker asked rhetorically. It meant, of course, that England had broken her covenant with the Lord. For the moment God's fierce anger was expressed primarily through the crisis of the economy. The entire sermon is laced with metaphors of debt and broken contracts. Addressing this congregation of clothiers and weavers, Hooker observed, "You complain of trading in the world: almost no trust to be put in any; every man almost is turned bankrupt. I am sure, brethren, it is true in religion."[69]

The trade depression was merely the reflection of England's spiritual bankruptcy; breaking faith with God had severed the threads of commerce. And yet, their economic sufferings were trivial compared to the punishment the Lord would inflict by means of the Spanish unless the nation repented. Hooker warned his auditors that as townsmen of Dedham, who had enjoyed a godly ministry for half a century, more would be demanded of them than of less fortunate Christians. He compared them to tenants farming bountiful lands at correspondingly high rents. There was great rejoicing in Hell, he told them, when a drunkard or hypocrite arrived from Dedham. The devils lit bonfires and stood on tiptoe to gawk at him.[70] Many in the congregation took Hooker's warnings to heart. In the Civil War, Dedham was one of the most loyally Parliamentarian towns in the county—"an officious race of traitors," in the words of one Royalist.[71]

Collins's mediation in June secured a temporary respite for Hooker. But in November of 1629 John Brownrigg, the Laudian rector of Rawreth, begged the bishop for help in "the oppressing and rooting out . . . of such a one from amongst us." Brownrigg admitted that since the people of Essex were, in his words, "over-much addicted to hearing the Word," the suppression of Hooker's lecture would kindle "great heart-burnings" against the authorities. Brownrigg felt, however, that the people could be pacified by a weekly lecture preached in rotation by the orthodox divines of the Chelmsford neighborhood.[72]

Hooker had his defenders as well as opponents among the conforming clergy. On November 10 forty-nine beneficed Essex ministers, including Samuel Collins, signed a letter to Laud declaring that Hooker was "for doctrine orthodox and life and conversation honest, and his disposition peaceable, in no ways turbulent or factious." This testimonial elicited a petition from forty-one ministers describing themselves as conformable, demanding the suppression of heterodoxy, and clearly aimed at Hooker, though he was not mentioned by name.[73] Collins had given Laud excellent advice, but the bishop listened to Brownrigg. Hooker's lectureship had been suppressed by February 1630.

The suppression of Hooker was merely a first step in Laud's campaign to reduce the county to conformity. In the next two years the godly in Essex were subjected to a repression more severe than any they had endured since Elizabeth's accession. The immediate consequence was to drive the leading preachers into exile or a politic conformity; the long-term result was to make them, and their lay supporters, irreconcilable to the established church and to destroy all hope of the compromise solution sought by men like Collins.

Nathaniel Rogers, the son of John, was among the first of Hooker's disciples to be driven from the county. Rogers was serving as curate to Dr. Barkham, the dean of Bocking. At about the time of Hooker's suppression, he refused to don the surplice at a funeral service. Hooker had convinced him that the use of the surplice was against the Word of God. Thereupon Dr. Barkham "gave him private advice to provide for himself in some other place." Rogers moved first to Suffolk and five years later followed Hooker across the North Atlantic.[74]

Other Puritans were treated less gently. Thomas Shepherd was summoned to appear before Laud in December 1630. Shepherd has left us a vivid account of their meeting:

> He asked who maintained me . . . charging me to deal plainly with him, adding withal that he had been more cheated and equivocated with by some of my malignant faction than ever was man by Jesuit. At the speaking of which words he looked as though blood would have gushed out of his face, and did shake as if he had been haunted of an ague fit, to my apprehension, by reason of the extreme malice and secret venom. I desired him to excuse me. He fell then to threaten me, and withal to bitter railing, calling me all to naught, saying "You prating coxcomb, do you think all the learning is in your brain?"

Laud forbade Shepherd to "preach, read, marry, bury, or exercise any ministerial function" in any part of the diocese of London.[75]

In the autumn of the following year, Laud conducted a visitation of the county *in propria persona*. As Thomas Shepherd recalled it, he and Thomas Weld, Daniel Rogers, Nathaniel Ward, Stephen Marshall, and Samuel Wharton "consulted together whether it was best to let such a swine to root up God's plants in Essex, and not give him some check." But Laud struck first. John Rogers was suspended. Thomas Weld was excommunicated, and when he protested, he was seized by the pursuivant and bound over to the High Commission. Shepherd barely escaped. He was whisked to safety by Martin Holbeach, the famous Puritan schoolmaster of Felsted. Stephen Marshall, Samuel Wharton of Felsted, and Edward Brewer of Castle Hedingham were charged with nonconformity but let off with warnings.[76] (Ward was excommunicated two years later).

Samuel Collins of Braintree was also in trouble by the end of 1631. He had received a sharp letter from Laud, which, as he wrote to Duck, "hath renewed the colic and stone lately grown upon me for the waywardness of some of my people." He was already under attack from radical Puritans and was doing his best by "moderate and slow proceedings" to bring his congregation back into line. If he had insisted on "the strict practice of conformity," Collins claimed, "I had undone myself and broken the town in pieces." If Laud would neither relax his demand for conformity nor transfer him to some less dissident parish, then he expressed a wish to be "ere long at rest with the greater Bishop of our souls."[77]

Matthew Newcomen, however, was probably right when he insisted, at Collins's funeral, that Collins had never seriously considered leaving Braintree. He refused the smaller and quieter rectory of Barnston, which Laud offered him, recommending instead his kinsman John Bedle, who was a disciple of Thomas Hooker and a client of the Earl of Warwick. On May 31, 1632, Collins wrote a fascinating letter to Laud, which shows him still trying to maintain a difficult balance between the Puritans and Arminians. Collins urged that when he and Bedle appeared before Laud, the bishop should take a hard line with Collins, warning him to suppress conventicles, to enforce conformity in the service of communion, "and withal to intimate that your Lordship hath so watchful an eye over us in Braintree as that few things can be spoken or done, but they come to your Lordship's ear." Collins predicted that "these things spoken at this present will both settle this young man in the comfortable way wherein he now is, and may procure me much peace." Thus, Collins hoped to reassure Laud of his own orthodoxy, prove to the more radical Puritans that his own hands were tied, and still exercise influence on their behalf. The performance, if it was ever staged as Collins proposed, had little enough effect on Bedle, who was censured for nonconformity during the following year.[78]

One of Collins's arguments against the enforcement of strict orthodoxy was that many of his congregation were prepared to emigrate to New England at the first sign of a change in their habitual forms of worship. In fact, in the preceding two years at least 157 men and women had already left Essex for Massachusetts, together with 185 of their neighbors from Suffolk, most of whom came from the southeast of the county, which formed a single economic region with the clothing district of Essex. Only one of these emigrants is known to have come from Braintree, but Collins's fears were realized in 1632, when eighteen inhabitants set sail, along with another eight from Bocking. In all, at least 565 individuals set forth from Essex for the New World between 1630 and 1639. Of these Braintree provided forty-one and Bocking and Dedham thirty each.[79]

The people of Essex, and especially those in clothing towns like Braintree, Bocking, and Dedham, had compelling secular incentives to cross the Atlantic. But segregation of religious and secular motives would have seemed obtuse to the founders of the Massachusetts Bay Colony. Puritan ideology provided a unified theory of the relationship between spirit and matter. Nothing in the Puritan universe was merely secular; everything, in its innermost meaning, was religious. Plague, famine, and war, said William Gouge, were "God's three arrows," the weapons of divine vengeance against a sinful nation. Among the sins of England, Gouge listed idolatry, the profanation of the Sabbath, the neglect of preaching, the oppression of the poor, and "magistrates' abuse of their authority." Gouge dedicated his sermon to his old schoolmates at Eton and Cambridge, Sir Nathaniel Rich and the Earl of Warwick.[80]

It was this way of reading contemporary events that inspired John Winthrop, a friend of both Rich and Sir Francis Barrington, to organize in 1630 the first sizable emigration to Massachusetts Bay.[81] "I am verily persuaded," he had written his wife in May 1629, two months after the dissolution of Parliament, "God will bring some heavy affliction upon this land, and that speedily." The English had learned nothing from their own afflictions, nor from the catastrophes visited upon the Protestants on the Continent. The Lord's patience was bound to run out soon. Yet, he might provide "a shelter and a hiding place" for the righteous, as he had once done for Lot. Winthrop also advocated colonization as a solution to poverty and overpopulation.[82]

A few months after Winthrop's fleet had landed in Massachusetts, his agents in England were trying to persuade Thomas Hooker to emigrate as well. Since the suppression of his lectureship, Hooker had been teaching school at Little Baddow, where his usher was John Eliot, the future apostle to the Indians; he also spent some months in Lincolnshire. Laud, however, was not done with him. He was ordered to appear before the Court of High Commission, and a bond of £50 for his appearance was put up for him by one of the Earl of Warwick's tenants, a wealthy yeoman of Great Waltham named Nash. As the appointed date drew near, Hooker's friends— probably including the Earl himself—advised him to forfeit the bond rather than face Laud's malevolence. A collection was taken up around Chelmsford to reimburse Goodman Nash, and Warwick provided "a courteous and private recess" for Hooker's family, while the preacher prepared to embark for Holland.[83]

On the eve of his departure, probably on April 17, 1631, Hooker preached to a congregation assembled either in Chelmsford or at the Earl of Warwick's hall in Great Waltham, the most dramatic sermon of his English career: "The Danger of Desertion." Puritan preachers normally considered themselves, by virtue of their office, to be the successors to the biblical prophets. On this occasion, however, Hooker felt the breath of the spirit at gale force. God had spoken to him the night before and entrusted him with a fearful message: the destruction of England was at hand. Like a peddler whose wares none would buy, God was packing up his Gospel and preparing to leave England forever. The signs were unmistakable: England had lost those "two great means of safety, Magistrates and Ministry." Hooker did not need to explain to his audience the obvious reference to the dissolution of Parliament and his own suppression. The land that had been the mirror of God's mercies would be delivered to the fury of the papists. Her men would be slaughtered, her women defiled, her children impaled on the pikes of the Spanish *tercios*. Already the righteous were fleeing the wrath to come. Alluding to the folk who had sailed to New England the preceding year under the leadership of John Winthrop, Hooker observed that "God begins to ship away his Noahs, which prophesied and foretold that destruction was near."[84]

Hooker exhorted the congregation one last time to undertake a great effort of national repentence, which might yet, even at this late hour, avert disaster. "O, therefore, my brethren, lay hold on God, and let him not go out of your coasts. (He is going!) Look about you, I say, and stop him at the town's end, and let not thy God depart . . . Suffer him not to say farewell, or rather fare-ill, England!"[85] But the people of Chelmsford would have to lay hold on God without the help of Thomas Hooker. This sermon was his own farewell to England. After three years in Holland he sailed to New England himself, to join the other Noahs.

As Collins had predicted, Laud's program encountered increasing popular opposition. An anonymous ballad appeared in Colchester in the summer of 1631, lampooning three Laudian ministers. Theophilus Roberts of St. Nicholas parish was compared not only to the persecuting Bishop Bonner of Marian times but to Judas Iscariot as well. Roberts was alleged to be an incompetent and infrequent preacher, despised by the rank and file of his congregation, although he was considered "a great gallant" by the "courtly knaves." William Eyres would make "a dainty friar" if popery were restored, while Gabriel Honifold preferred wine and wenches to the study of divinity. Thomas Newcomen came in for similar abuse. The anonymous balladeer was not alone in his opinion of Honifold and Newcomen. Both men were nearly murdered by a Parliamentary mob in 1642, and both were sequestered, Newcomen for supporting Laudian innovations and opposing Parliament, Honifold for "non-residence, seldom preaching, swearing, and playing at cards and tables on the Lord's day."[86]

Laud's program to enhance the "beauty of holiness" by repairing churches imposed new burdens on a society already suffering from rising poor rates and antagonized by the extralegal exactions of the Crown. On the parish level there was an inevitable trade-off between funds levied for church repairs and for poor relief.[87] In Chelmsford during the 1630s, for example, the beauty of holiness was quite expensive. The churchwardens' rate came to £169 in 1631, and £181 the next year. In Colchester, Laud's commissary, Robert Aylett, found it hard in 1632 to collect money for the repair of London's disintegrating cathedral. The taxpayers of Essex had more pressing concerns than shoring up that dilapidated pile. "The people of Colchester," Aylett complained, "are like them of Ephesus. Their Diana is their liberty."[88] Things were little better elsewhere in the county.

Resistance to the whole Laudian program was growing. "There is a foul cloud arising," warned Aylett, "which threatens a foul storm." Late in 1634 the rector of Great Horkesley blamed the refusal of his flock to contribute to St. Paul's on "certain sectaries in these parts, whose examples guide the inferior sort."[89] One sectary in the area was John Bastwick, who was arrested in Colchester earlier in the year as the author of two antiepiscopal pamphlets.[90] Bastwick opposed the hierarchy on social as well as theological grounds. He condemned the bishops for wasteful extravagance and neglect of the duties of charity.[91] Another subversive in Colchester was Bastwick's brother-in-law, Thomas Cotton, described by an informant as "a great depraver of government." Cotton's library was reported to contain "all the discontented books and speeches invective against the church and state that have been published of old or lately," and he maintained a "peevish intelligencer" in London who pro-

vided him with weekly news reports. Cotton read these reports in the
streets of Colchester on market days, when "zealants" flocked about
him "as people use where ballads are sung." Cotton had recently arranged for Henry Burton to come up from London to preach, first in
Cotton's private chapel and then at a public lecture. When Cotton's
study was searched, he was found to possess three parliamentary
diaries and books by Henry Burton and William Prynne, as well as
the works of Bastwick. Aylett's "foul storm" was rising.[92]

The Puritan gentry, however, were not yet prepared to place
themselves at the head of this popular disaffection. While they
might be appalled by Laud's offensive against preachers and against
Calvinism itself, they offered no direct resistance. As we have seen,
Warwick, Barrington, and Masham continued to serve the Crown
loyally and efficiently in the government of the county. In 1632 Barrington and Masham even helped collect contributions for Laud's
pet enterprise, the rebuilding of St. Paul's in London.[93]

There is reason to believe that some of Laud's victims felt betrayed by Barrington's failure to oppose the repression. We have already heard Barrington's anguished complaints that his character
and behavior were being subjected to merciless censure. The location of these undated letters in the collection suggests that they were
written in the autumn of 1631, at the time of Laud's visitation. It is
quite likely that Barrington's tormentors included preachers like
Thomas Shepherd and Thomas Weld, who were trying to find some
way of obstructing the episcopal offensive. The inquisition that
made Hatfield uninhabitable for Barrington may have been an attempt to goad him into a more vigorous defense of the harried
preachers. To a man like Barrington, however, the ecclesiastical situation probably appeared more fluid in 1631 than it looks to us in
hindsight. The Barringtons followed the Crown's episcopal appoint-
ments during these years with mingled hope and anxiety. Laud,
after all was not yet primate, and the depth of Charles's personal
commitment to Arminianism had yet to be disclosed.[94]

But as long as Laud and his ecclesiastical party enjoyed the full
confidence of the king, there was in truth little enough that the gentry could do to check the apparent drift of the English church toward Rome. Just how little was made clear by the case of William
Innes, a minister in Harwich. A series of disputes dating back to
1624 between Innes and his congregation had produced a tangled

skein of accusations and countercharges. Innes was accused of popery as well as perjury and extortion. His opponents were charged with acts of heretical blasphemy, such as the baptizing of a dog. A commission of justices, including the Earl Rivers and Sir Harbottle Grimston, lately M.P. for Harwich, determined that the congregation's accusations were justified. Among other misdemeanors Innes had allegedly claimed that Henry VIII was "frying in Hell," a proposition that could no doubt be persuasively defended on a number of grounds but that in Innes's case merely denoted his own hostility to the Reformation. He also believed that Catholic Italy was better governed than Protestant England, and that not three of his parishioners in Harwich would be saved.[95]

The commissioners' report was thoroughly documented, and at least one of the signatories—the Earl Rivers—was probably a papist himself, while Harbottle Grimston was no friend of schism or nonconformity. But the Court of High Commission chose to regard the case as a struggle for power between clergy and laity. They ruled in favor of Innes and denounced "the strangeness, insolency, and ill consequence of this proceeding by private men against the highest ecclesiastical court in England."[96] The burden of this charge, presumably directed against Innes's opponents in Harwich, is not entirely clear to me, and the whole case would repay more thorough investigation. But the behavior of the High Commission must have demonstrated to many in Essex the magnitude of the threat posed by Laud's party to the ecclesiastical power of the laity.

Frustrated at home, the Puritan aristocrats turned their attention across the sea, where the power of Antichrist might be more effectively contested. In April of 1629 Sir Nathaniel Rich received a letter from the West Indies describing an uninhabited island named Catalina, off the coast of Central America, which might prove suitable for colonization. In the following year Warwick, Pym, and Rich organized their friends and allies into a corporation for settling the island, whose name they changed to Providence.

The history of the Providence Island Company has been recounted in exhaustive, and rather disorderly detail by A. P. Newton.[97] Its members included virtually all the leading Puritan aristocrats, many of whom were related by ties of blood and marriage as well as by religious affinity. There were Sir Thomas Barrington, who served as deputy governor in 1633–34, his brothers-in-law Sir Richard Knightley and Sir Gilbert Gerrard, his cousin John Hampden, and his nephew-in-law Oliver St. John. Other members included Lord Brooke, Lord Saye and Seale, Benjamin Rudyerd, Sir William Waller, and Warwick's brother-in-law Sir Thomas Cheke. As Christopher Hill was observed, the roster of Providence Island adventurers is very nearly a roll call of opposition leaders in the Long Parliament.[98]

The name Providence was richly connotative. It suggested that the island, whose existence had been disclosed just a month after the dissolution of Parliament, had been provided by God as an instrument of His grand design. Providence Island was insignificant in itself. True, it abounded in parrots, tobacco, cedars, wild vines, and fig trees, and the surrounding waters teemed with fish.[99] But it was not the island's natural resources that attracted the attention of these Puritan gentlemen—not even the tobacco. The value of the island lay in its strategic location. Providence was close enough to the Mexican coast to serve as an advance base for English penetration into Central America, which would be facilitated by the conversion of the natives to Protestant Christianity. The purpose of the enterprise was defined by John Pym as "the furtherance of that great work of subverting the Spanish tyranny in those parts and planting the Gospel." Providence Island could also furnish a haven for privateers seeking to sever the main artery of the Spanish Empire by intercepting the annual treasure fleet. It could become a Caribbean (and Protestant) Dunkirk, at a time when the Dunkirkers were inflicting cruel losses on English shipping, especially that of Colchester. Since American treasure, which sustained the Spanish war effort, was, in Pym's words "the great support of popery in all parts of Christendom," its capture would therefore be the most effective way to defend the Reformed church in the Old World as well.[100]

In 1626 Sir Nathaniel Rich had proposed to Parliament the formation of a joint-stock company to wage war on Spain. The Providence Island Company was the realization of that design. The policy of imperial aggrandizement, which Charles refused to embrace, would be carried on through private enterprise. Our knowledge of its ultimate failure should not lead us to dismiss this project as inherently fantastic. The aspirations of Warwick, Rich, and Pym were no wilder, after all, than those of Cortes and Pizarro. If a band of papist cutthroats could conquer the Americas for Satan, then a few resolute Englishmen, having converted the natives to the true Gospel, might win it back for the Lord.

Modern historians are inclined to regard as anachronistic the Warwick group's animus against Spain, which would later inspire the foreign policy of Oliver Cromwell. Since a declining Spain no longer posed a serious threat to English security, it is suggested that Hispanophobia had become an obsolete prejudice, the relic of an age of lethal fanaticism now happily gone by. The argument may have some force when applied to Cromwell's Caribbean expedition in 1656, but it has little relevance to the 1630s. Throughout that decade European Protestantism was threatened with extinction by Catholic armies that were being financed by gold and silver from Spanish America. The increasingly visible symptoms of Spain's fundamental weakness merely made the fabulous wealth of her colonies a more tempting and accessible prize.[101] The Protestant imperialists were not interested in preserving a balance of power between Christ and Antichrist.

Given this eschatological and geopolitical perspective, the leaders of the Providence Island Company were bound to regard with mixed feelings the flow of settlers to Massachusetts Bay. Warwick, it is true, had granted them the land in the first place, assigning to John Humphries and John Endicott in 1628 the territory he had received by lot as a member of the Council for New England.[102] Other members of the company, especially Lords Saye and Brooke, were involved in a premature venture to colonize southern Connecticut. There is even evidence that Sir Thomas Barrington considered emigration to New England himself in 1634–35.[103] But New England was remote from the main theater of conflict. Warwick could heartily endorse John Winthrop's ambition "to raise a bulwark against the kingdom of Antichrist which the Jesuits labor to rear up in all places of the world," but he could not believe that Armageddon would be fought out anywhere near Boston.[104] Warwick and Pym therefore repeatedly attempted to divert the flow of emigrants from New England to the Caribbean, and even to encourage settlers to migrate from Massachusetts to Providence Island, just as Cromwell later attempted to transplant New England colonists to Jamaica. As one can readily imagine, these efforts were not appreciated by the leaders of the Bay Colony.[105]

The strategy of the Warwick group, and its dependence on divine assistance, required that the colony on Providence Island become both a pirates' nest and a Puritan utopia. Would-be pirates were easy enough to recruit in the economically stricken England of the 1630s, but godly ones were harder to come by. Despite the efforts of Sir Thomas Barrington to enlist suitable colonists, the emigrants who were most committed to planting the Gospel in the New World tended to prefer New England to the Mosquito Coast.[106] Few of the Providence Islanders were remarkable for piety or discipline. There was constant conflict between the colonists and their Puritan ministers. By 1635 the hope of creating an insular Geneva had been abandoned, and the island was treated merely as a base for privateers.[107] In 1641 the settlement was wiped out by the Spanish.

The Providence Island venture is of scant importance in British colonial history, except as the forerunner of Cromwell's Western Design. Its significance for English political development is considerably greater. It was largely through the Providence Island Company that the continuity of political puritanism and the coherence of its leadership were preserved during the eleven years of Personal Rule, until royal policy could once again be challenged in the two houses of Parliament.

The coincidence of severe economic depression with the suspension of Parliament made the taxpayers of Essex doubly resentful of royal exactions, and doubly suspicious of fiscal innovations. During the years of dearth, 1629–1631, there were repeated protests by the grand jury against the amount levied on the county in composition for purveyance. It was alleged that at £3,000 per annum Essex was the most heavily assessed shire in the kingdom.[108] In 1633 even the future Royalist leader Sir John Lucas complained that his rate had been unwarrantably increased.[109] It was charged that His Majesty's commissioners were making new infringements on gentlemen's property rights, confiscating firewood laid up for the winter and seizing pigeons and poultry to feed the falcons of the royal mews. It was probably in connection with purveyance that a royal servant named Andrew Windsor suffered "violence and wrong" at the hands of the officers of Colchester in July 1631.[110]

Most offensive of all were the activities of the saltpeter men. The principal source of saltpeter, essential to the manufacture of gunpowder, was pigeon dung. The farmers of Essex were irritated by the saltpeter men invading their barns and dovecots, and, on one occasion, by their attempt to commandeer farm buildings for use as workhouses to refine the saltpeter. Both Sir Thomas Barrington and Sir William Masham took up the cause of the farmers, for which they were summoned to London and reprimanded by the lords of the Admirality.[111]

Purveyance was, at least in principle, a familiar and well-established tax. More alarming were the Crown's fiscal innovations. In 1630–31 at least £1,389 was extracted from 121 Essex men on the pretext that they had failed to purchase knighthoods on Charles's coronation. These fines "in distraint of knighthood" fell most heavily on the gentry and clothiers of north-central Essex and Colchester—precisely the region most affected by the trade depression. By the spring of 1631 defaulters were being compelled to pay thrice their assessments in the subsidy rolls.[112] If the knighthood fines fell most heavily on clothiers, other industrialists were alienated by the Crown's attempt to establish monopolies in salt manufacture (1631) and brewing (1638).[113] But all these grievances were minor compared to the great fiscal schemes of the 1630s: Forest Fines and Ship Money.

The idea of reasserting royal title to lands within the medieval Forest of Essex had been considered as early as 1630, but it was not until August 15, 1634, that the sheriff of Essex was ordered to make a survey of encroachments on the forest since the reign of Henry III.[114] In September the Forest Court met at Stratford Langthorne, presided over by the king's Justice-in-Eyre, none other than Warwick's younger brother, the Earl of Holland.[115] At the first session the attorney-general, Sir John Finch, announced that he had unearthed a document from the reign of Edward I declaring the forest to cover the southern two-thirds of Essex, and demanded to know "how his master had lost every inch of it." According to Warwick's own account, he and the rest of the Essex gentry were dumbfounded at the extent of the royal claim. "If I had had the spirit of divination what Mr. Attorney would have been at," he wrote the council, "myself and many of the lords and freeholders would have been there with their evidences and charters." When Warwick begged for time to prepare the county's case, Finch replied "that I fought like a man-of-war at my lock, but he was resolved to give no longer time than till morning." The next day Finch bullied a reluctant grand jury into endorsing the Crown's claims. One juror who dared to hold out was summoned to appear before Star Chamber.[116]

The land in question had been alienated by the Crown and brought under cultivation centuries earlier. As the Venetian ambassador, Anzolo Correr, perceived, the reassertion of royal claims was merely another of Charles's "subtle devices to supply monetary necessities." The king hoped to exact 20 percent of the value of the land from its owners in compensation.[117]

At the Michaelmas Sessions for 1634, the Essex grand jury protested against this royal aggression.[118] The landlords of the county conducted a search of the Tower archives, at a cost to themselves of £2,000, for evidence of their titles, which the Earl of Warwick presented to the king. The government was undeterred. "The situation daily becomes worse and more embittered," wrote Correr in March 1635. There was a real danger, he believed, of a "troublesome rising."[119] On April 6, 1635, the Forest Court reconvened. At this session, according to the future Royalist Sir Humphrey Mildmay, the solicitor-general, Sir Edward Littleton, "played the devil" against the county. Finch, now Chief Justice, delivered his judgment, reluctantly endorsed by an uncomfortable Earl of Holland, that the ruling made at the previous session should stand.[120]

The issue of the forest lands seems to have lain dormant for the next year and a half, perhaps because the king's attention had shifted to the matter of Ship Money. Writs for the collection of the tax in coastal areas were issued in the fall of 1634, when Essex and Suffolk were jointly charged to provide £6,615. The next summer the levy was extended to inland parishes. Essex was rated at £8,000 per annum from 1635 through 1637, at £2,750 in 1638, when the tax was reduced throughout England, and again at £8,000 in 1639.[121]

It was an unfortunate time to introduce a new tax of questionable legality and lacking parliamentary sanction. Plague was raging in the county. The harvest of 1636 was a disaster.[122] After several years of recovery the cloth trade had collapsed again. Conditions were as bad in the clothing districts in 1636 as they had been in 1629. Clothiers went bankrupt, and once again cloth workers were threatening to rebel sooner than starve.[123] And yet, one of the objects of the Ship Money levy was precisely to tap commercial and industrial wealth more effectively, thereby shifting the burden of taxation from land to liquid capital.[124]

It is no wonder, therefore, that there was a good deal of foot dragging and prevarication over Ship Money. Constables refused to assess their neighbors; towns and individuals quibbled over the rating.[125] "I profess there is no penny that is not forced, God help me, amongst the people," complained the sheriff, Sir Humphrey Mildmay, in July 1636. By the end of the year Mildmay's collection was £1,900 short of the required sum. The arrears for Essex were the highest in the country.[126]

Sir Humphrey Mildmay's elder brother, Sir Henry Mildmay of Wanstead, was a self-seeking courtier but a consistent opponent of the Arminian faction. Unlike his brother, however, Sir Humphrey made not the slightest pretense of puritanism. His diary reveals him as a whimsical and feckless country gentleman, fond of the bottle and no stranger to the brothel. As a diarist, though not as a public servant, he reminds one a bit of Pepys. His religion was an unreflective Anglicanism. He had no great objection to popery, however; he admired a sermon he heard preached by a Catholic priest in London. Sir Humphrey's rare fits of piety tended to coincide with hangovers. He enjoyed the company of parsons who shared his taste for gaming and boozing—exactly the kind of "scandalous minister" that the Puritans were determined to extirpate from the Church of England. But Sir Humphrey laughed at Puritans.[127]

Such a man was not likely to wield much moral authority among his godlier neighbors, and it was from Puritans that Sir Humphrey encountered the most troublesome opposition. Many of the chief constables, he complained, were "discipliners" and as such "very zealous in all causes that concern the hindrance of his Majesty's service." Furthermore, the common folk were being encouraged to resist by their betters: "such as I hope the board knows right well," Mildmay remarked significantly, "and what their good wills are to this service."[128] He was clearly referring to the Earl of Warwick and his friends. Ship Money was particularly hard to gather in the hundreds of Harlow, Rochford, and Barstaple, where the earl held the right of appointing bailiffs. Warwick and Masham were among the eight "persons of quality" who in November of 1636 were still flatly

refusing to pay. Sir Thomas Barrington apparently paid his own assessment, but his parish of Hatfield Broad Oak was among the most
refractory in the county.[129]

Warwick and Masham were not the only members of the Providence Island Company to withhold Ship Money; they were joined
by Lord Saye and Seale and John Hampden. Their behavior may
have been part of a concerted strategy to force a legal test of the con-
stitutionality of the new tax. If so, it succeeded in May of 1637, when
the government began proceedings in the Court of Exchequer
against John Hampden, with results that are well known.

On January 16, 1637, Warwick appeared before King Charles to
explain his opposition to Ship Money and to urge the recall of Parliament. According to the Venetian ambassador, Warwick virtually
admitted that he had used his influence to obstruct the levy. His
tenants, he said, "were all old and accustomed to the mild rule of
Queen Elizabeth and King James." They were unwilling to die
"under the stigma of having, at the end of their lives, signed away
the liberties of the realm." They held themselves in honor bound to
transmit to their posterity the "sacred treasure" of law that they had
inherited. Warwick, for his part, could neither condemn nor coerce
them. If Charles would only recall Parliament, ally himself with
France to recover the Palatinate, and assert British hegemony on the
high seas, then Warwick was prepared to stake his head that Parliament would grant whatever Charles might ask. For his own part, he
was ready "to sacrifice his blood as well as his goods for his Majesty."[130]

It is significant that Warwick raised no objection to the weight of
taxation per se, nor did he allude to the depressed state of the Essex
economy. Not that he was either ignorant or unconcerned; throughout the previous summer he had been meeting with weavers and
clothiers, attempting to seek solutions to the crisis of the industry.
But for Warwick, as for the Puritan opposition generally, the solution to the domestic crisis was imperial expansion, which necessitated an aggressively Protestant foreign policy. Such a policy might
prove expensive at first, but ultimately the plundering of the Spanish Empire would not only pay for itself but return stupendous profits. There is no reason to doubt the sincerity of Warwick's offer to
spend blood and treasure in this cause. Whether many Essex taxpayers shared the zeal of the Puritan leadership may well be doubted,

however. Warwick's declaration contained the germ of later conflicts. For all the piety of their objectives, Cromwell's taxes were no
more popular than those of Charles.

The Venetian ambassador was impressed with the "subtlety and
sagacity" of Warwick's performance but observed that the king was
not. Charles listened to his speech with a frosty smile, thanked him
for his expression of loyalty, and ignored his advice. "We see this
grave matter approaching greater dangers," Correr concluded,
"with little hope of any remedy that may not prove very unpleasant
and bitter."[131]

Warwick's appeal to Charles was part of a broader agitation
among the aristocracy for the recall of Parliament. Correr reported
that secret meetings were being held to prepare a remonstrance to
the king, wherein the petitioners promised, if Parliament were summoned, to augment by one-fourth any subsidies that might be voted.
The very day after this dispatch, Warwick was meeting in London
with his fellow Providence Island adventurers, Saye and Seale and
Brooke. Ostensibly they were negotiating a marriage settlement for
Warwick's son Charles, but it is very probable that they talked of
more than dowries and entails.[132]

Nothing seems to have come of this remonstrance. There was a
brief surge of hope that the king would adopt at least a part of the
program proposed to him by Warwick by concluding a French alliance. But on Wentworth's advice the treaty fell through.[133] In the
event, Charles's only concession to the imperialists was an enlarged
commission to the Providence Island Company to privateer in the
West Indies. The members invested an additional £100,000 in this
enterprise in the summer of 1637.[134]

Meanwhile, resistance in Essex to Ship Money had collapsed.
This may have been due in part to the declaration of the royal
judges in February in favor of the tax's legality; in part to the prosecution of sixty defaulters in the Exchequer; in part to the willingness
of Warwick and his allies to attend the outcome of Hampden's case;
in part perhaps to some lingering hope that Holland's faction at
Whitehall might yet prevail with Charles to revive the French alliance.[135] But the decisive factor was the character of the new sheriff,
Sir John Lucas of Colchester, who demonstrated what the determined execution of royal policy might achieve, even in a county as
obstinate and troublesome as Essex.[136]

Lucas was a man of an entirely different stamp from the engagingly disreputable Mildmay. He was a kind of provincial Strafford, loyal, arrogant, and unpopular. He was a High Churchman by upbringing. His father had been a close friend of Bishop Harsnett, who had taken a personal interest in young John's religious education.[137] Sir John had already been involved in bitter litigation with his neighbors in Colchester. He had attempted to suppress windmills that competed with a water mill in his possession; he had torn up the town's water pipes that ran through his property.[138] He was also an extraordinarily efficient sheriff. In January of 1637, when the high constables of one Essex hundred refused to assess the inhabitants, Lucas himself drove half a dozen wagons to the constables' homes and distrained their possessions to the value of the entire sum levied on their district.[139] In May the king commended Lucas for his zeal. He had assessed the entire county, with the exception of two parishes, an accomplishment that, as Charles noted, had never been achieved before.[140] One hopes Sir John savored this commendation, because in 1642 he was to pay very dearly for having antagonized his neighbors.

The rates imposed by Lucas were neither inequitable nor particularly onerous. Of 1,366 taxpayers in twenty-one parishes, 1,056, or 77 percent, were assessed at less than 10s. (Of 597 individuals rated at less than 10s., 438, or 73 percent, paid less than 5s.) The median assessment for fifteen members of the Braintree vestry was 14s. The leading clothiers of Braintree (Adrian Mott) and Dedham (Samuel Sherman) paid £1 12s. 8d. and £1 13s. 0d. respectively. Only a few really wealthy clothiers were rated over £2, like Thomas Guyon (£2 11s. 6d.), Robert Crane (£2 15s. 0d.) and Henry Ennew (£2 15s. 0d.), all of Coggeshall.[141]

The landed magnates of the county paid a great deal more, but then they were a great deal richer. There is no evidence of political favoritism or persecution. Warwick's assessment, at £40, was exceeded by those of Lord Petre, Viscount Bayning, and Earl Rivers, all of whom paid £50. Henry Neville of Cressing Temple, the court candidate in the elections to the Short Parliament, paid £18. Sir Thomas Wiseman, who had participated in the attempt to deny the election of 1628 to Sir Francis Barrington, paid £16. Sir Thomas Barrington and Sir William Masham were assessed at only £15.[142]

Lucas was able to collect the entire sum of £8,000 imposed on the county, and he established a precedent that his successors as sheriff were able to follow. According to M. D. Gordon, the Ship Money writs for 1635–1638 brought in a total of £25,698 from Essex, leaving a mere £1,052 uncollected. If this was absolutism, it seemed to be working tolerably well.[143]

Meanwhile, the government pressed forward with its scheme to extract swingeing fines from landholders within the old royal forest. In February 1637 the Forest Court convened again under the Earl of Holland. Holland ordered all fences and enclosures in the forest to be pulled down to allow the deer full range over the inhabitants' crops.[144] Garbled by rumor, this proclamation may have encouraged the rioters who in 1639 tore down enclosures on the land of Sir Thomas Barrington and Lord Morley, within Hatfield Forest.[145] But its intent was merely to force tenants to compound with the king. Some did so; Sir Humphrey Mildmay compounded for £150.[146]

The added revenue, however, hardly compensated for the political damage done by such measures. Holland lost such credit as he possessed in the county. His attempts to influence the elections of 1640 in favor of the Crown was foredoomed by his behavior in 1637.[147] In June a newsletter reported that most of the gentry were preparing to give in, but added that "what the peasants will do is not yet known." The humbler tenants were angry but leaderless. "When they meet together they talk at large, but being divided they soon become crestfallen."[148] Despite this lack of leadership, however, Correr wrote in October of 1637 that Charles had been forced by the threat of revolt to delay the proceedings. "The question of the forests," the ambassador believed, was "at once more difficult and odious" than Ship Money, because it posed a more urgent threat to the rights of property.[149]

As the Venetian ambassador perceived, Charles's unwavering support for Laud's ecclesiastical program made a reconciliation with Parliament impossible, since Parliament would immediately attack the archbishop. The king, Correr believed, had even more to fear from religious than from secular discontent.[150] But we need not contrast the two. The combination of arbitrary taxation with ecclesiastical innovation magnified popular hostility to both, since tyranny and popery were so intimately associated in the minds of English Protestants.

Furthermore, the seemingly endless succession of temporal disasters provided incontrovertible evidence that God was angry with
England. These judgments, tokens of divine displeasure, fatally undercut the legitimacy of royal authority in church and state. In November 1635 John Dod preached in Coggeshall that "the new mix-
ture of religion that is commanded in the churches" had brought
down "the plague of God" upon the land. In the same town a year
and a half later, a suspended minister named Edward Sparhawk explained that "the true cause of judgments in the land"—of the bad
harvests, the visitations of the plague, the decay of trade, and the
"doubling of taxes"—was the Laudian counter-reformation: the
railing of altars, bowing at the name of Jesus, "treading down of
God's people," and the officially sanctioned "profanation of the
Lord's day." King Charles was again compared to Manasseh, who
had erected altars to strange gods and consorted with witches and
wizards, and whom God therefore had delivered into the hands of
the Assyrians. "Until these causes be removed," Sparhawk concluded, "the plague will not cease." Robert Aylett, in reporting this
sermon to Laud, observed that the town where it was preached was
still refusing to pay Ship Money.[151]

The godly sought to deflect divine wrath by holding fasts and
days of public repentence—a practice that was to be continued by
the Long Parliament. In June 1636 Laud's commissary reported
that the people of Leighs in Rochford hundred spent the entire day
in church fasting and praying and listening to the preaching of a
Scottish minister. Such activities were common, he added, throughout the surrounding area. Rochford was, of course, Warwick's territorial base; we can safely assume that there was fasting and preaching wherever godly gentlemen held sway.[152] The government
naturally rejected as subversive this metaphysical explanation of
temporal misfortune and therefore sought to suppress the public
fast. The Laudians, according to the Suffolk minister Robert Reyce,
thought fasting "as hateful as conventicles" and identified it with
puritanism. Thus, the godly were deprived of what they considered
their most effectual means of collective deliverance from calamity.[153]

The godly had learned from John Foxe—whose works Laud attempted to suppress in 1637—that the faithful must expect to endure persecution until the ultimate, and inevitable, victory of Christ
over Antichrist. As James Harrison reminded the Barrington house-

hold early in 1635, "It is a good sign that the case is good with us, when we have affliction and when Satan troubles us." The godly might comfort themselves with the reflection that "tyrants are not always masters of their own works." Even oppression and apostasy were part of God's plan, since "all the enemies of God's church are in His power."[154]

In the summer of 1636 the funeral of John Rogers of Dedham afforded the godly an opportunity to affirm their solidarity in the face of persecution. Rogers had expressed his willingness to die on the gallows if it would help rid the church of idolatry. As it happened, he died in bed, although it was rumored that his end had been hastened by the prospect of losing his lectureship. Just four years later Rogers's successor would urge this same congregation to fortify themselves against the halter and the stake by meditating on Foxe's *Book of Martyrs*. But Rogers's funeral very nearly ended in a less edifying tragedy. The Dedham church was packed to three times its normal capacity. The gallery began to give way beneath the weight, and it seemed for a few agonizing moments that the congregation below would be crushed. It would have been a dreadful blow to the entire household of faith, especially since the godly had recently hailed as an act of divine justice the death of some papists in a similar accident during a secret conventicle in Blackfriars. But, as Henry Jacie wrote to John Winthrop in Massachusetts, God honored the great preacher, even in death, with a miracle: the gallery held. Jacie's letter is a caveat against exaggerating the contrast between Protestant rationalism and Catholic superstition. A Jesuit might reasonably have asked how Rogers's posthumous miracle differed from those attributed to Catholic saints, which Puritans found so objectionable.[155]

With John Rogers's death, the informal leadership of the godly preachers in Essex passed to Stephen Marshall of Finchingfield, who by 1637 was said to have gained control of the consciences of all the leading lay Puritans of the county and to have grown very rich in the process. He was raising money among the faithful to finance the preaching of the Gospel in Wales, and to aid John Dury's schemes for the union of all Protestants.

Marshall was to become one of the great clerical tribunes of the English Revolution. In a few years he would be exhorting the godly—in Parliament and on the field of battle—to smite the Amalekites hip and thigh. For the moment, though, he was waiting on the Lord. Laud's vicar-general, Sir Nathaniel Brent, found Marshall's circumspection extremely frustrating. Marshall, he said, "is held to be a dangerous person, but exceeding cunning. No man doubteth but he hath an inconformable heart, but externally he observeth all."[156]

So not even Marshall, the future radical, was yet prepared to advocate rebellion. Nor did the analogy with Manasseh, invoked by Dod and Sparhawke, encourage overt resistance. Manasseh, after all, had repented, so might Charles. But at the same time, even a preacher as moderate as old James Harrison, who made obsequious professions of conformity to Brent in 1637, insisted that the Christian must obey God rather than man.[157] This principle served to justify popular resistance to the railing of altars, which began in earnest in 1636.[158] Opposition to the new scheme was strongest, according to Robert Aylett, in the large clothing towns. Dissidents cited the example of the churches in London, where it was alleged that the altars had not been railed. Even when Laud's orders were obeyed and the communion table placed altarwise in the chancel, it was often moved back again into the body of the nave during the celebration of communion, thus defeating the whole purpose of the operation.[159]

The struggle was particularly acute in Colchester. When James Wheeler, the churchwarden of St. Botolph's, refused to rail the altar, his house was ransacked by the authorities, and Wheeler himself was excommunicated and imprisoned.[160] In St. Runwald's parish, however, the dissidents took the offensive. When the rector, Thomas Newcomen, denied communion to all who refused to receive it kneeling at the altar rail, he was indicted at the borough Quarter Sessions for violation of the Elizabethan settlement. The case became a Puritan *cause célèbre*. The redoubtable William Prynne published a detailed account of the proceedings in the hope that it would provide "a precedent for all England to follow."[161]

The unpopularity of the Laudian regime was heightened in June 1637 by the public mutilation of John Bastwick of Colchester and his fellow sufferers, Henry Burton and William Prynne. Eight months later the young John Lilburne was flogged through the streets of London for distributing Bastwick's books, which were no doubt being read in Bastwick's native Colchester as well. Already there were signs of increased separatist activity in the town. A baker named Cole was holding conventicles and maintaining "that it is impiety to hinder any man from preaching to whom God hath given extraordinary understanding and the gift of utterance."[162] Thomas Lambe, a Baptist evangelist later associated with the Levellers, was also preaching in Colchester.

In Maldon, too, where in the previous generation George Gifford had led "God's little flock" against "Satan's legions," there were signs of increasing radicalism. An itinerant preacher named Enoch Grey alluded to the punishment of Bastwick, Burton, and Prynne by warning Laud and Charles that there was "a Star Chamber in heaven" that also had power to crop ears and slit noses. Grey took up the thesis of Hooker, Dod, and Sparhawk that "the sins of the King, as the sins of Manasseh, are visited upon the kingdom." Chief among Charles's sins was his marriage to a "Babylonish woman." Grey prayed for the king's conversion, but he hinted that the people should arm themselves if all prayers failed.[163]

Even as late as the spring of 1638, however, very few men were prepared to contemplate forceful resistance. For most, the only alternative to acquiescence or passive resistance was exile. In New England, as Thomas Weld wrote back to his former congregation in Terling, the godly were the majority. "Here, blessed be the Lord God forever, our ears are not beaten nor the air filled with oaths." The sacrament was properly administered, fast days were observed, scandalous behavior was suppressed. Naturally, God favored the colonists with the good weather and abundant harvests that he denied England.[164]

It was a tempting prospect. In March 1639 Lord Maynard informed Laud that "incredible numbers" of well-to-do clothiers—the social group most opposed to both Ship Money and Arminianism—were planning to emigrate, which would desperately impoverish the parishes that they left behind. Maynard's report may have contributed to the government's decision the following month to forbid ships to sail for New England without license.[165] It was no doubt this order that inspired Enoch Grey's prayer that God would "utterly destroy those who are enemies to the plantations."[166] In August 1637 the Star Chamber decreed that no more nonconforming ministers were to emigrate, and that those who had departed without permission were to be returned to England. The noose was tightening. The familiar stories of John Foxe were becoming uncomfortably pertinent.[167]

Not even Foxe, however, provided a theory of insurrection. The suspension of Parliament still held the opposition spellbound. The collection of Ship Money proceeded in 1637 and 1638. Only £145, or 1.3 percent of the total remained uncollected during these two years.[168] There is thus no sign whatever that popular discontent was about to flare spontaneously into rebellion. A spark was needed to touch off an insurgent movement. That spark was provided by the Scottish rebellion in the summer of 1638.

On August 5, 1638, an interesting discussion took place in the Earl of Warwick's garden at Great Leighs between a suspended preacher from Norfolk named Jeremiah Burroughs and the parson of Chelmsford, Dr. John Michelson. Burroughs enthusiastically defended the behavior of the Scottish people in binding themselves by solemn covenant to the defense of their Protestant religion. He advanced a theory of popular sovereignty. It was lawful, thought Burroughs, to take up arms against a tyrant who had violated his coronation oath. Dr. Michelson was horrified. He had signed a petition in support of Thomas Hooker. Cotton Mather has a good word for his learning and piety. But Michelson firmly believed that prayers and tears were the only weapons that Christians might wield against duly constituted authority. Burrough's apology for revolution scandalized him so much that he sent a complete report of the conversation to Dr. John Lambe, Laud's Dean of the Arches.[169] It was Burroughs, rather than Michelson, who had the future (at least the immediate future) in his bones. Three years later Michelson's commitment to passive resistance would cost him his living, and very nearly his life, at the hands of Parliamentary soldiers.

11 / The Puritan Moment

'Tis prophesied in the Revelation, that the
Whore of Babylon shall be destroyed with fire
and sword, and what do you know, but this is
the time of her ruin, and that we are the men
that must help to pull her down?

—*Edward Symmons, quoting captured Parliamentary
soldiers, in* Scripture Vindicated, *1644*

The Greeks have a proverb, "If a stone falls on an egg, alas for the
egg; if an egg falls on a stone—alas for the egg."[1] The proverb expresses the sensible desire of most ordinary men and women to have
as little as possible to do with history. Plebeian wisdom recognizes
that when great events impinge on unimportant people, the latter
are likely to suffer.

The stone fell on Hugh Harr, a laborer of the parish of Vange, in
April 1639, when he was conscripted for service in Scotland in the
first Bishops' War. In Scotland, Harr fell lame, "partly by the coldness of the air, and partly by a stab in the thigh," and was sent home
in a carrier's wagon. He never regained his strength, despite unsuccessful trips to Bath to take the waters and to London for treatment
at St. Bartholomew's hospital. He was unemployable; he had no
pension. The small village of Vange, having financed Harr's fruitless
expeditions, denied him further relief. Two years after his service to
king and country, Harr was "utterly destitute of means whereby he
may subsist."[2]

Harr's bad luck was not uncommon. Soldiers maimed in the service of their king, or for that matter of Parliament, counted themselves lucky to secure a pension of £3 per year.[3] It is not surprising
that freedom from conscription was one of the demands of the New
Model Army. But if conscription was detested by the lower orders,
it was feared by men of property. Educated Englishmen knew of
the havoc wrought by marauding soldiers in Germany, where the
wars of religion still raged. Even in Essex there had been alarming

mutinies in the 1620s. Since time out of mind, the disbanded soldier was the most dreaded of sturdy vagabonds.

Conscription was thus a dangerously unpopular expedient, even in a just and necessary war, and in the minds of most Englishmen the Scottish Protestants were precisely the wrong enemy. Hugh Harr had submitted docilely, but in the same spring of 1639 a husband-man of Rettendon declared that if he were pressed, the king would be the first person he would aim at. Such expressions of disloyalty had not been recorded since the accession of King James. Despite the economic hardships of the preceding decades, lower-class mal-contents had refrained from attacking the Crown directly. But now the king's very sovereignty was impugned. When a loyalist in Saffron Walden maintained that Charles was the lawful ruler of the three British kingdoms, a laborer commented ominously, "the more's the pity."[4]

The first Bishops' War ended ignominiously. By July the soldiers were straggling back, "not well-contented," as the future Royalist Sir Humphrey Mildmay noted.[5] Many of them failed to return their arms to the magazine at Harwich, probably because they had sold them on the way. The Scots' revolt destroyed what legitimacy Charles's Personal Rule possessed. In 1639 the Crown's most lucra-tive new source of income almost completely dried up; only £331 of the £8,000 Ship Money for which Essex had been assessed could be collected. (In the previous four years the government had been able to bring in all but £1,052 of the £26,750 demanded—a return of 96 percent).[6] The government's insolvency, and the defeat of English forces by the rebellious Scots, compelled Charles to summon Parlia-ment in the spring of 1640. In Essex the elections proved to be a trial of strength between what would soon become the Royalist and Par-liamentary parties in a civil war.

In the weeks before the election, preachers associated with War-wick and his friends campaigned energetically for the return of Puri-tan members. Foremost among these clerical activists was Stephen Marshall of Finchingfield. Even Marshall's enemies acknowledged his ability to stir a popular audience. The son of a glover, Marshall was described by one hostile observer as being "of middle strature, thick-shouldered with a swarthy complexion, his eyes always rolling in his head." He dressed negligently and was "acquainted with all the vulgar proverbs and odd country phrases and by-words, which he would sprinkle up and down in his sermon, which captivated people at a strange rate."[7] Another activist was John Powtey, the Scots curate of Dunmow Priory, who accused Lord Maynard, now the leader of the court faction in the county, of "lacking zeal to the Gospel"—a "notorious scandal," according to his lordship. Warwick, meanwhile, sent letters to the captains of the county's trained bands, urging support for the opposition.[8]

The godly candidates did well in the boroughs, where, as one disgruntled Royalist put it, most of the inhabitants were "mean-conditioned, most factious, and few subsidy-men." Naturally, therefore, they were mostly Puritan as well. In Colchester, despite the efforts of the Earl of Holland to promote a supporter of the court, the corporation returned Sir William Masham and Harbottle Grimston, the son of Sir Harbottle and recorder of Colchester.[9] At Harwich and Maldon the results were less clear. Of the Harwich members, Sir Thomas Cheke was Warwick's brother-in-law, but Sir John Jacobs, the farmer of the royal customs, was aligned with the court. The political sympathies, if any, of John Porter, the recorder of Maldon and the member for that borough, are unknown, but the other Maldon representative, Sir Henry Mildmay of Wanstead, was in Warwick's camp. Sir Humphrey Mildmay disgustedly described his brother riding "in triumph with his rabble." After his election Sir Henry rode on to the Earl of Warwick's home at Great Leighs to help out with the election of the knights of the shire.

The conflict was hottest at the county elections in Chelmsford. The Crown sought the return of Henry Neville of Cressing Temple, an energetic supporter of the Laudian program. The opposition's candidates were Sir Thomas Barrington and Sir Harbottle Grimston, the father of the new member for Colchester. Sir Humphrey Mildmay rode up to Chelmsford with a crowd from Maldon and found there "such a multitude of all sorts of people as I never before saw." Court supporters found the mood of the crowd ugly. "Threatening speeches" were addressed to the Earl of Carlisle, Lord Maynard and "the rest of the gentry"—those, that is, in Neville's camp. One man was arrested for brandishing a sword and shouting "that if Neville had the day, they would tear the gentlemen in pieces." The man was arrested but later bailed, "to his great popular glory," by no less a personage than the Earl of Warwick himself, who was obviously willing and able to channel popular turmoil toward political ends. The possibility of violence was averted when Neville lost heavily.[10]

Neville's account of his defeat is instructive. He blamed it on the demagogy of the Puritan ministers, like Stephen Marshall, who had packed the county elections with Puritans from the corporate towns, and on the price revolution of the preceding century and a half, which had eroded the value of the electoral property qualification. When the franchise had been limited to 40s. freeholders, he correctly observed, "that sum was then worth £20 in present value." "It would be a great quiet to the state," Neville argued, if the property qualification were adjusted for inflation, "for then gentlemen would be looked up to, and it would save ministers a great deal of pains in preaching [away] from their own churches."[11] It was a tidy synthesis of social, economic, and ideological explanations.

Neville's reaction betrays a conservative's premonition of the social dangers posed by Puritan populism. Neville's fears—very well founded ones as the event would prove—were shared by his principal supporter, William Lord Maynard, who was yoked in uneasy tandem with Warwick in the lord lieutenancy. "I shall not," Maynard wrote petulantly to Barrington, "suffer myself hereafter upon the persuasion of others to appear in any popular assemblies, where fellows without shirts challenge as good a person as myself."[12] Maynard was not giving up public life; indeed, he reaffirmed his commitment to serving his king. Rather, he was repudiating the parliamentary process, on the grounds that it was rigged against the aristocracy.

The first Parliament of 1640 lasted for only twenty-two days. During the brief session, Harbottle Grimston the younger emerged as the chief Essex spokesman, Sir Nathaniel Rich having died in 1636. Grimston was the recorder of Colchester and one of the great lawyers of the seventeenth century. He was already self-confident enough to swap syllogisms on the floor of the Commons with John Selden.[13] At thirty-seven Grimston was on the threshold of a brilliant, if checkered, parliamentary career, which cast him finally in a piquant role of Speaker in the Restoration Parliament.[14] But this exaltation came only after a spell in prison at the time of Pride's Purge and an ensuing decade of political obscurity had moderated his radicalism. In 1640 he was one of the firebrands of the opposition, and the mouthpiece for the commercial and religious grievances of his Colchester constituents. The commonwealth, he declared, "hath been torn and macerated, and all the proprieties and liberties shaken; the church distracted, the Gospel and professors of it persecuted and the whole kingdom over-run with multitudes and swarms of projecting cater-worms and caterpillars, the worst of all the Egyptian plagues." Grimston minimized the danger from Scotland, since "a danger without the door" was of less moment than "the danger already upon our backs."[15]

The Short Parliament was dissolved in May, "to the much sorrow of all good men," wrote the Royalist Sir Humphrey Mildmay.[16] In the summer of 1640 the Crown attempted a counterattack. Opposition leaders were harassed and their studies rifled; London aldermen were imprisoned for refusing a new Forced Loan. The sheriff of Essex, Sir Martin Lumley, was summoned with seven colleagues before the Star Chamber to answer for "great and supine negligence" in collecting Ship Money, and delinquents owing forest fines were summoned before the Earl of Holland's Forest Court.[17] Above all, the Crown was determined to silence the clerical opposition. When Convocation passed its new canons, requiring subscription to the suspicious "etcetera oath" and quarterly sermons in support of the royal prerogative, Matthew Newcomen preached a sermon in Dedham that conveys the desperation felt by Puritans in that summer. "I have now done with my text," he declared, "and so far as I know with my preaching in this place." He lamented the suppression of godly ministers and lecturers— "so many burning and shining lights . . . quenched, so many fountains that were wont to send forth streams of living water dammed up"—and predicted his own imminent silencing. Newcomen warned his flock against apostasy. If in the coming months "seducers" tried to mislead them, they must "cease to hear their instructions, whosoever they be." His followers should fortify themselves against possible death at the stake by meditating on Foxe's *Acts and Monuments*. (For those parishioners too poor or parsimonious to buy the complete work, Newcomen suggested an abridgement called *The Mirror of Martyrs*.) But Newcomen still urged nonresistance. "Never for anything resist or rise against the magistrate," he told listeners. "Avenge not yourselves, but commit your case to the Lord, to whom vengeance pertaineth."[18]

God's vengeance was not long in descending upon Charles, in the carnal form of the Scots army. The county of Essex was ordered to levy and arm seven hundred men and ship them north.[19] Thus, men were forced to choose between resisting the magistrate and supporting a war that most considered unnecessary at best and at worst downright wicked.

The attempt to raise a force from Essex against the Calvinist Scots was a fiasco. The county was charged to raise £2,400 in Coat and Conduct Money for the troops. Barely a quarter could be collected.[20] One reason for this reluctance was the conviction, expressed by Harbottle Grimston, that the real danger was "already upon our backs." In Colchester there were wild rumors in June that Irish saboteurs were planning to fire the town. Suspicious strangers had been seen inspecting "the oldest houses and those most combustible" in the narrow lanes under the city walls; an army of papists was said to be assembling "with great stores of armor" at Berechurch, the seat of the recusant Audleys. Some believed that the papists were led by Matthew Wren, the hated former bishop of Norwich; others thought Laud had arrived in person.

The mayor mustered fifty men of the trained bands, ordered the watches strengthened at the gates, and instructed the constables to make a privy search for the incendiaries. Some Irishmen (the wrong ones, it turned out) were duly apprehended. The trained bands, who had been issued powder and shot, took to drinking and firing their muskets at random. Someone beat up the drum and led a few apprentices straggling off to Berechurch; they returned without having engaged the papist host.[21] The affair had no immediate consequence, but in 1642 similar rumors were to touch off riots of a much more serious kind.

The soldiers, understandably enough, were even more recalcitrant than the taxpayers. They had, after all, substantially more to lose. We have already considered the case of Hugh Harr, who had the bad luck to be nabbed by the constables for the first Bishops' War. In the summer of 1640 those soldiers who did not desert became increasingly insubordinate. They demanded higher pay; they insisted on going north by land rather than sea; they insulted their officers; they extorted money and food by threats of violence.[22]

Some of the soldiers' outrages were no doubt mere acts of plunder. But a considerable number of the men had strong religious and political antipathies, if not yet very positive convictions. At Sampford

one Henry Crane incited fifty soldiers to loot the house of a gentleman named Henry Greene. Greene was a "base fellow," he declared,
and "they should do their country good to tear him in pieces."
Greene, who bought himself off with "money, victuals, and fair
speeches," was later sequestered as a Royalist.[23] The men of Captain
Rolleston's troop were reading Scottish propaganda which had been
smuggled to their quarters in Braintree by a Suffolk clothier.[24]

The Earl of Warwick was surprised to find the men "very jealous
in point of their religion." They had often asked him that their officers might take communion with them. The spirit of the New Model
was already afoot. Moreover, they were organizing themselves.
"Though they lie twelve or fifteen miles asunder," Warwick noted,
"yet they have continual intelligence one from another." In July
and August these soldiers took it upon themselves to "reform
churches" (the phrase comes from the Royalist Lord Maynard).[25]
More precisely, they set about destroying the Laudian innovations
and terrorizing the ministers who had supported them. At Radwinter they smashed the cherubim that the rector, Richard Drake,
had installed at his own expense.[26] At Bocking, whence the dean,
Dr. Barkham, had expelled Nehemiah Rogers,[27] they pulled up the
altar rails and burned them in front of their captain's quarters.
Then, they moved on to the neighboring village of Panfield, whose
rector, Edward Jenkinson, had preached that those who refused to
bow at the name of Christ "should bow in Hell hereafter." They
forced him to flee across the river in terror of his life. It is true that
the men's religious zeal had been quickened by a barrel of beer with
which Dr. Barkham had imprudently tried to pacify them.[28] But
they had also been reading Scottish propaganda while presumably
in their right wits.

More altar rails were smashed and burned at Chelmsford, Great
Braxted, Kelvedon, Great Holland, Chich St. Osyth, Elmstead, and
Icklinton, just across the Cambridgeshire border. At Stebbing the
home of a recusant was plundered; there were unspecified "outrages" at Great Bardfield. We know almost nothing about these rioters except, in a very few cases, their occupations. Those indicted for
the disturbance at Great Braxted, for example, included three husbandmen, a clothier, a comber, a weaver, a carpenter, and a blacksmith—a pretty fair cross-section of the middle third of the population. (The mass of laborers were relatively uninvolved in

ideologically motivated violence). The Braxted rioters came from seven different parishes. Conscription had made possible collective action by men who, in the normal course of things, would never have met. Moreover, the rioters showed solidarity with those arrested as ringleaders. The council had to order extra guards posted at Colchester Castle for fear the prisoners would be rescued by their comrades.[29]

Except perhaps at Chelmsford, where the culprit was a man reputedly "crazy in his brains," the rioters were purposeful and selective. The ministers of all the affected parishes were later sequestered, either for scandalous life and doctrine or for royalism. Most had already antagonized their congregations in one way or another. At Great Bardfield the curate was a Scot who had fled south to avoid taking the Covenant, and had denied poor relief to parishioners who attended Puritan sermons; the minister had refused communion to those who refused to kneel at the rail.[30] Edward Cherry, who held the livings of both Great Holland and Chich St. Osyth, supported Sunday sports, drank to excess, and devoted his infrequent sermons to promoting the Laudian reforms. Crackenthorpe of Bradwell was another notorious tippler.[31]

The political implications of these riots naturally aroused the council's suspicions that they were connived at by Warwick's faction.[32] The disorders certainly strengthened the position of the godly party. One trooper was overheard drinking Warwick's health as the "King of Essex." Warwick arrested him, it is true, but he used the incident to impress the government with the strength of his popular following. He pointedly informed the council that if anyone else had attempted the arrest, the entire company would have risen in arms.[33]

By September 1640 it was reported that the roads between London and Cambridge were unsafe for ministers to travel. In fact, it was only Laudians who were molested. When Richard Drake of Radwinter preached at the Bishop's Triennial Visitation that autumn in Great Dunmow, he needed an entire troop of foot (presumably supplied from the capital) to protect him against the rabble.[34] Lord Maynard, the king's leading supporter among the Essex laity, was physically and politically a broken man. His wife reported to the king that "his good name was blasted by the multitude only for the fervor and zeal to your Majesty's service." Maynard was dead within the year.[35] Warwick's position as the "King of Essex" was, for the moment, secure.

The elections to the Long Parliament were held in October, and this time the Country made a clean sweep of the borough seats. Sir Thomas Barrington now stood for Colchester (along with Harbottle Grimston), in order to clear a seat as knight of the shire for Warwick's son and heir.[36] When Holland tried again to intervene, on behalf of one Sir Thomas Ingram, the Colchester burgesses tartly replied that they had no intention of electing "a stranger, whose name was never heard of in these parts." Instead they needed representatives who understood the town's problems, chief among which were the "many impositions now laid upon trades."[37] Barrington and Grimston were chosen without incident. Sir John Jacobs was dropped by the borough of Harwich, and Sir Thomas Cheke and Sir Harbottle Grimston were returned. At Maldon, Sir Henry Mildmay retained his seat, while the town recorder, John Porter, was replaced by the Irish carpetbagger and land speculator John Clotworthy.[38] (Determined to secure Clotworthy's presence in the House, the opposition had arranged to elect him from a seat in Cornwall as well as Maldon.)

The county elections were a foregone conclusion. Sir Humphrey Mildmay rode to town three days before the polling but found "the news such that made me and Parson Webb come home without any stay at an early hour."[39] John Wenlock, a lawyer with similar views, stayed home in disgust; he knew what to expect after hearing of the elections in Suffolk.[40] This time the county members were Sir William Masham and Robert Rich, Warwick's son and heir. (Rich was raised to the peerage the following year, presumably in an attempt to buy Warwick off. His place in the House of Commons was taken by Sir Martin Lumley.) The younger Rich later turned Royalist, but we can assume that it was his father's name rather than his own qualities that won him the seat.[41]

At Westminster, Harbottle Grimston returned to the attack on monopolies, forest fines, extralegal taxation, and above all, Archbishop Laud—"the stye of pestilent filth that hath infected the state."[42] In Essex continued rioting provided a counterpoint to the proceedings in Parliament. Already in August at Chich St. Osyth and Great Holland, local civilians had followed the example of the soldiers. In October three women and five men rushed into the church at Halsted, where they seized the clerk by the throat, stripped him of his surplice and hood, and denounced the prayer book as a popish idol. A crowd rescued the rioters from the arresting constables.[43]

On New Year's Day, 1641, the bell-ringers of Latton pulled down the altar rails and burned them at the town whipping post. The rioters included a yeoman's servant and the apprentices of a potter and a dishturner. One of them offered a reasoned justification for his actions. He had torn down the rails, he said, "because they gave offense to his conscience, and [because] the placing of them was against God's law and the king's, as appeareth by the twentieth chapter of Exodus and about the twentieth verse." The young men had probably heard of the Commons' resolution passed two weeks earlier, which condemned the new church canons as contrary to the king's prerogative and the liberty and property of the subjects.[44]

Despite the invocation of Scripture and statute, however, there was a carnival quality about the Latton affair. A local carpenter brought a barrel of beer into the church to assist the good work. A month later the women of Sandon burnt the rails of their church "bravely like devils" on the village green. ("God send them a day of payment," wrote their neighbor Sir Humphrey Mildmay in his diary.) At Great Waltham the surplice was repeatedly mutilated; at Danbury the service of Holy Communion was disrupted.[45]

Like the soldiers, the civilian rioters were selective. The incumbent of the Puritan clothing town of Halsted was an appointee of the Bishop of London; he was sequestered two years later.[46] The patrons of Latton were the Royalist Altham family.[47] The parson of Sandon, the distinguished biblical scholar Brian Walton, was also a pluralist and royal chaplain.[48] At Great Waltham, a living held by Trinity College, Oxford, the influence of the Laudian vicar had been undermined in the preceding decade by a Puritan lecturer named John Fuller, "a young hot fellow," as Aylett described him to Laud, "who I fear will pull down faster than the vicar can build up in conformity." As for Danbury, even Clement Vincent's friend and patron Sir Humphrey Mildmay admitted that he was an indolent alcoholic.[49]

The strength of Parliament lay in its ability to call on these reserves of popular energy to carry through the great destructive ordinances of 1640–1642. Pointing to Pym's manipulation of the London crowd in support of the Grand Remonstrance, some historians have concluded that the rank and file were merely passive tools in the hands of the opposition leadership. Richard Baxter, however, saw it the other way around. In his view "the headiness and rashness of the younger inexperienced sort of religious people made many Parliament men and ministers overgo themselves to keep pace with these hot spurs."[50] It is best to think of a constant interplay between the action of the opposition at Westminster and a relatively autonomous (and heterogenous) popular movement in the country at large. The influence was reciprocal.

At the same time, the association of the Parliamentary opposition with lower-class violence helped to drive conservative gentlemen over to the side of the king, a process that has been described in great detail by Brian Manning.[51] Sir Humphrey Mildmay is a case in point. On November 25, 1640, he recorded with apparent satisfaction the imprisonment of "Black Tom"—the Earl of Strafford—in the Tower. On February 16, 1641, he was delighted by the "joyful news" of the passage of the Triennial Act. Yet, the increasing power of the Puritans and their plebeian supporters disgusted and alarmed him. Attending the annual bailiff's feast in Maldon, he was "met with base company and rascally, saucy ministers."[52]

The first phase of the revolution culminated with the execution of Strafford on May 12, attended by great crowds from the surrounding counties, who returned home that night tossing their caps in the air with cries of "His head is off! His head is off!" and smashing the windows of those who failed to light bonfires in celebration.[53] Sir Humphrey did not share their jubilation. Instead, he described "the good behavior of the noble Earl of Strafford, who died like a saint to the shame of his enemies."[54] In Mildmay's eyes "Black Tom" had become a martyr.

The alarm of conservatives like Mildmay can only have been heightened by the spread of increasingly radical religious ideas among the common people. Separatism had been no more than a minor nuisance in Essex before the Bishops' War, and a few cases had been serious enough to warrant presentment at the Quarter Sessions. But the collapse of censorship and church discipline opened the floodgates.

In 1639 one William Cartwright was imprisoned as a Brownist. At the Michaelmas sessions of 1640 a cordwainer and a chapman were accused of maintaining conventicles in Moulsham. One of them, the cobbler Thomas Staines, was later active in what looks like Leveller agitation in 1647. The following spring, artisan separatists appeared at Bocking, Sible Hedingham, Castle Hedingham, Ridgewell, and Halsted. In the summer two women, later identified as Anabaptists, declared that "the church is a den of thieves, and none but rogues come thither."[55] At Chelmsford, according to one source who seems to have known the minister, there was no dissent before the calling of Parliament. "But since this magnified Reformation was set on foot, this town ... is so filled with sectaries, especially Brownists and Anabaptists, that a third part of the people refuse to communicate in the church liturgy, and half refuse to receive the blessed sacrament unless they may receive it in what posture they please to take it." Early in 1642 Ralph Josselin, too, "began a little to be troubled by some in matter of separation."[56]

The Essex gentry in 1641 had real cause for alarm. In April Sir John Coke the younger wrote of "tumults in Essex in the throwing open of commons," and a few months later the enclosures of Sir John Lucas at Rovers Tye were leveled and his brick kilns destroyed by the weavers of Colchester.[57] This incident shows how religious and social grievances might fuse. Roger Roberts, the leader of the crowd, was a bitter opponent of episcopacy, who with fine irony took the title of Bishop Blaze as his *nom de guerre*.[58] (St. Blaze was the patron saint of weavers.) Lucas, a staunch Royalist, had antagonized popular opinion in the town by obstructing the town's waterworks, and, more seriously, by collecting Ship Money with great efficiency during his term as sheriff. There were strong grounds for suspicion that the town chamberlains had encouraged the weavers to attack him. John Langley, the Puritan captain of the trained band, had already tangled with him in a dispute over the collection of saltpeter.[59]

It was above all this threat to property that caused a section of the gentry, even in Essex, to rally to the Crown. One gentleman who did so was Sir Francis Coke of Pleshey, who had been brought to the point of apoplexy by the unwonted insolence of the lower orders. In September 1641 Coke and a fellow justice, attempting to suppress the "surfeiting and drunkenness and other luxurious riotings" that desecrated the Sabbath in Pleshey, were abused by a woman named Joan Allen, a particularly notorious tavern keeper. Coke's hysterical letter to Warwick reveals as much by its style as its content:

If such opprobrious and scandalous speeches shall be suffered to blemish the names and persons of any, much more those who are in authority and should suppress the vices of such wicked offenders who contrary to all law and order do what they please by the calumnious abuses of her and others ... if those sufferances have no redress nor find a sharp correction by example and terror to others to be warned by, I shall lay aside the authority and power that is imposed on me and give such offenders their own free will, to vomit out the foulness of their malice and odium of reproach as well to others as myself.[60]

Concealed in this syntactical thicket is the accusation that Warwick's party had allowed the social hierarchy to collapse, and a warning that unless order were restored, ruin would engulf the gentry as a class, regardless of political or religious persuasion. Coke achieved his immediate objective, since Joan Allen was sent to the House of Correction. A year and a half later, however, Warwick placed Coke himself in the Tower of London.[61]

The opposition had passed the point of no return. At the beginning of the Long Parliament, Sir Thomas Barrington had merely wished to see the powers of the bishops reduced. By June 1641, exasperated by the obstructionism of the prelates in the House of Lords, he was demanding that episcopacy be abolished root and branch.[62] In July the news reached England that the Providence Island settlement had been wiped out by the Spanish; in October the Irish rebellion broke out. The international Protestant cause, as well as the personal investments of colonizers like Warwick, Barrington, Masham, and Clotworthy, now depended on carrying the revolution further. But this in turn meant giving freer reign to popular violence, with all its attendant risks.

In the last months of 1641, while Parliament drew swords over the Grand Remonstrance and the "No Bishop" mobs surged through the streets of London, local officials carried out Parliament's ordinance for the removal of idolatrous images from all parish churches. In Royalist districts, like Baxter's Kidderminster, the rabble defended the familiar images of Christ, the Virgin, and the saints.[63] There seems to have been none of this in Essex. In most parishes the order was carried out without incident.[64] But at Chelmsford a riot ensued that can help us recover some of the social attitudes that underlay popular iconoclasm.

The glory of the Chelmsford church was a medieval stained glass window in the east chancel, depicting the life of Christ from conception to ascension. Like many such windows, however, it was a monument to social subordination as well, since the escutcheons of the church's gentle benefactors were interspersed with the biblical images. Such monuments make it easy to understand why lower-class schismatics hated both "idols" and the doctrine of good works. In medieval Catholicism good works included benefactions such as those commemorated in the Chelmsford window. Thus, if good works availed for salvation, then the chancel window, with the dawn light streaming through it, prefigured the appearance in glory of the families whose arms it bore. To the vulgar it must have symbolized the most oppressive feature of feudal Catholicism: the eternalization of secular class privilege. When the churchwardens, in obedience to Parliament's order, replaced the pictures of Christ with clear glass but left the rest intact, the local sectaries "very ill-satisfied with this partial imperfect reformation," assembled with stones and staves on Guy Fawkes day and smashed the whole window to pieces.[65] One must regret the loss to posterity; one should also remember what such imagery stood for.

If the Irish rebellion marks a watershed in the revolution, the Chelmsford riot initiates a new phase of popular action. Altar rails and surplices were opposed by a considerable number of men of property, but the chancel window was the collective inheritance of the county's ruling class. Most of the earlier episodes had occurred where the minister was either scandalous or Laudian. Michelson was a moderate Puritan. But he felt the crowd had gone too far, and the following Sunday he preached against "popular tumultuous reformations, though to the better." Since lawful authority could not reside in the people, such actions would "cast out one devil by another, abolishing superstition by sedition."[66]

His sermon split the congregation. Many, including Mark Mott, who succeeded to the living upon Michelson's sequestration, sided with the doctor. But the sectaries were enraged. Someone fired a carbine into Michelson's study; he was providentially absent at the time. A fortnight later a young clothier led a mob into church after the service and tried to rip the surplice from his back, reviling him as "Baal's priest and popish priest for wearing the rags of Rome," and accusing him of perjury for swearing to the Protestation. Michelson was rescued by his supporters. For the time being there was stalemate.[67]

Superstition versus sedition: Michelson had neatly formulated the alternatives. As Parliament drifted toward war with the king, the godly found themselves in alliance with forces that might escape their control. Underlying the whole struggle was the dreadful prospect that the many-headed monster might play *tertius gaudens.*

Political instability worsened the economic depression. Plague broke out in Witham in 1641 and spread to Bocking the following year. There were more disputes over the allocation of the poor rate in West Ham and Great Horkesley.[68] Panic over the Irish rebellion and lack of confidence in the government, particularly over the control of the Mint, precipitated the utter collapse of the cloth trade.[69] Since the Irish Catholics were visibly massacring English settlers, it seemed plausible to assume that the English Catholics, the papal fifth column, were the cause of England's domestic woes. The petitions from Essex and Colchester to the Commons on January 18th, 1642, made this accusation explicitly. The petitioners included the toleration of Catholics and the failure to execute papist priests as among the factors that had caused "such a decay of clothing and farming (the two trades of our country, whereby the multitudes of our people have lived) that we tremble to think what may follow thereon." Parliament was urged to rectify the situation by expelling the Catholic peers, relieving Ireland, and placing the Tower under reliable commanders.[70]

The reasoning behind these petitions, as behind Grimston's speeches in 1640, will astonish only those who still conceive of the revolution in narrowly constitutional terms. The relationship between economics, politics, and religion that modern historians find so subtle and elusive are not even articulated; they are assumed. There is evidence, moreover, that these attitudes were widespread among the lower classes, at least in the clothing industry. When mobs of weavers plundered the homes of Catholics and Royalists in the summer of 1642, they did so because they believed the malignants "were the causes of the present troubles and distractions in the

kingdom, and were the occasions that they and their wives and children were brought into great want and extremity by reason of the
want of tradings."[71]

When Grimston presented the Essex petitions on January 9, 1643,
he placed the cloth depression at the head of the county's complaints, and treated the House to a thoughtful disquisition on its
causes and effects. Grimston, however, blamed royal taxation more
than the machinations of papists. He also explained how industrial
depression ramified through the county's entire economy. Clothiers
were turning to farming, grazing and innkeeping, "whereby the
rents of farms are increased by the multitude of tenants, [which]
hath almost beggared the most part of that county."[72]

On January 25 Pym elaborated on Grimston's theme, reiterating
the identity of religious, political, and economic reform. Reverting
to organic analogy, he blamed the "distempers" of the body politic
on the simultaneous obstruction of trade and of religious zeal. Unless the "ill vent" of cloth and other products was remedied, Pym
predicted an insurrection of the poor that would spread to the farmers and husbandmen. Pym then affirmed Parliament's support of
free trade, citing the abolition of monopolies, and the attempt to secure the Tower and restore commercial confidence.[73] An Essex Royalist wrote that the clothiers were "rebels by their trade" because
"the Parliament's constant style was tenderness of commerce."
Moreover, the employers "derived their impressions to their workmen," so that the industry as a whole became the social core of the
Parliamentary and later of the Cromwellian bloc.[74]

The integration of religious, political and economic issues prevented the general insurrection that Pym, as much as Sir Francis
Coke, dreaded. To be sure, within a week of Pym's speech, a hundred laborers and artisans rioted for two days on the estate of Edward Church at Mucking, smashing his barn and making off with
his stock of rye.[75] During the next year and a half there was plundering, poaching, and enclosure leveling on an impressive scale. But
the victims were all, like Church, either Royalists or recusants. Parliament men experienced no riots such as the one directed against
Sir Thomas Barrington in 1639.

When Parliament ordered Essex to mobilize in the summer of
1642, the county's response contrasted strikingly with its obstinacy
two years earlier. Warwick, executing the Militia Ordinance on

June 7 at Brentwood, found that the trained bands and volunteers had themselves made good the losses of equipment in the Scots campaign. Four companies had their full complement of five hundred men, and a fifth, under the son of Sir William Masham, had twice that number, so that an additional company was hived off and placed under the younger son of Sir Thomas Barrington. The soldiers engaged themselves to support Parliament against the "late hellish designs and actings of a malignant party." Three days later the northern bands mustered at Dunmow, resolving "with our hands upon our swords" to deliver the king from the "false flatterers and traitors" who had abused his favor. The Dunmow resolution, carried "with universal approbation, by holding up of hands, throwing up of hats, and acclamations," was circulated through the county and presented to the Commons with ten thousand signatures. Robert Smyth, the High Sheriff, told the House that ninety thousand more would sign if given the chance.[76]

As Clive Holmes has demonstrated, this impression of unanimous zeal is deceptive. It is true that there was a good deal of genuine enthusiasm for the Parliamentary cause. Moreover, the Earl of Warwick, as the defender of the county's liberties and the champion of aggressive Protestantism and colonial expansion, enjoyed unrivaled personal prestige. But there was a significant body of neutralist, even Royalist, opinion in the county as well. In mid-July twenty-five justices and six members of the grand jury subscribed to a petition pledging their loyalty to Charles. In January of the following year a petition for an immediate peace received more than six thousand signatures, including those of more than two hundred gentlemen. When the fighting began in earnest, soldiers from Essex proved as likely to desert as those from other counties, especially when they were commanded to serve far from home.[77] Even in Essex, which was called "the first-born of Parliament" for its alacrity in executing the Militia Ordinance, true zealots were in a minority. But this minority received prompt and determined leadership from Warwick and his friends. In contrast, no coherent Royalist party ever emerged in. Essex, because its potential leaders were isolated and neutralized at the outset.

The impotence of the would-be Royalists in Essex was due, in large measure, to the fact that the godly had seized control of the pulpit. In February 1642 Stephen Marshall preached one of the great incendiary sermons of the revolution, entitled "Meroz Cursed." In Judges 5:23 the tribe of Meroz is cursed for its failure to come forth and fight in the Lord's cause. This rather obscure text had been used in 1626 by another Essex preacher, Thomas Barnes, to urge English intervention on the side of the German Protestants.[78] Marshall now used it to castigate those who hoped to remain neutral in the conflict between Crown and Parliament. God, says Marshall, "curses all them who come not out to help him, as well as those who come out to fight against him." He offered a clear justification not only for parliamentary resistance to the king but for popular insurrection. "It is no new thing," he observed,

to find the mighty ... to engage all against the Lord, his church and cause. The Lamb's followers and servants are often the poor and off-scouring of the world, when kings and captains, merchants and wise men, being drunk with the wine of the whore's fornications, proceed to make war with the Lamb ... When the mighty of the world do oppose the Lord, God's *meanest servants* must not be afraid to oppose the *mighty*.[79] [Emphasis in the original.]

Nor was Marshall talking merely of civil disobedience or passive resistance. "If this work be to revenge God's church against Babylon," he tells us, "he is a blessed man that takes and dashes the little ones against the stones." Marshall delivered this message to sixty different audiences, including, one assumes, his own congregation at Finchingfield.

At Earls Colne, Ralph Josselin urged his parishioners to contribute money and arms, and himself financed a volunteer.[80] Matthew Newcomen, who preached a bloodcurdling sermon against Catholic treachery on November 5, comparing the king's advisers to Guy Fawkes, must have been mobilizing the godly of Dedham.[81] Obadiah Sedgwick was no doubt doing the same in Coggeshall; in October he would ride with Stephen Marshall through front lines at Edgehill, exhorting the Parliamentary troops.[82]

Some preachers had already abandoned the fiction that Parliament fought merely to save the king from evil counsel. Lemuel Tuke, a lecturer at Rayne with a rather shady reputation (his enemies called him a drunken, ignorant, and lecherous weaver) "labored to poison his people with sedition and rebellion, affirming openly that it was lawful, not only to resist, but ... to kill the king, instancing in the example of Athaliah, 2 Kings II." At Colchester one Mr. Archer called Parliament "the Lord's annointed" and urged his congregation to disregard the scruples of "the gentry ... and the learned," who thought resistance "erroneous and damnable."[83]

In addition, the godly used the Puritan Sabbath and the special fast days of thanksgiving and humiliation to orchestrate the loyalty of their supporters and to expose and intimidate potential dissidents. One of the nastier aspects of this policy was the encouragement of moral espionage between neighbors. This led to cases of manifest injustice, as in 1641, when local busybodies locked up a widow for not appearing in church on the Sabbath, although she was exhausted from a fifteen-mile trip on foot the day before.[84] But it had its effect. Royalists like Sir Humphrey Mildmay, who ignored the Parliamentary fasts and kept those of the king, and ministers like Thomas Staple of Mundon, who kept "a day of profaneness by drinking of healths ... singing of profane songs, with hollowing and roaring," in derision of a day of humiliation were exposed as dangerous dissidents, just as a man would be today if he were caught listening in Russia to Radio Free Europe.[85]

In contrast, the efforts of the loyal clergy were pitifully ineffective. Some merely grumbled morosely or, like Richard Nicholson of Stapleford Tawney, sang seditious ballads against Parliament in the alehouse. Others made a more serious effort. James Mowe of Bardfield argued against the exclusion of Catholic lords, taught that "Parliaments were not ordained by the word of God as kings were, but were merely by the favor of the king to his subjects," and later helped circulate a neutralist petition for peace. Edward Cherry of Chich St. Osyth published a libelous attack on the Earl of Warwick and his brother the Earl of Holland.[86] But Mowe and Cherry had already lost control of their parishes, which both experienced iconoclastic riots in 1640.

The examples of Richard Drake of Radwinter and Edward Symmons of Rayne, both of whom left accounts of their tribulations, may serve to illustrate what went on in many parishes. Drake had been molested by soldiers in 1640. In February 1641 he was censured by the Grand Committee on Religion of the House of Commons, with Sir Thomas Barrington directing the prosecution, but was allowed to continue preaching pending the decision of the House of Lords. The Puritans in the parish, incited by one of the churchwardens, subjected him to continuous harassment through the first half of 1642. First, the tables were removed from the east end, and the monthly communion made quarterly. Then, in February a cobbler stole the service books and a tailor twice broke up the sacrament. In March forty children ran into the church and rang the bells during divine service.

Baptisms and burials were constantly disrupted. On March 17, while Drake was reading the lesson, one George Traps came up to the desk and threw a Parliamentary tract, *An Answer of the Roundheads to the Rattleheads,* in Drake's face, saying, "There is reading work for you, read that." In June a man named Edward Montford interrupted the lesson "with blasphemous answers, impious mockeries, unseasonable 'amens,' crying out 'Hold your peace, Hob, Down on your knees, Hob,' with much laughter, scornfully pulling off his hat and clapping it on again, bending the knee and bidding others to do so in derision." Then, Montford climbed to the bellfry and began jangling the bells "with incredible performances as words and gestures." One of these rioters told Drake's curate, "he had been well enough served to have been taken by the heels and his brains beaten out."[87]

At Rayne, Edward Symmons had lost his congregation to the radical lecturer Lemuel Tuke, who, according to Symmons, "bawleth against the reverend and learned ministers of the country, and raileth upon the worshipful gentry." The leader of the Puritan faction among the laity was Samuel Burrowes, the brother of Thomas, the Independent minister of Pebmarsh. In the summer of 1642 Symmons urged his parishioners to resist parliamentary taxation. They responded by sending him up before the House Committee on Religion, which referred him to its Committee on Scandalous Ministers. Symmons thought this was done to discredit him among the people, which seems plausible. (At the hearing Sir Thomas Barrington is supposed to have conceded that the doctrine of nonresistance was a divine truth, but said it was inexpedient to preach it at the moment. It sounds like him.) Symmons was allowed to return to Rayne on the condition that he steer clear of political subjects, but he faced mounting hostility. Only the intervention of Stephen Marshall saved Symmons from being plundered, and possibly lynched, in the August riots.[88]

Elsewhere the story was the same. In July, Brian Walton of Sandon complained that a lecturer named Prynne had ousted him from the pulpit and now officiated at baptisms and burials with a service of his own devising.[89] Probably most of the hundred and sixty-odd ministers who were sequestered experienced some kind of harassment during these months. No wonder the king's party lacked leadership. With the Laudian clergy silenced, there was no one left to agitate for the royal cause. The loyal gentry were not uncouth rustics, but they were unused to mass oratory. Accustomed to command rather than persuade inferiors, they were incapable of offering effective resistance to the mobilization of the Parliamentary army. When they finally moved into action in December with a petition for peace, it was too late.[90]

One lay Royalist who did agitate publicly for the king was a lawyer named John Wenlock. In Whitsunweek, Wenlock spoke in favor of the King's Proclamation at a public meeting in his native Langham, elucidating the king's strong constitutional case. Wenlock's reasoning sounds more persuasive today than it did to his audience, and the meeting voted overwhelmingly to send arms to Parliament. As the troops were mustering, Wenlock rode among them and explained the reasons for his refusal to contribute. The crowd threatened to rifle his house and pull it down. Wenlock was on the run for most of the next ten years. Along the way he scored a number of debating points and claimed to have converted a number of deluded lower-class Roundheads.[91] But reason, like God, is often on the side of the big battalions, and in Essex in 1642 the big battalions of preachers and lawyers were for Parliament.

With a Parliamentary army in force, suspected Royalists were at the mercy of the godly, and the less tender mercy of the mob. From June to August volunteers from Essex, Suffolk, and Norfolk, destined for service in the Earl of Essex's army under Lords Brooke and Saye, were billeted in Chelmsford until they were made up into companies of three to four hundred and sent on to London. In Chelmsford the troops joined forces with the local sectaries, who proceeded to a final reckoning with Dr. Michelson. The troopers quartered themselves in the minister's house and ordered him to refrain from reading the Common Prayer or mentioning episcopacy. When the curate defied them (on Michelson's orders), the volunteers of Colchester and Ipswich, who sat with their hats on, shouted at him to "come down out of his calves' coop, and make an end of his pottage." As the curate withdrew in confusion, the soldiers began mutilating the Bible, until their sergeant redirected their rage to the prayer book, which they dismembered. They trampled some pages under foot, threw others in the river Chelmer, while "some they pissed upon and some they fixed on the end of their clubs and cudgels, and in triumphant manner marched with them up and down the town."[92] (There was nothing unique about this extravagance. The previous year a weaver from Earls Colne confessed to stealing the prayer book after one of Josselin's sermons and hurling it into a pond. The next day he returned to mutilate and burn it. Similar events occurred in 1642 in Shelley and High Ongar.)[93]

The soldiers continued to bully and threaten Michelson throughout the summer. While he was burying one of the local gentry in the chancel, they rushed in and made a show of trying to bury the doctor as well. When bonfires were lit to celebrate the abolition of episcopacy, they tried to throw him on the pyre. Although these can hardly have been serious attempts at assassination, they were bloodchilling enough to their victim. After a few months of it Michelson fled Chelmsford in fear of his life, and the living passed to the Presbyterian Mark Mott, the brother of Adrian Mott, the leading member of the Braintree vestry. The text for Mark Mott's first sermon was, "Curse ye, Meroz." But the sectaries got little profit from the exchange, for once the soldiers had gone, Mott imposed an orthodoxy as rigorous as that of his predecessor.[94]

The behavior of the soldiers after joining Essex's army is entertainingly recorded in the letters of a subaltern officer named Nehemiah Wharton.[95] Judging from their activities on the march to Northampton—poaching papists, ducking whores, smashing relics—one assumes that the newly raised troops may have also been responsible for the sudden rash of poaching that broke out in Waltham Forest in May and June, when thirty-four known and sixty-four unknown poachers were reported. (There were sixty-one cases between November 22 and 30, at which time many of these soldiers would have been returning home.)[96]

Parliament immediately became concerned at the threat to property posed by these armed bands. On August 17 the House of Lords issued two orders against the plundering of churches or private homes, and the deputy lieutenants in each county were instructed to prevent all "riots, tumults . . . or the taking of victuals without due payment."[97] Four days later the worst riots of the century broke out along the Stour Valley.

Overpowered in their home county, the more militant Essex Royalists tried to make their way north to join the king at Nottingham. Sir John Lucas planned to depart in the early hours of August 22, at the head of a party of horsemen, accompanied by Thomas Newcomen, rector of St. Runwald's, Colchester, who had administered an oath of secrecy to the Cavaliers.[98] (Newcomen was the brother of Matthew, but was himself a Laudian. He had been engaged in acrimonious litigation with his parishioners in 1637.) On August 20 the town carrier was intercepted bringing a shipment of arms to the Lucas house, and a servant betrayed his master's plans to John Langley, the captain of the trained bands. Langley, in addition to being one of Colchester's leading Parliamentarians, had personal scores to settle with Lucas, since the two men had quarreled over the collection of saltpeter in Lucas's home two years earlier. On the following day, a Sunday, Langley and Henry Barrington, an alderman and brewer, rode to the towns of Coggeshall, Bocking, Braintree, and Halsted, ordering them to mount armed guards on the highway to intercept Lucas's party.

The Parliamentarians apparently feared a Cavalier uprising. On Sunday night Langley ordered the high constable to set a watch on the house, which at midnight stopped a small party coming through the rear gate. Rumors now spread to the town that Lucas was leading hundreds of armed Cavaliers. The drum was beaten up, and the trained bands besieged the place, where they were joined by a mob variously reckoned at from two to five thousand from town and country. Mayor Thomas Wade and the Colchester aldermen arrived at one o'clock on Monday morning to dismiss the crowd, but as Wade wrote Parliament later that day, they "regarded us no more than they do a child." Wade now ordered the trained bands to guard the house against plunder. But at daybreak the crowd broke through and began looting, while the mayor and aldermen stood by helplessly. Eight horses and a considerable amount of armor and ammunition were discovered, and this, amplified by a rumor that two hundred Cavaliers still lurked in the vault, incited the crowd's fury. The house was thoroughly rifled, its walls and gardens defaced, the deer slaughtered, the cattle driven out, and the Lucas ancestral tombs desecrated. The corpses were dismembered, and the rioters paraded through the town with the hair of the dead in their caps.[99]

Yet, there was surprisingly little violence to the living. John Brown, an old servant of the family, was briefly interrogated with a musket at his chest and lighted matches between his fingers. If the Royalist Bruno Ryves can be trusted, the crowd carrying Thomas Newcomen through the streets debated wildly whether to drown him, stone him, or beat out his brains. In fact, he escaped with a cudgeling. The crowd was adamant, however, that Newcomen, Lucas, his mother, and his servants be arrested. When Mayor Wade tried to remove them to his own house for safety, the crowd threatened to pull the mayor's house down on his head. The Royalists were accordingly transferred to the Moot Hall. On Monday afternoon Mayor Wade wrote, "They are come to such a head . . . that we know not how to quiet them. [I] believe we could not repress them if we had five trained bands, unless they were killed."[100]

While Lucas was being pillaged, smaller crowds looted Henry Audley at Berechurch and robbed Erasmus Laud, the rector of Little Tey, of cattle, cash, and clothes. Another contingent struck at Gabriel Honifold of St. Mary Magdalen's, Colchester; when Honifold sought justice, he was mobbed in the streets and had to put himself in protective custody. The recusant Henry Audley had been thought to be raising a popish army at Berechurch in the summer of 1640.[101] Even Clement Walker, in his *Sufferings of the Clergy*, admits Laud to have been of "no good character," while Honifold, a pluralist, was sequestered for nonresidence, swearing, and card playing. As early as 1632 a scurrilous doggerel had lampooned his weakness for women and the bottle.[102]

The main body of rioters at Colchester now spoke of going on to plunder all the Catholics in the county, believing, as the Parliamentary *Perfect Diurnall* reported, that "they were the causes of the present troubles and distractions in the kingdom, and were the occasions that they and their wives and children were brought into great want and extremity by reason of the want of tradings."[103]

Their first target was the estate of Elizabeth Savage (née D'Arcy), Countess Rivers, who was not only a great Catholic landowner but lady of the bedchamber to the Catholic queen. The day after the Lucas riot, the crowd attacked her estate at St. Osyth's, wrecked her gardens and crops, scattered her livestock, and made off, by the lady's account, with £50,000 worth of plate and pewter. The depositions surviving from this affray indicate that most of the rioters were weavers.[104]

When Lady Rivers fled across the Stour to her estate at Long Melford, the crowd pursued her. Just across the border, at Sudbury, it was reported on Wednesday, August 24, that the people there "begin to take example by the insurrection at Colchester, and rescue prisoners, plunder houses, not only papists but Protestants, alleging them to be persons disaffected to the Parliament." On Thursday there were rumors that the crowd planned to attack the Earl of Suffolk at Audley End, but they held on for Long Melford instead.[105] They were reinforced by rioters from Suffolk, two thousand of whom assembled at Bury St. Edmunds. While the trained bands hesitated to move against them, they attacked the countess's second residence, ripping down the elaborately wrought ceiling, slaughtering deer, and letting wine and beer run knee deep in the cellars after they had drunk their fill.

Lady Rivers estimated her losses at Long Melford at £40,000. Some of her neighbors suffered as well. Sir Francis Mannock lost important documents, and the house of one Dr. Warren was rifled for his "gods"—perhaps classical statuary mistaken for popish images. These were set up derisively around the market cross and called "his young ministers." Warren himself was "huffed and shuffed" and robbed, but not otherwise injured. Again, the fury of the rioters stopped short of real bodily harm.[106] Indeed, Bruno Ryves reports only a single death during all these disorders: an old woman hiding the silver of Parson Stevens of South Hanningfield was beaten with a club "with such violence that her brains came out at her nostrils."[107]

Lady Rivers, meanwhile, had appealed to the Earl of Warwick for help. The earl was at sea securing the fleet for Parliament, and his feckless heir was hunting stag at Rochford, so Arthur Wilson, Warwick's steward, was ordered to fetch her to Leighs for safekeeping. Wilson passed safely northward through Braintree and Haverhill, assured of passage in a coach bearing the Rich coat of arms. But across the border at Sudbury he was stopped by a mob that mistook him for Lord Rivers. Wilson identified himself, disingenuously explained that he was going about the Earl of Warwick's business at Bury, and produced letters in his master's handwriting. The mayor was dubious; the letters might be forged. (Meanwhile, Wilson re-called, "The tops of all the trees and all the windows were thronged with people, all vociferating for 'the letters! the letters!' ") At last he was recognized by the town clerk, whose father had been in War-wick's employ, and allowed to drive on to Melford.

The lady herself was already out of harm's way. She had first taken refuge with Sir Robert Crane, the Parliamentary leader, at Melford. From there she fled to Bury, which for an anxious hour re-fused to admit her, and she finally escaped to London. When Wilson reached Melford, he found Sir Robert obliged to keep a trained band in his house to protect himself from the rabble, whom he had antagonized by harboring the countess.[108]

Wilson's fruitless mission, and his experience in the course of it, should dispel the notion that these riots were engineered by the Par-liamentary leadership. On August 23, as the crowds were digging up Lady Rivers's corn at Long Melford, the Commons ordered they should be thanked for their zeal and quietly dispersed. On the fol-lowing day Sir Thomas Barrington and Harbottle Grimston, the members from Colchester, rode down from London to take matters in hand. They charged Newcomen and Lucas with treason and or-dered them conveyed to London. Newcomen had to be personally escorted through a hostile mob, which only refrained from stoning him through fear of hitting Sir Thomas Barrington.[109]

Barrington and Grimston found that a printed paper was circu-lating among the rioters that purported to give parliamentary sanc-tion to the plundering of Royalists.[110] Earlier in the summer the sol-diers at Langham who threatened John Wenlock also claimed official authority. But the myth of a license to rebel from some higher authority—the "good king," the Pope, the czar as "little fa-ther"—is common to many preindustrial revolts. Had the printed order not existed, rumor would probably have invented it. Some-times, however, the pretense of legitimacy was a conscious fraud. In December one rioter claimed to be acting on the orders of the Col-chester aldermen, but later declared he cared nothing for king *or* Parliament.[111]

Barrington denounced the paper as a forgery contrived by Royal-ist provocateurs to discredit the Parliament. On August 29 he wrote that throughout Essex, the crowds disbanded as soon as he ex-plained matters, and returned the goods they had taken. Meanwhile, Parliament had passed another ordinance forbidding soldiers to pillage, and made the offense felonious. The high sheriff of Essex was especially instructed to protect the house of Sir Humphrey Mildmay, an especially tempting prize now that the master was in Somerset. On September 9 an order was issued for the recovery of Lady Rivers's goods. All county officials, from deputy lieutenants to parish ale conners, were to make "strict and narrow search . . . in such creeks, vessels, wagons, and carts as are expected to harbor the same." Harbottle Grimson was given charge of the operation and instructed to encourage Lady Rivers's tenants to resume their rents.[112]

Thus, Parliament tried to reassure the county of its commitment to law, order, and property rights. Few Royalists can have been convinced. Sir Humphrey Mildmay, who sweated through November in constant terror of looters, referred to them as "the Barringtons." The rioters' victims received no real redress. In some instances this was due to the reluctance of juries to convict, as was the case when Richard Drake tried to prosecute his tormentors at the summer sessions, or later when John Cornelius of Peldon brought charges against the men who had plundered him in December. But elsewhere the authorities themselves simply ignored their complaints. When Erasmus Laud identified some Colchester men among the crowd that plundered him, Alderman Cole threw him out. Cole gave the same treatment to Gabriel Honifold.[113] Even if the crowds Sir Thomas Barrington met with voluntarily returned their booty, the tenants of Lady Rivers were still defaulting on their rents a year and a half later. When a man was arrested in London in the act of fencing her stolen goods, he was released after appealing to Parliament.[114] None of this inspired confidence.

Herein, perhaps, lay the real achievement of the riots. For, as the Parliamentary leaders no doubt realized, if the Royalists were alienated, they were also terrorized. The result, at least in the short term, was to secure the county for Parliament. At Sudbury men professed their loyalty, whatever their private opinions, to avoid being plundered. It was the same at Long Melford. "This insurrection," wrote the diarist John Rous, "scareth all the malignant party." On September 8 Harbottle Grimston reported that the hundreds around Colchester had brought in £6,000 on the Parliament's Propositions; in a week the figure had reached £30,000.[115] This was three times the Forced Loan of 1626, and nearly four times the annual levy of Ship Money. The fate of families like the Riverses, Lucases, and Audleys must have helped loosen the purse strings of their neighbors.

The rioting itself slackened off in September and October, although the enclosures of Sir Thomas Dacre were leveled at Waltham Abbey. In November, with the return of the soldiers, Royalist fears quickened again, but the main victims were the stag of Waltham Forest. There were sixty-one recorded cases of poaching and another thirty in December.[116] It was not only deer that were poached. Early in the following year, George Asser of Barking organized a band of fellow fishermen to dredge for oysters in the mouth of the Burnham River. These beds, source of the highly prized Wallfleet oysters, were the monopoly of the Earl of Sussex.[117]

In December there were sporadic incidents—an assault on the minister of Witham[118] and the rather desultory plundering of John Cornelius, the minister of Peldon.[119] Parliament now moved to institutionalize the repression of the Royalists, and to insure that the spoils of their estates would go to fill coffers of Goldsmiths' Hall rather than the pockets of weavers. The laborers of Newport had a last fling in April of 1643, when they tore down the enclosures of the Earl of Suffolk, "alleging that if they took not advantage of this time, they shall never have the like opportunity again."[120] They were right; they never did. Four years later, when the revolution entered a more radical phase, there was a resurgence of popular activity in Essex, but it took the form of religious revivalism rather than riot or insurrection. The only recrudescence of popular violence in Essex occurred during the abortive Royalist rising of 1648, and this was directed against the godly members of Chelmsford's Parliamentary committee.[121]

The rioting soldiers of 1640, the altar-rail burners and iconoclasts of 1641, and the plunderers of the summer of 1642 had done their work in securing the county for Parliament. Potential Royalists were intimidated, and would-be neutralists were coerced into active compliance, by the relatively mild reign of terror.

We should not exaggerate the spontaneous enthusiasm of the Essex gentry for the Parliamentary cause. Austin Woolrych is probably right, even for Essex, in believing that most gentlemen wished to

remain "as neutral as they expediently could."[122] There was a significant "peace party" in the county,[123] and as many aristocrats were
sequestered for delinquency as served on the Parliamentary committee.[124] Richard Baxter claimed that the gentry in East Anglia
were Parliamentarian only because the royal army never appeared
there.[125] Expediency meant giving at least tacit support to the
stronger party in one's own neighborhood.

But why had the king no army in Essex? In large part because
more men chose to obey the Militia Ordinance than the Crown's
Proclamation. This was one of those occasions when the beliefs and
prejudices of ordinary people really made a difference. Charles had
aristocratic supporters everywhere in England, but his writ ran only
where his agents could exact compliance. In many areas there was
considerable popular support for church and king. In Richard
Baxter's Kidderminster, for example, it was the godly who were
plundered, while crowds rallied to defend the religious images that
Parliament ordered to be removed.[126] Even in Essex, the Chelmsford
mob in 1648 would support the Royalist insurgents. But popular
royalism was virtually unknown in the county at the beginning of
the Civil War. There were only three lower-class Royalists reported
to the Colchester Quarter Sessions, and none to the county sessions,
during the first six months of hostilities.[127]

What sort of people made up these crowds, and how representative were they of the population as a whole? From the fragmentary
evidence available, they seem to have represented a cross-section of
what we might call the lower-middling sort: the precariously situ-
ated group III of the first chapter. We know that the crowds included women as well as men, though the proportions are impossible
to determine. Weavers and rural artisans seem to have predominated, with a sprinkling of husbandmen and yeomen.[128] The laborers, at the bottom of rural society, were relatively inactive. They
formed a majority of the rioters in only one episode—an apparently
apolitical act of plunder—although among all accused felons during
this period, those designated as laborers represented 80 percent of
the total.[129] Given what we know of the experience of Hugh and
Gillett, their political passivity is hardly surprising. The politically
and religiously motivated rioters were artisans who enjoyed at least
some degree of economic independence.

The actual rioters, of course, were only a small minority of the social strata from which they were drawn. (Still, if we could accept the figure of five thousand at which the panic-stricken mayor estimated the Colchester mob, this might have been close to 10 percent of the county's adult population.)[130] But there is evidence that they had broader popular support. The three women and five men who assaulted the minister of Halsted in 1640 were rescued from arrest by the crowd.[131] Two years later no jury could be found to convict the rioters who had sacked the home of John Cornelius at Peldon, despite the fact that several of them had already confessed. One juryman bluntly declared "that these men arraigned at the bar were honest men, that they had an intent to do them favor, and they would do it."[132]

These crowds were, for the most part, surprisingly unbloodthirsty. The Tudor and Stuart upper classes always claimed to believe that they would be butchered en masse if the "many-headed monster" broke loose.[133] Yet, despite the collapse of authority, there was little violence to life or limb. The Royalist Bruno Ryves, a meticulous connoisseur of popular atrocities, could lay only a single death to the rioters.[134]

Yet, the crowd attacked *symbols* with an almost insane ferocity. Desecration like that visited upon the Chelmsford church was not uncommon during the early stages of the war. At Worcester Cathedral the troops smashed organs and statues, defecated in the aisles, and urinated in the baptismal font.[135] At Canterbury they fired their muskets at the statue of Christ, "triumphing much when they hit it in the head or face."[136] As Keith Thomas has shown, ritual desecration has a long history; it belongs to a tradition of anticlericalism extending back at least to the Lollards.[137] One may attribute it, perhaps, to the subliminal dread that these religious objects still inspired. For the naïve trooper, haunted by vestigial peasant superstitions, an aura of tabu must have clung to the images of Christ and Virgin that could be dispelled only in a frenzy of destructive (and often drunken) ridicule.

At the same time, symbolic violence was a form of social protest. The smashing of the Chelmsford window, for example, was an act of secular as well as religious iconoclasm. Social resentment was even more obvious in the plundering of aristocratic tombs. In Essex rioters destroyed the Lucas vaults, just as at Worcester soldiers defaced the monument of Bad King John. Secular iconoclasm was a crude affirmation of human equality in the face of death, the Great Leveler, as well as an act of retroactive vengeance.

The rioters were very selective. They attacked not clergy and aristocrats as such but Laudians, Royalists, and especially Catholics. The victims of enclosure riots were all "malignant." Even the numerous poachers, whom one would not normally expect to be politically fastidious, confined their activities to the parks of Royalists and recusants. The spacious preserves of Warwick and Barrington were unmolested.[138]

In speaking of a Puritan Moment I do not claim that Essex contained 150,000 Saints. Many of the rioters were Puritan only in their animosities. If they burned altar rails and terrorized Catholics, they also got drunk and stole silverware, poached deer, and leveled enclosures. These were acts that the leaders of the godly party might choose for the Moment to ignore, but of which they could scarcely approve. There were enormous differences of outlook between gentlemen like Warwick, Masham, and Barrington, who believed in the culture of discipline, and the drunken weavers who blamed Catholics for the crisis of the cloth trade. Nonetheless, it is impossible to deny a degree of practical solidarity between the crowd and the godly aristocrats at the outbreak of the Civil War. Popular violence was directed exclusively against Royalists and recusants. At the same time, the godly gentlemen refrained from closing ranks with their recusant and Royalist fellow aristocrats, although they might, as in the case of Countess Rivers, intervene to save them from physical harm.

This solidarity across class lines was very largely the achievement of the more radical Puritan preachers. Their great contribution was to channel hostility that might have been directed against the rich in general toward that section of the upper class that clung to the old religion or displayed obtrusive loyalty to the Crown. However progressive one may consider the Parliamentary cause, this process seems disturbingly akin to anti-Semitism—and to witch-hunting, which revived tragically in Essex in the year of Naseby.[139] Catholics, and by extension Royalists in general, were scapegoated for hardships that men and women could not otherwise comprehend. Richard and John Rogers, George Gifford, Thomas Hooker, Stephen Marshall, and their colleagues had gradually taught godly aristocrats to identify more closely with the household of faith than with the profane (or Roman Catholic) members of their own class. And they had encouraged men and women of a humbler station to see themselves as instruments of God's metahistorical plan.

Stephen Marshall, who in 1637 was said to govern the consciences of all the *rich* Puritans of Essex, declared in 1642 that "the Lamb's followers and servants are often the poor and offscourings of the world, when kings and captains . . . give all their strength to the Beast."[140] Surely, at least some of the rioters of 1642 had been inspired by such sermons, especially since Marshall himself preached this one in more than sixty churches. Two years later Edward Symmons, Marshall's neighbor and erstwhile friend, met captured Parliamentary soldiers who had read Marshall, and who told Symmons, " 'Tis prophesied in the Revelation, that the Whore of Babylon shall be destroyed with fire and sword, and what do you know, but this is the time of her ruin, and that we are the men that must help to pull her down?"[141]

12 / Conclusion

> Ideas were all-important for the individuals
> whom they impelled into action, but the histo-
> rian must attach equal importance to the cir-
> cumstances that gave these ideas their chance.
> Revolutions are not made without ideas, but
> they are not made by intellectuals. Steam is es-
> sential to driving a railway engine; but neither a
> locomotive nor a permanent way can be made
> out of steam.
>
> —Christopher Hill, in *Intellectual Origins of the
> English Revolution*, 1965

Between 1640 and 1642 one of England's richest and most strate-
gically located counties flared into open rebellion against the
Crown. I have called this the Puritan Moment in order to emphasize
the decisive role of religious conviction and prejudice in catalyzing
this rebellion. The Puritan Moment was not a provincial revolt
against centralized government as such. The currently fashionable
concern with localism will not get us very far toward an understanding of how Essex became the "first-born of Parliament." The
concerns of the godly were not merely, or even primarily, provincial.
They were national, imperial, and cosmic in scope. When the
trained bands vowed with hands on swords to defend Law, Liberty,
and "Religion more precious than both,"[1] and when the weavers of
the Stour Valley plundered Catholics and Royalists, these were not
manifestations of regionalist sentiment. It may well be true that
most men and women—even in Essex at the height of the Puritan
Moment—were indifferent or self-interested. It is not news that history is often made by minorities; but this is hardly a reason to ignore
the history that minorities do in fact make.

I have already cited the Venetian ambassador's remark in 1637
that Charles had more to fear from religious than from secular discontent. The Essex evidence convinces me that, in an important
sense, Anzolo Correr was right. Above all else it was militant Protes-

tantism—called puritanism by its enemies—that gave rebellion its cultural validation, and that resolved a host of conflicts into the encounter of Roundhead and Cavalier. It was the Bishops' War and the Irish Rebellion that precipitated the crisis, not Ship Money or the Forest Fines.

But my whole argument has been that in dealing with the early seventeenth century, it is always wrong to discriminate too sharply between the religious and the secular. Contemporaries, I have suggested, assumed the interpenetration of the two spheres. This was especially true of serious Calvinists, since predestination kept God ubiquitously busy in human affairs. What I have called the Puritan Moment was an evanescent synthesis of religious, political, and economic discontent.

To recapitulate briefly: the social trends of the sixteenth century—especially population growth and the commercialization of agriculture—had produced a redundant population of landless men and women, the tribe of Hugh Make-Shift. The creation of this superfluous class inspired a reorientation of social policy at the local as well as national level. The late medieval preoccupation with scarce labor and high wages gave way to alarm at the growth of poverty, underemployment, and crime. With the decline of the manor, and the enactment of Poor Laws and the statute against cottaging, parish elites assumed new powers and responsibilities. Calvinism—still, under Elizabeth and James, the official doctrine of the Church of England—provided these elites with an appropriate world view. It gave them the self-confidence to impose a culture of discipline in the face of traditionalist resistance.

Despite the misgivings of both Elizabeth and her successor, there was nothing socially subversive about this social puritanism, though a full-blown presbyterian system might well have posed a threat to the political authority of the Crown. The Puritan Moment required the coincidence of two intrinsically unrelated phenomena: a commercial crisis and what looked like a domestic counter-reformation. The decay of trade, by cutting off the growth of the cloth industry, worsened the plight of the new proletariat and made the culture of discipline more necessary. The Laudian reforms struck at the heart of the social puritanism in which that culture was grounded. Moreover, the church gave enthusiastic support to the Crown's attempts, during a time of great economic hardship, to increase its share of the national income without parliamentary consent. Between 1640 and 1642 a society fissured by social and constitutional conflicts broke apart along essentially religious lines. The Puritan preachers, with a persuasively simple explanation for all of England's woes, found themselves launching an insurrection.

Now, it is quite possible to imagine a rebellion in seventeenth-century England without this religious dimension. The price revolution, the mounting costs of war, and the "adamantine resistance to honest taxation" displayed by Countrymen like Edward Alford had probably made some sort of crisis inevitable. It is much harder to imagine a purely secular rebellion, an English Fronde, succeeding. It was puritanism that inspired godly aristocrats to transcend those venal and parochial concerns to which historians are rightly devoting more attention, but which could never, in themselves, have triggered a major revolution. It was puritanism and anti-Catholicism that brought those aristocrats into a temporary coalition with disaffected members of the middle and lower classes. Without that unstable, ephemeral, but historically decisive alliance, it is doubtful that a county like Essex could have been secured for Parliament or that a civil war could have been waged, let alone have been won, by the rebels. But for a moment—the Puritan Moment—class resentments and fears could be forgotten by men and women who believed, with Stephen Marshall, that "the question in England is whether Christ or Antichrist shall be Lord."[2]

Abbreviations

A.P.C.	*Acts of the Privy Council*
Barnes	Thomas G. Barnes, *Somerset, 1625–1640* (Cambridge, Mass., 1961)
B.I.H.R.	*Bulletin of the Institute of Historical Research*
Bod.	Bodleian Library, Oxford.
B.M.	British Museum, London.
Burley	K. H. Burley, "The Economic Development of Essex in the Later Seventeenth and Early Eighteenth Centuries" (Ph.D. diss., University of London, 1957)
C.J.	*Journals of the House of Commons*
C.S.P.D.	*Calendar of State Papers Domestic*
C.S.P. Ven.	*Calendar of State Papers Venetian*
Davids	T. W. Davids, *Annals of Evangelical Nonconformity in the County of Essex* (London, 1863)
Dedham Minutes	Minute book of the Dedham Classis, ed. R. G. Usher, as *The Presbyterian Movement in the Reign of Queen Elizabeth* (London, 1905)
D.N.B.	*Dictionary of National Biography*
D.W.L.	Doctor Williams's Library, London
Econ. H. R.	*Economic History Review*
Emmison, *Disorder*	F. G. Emmison, *Elizabethan Life: Disorder* (Chelmsford, Essex, 1970)
Emmison, *Morals*	F. G. Emmison, *Elizabethan Life: Morals and the Church Courts* (Chelmsford, Essex, 1973)
E.R.O.	Essex Record Office, Chelmsford
Everitt	Alan Everitt, *The Community of Kent and the Great Rebellion, 1640–1660* (Leicester, 1966)
Fletcher	Anthony Fletcher, *A County Community in Peace and War: Sussex, 1600–1660* (London, 1975)
Harrison	William Harrison, *Description of England,* ed. Georges Edalen (Ithaca, 1968)
H.M.C.	*Historical Manuscript Commission Reports*
Holmes	Clive Holmes, *The Eastern Association in the English Civil War* (Cambridge, 1974)
Hull	Felix Hull, "Agriculture and Rural Society in Essex, 1560–1640," (Ph.D. diss., University of London, 1950)

Josselin	*The Diary of the Rev. Ralph Josselin, 1616–1683,* ed. E. Hockliffe, (London, 1908)
L. J.	*Journals of the House of Lords*
Macfarlane, *Josselin*	Alan Macfarlane, *The Family Life of Ralph Josselin* (Cambridge, 1970)
Macfarlane, *Witchcraft*	Alan Macfarlane, *Witchcraft in Tudor and Stuart England* (New York, 1970)
Morant	Phillip Morant, *The History and Antiquities of . . . Essex* (Colchester, Essex, 1768)
Norden	John Norden, *Speculi Britanniae Pars,* ed. Henry Ellis (London, 1840)
O.E.D.	*Oxford English Dictionary*
P.R.O.	Public Record Office, London
Quintrell	B. W. Quintrell, "The Government of the County of Essex, 1603–1642" (Ph.D. diss., University of London, 1965)
Reyce	Robert Reyce, "Breviary of Suffolk," in *Suffolk in the Seventeenth Century,* ed. Francis Hervey (London, 1902)
Shipps	Kenneth W. Shipps, "Lay Patronage of East Anglian Clerics in Pre-Revolutionary England" (Ph.D. diss., Yale University, 1971)
Smith	Thomas Smith, *De Republica Anglorum* (London, 1583)
Stat.	Statutes of the Realm
T.E.D.	*Tudor Economic Documents,* ed. R. H. Tawney and Eileen Power (London, 1924)
Thirsk	Joan Thirsk, ed., *The Agrarian History of England and Wales* (Cambridge, 1967), vol. 4, *1500–1640*
Thirsk and Cooper	Joan Thirsk and J. P. Cooper, eds., *Seventeenth Century Economic Documents* (Oxford, 1972)
Tusser	*Thomas Tusser . . . His Good Points of Husbandry,* ed. Dorothy Hartley (London, 1931)
Tyack	N. C. P. Tyack, "Migration from East Anglia to New England before 1660" (Ph.D. diss., University of London, 1951)
V.C.H. Essex	*Victoria County History of Essex* (London, 1903–)
Wills	*Wills at Chelmsford,* ed. F. G. Emmison (London, 1958–)
Wrightson and Levine	Keith Wrightson and David Levine, *Poverty and Piety in an English Village: Terling, 1525–1700* (New York, 1979)

Notes

Preface

1. The list of such studies is already long and growing almost by the hour. Some of the more influential titles, in order of publication, are: Wallace Mac-Caffrey, *Exeter, 1540–1640* (Cambridge, Mass. 1958); Thomas G. Barnes, *Somerset, 1625–1640* (Cambridge, Mass., 1961); Alan Everitt, *The Community of Kent and the Great Rebellion* (Leicester, 1966); Alan Everitt, *The Local Community and the Great Rebellion* (London, 1969); J. T. Cliffe, *The Yorkshire Gentry from the Reformation to the Civil War* (London, 1969); R. C. Richardson, *Puritanism in North-West England* (Manchester, 1972); David G. Hey, *An English Rural Community* (Leicester, 1974); Clive Holmes, *The Eastern Association in the English Civil War* (Cambridge, 1974); J. S. Morrill, *Cheshire, 1630–1660* (Oxford, 1974); Anthony Fletcher, *A County Community in Peace and War: Sussex 1600–1660* (London, 1975); J. S. Morrill, *The Revolt of the Provinces* (London, 1976); Peter Clark, *English Provincial Society from the Reformation to the Revolution* (East Brunswick, N.J., 1977); Keith Wrightson and David Levine, *Poverty and Piety in an English Village* (New York, 1979).

2. E. W. Ives, ed., *The English Revolution, 1600–1660* (New York, 1971), pp. 40, 48, 159.

3. *H.M.C. Beaufort*, p. 20; Barbara Donagan, "The Clerical Patronage of Robert Rich, Second Earl of Warwick, 1619–1642," *Proceedings of the American Philosophical Society* (October 1976), 388; *L.J.*, IX, 72.

1. The English Goshen

1. Burley, pp. 10–12, 21, 393–395. Dr. Burley estimates the population of Essex at 120,000 in 1670. There is reason to believe that the population had grown somewhat in the course of the seventeenth century. Burley's figures are derived from the Hearth Tax Returns, E.R.O., Q/R Th 5.

2. William Camden, *Britannia* (London, 1607), p. 405.

3. Thirsk and Cooper, p. 618. The original source is P.R.O., SP 16/376, no. 104.

4. A. J. and R. H. Tawney, "An Occupational Census of the Seventeenth Century," *Econ. H. R.*, 5 (October 1934), 25–64.

5. Norden, p. 7.

6. Michael Drayton, *Poly-Olbion* (London, 1890), pt. 3, p. 3.

7. John Brome, *Travels over England, Scotland, and Wales* (London, 1707), p. 108.

8. *V.C.H. Essex*, I, 1.

9. Norden, pp. 7–9.

10. *V.C.H. Essex*, I, 1–13; Joan Thirsk, "The Farming Regions of England," in Thirsk, pp. 54–55.

11. Hull, p. 50.

12. Thirsk, p. 53; Norden, p. 8; Hull, pp. 112–113. The hundreds of Essex were administrative subdivisions of the county. There were twenty of them, varying in area from Hinckford and Chelmsford (136.7 and 127.4 square miles, respectively) to Clavering, with 25.1 square miles. The median is 61.3 square miles. Technically, Becontree is a half-hundred, and Havering is a liberty. See Burley, p. 21. On the growing of hops, see also Thomas Fuller, *Worthies of England* (London, 1662), I, 493.

13. Norden, pp. 8–9; Brome, *Travels,* p. 109; Thirsk, p. 53.

14. Hull, pp. 13–16, 96–97, 327, 344, 534.

15. Norden, p. 8; Fuller, *Worthies,* I, 497; Daniel Defoe, *Tour through . . . England and Wales,* ed. G. D. H. Cole (London, 1928), I, 9; E.R.O., Q/SR 138/43 (1597).

16. Hull, pp. 63–65. Leases frequently included the tenant's obligation to keep the salt-sluices in order. See also F. G. Emmison, "A Grazing Agreement in Essex in 1605," *Essex Review,* 48 (1939), 203–207.

17. Hull, pp. 89, 111; C. B. Sworder, "Epping Fairs, Markets, Alehouses," *Essex Review,* 32 (1923), 17–21.

18. E.R.O., Q/SBa 2/34, petition of East Doniland.

19. *V.C.H. Essex,* II, 313–314; Fuller, *Worthies,* I, 498; Defoe, *Tour,* p. 12.

20. *L.J.,* IV, 699; V, 32, 66; VI, 625; VII, 32, 352, 385, 389; XI, 306, 335; XII, 536; XVII, 443.

21. Defoe, *Tour,* p. 11.

22. See E.R.O., Q/S Ba 2/1–40, for innumerable depositions relating to poaching. For Elizabethan examples, see Emmison, *Disorder,* pp. 232–255.

23. Harrison, pp. 253, 256, 327–329; Hull, p. 54; Sworder, "Epping Fairs," p. 18.

24. Hull, pp. 115–117, 156–166.

25. Calculated from figures in Burley, p. 393. Unlike Dr. Burley, I cannot consider Thaxted a cloth town. However, I do so regard Finchingfield. The exchange makes little difference to the overall figures.

26. Burley, pp. 3–4.

27. Stephen A. Warner, ed., *Letters from a Lieutenancy Book* (Chelmsford, Essex, 1910), p. 1. In 1615 it was reported that, at the accession of Elizabeth, Bocking, West Bergholt, Dedham, and Coggeshall had long been famous as clothing towns. B.M. Egerton. MS. 2651, fol. 24.

28. E.R.O., Assize File 35/9/2/9.

29. Warner, *Letters,* p. 1; J. E. Pilgrim, "The Rise of the New Draperies in Essex," *University of Birmingham Historical Journal,* 7 (1958–59), 36–39; Hull, pp. 253–256.

30. Norden, p. 9; *C.S.P.D.* 1547–1580, p. 697; *A.P.C.* 1597–1598, p. 69; E.R.O. Q/SR 136/82; Hull, p. 483.

31. *Wills,* I–II, passim.

32. For the higher estimate, see B.M. Egerton. MS. 2651, fol. 24; for the lower, see Burley, p. 103. In 1621 it was alleged in the House of Commons that a single loom would "set on work" forty people; Thirsk and Cooper, p. 2.

33. Fuller, *Worthies,* I, 494; Thirsk and Cooper, pp. 224–232; Burley, p. 103.

34. *Wills,* I–II, passim; E.R.O., Q/SR 208/50; Fuller, *Worthies,* I, 494–495.
35. *C.S.P.D.* 1591–1594, p. 153.
36. Emmison, *Disorder,* pp. 12–26; P. H. Reaney, *Essex* (East Ardley, York-shire, 1970; first published 1928), p. 85.
37. *V.C.H. Essex,* II, 313; Defoe, *Tour,* p. 17.
38. *V.C.H. Essex,* II, 274–279; Hull, pp. 3, 184.
39. But see Doris Willard, *Bibles in Barrels* (Southend, Essex, 1962).
40. Thirsk, p. 55.
41. Drawn from P.R.O., SP 16/358. The parishes are Finchingfield, Brain-tree, Halsted, Dedham, Felsted, Bocking, Hatfield, Little Leighs, Chelmsford (with Moulsham hamlet), Coggeshall, Ashen, Great Saling, Mount Bures, Middleton, Belchamp, Gosfield, Little Maplestead, Wickham, Bradwell, and White Colne.
42. Burley, p. 338.
43. Ibid.
44. Holmes, p. 229.
45. Christopher Hill, *Reformation to Industrial Revolution,* vol. 2 of *The Pelican Economic History of Britain* (London, 1969), p. 87.
46. Morant, I–II, passim; Holmes, p. 230.
47. Hull, pp. 283–289.
48. See J. P. Cooper's famous article "The Counting of Manors," *Econ. H. R.,* 2nd ser. 8 (April 1956), 377–389, and the brief, witty restatement of Coo-per's argument by J. H. Hexter in *Reappraisals in History* (New York, 1963), pp. 127–129.
49. Hull, p. 289.
50. Holmes, pp. 12, 231, 242; Everitt, pp. 15–35.
51. On this difficult and complex subject, see Eric Kerridge, *Agrarian Prob-lems in the Sixteenth Century and After* (London, 1969).
52. Hull, pp. 292–313, 391.
53. Ibid., p. 76.
54. Stat. 5 Eliz., c. 4.
55. *O.E.D.,* s.v. "ploughland."
56. Stat. 4 Hen. VII, c. 19; 2 & 3 Phil. & Mary, c. 2; 5 Eliz., c. 2.
57. Quoted in H. N. Brailsford, *The Levellers and the English Revolution,* ed. Christopher Hill (London, 1961), p. 613. Lilburne actually proposed to grant each family lands worth £5 to £6 per annum. In calculating the acreage this would represent, I have assumed an average rent of 5s. per acre, which seems the best estimate for the 1650s. See Eric Kerridge, "The Movement of Rent," in E. M. Carus-Wilson, ed., *Essays in Economic History* (New York, 1962), II, 208–226.
58. Peter Bowden, in Thirsk, pp. 650–663.
59. To be precise, 186 of 674 households, or 27.6 percent. E.R.O., Q/SR 188/80–83, 91–93; 241/37; 259/23; 267/31; 271/44; 275/37; 284/13; 301/42.
60. On a sample of thirteen manors scattered about the county the average size of holdings under 5 acres was only 1.3 acres. Calculated from Hull, p. 81.
61. Hull, pp. 76, 476–478; Burley, p. 21.
62. E.R.O. Q/SR 216/109, 140; 298/116.
63. Burley (p. 103) estimates that there were 4,800 combers and weavers in the later seventeenth century, out of a total population of twenty thousand. Adult males cannot have accounted for more than one-quarter of the population, or thirty thousand, and since the percentage of children is generally higher in preindustrial societies, the number may have been substantially less. Assuming

an adult male population of thirty thousand, weavers and combers would form
16 percent of the total. For the problem of the age structure of the society, see
D. C. Coleman, "Labour in the English Economy of the Seventeenth Century,"
in Paul S. Seaver, ed., *Seventeenth-Century England* (New York, 1976), pp. 117–119.

64. Reyce, p. 57.

65. E.R.O., D/DEb 7/2, 7.

66. Burley, p. 103.

67. J. E. Pilgrim, "The Cloth Industry in Essex and Suffolk, 1558–1640,"
B.I.H.R., 17 (1939–40), 144. Pilgrim himself acknowledges that "state and local
regulations were disregarded, sometimes on an astonishing scale."

68. Reyce, p. 22.

69. *C.S.P.D.* 1637, p. 88.

70. J. E. Pilgrim, "The Cloth Industry in Essex and Suffolk, 1558–1640"
(M. A. thesis, University of London, 1939), pp. 148–151.

71. Hull, p. 284; P.R.O., SP 16/358.

72. Everitt, p. 24; Fletcher, pp. 19, 26.

73. For Mott's activities over four decades, see E.R.O., D/P 264/8/3, passim.

74. P.R.O., SP 16/358.

75. Burley, p. 356.

76. One of the earliest and still most influential taxonomies is that devised
in 1695 by Gregory King. It is reprinted in Thirsk and Cooper, pp. 780–781. For
a more recent model, see Lawrence Stone, in Seaver, *Seventeenth-Century England,*
p. 28. My own scheme is close to that proposed by Wrightson and Levine for the
village of Terling; see Wrightson and Levine, passim.

77. For a discussion of this point, see Wrightson and Levine, pp. 96–97.

78. Oliver Cromwell, for example, was a mere leaseholder from 1631 to
1636, although he had already served in Parliament; Christopher Hill, *God's
Englishmen: Oliver Cromwell and the English Revolution* (New York, 1970), pp. 45–46.

79. Harrison, pp. 120–121; Smith, p. 31.

2. Make-Shift's Inheritance

1. E.R.O., parish registers.

2. Macfarlane, *Witchcraft,* p. 147; Wrightson and Levine, pp. 44–45; D. C.
Coleman, *The Economy of England, 1450–1750* (Oxford, 1977), p. 20.

3. Hull, p. 156; F. J. Fisher, "The Development of the London Food Market, 1540–1640," *Econ. H. R.,* 5 (April 1935), 46–64.

4. E.R.O., Q/SR 151/99; 155/31; 185/13; 157/30; 209/108.

5. *Wills,* I–II, passim.

6. Harrison, pp. 247–248.

7. E.R.O., Q/SR 183/62.

8. Hull, pp. 127, 141–142; on changes in the marketing of agricultural produce, see Alan Everitt, in Thirsk, pp. 466–592.

9. Harrison, pp. 200–201; W. G. Hoskins, "The Rebuilding of Rural
England, 1570–1640," *Past and Present,* no. 4 (November 1953), 44–59.

10. On these developments, see F. G. Emmison, *Elizabethan Life: Home, Work
and Land* (Chelmsford, Essex, 1976), esp. pp. 1–6.

11. Ibid., p. 6.

12. Harrison, pp. 200–201; Reyce, p. 58.

13. Quintrell, p. 15.

14. Hull, pp. 246–264. A case in point was William Lord Maynard, who leapt into the front ranks of the Essex gentry when marriage with Anne Everard brought him the manor of Sandon "and many other fair lordships"; Morant, II, 25.

15. Quintrell, pp. 12–22.

16. Hull, pp. 306–307.

17. Harrison, p. 204.

18. Hull, pp. 307, 391.

19. Eric Kerridge, *Agrarian Problems in the Sixteenth Century and After* (London, 1969), pp. 65–93.

20. Hull, p. 318.

21. Wrightson and Levine, p. 30.

22. John Norden, *The Surveyor's Dialogue,* 3rd ed. (London, 1618), dedication.

23. Hull, p. 299.

24. Norden, *Dialogue,* pp. 14–15, 8.

25. Ibid., p. 3.

26. Norden, *Dialogue,* p. 4; Kerridge, *Problems,* p. 27.

27. Wrightson and Levine, pp. 27–29.

28. Hull, pp. 318, 380; Burley, pp. 71–73.

29. Harrison, p. 202; Norden, *Dialogue,* p. 9; Reyce, p. 52.

30. Hull, pp. 371–372.

31. Lawrence Stone, *The Crisis of the Aristocracy, 1558–1641* (Oxford, 1965), pp. 37, 754.

32. Tyack, p. 109.

33. Wrightson and Levine, pp. 26–27.

34. Harrison, p. 202.

35. George Gifford, *Eight Sermons upon . . . Ecclesiastes* (London, 1589), p. 105.

36. Richard Rogers, *Seven Treatises,* 3rd ed. (London, 1610), p. 115.

37. Harrison, p. 202.

38. Hull, pp. 334–335.

39. Ibid., pp. 347–348, 350–351.

40. Harrison, p. 202.

41. E.R.O., Q/SR 181/100. Between 1611 and 1618 the royal manor of Havering was surveyed and a list of quit-rents prepared, possibly with a view to raising them; *C.S.P.D.* 1611–1618 pp. 508, 579.

42. *H.M.C.* Salisbury, IV, 44–45. "Barbaric," wrote Lord Burghley (in Greek) in the margin of Smith's letter.

43. Norden, *Dialogue,* pp. 61–65.

44. Hull, p. 299.

45. Norden, *Dialogue,* pp. 61, 64.

46. Hull, p. 408; Norden, *Dialogue,* p. 35.

47. Gifford, *Ecclesiastes,* p. 105.

48. *A.P.C.* 1558–1570, p. 137.

49. *C.S.P.D.* 1591–1594, p. 153.

50. *C.S.P.D.* 1623–1625, p. 41; E.R.O., D/B 3/3/217.

51. Emmison, *Disorder,* p. 102.

52. E.R.O., Q/SR 193/11; D/DBa L11.

53. *C.S.P.D.* 1611–1618, p. 462.

54. E.R.O., Q/SR 219/47; 199/35; 180/49.
55. E.R.O., Q/SR for years 1570–1619.
56. Emmison, *Disorder,* p. 131.
57. Ibid., pp. 124–126. Weapons used in other frays included pikestaves, hatchets, halberds, an occasional firearm, and cheeses.
58. E.R.O., Q/S Ba 2/30, report of arbitrators between John Chawkes and John Totman; petition of John Totman.
59. E.R.O., Q/SR 403/84–85.
60. E.R.O., Q/SR for years 1570–1630.
61. E.R.O., Coggeshall manorial rolls.
62. Margaret Spufford, *Contrasting Communities: English Villagers in the Sixteenth and Seventeenth Centuries* (Cambridge, 1974), pp. 165–166.
63. Kerridge, *Agrarian Problems,* passim.
64. For evidence of the complexity of the tenurial hierarchy, see the account of an Elizabethan disseisin case by John Holmes, "The Affair at Paternosters," *Essex Review,* 64 (1955), 259–266.
65. David G. Hey, *An English Rural Community: Myddle under the Tudors and Stuarts* (Leicester, 1974), pp. 31–48.
66. Norden, pp. 7–9; Hull, pp. 57–58.
67. Hull, p. 55.
68. E.R.O., Q/SR 257/30.
69. Tyack, p. 112; *C.S.P.D.* 1623–1625, p. 41; E.R.O., D/B 3/3/217; E.R.O., Assize File 35/10/22.
70. Hull, pp. 55, 63–65.
71. *C.S.P.D.* 1611–1618, pp. 37, 58, 381; 1619–1623, p. 430; 1623–1625, p. 135.
72. Hull, pp. 348, 375.
73. Wrightson and Levine, pp. 33–35.
74. Peter Bowden, in Thirsk, p. 865.
75. E.R.O., Q/S AA/1; D/DBa/08/2,3. In 1613 Ralph Loder reckoned that his five servants each cost him £10 5s.; Thirsk and Cooper, p. 121. For similar estimates, see Macfarlane, *Josselin,* p. 44.
76. D. C. Coleman, "Labor in the English Economy of the Seventeenth Century," in Paul S. Seaver, ed., *Seventeenth-Century England* (New York, 1976), p. 125.
77. Harrison, p. 217.
78. Gifford, *Ecclesiastes,* pp. 16, 118; Rogers, *Seven Treatises,* p. 115.
79. *H.M.C.* Tenth Report, appendix 4, pp. 473–474; E.R.O., Q/SR 44/27; 45/29.
80. E.R.O., Q/SR 77/57; 111/51; 126/58; 128/18a; 117/71; 123/83–84; 112/69; 135/21; 138/43.
81. E.R.O., Q/SR 202/99; D/P 94/5/1, fol. 165v.
82. Keith Wrightson, "An Essex Village and the Courts, 1590–1650" (unpublished typescript), p. 1.
83. Hull, pp. 474–478.
84. Harrison, p. 216; Coleman, "Labor," p. 116; Thirsk and Cooper, pp. 780–781.
85. Tusser, pp. 99–100.
86. E.R.O., Q/SR 195/28; 216/52; 186/10; 198/34; 215/39; 225/17.
87. Harrison, p. 217.

88. Hull, p. 604.

89. P.R.O., SP 14/150/7; *C.S.P.D.* 1636–37, p. 361.

90. On the whole subject of servants in seventeenth-century England, see Peter Laslett, *The World We Have Lost,* 2nd ed. (London, 1971), pp. 1–22.

91. Thomas Hardy, "The Dorsetshire Laborer," in Harold Orel, ed., *Thomas Hardy's Personal Writings* (Lawrence, Kansas, 1966), p. 175.

92. E.R.O., Q/SR 52/29.

93. E.R.O., Q/SR 154/3, 49; D/B 3/3/397/9.

94. E.R.O., Q/SR 207/96. For other cases of laborers going lame, see E.R.O., Q/S Ba 2/34, petition of Roger Bridge; Q/S Ba 2/105, petitions of Richard Warrakers and Joan Godfrey.

95. E.R.O., Q/S Ba 2/30, petition of John Greene.

96. E.R.O., Q/S Ba 2/30, examination of John Bum.

97. Joel Samaha, *Law and Order in Historical Perspective: The Case of Elizabethan Essex* (New York, 1974); Jeremy C. M. Walker, "Crime and Capital Punishment in Elizabethan England" (B.A. thesis, University of Birmingham, 1971).

98. The adjustment is only approximate, however. I have controlled only for the survival of Assize files, although about one-sixth of felony cases come from the Quarter Sessions rolls. Any finer tuning was beyond my slender statistical capacities, and would in any case have made little difference to the general picture.

99. Quoted in Walker, p. 12.

100. Printed in James Bruce Ross and Mary Martin McLaughlin, eds. *The Portable Renaissance Reader* (New York, 1953), p. 225.

101. Stats, 3 & 4 Ed. VI, c. 16.

102. William Harrison, *Elizabethan England,* ed. Lothrop Withington (London, n.d.), pp. 246–247.

103. E.R.O., Q/SR 76/23–23a; 113/36.

104. Act IV, sc. iii.

105. E.R.O., Q/S Ba 2/105, petition of ministers and inhabitants of West Bergholt.

106. For examples, see Gamini Salgado, ed., *Cony-Catchers and Bawdy Baskets: An Anthology of Elizabethan Low Life* (London, 1972).

107. Harrison, *Elizabethan England,* p. 127; E.R.O., Q/SR 76/57.

108. E.R.O., Q/SR 79/92.

109. E.R.O., Q/SR 113–139; 122/166; 120/46.

110. *Stanleyes Remedye* (London, 1646), p. 5.

111. R. Younge, *The Poores Advocate* (London, 1655), pp. 10–11.

112. E.R.O., Q/SR for years 1564–1572, passim.

113. E.R.O., Q/SR 79/92; 214–275; 113/40–40a.

114. E.R.O., Q/SR 304/154; 256/49.

115. The following paragraphs are drawn principally from the liner notes by Charles Parker for the record album *The Traveling People,* a "radio ballad" by Ewan MacColl, Peggy Seeger, and Charles Parker (London, Argo Records, 1969). Produced for the BBC, this radio ballad combines interviews with gypsies and tinkers with traditional and original music by MacColl and Seeger.

116. E.R.O., Assize File 35/8/4/16; 35/12/6/24; 35/20/5B/24; Q/SR 181/64; 196/17, 109.

117. E.R.O., Assize File 35/54/H/89.

118. Jeremy Sandford, *Gypsies,* (London, 1975), p. 20.

119. I owe this point to W. K. Jordan.

120. I have this story from MacColl's wife, Peggy Seeger, who adds, "It's funny now, but the BBC only gave us a £20 allowance."

121. Keith Thomas, *Religion and the Decline of Magic* (New York, 1971), pp. 435–468.

122. Macfarlane, *Witchcraft*, p. 23.

123. Geoge Gifford, *A Dialogue Concerning Witches* (London, 1593), p. 2.

124. Macfarlane, *Witchcraft*, p. 61.

125. For general interpretations of continental witchcraft, see H. R. Trevor-Roper, "The European Witch-Craze of the Sixteenth and Seventeenth Centuries," in *Religion, Reformation and Social Change, and Other Essays* (London, 1967), and Norman Cohn, *Europe's Inner Demons* (New York, 1975).

126. Thomas, *Religion*, pp. 552–558.

127. ibid., p. 554.

128. Ibid., pp. 563–564.

129. Ibid., pp. 554–555; Peter Haining, ed., *The Witchcraft Papers: Contemporary Records of the Witchcraft Hysteria in Essex, 1560–1700* (London, 1974), p. 63.

130. Thomas, *Religion*, p. 506.

131. Haining, *Papers*, p. 26.

132. Thomas, *Religion*, p. 512.

133. Gifford, *Dialogue*, p. 18.

134. On the social status of witchcraft "victims," see Macfarlane, *Witchcraft*, p. 150.

135. Thomas, *Religion*, p. 7.

136. Gifford, *Dialogue*, p. 18.

137. *H.M.C.* Salisbury, IV, 5.

138. Quoted in Christopher Hill, *Change and Continuity in Seventeenth-Century England* (London, 1974), p. 181.

139. Anthony Fletcher, *Tudor Rebellions*, 2nd ed. (London, 1973), p. 76.

140. E.R.O., Assize File 35/9/2/6–9.

141. *A.P.C.* 1575–1577, pp. 187–188, 263.

142. E.R.O., Assize File 35/25/T/37. Tusser was a crackpot, no doubt, but by contemporary standards his prophecies were not as eccentric as they look. As Keith Thomas notes, they derived from the medieval prophetic tradition; Thomas, *Religion*, pp. 406, 422.

143. E.R.O., Assize File 35/23/H/36.

144. E.R.O., Assize File 35/28/H/32.

145. E.R.O., Assize File 35/27/T/47.

146. E.R.O., Q/SR 113/49.

147. E.R.O., Assize File 35/33/T/53.

148. E.R.O., Assize File 35/36/T/39–40.

149. E.R.O., Q/SR 136/111; 171/57.

150. E. P. Thompson, "The Moral Economy of the English Crowd in the Eighteenth Century," *Past and Present*, no. 50 (February 1971), 76–136.

151. For these and other sixteenth-century beverages, see Harrison, p. 247.

152. *H.M.C.* Salisbury, IV, 5.

153. *D.N.B.*

154. *H.M.C.* Salisbury, IV, 4.

155. *C.S.P.D.* 1595–1597, pp. 237–253, 421–424; *D.N.B.*

156. J. E. Neale, *Elizabeth I and Her Parliaments* (New York, 1966), II, 336.

3. The Crisis of Social Policy

1. Stat. 5 Eliz., c. 4, printed in *T.E.D.*, I, 338–350. See also W. E. Minchinton, ed., *Wage Regulation in Pre-Industrial England* (Newton Abbot, Devon, 1972).

2. E.R.O., Q/SR 3/2.

3. E.R.O., Q/SR 34–37, passim.

4. E.R.O., Q/SR, for years 1571–1650, passim.

5. See, for examples, E.R.O., Q/SR 52/37, 378/18.

6. E.R.O., D/P 232/8/1, 25 December 1603.

7. Harrison, pp. 182, 218.

8. D. B. Quinn, "Sir Thomas Smith (1513–1577) and the Beginnings of English Colonial Theory," *Proceedings of the American Philosophical Society*, 89 (1945), 543–560.

9. J. E. Neale, *Elizabeth I and Her Parliaments* (New York, 1966), II, 282, 348; Emmison, *Disorder,* pp. 237, 241.

10. On this whole subject, the standard general works remain Sidney and Beatrice Webb, *The Old Poor Law,* vol. 7 of *English Local Government* (London, 1927), and, less reliably, E. M. Leonard, *The Early History of English Poor Relief* (Cambridge, 1900). For a recent synthesis, see John Pound, *Poverty and Vagrancy in Tudor England* (London, 1971), which contains a useful bibliography of more specialized studies.

11. B.M. Harleian MS. 7020, fols. 267, 267v.

12. E.R.O., Q/SR 145/2a.

13. It is obviously illegitimate to assume that the extant accounts represent more than a fraction of the actual amount of public poor relief. The Essex Quarter Sessions rolls, for example, contain references to poor rate collections in at least sixteen parishes for which no rates have survived. They are: West Hanningfield (Q/SR 78/45; 110/46); Goldhanger (Q/SR 93/21); Thundersley (Q/SR 78/45; 110/46); Netteswell (Q/SR 133/43); West Ham (Q/SR 138/43; Q/S Ba 2/43); Runwell (Q/SR 163/10); Hatfield Peverel (Q/SR 199/50); Danbury (Q/SR 202/97); Latton (Q/S Ba 2/27; 2/30); Great Burstead (Q/S Ba 2/34); Bocking (Q/S Ba 2/29); Great Waltham (Q/S Ba 2/28); Great Oakley (Q/S Ba 2/38); Rainham (Q/SR 312/80); Great Horkesley (Q/S Ba 2/43); and Boxted (Q/SR 1/1, fol. 1). A reference to rates in Stanstead Mountfichet postdates the Restoration but declares that the rates had existed since "time out of mind" (Q/S Ba 2/108). In addition, there were in the 1590s occasional hundredal collections, as in Chafford and Barstaple hundreds in 1593. These were compulsory rates, and defaulters were presented at the sessions (Q/SR 124/24).

14. E.R.O., D/P 18/8/1; 264/8/3, 1 February 1630; 167/1/1, p. 308.

15. E.R.O., D/DBa/08/1,2,4; Q/R Th 5.

16. W. K. Jordan, *Philanthropy in England* (London, 1959).

17. John R. Rilling, "The Administration of Poor Relief in the Counties of Essex and Somerset during the Personal Rule of Charles I, 1629–1640" (Ph.D. diss., Harvard University, 1959), pp. 117–130.

18. E.R.O., D/DBa/08/2–5. For further details, see Chapter 7.

19. E.R.O., D/DBa/08/1–2.

20. Tusser, p. 157.

21. *T.E.D.* I, 353 ff.

22. A. E. Bland, P. A. Brown, and R. H. Tawney, eds., *English Economic History* (London, 1914), p. 344.

23. Harrison, p. 256.

24. Stat. 31 Eliz., c. 8.

25. Stat. 3 & 4 Ed. VI, c. 3.

26. E.R.O., Q/SR 109/53.

27. E.R.O., Q/SR 109/54. See also Q/SR 109/55–56, 56a; 110/40–41; 111/2, 51–53.

28. E.R.O., Q/SR 114/6.

29. E.R.O., Q/SR 122/67–68.

30. E.R.O., Q/SR 118/41; 123/83–85; 154/52. See also Q/SR 115/61; 117/1, 70, 72; 122/71; 123/87; 126/59, 61; 140/128–129.

31. E.R.O., Q/SR 250/54.

32. E.R.O., Q/SR for years 1580–1630.

33. Hull, pp. 604–605.

34. Dedham Minutes, p. 100.

35. E.R.O., D/P 232/8/1.

36. Bod. MS. Top. Essex, c. 18, fol. 44.

37. E.R.O., D/P 264/8/3, 12 July and 1 November 1619; 4 February, 1 April, 4 November 1622. In the 1620s alone the vestry expelled at least forty-eight inmates and cottagers; most of these evictions left no trace in the Quarter Sessions rolls.

38. E.R.O., D/P 14/8/7, 23 October 1626.

39. E.R.O., D/P 167/1/1, pp. 185, 308.

40. E.R.O., Q/SR 126/37, 60.

41. E.R.O., D/P 264/8/3, 1619, passim, 1 April 1622; D/P 14/8/7, 23 October 1626; Q/SR 207/58.

42. Emmison, *Disorder,* pp. 206–207; E.R.O., Q/SR 273/15.

43. Thirsk and Cooper, p. 80.

44. I owe this point to Arthur Searle of the British Library, formerly of the E.R.O.

45. W. J. Pressey, "Essex Affairs Matrimonial," *Essex Review,* 49 (1940), 86.

46. E.R.O., Q/SR 181/95–96; D/P 14/8/7, 19 February 1628.

47. Thirsk and Cooper, p. 759.

48. R. Younge, *The Poore's Advocate* (London, 1655), pp. 10–11.

49. David Levine and Keith Wrightson, "The Social Context of Illegitimacy" (unpublished typescript, 1970).

50. E.R.O., D/Ba/08/3.

51. E.R.O., D/P 264/8/3, 6 September 1619.

52. E.R.O., Q/SR 266/12; Q/SBa 2/37, petition of Theydon Garnon. See also Q/SR 419/61.

53. E.R.O., Q/SR 53/51, 97; 60/47; 67/51; 70/25; 90/33.

54. E.R.O., Q/SR 104/59–59a; 109/19.

55. E.R.O., Q/SR 125/1; 147/28; 158/34.

56. Stat. 7 Jac. I, c. 4.

57. Phillip Stubbes, *The Anatomie of Abuses,* ed. F. J. Furnivall (London, 1879), p. 99.

58. P.R.O., E 134/8 Car. I / Mich. 18, deposition of Thomas Lawrence.

59. Colchester Castle, Colchester Assembly Book, 1620–1647, p. 16.

60. Joan Kent, "Attitudes of Members of the House of Commons to the Regulation of 'Personal Conduct' in Late Elizabethan and Early Stuart

England," *Bulletin of the Institute of Historical Research,* 46 (May 1973), pp. 41–71.

61. Kent, "Attitudes," pp. 43–44.

62. Ibid., p. 62.

63. Emmison, *Disorder,* pp. 204–206, 209; E.R.O., Q/SR 348/74.

64. Emmison, *Disorder,* pp. 209, 224; E.R.O., Q/SR 231/17.

65. E.R.O., D/P 167/1/1, fol. 165; Q/SR 231/17; Q/S Ba 2/37, letter of James Heron. See also Q/SR 316/89, for a similar complaint from Upminster in 1642.

66. On this general subject, see Christopher Hill, *Society and Puritanism in Pre-Revolutionary England* (New York, 1967), pp. 259–297, 420–443.

67. Dedham Minutes, pp. 99–100.

68. Bod. MS. Top. Essex, c. 18, fols. 44–45.

69. E.R.O., D/P 14/8/7, 23 October 1626, 10 April 1627.

70. E.R.O., D/P 264/8/3, 3 February 1623.

71. E.R.O., D/P 14/8/7, 5 June 1627.

4. Preachers, Prelates, and Parliaments

1. *H.M.C.* 7th Report, appendix, p. 516; Thomas Shepherd, "A Memoir of his own Life," in Alexander Young, ed, *Chronicles of the First Plantation of the Colony of Massachusetts Bay* (Boston, 1846), p. 515.

2. W. K. Jordan, *Edward VI: The Young King* (London, 1968), pp. 150, 165.

3. Brian Dale, *Annals of Coggeshall* (Coggeshall, Essex, 1863), pp. 124–125; John Foxe, *Acts and Monuments,* ed. Josiah Pratt (London, n.d.), III, 598; IV, 242–243; John Strype, *Ecclesiastical Memorials* (Oxford, 1822), I, pt. 1, 114.

4. Strype, *Memorials,* I, pt. 1, 113–133; Foxe, *Acts and Monuments,* pp. 150, 165.

5. Harold Smith, *The Ecclesiastical History of Essex during the Long Parliament and Commonwealth* (Colchester, Essex, c. 1930), p. 8; Foxe, *Acts and Monuments,* VI, 722, 729, 740; VII, 97–98, 114–123; VIII, 303–310, 383–384, 389, 393, 405–407, 413–414, 417–420, 467; Strype, *Memorials,* III, pt. 1, 552–554; *A.P.C.* 1558–1570, p. 26.

6. John Strype, *Annals of the Reformation* (Oxford, 1824), II, pt. 2, 282.

7. M. M. Knappen, ed., *Two Elizabethan Puritan Diaries, by Richard Rogers and Samuel Ward* (Chicago, 1933), p. 83.

8. Arthur Dent, *The Ruine of Rome,* 2nd ed. (London, 1607), sig. A2.

9. Harvard University, Houghton MS. Eng. 109.

10. William Haller, *Foxe's Book of Martyrs and the Elect Nation* (London, 1963).

11. Arthur Dent, *The Ruine of Rome* (London, 1603), "To the Christian Reader."

12. George Gifford, *Sermons upon the Whole Book of the Revelation* (London, 1956), sig. A2, p. 184.

13. Dent, *Ruine,* p. 240.

14. Dent, *Ruine,* "To the Christian Reader"; Gifford, *Revelation,* p. 2.

15. Stephen Marshall, *The Song of Moses* (London, 1643), p. 3.

16. Edward Symmons, *Scripture Vindicated* (London, 1645), sig. A3.

17. William Lamont, *Godly Rule: Politics and Religion, 1603–1660* (London, 1969).

18. E.R.O., Q/SR 48/41.

19. E.R.O., D/ACA 11/50; Patrick Collinson, *The Elizabethan Puritan Movement* (Berkeley, Calif., 1967), p. 92.

20. E.R.O., Q/SR 96a/4.

21. D.W.L. 31/B/II/92.

22. D.W.L. 31/B/I/112–121.

23. George Gifford, *Country Divinity* (London, 1583), fol. 63v.

24. For examples, see John Strype, *Life of Parker* (Oxford, 1821), II, 381–385; Richard Rogers, *Seven Treatises* (London, 1603), pp. 477–492; Collinson, pp. 381–382.

25. Rogers, *Seven Treatises* (1603), p. 477.

26. Kenneth W. Shipps, "Lay Patronage of East Anglian Puritan Clerics in Pre-Revolutionary England" (Ph.D. diss. Yale University, 1971), appendix vii.

27. William Harrison, *Elizabethan England,* ed. Lothrop Withington (London, 1889), p. 66.

28. Collinson, *Movement,* p. 176.

29. Collinson, *Movement,* pp. 171–174.

30. Harrison, *Elizabethan England,* p. 67.

31. Davids, pp. 67–68; Collinson, *Movement,* pp. 150–151.

32. Collinson, *Movement,* pp. 187, 191.

33. Harrison, *Elizabethan England,* p. 67.

34. Davids, pp. 70–71; John Strype, *Life of . . . Aylmer* (Oxford, 1821), pp. 54–56; *Annals of the Reformation* (Oxford, 1824), III, i, 178; III, ii, 228–237.

35. Collinson, *Movement,* pp. 211–212.

36. *Dedham Minutes,* passim.

37. Collinson, *Movement,* pp. 225–229, 287–288, 305, 319.

38. Dedham Minutes, p. 31; Davids, pp. 77–78; Collinson, *Movement,* p. 256.

39. Albert Peel, *The Seconde Parte of a Register* (Cambridge, 1915), I, 225; D.W.L. 31/B/I/171.

40. Collinson, *Movement,* p. 256.

41. D.W.L. 31/B/I/177.

42. Dedham Minutes, p. 36; Davids, p. 88; D.W.L. 31/B/I/112–121; Peel, *Seconde Parte,* II, 80, 156ff; Smith, *Ecclesiastical History,* pp. 10–11.

43. Davids, pp. 79–80; Collinson, *Movement,* pp. 263–272.

44. Collinson, *Movement,* pp. 304–305.

45. B.M. Lansdowne MS. 50, fol. 89.

46. B.M. Lansdowne MS. 68, fol. 110.

47. Peel, *Seconde Parte,* II, 28–30.

48. B.M., Additional MS. 38,492.

49. J. E. Neale, *Elizabeth I and Her Parliaments* (New York, 1966), II, 209–210, 267–279, 288, 291.

50. D.W.L. 31/B/I/143–145, 185–187; Peel, *Seconde Parte,* II, 188–191; Davids, p. 81.

51. Davids, p. 84; Neale, *Parliaments,* II, 148–150, 157.

52. *A.P.C.* 1588, pp. 318–319.

53. D.W.L. 31/B/I/139–142; Peel, *Seconde Parte,* II, 258–259; Neale, *Parliaments,* II, 237–239.

54. D.W.L. 31/B/II/92.

55. Knappen, *Diaries,* pp. 64, 76, 78.

56. Dedham Minutes, p. 74; Knappen, *Diaries,* p. 84; George Gifford, *Eight Sermons upon . . . Ecclesiastes* (London, 1589), dedication.

57. *D.N.B.,* "Richard Rich." Rich converted back to Protestantism at the

accession of Elizabeth. In fairness to his memory it should no doubt be added that he founded Felsted School, which educated hundreds of children of Puritan families during the Elizabethan and early Stuart period. See Quintrell, p. 29.

58. Davids, pp. 72–73; Strype, *Aylmer*, pp. 54–57.

59. *D.N.B.*, "Penelope Rich"; *H.M.C.* 7, appendix, p. 527; Cyril Falls, *Mountjoy: Elizabethan General* (London, 1955), pp. 57–58, 88.

60. *D.N.B.*, "Penelope Rich."

61. Davids, pp. 70–72; Strype, *Aylmer*, pp. 54–57.

62. E.R.O., Q/SR 84/28, 43.

63. Ogbu Uke Kalu, "The Jacobean Church and Essex Puritans" (Ph.D. diss., University of Toronto, 1972), p. 379. *D.N.B.*, "Robert Rich, Second Earl of Warwick." Knappen, *Diaries*, p. 78.

64. Kalu, "Jacobean Church," p. 365; D.W.L., 31/B/I/185–7; Peel, *Seconde Parte*, II, 191–192.

65. Davids, p. 81; Collinson, *Movement*, p. 278 Knappen, *Diaries*, p. 29; Neale, *Parliaments*, II, 156, 256, 267–276, 396, 402–404; *British Sessional Papers: House of Commons* (London, 1878), LXII, pt. 1, 414–437.

66. Collinson, *Movement*, p. 223; Emmison, *Disorder*, p. 193.

67. Neale, *Parliaments*, II, 267–279.

68. Collinson, *Movement*, pp. 450–457.

69. B.M. Additional MS. 38,492, fol. 89.

70. Lambeth MS. 2442, fol. 7.

71. Mark H. Curtis, "The Hampton Court Conference and its Aftermath," *History*, 46 (February 1961), 5–6.

72. Curtis, "Hampton Court," pp. 1–16, passim.

73. B.M. Additional MS. 38,492, fols. 81–85.

74. For a complete account of this interesting election, see Mary E. Bohannon, "The Essex Election of 1604," *English Historical Review*, 48 (1933), 395–413.

75. B.M. Additional MS. 38,492, fol. 6.

76. Curtis, "Hampton Court," p. 16.

77. S. R. Gardiner, *History of England* (London, 1894–1896), I, 179.

78. J. P. Kenyon, *The Stuart Constitution* (Cambridge, 1966), pp. 126–127.

79. B.M. Additional MS. 38,492, fol. 6.

80. *D.N.B.*, "Arthur Hildersam."

81. Curtis, "Hampton Court," p. 9; Kenyon, *Stuart Constitution*, p. 127.

82. Ogbu Uke Kalu, "Bishops and Puritans in Early Jacobean England: A Perspective on Methodology," *Church History*, 45 (December 1976), 469–489.

83. Kalu, "Bishops and Puritans," pp. 472–475.

84. Ibid., p. 480; Knappen, *Diaries*, pp. 29–31.

85. Kalu, "Bishops and Puritans," p. 481.

86. Douglas Bush, *English Literature in the Earlier Seventeenth Century* (Oxford, 1972), pp. 310–311.

87. William Haller, *The Rise of Puritanism* (New York, 1957), pp. 25, 36; Richard Rogers, *Seven Treatises*, 3rd ed. (London, 1610), sig. A4.

88. John Howe, *Works* (London, 1834), VI, 493; Giles Firmin, *The Real Christian* (London, 1670), "To the Christian Reader," pp. 75–76.

89. Cotton Mather, *Magnalia Christi Americana* (Hartford, Conn., 1852), I, 305–306.

90. Matthew Newcomen, *A Sermon Preached at the Funeral of . . . Samuel Collins* (London, 1658), pp. 50–52.

91. Kalu, "Jacobean Church," pp. 344, 377.

92. Samuel Clark, *The Lives of Sundry Eminent Persons in the Later Age* (London, 1683), pp. 58–59, 64, 159–160.

93. Kalu, "Jacobean Church," pp. 352, 379–384, 454–455.

5. The Code of Redemption

1. Arthur Dent, *The Plaine Man's Path-Way to Heaven* (London, 1607), pp. 23–24. On this whole subject, see Christopher Hill, *Society and Puritanism in Pre-Revolutionary England*, 2nd ed. (New York, 1967), pp. 30–78.

2. Richard Rogers et al., *A Garden of Spiritual Flowers*, 5th ed. (London, 1609), sig. A5v.

3. George Gifford, *The Country Divinity* (London, 1582), fol. 46.

4. Dent, *Path-Way*, pp. 17–18, 31.

5. Richard Rogers, *The Practice of Christianity* (London, 1623), p. 44.

6. Charles H. George and Katherine George, *The Protestant Mind of the English Reformation, 1570–1641* (Princeton, N.J., 1961), pp. 324–326.

7. Ibid., pp. 327–328.

8. Gifford, *Country Divinity*, fol. 11.

9. Ibid., fols, 6–6v.

10. J. P. Kenyon, *The Stuart Constitution* (Cambridge, 1966), p. 128.

11. George and George, *Mind*, p. 328.

12. The literature of semiotics is large and rapidly growing. A useful introduction is provided by Terence Hawkes, *Structuralism and Semiotics* (Berkeley, Calif., 1977), which contains a valuable bibliography. I have also found very stimulating the essays collected in Daniel P. Lucid, ed., *Soviet Semiotics: An Anthology* (Baltimore, 1977).

13. On the Russian formalists, see Fredric Jameson, *The Prison-House of Language* (Princeton, 1972), especially pp. 43–98.

14. Kenneth Burke, *Attitudes toward History*, rev. ed. (Boston, 1961), pp. 308–314.

15. For an introduction to the linguistics of Ferdinand de Saussure, see Jonathan Culler, *Saussure* (Glasgow, 1976).

16. Rogers, *Practice*, p. 43.

17. Gifford, *Country Divinity*, fol. 34v.

18. Dent, *Path-Way*, dedication.

19. Rogers, *Garden*, sigs. A4, A4v.

20. Thomas Hooker, *The Soules Preparation for Christ* (London, 1632), title page.

21. Rogers, *Garden*, sig. A4.

22. Hooker, *Preparation*, p. 10.

23. Ibid., p. 66; Gifford, *Country Divinity*, fols. 54–56.

24. Samuel Clark, *The Lives of Sundry Eminent Persons in the Later Age* (London, 1683), pp. 59, 64.

25. Ernest Axon, ed., *Oliver Heywood's Life of John Angier of Denton*, Chetham Society, n.s. 97 (Manchester, 1937), 50–51.

26. George and George, *Mind*, pp. 330, 337; Gifford, *Country Divinity*, fol. 49.

27. Rogers, *Practice*, pp. 7–9.

28. Giles Firmin, *The Real Christian* (London, 1670), dedication, p. 235.

29. Rogers, *Practice*, p. 57; Firmin, *Christian*, p. 67.

30. Jeremy Dyke, *Good Conscience* (London, 1624), p. 69.

31 Firmin, *Christian*, "To the Christian Reader," sig. G2.

32. Dent, *Path-Way*, p. 11.

33. Axon, *Angier*, pp. 50–51.

34. Ibid.

35. William Haller, *The Rise of Puritanism* (New York, 1957), pp. 3–48.

36. Cotton Mather, *Magnalia Christi Americana* (Hartford, Conn., 1852), I, 334.

37. Eliza Vaughan, *The Essex Village in Days Gone By* (Colchester, Essex, 1928), pp. 161–162.

38. Mather, *Magnalia*, I, 333, 346.

39. Rogers, *Practice*, pp. 54–57.

40. Richard Rogers, *Seven Treatises* (London, 1603), p. 488.

41. Rogers, *Garden*, sig. A7v.

42. Dent, *Path-Way*, pp. 16–18.

43. Ibid., pp. 8, 18.

44. Wallace Notestein, *The English People on the Eve of Colonization* (New York, 1962), p. 167.

45. Rogers, *Practice*, pp. 219–220.

46. J. Sears McGee, *The Godly Man in Stuart England* (New Haven, 1976), passim.

47. Gifford, *Country Divinity*, fol. 54v.

48. Ogbu Uke Kalu, "The Jacobean Church and Essex Puritans" (Ph.D. diss., University of Toronto, 1972), pp. 383–385.

49. Richard Rogers, *Seven Treatises*, 3rd ed. (London, 1610), p. 191; Hill, *Society and Puritanism*, p. 285.

50. Hooker, *Preparation*, p. 70.

51. George and George, *Mind*, p. 162.

52. Thomas Barnes, *The Court of Conscience* (London, 1623), pp. 139–140.

53. Gifford, *Country Divinity* (1598 ed.), p. 69.

54. George and George, *Mind*, p. 159.

55. *Winthrop Papers*, Massachusetts Historical Society Collections (Boston, 1929–), II, 122.

56. Rogers, *Seven Treatises*, 3rd ed., p. 489.

57. John Rogers, *The Doctrine of Faith*, 3rd ed. (London, 1629), pp. 474–489.

58. George Gifford, *Eight Sermons upon . . . Ecclesiastes* (London, 1589), fol. 17.

59. Jeremy Dyke, *Counterpoyson against Covetousness* (London, 1619), p. 14.

60. George Gifford, *Ecclesiastes*, fol. 16.

61. Firmin, *Christian*, pp. 269–270.

62. Rogers, *Seven Treatises*, 3rd ed., pp. 489, 572–573.

63. John Rogers, *A Treatise of Love*, 3rd ed. (London, 1637), p. 212.

64. Rogers, *Seven Treatises*, 3rd ed., pp. 194, 489.

65. Dent, *Path-Way*, p. 21.

66. Emmison, *Morals*, p. 215.

67. Dent, *Path-Way*, p. 24.

68. John Rogers, *Love*, p. 233.

69. Rogers, *Seven Treatises*, 1st ed., p. 485; Dyke, *Counterpoyson*, pp. 31–33.

70. Rogers, *Seven Treatises*, 3rd ed., p. 574.

71. Rogers, *Seven Treatises*, 1st ed., p. 484.

72. Christopher Hill, *Society and Puritanism*, p. 511.

73. Dent, *Path-Way*, p. 30.

6. *Society and Puritanism*

1. *O.E.D., s.v. "neighborhood."*
2. *A Collection of Seventy-Nine Black-Letter Ballads and Broadsides* (London, 1870), p. 135.
3. George Gifford, *The Country Divinity* (London, 1598), p. 6.
4. Richard Rogers, *Seven Treatises*, 3rd ed. (London, 1610), p. 115.
5. For a succinct description of these environmental perils, see Keith Thomas, *Religion and the Decline of Magic* (New York, 1971), pp. 3–21.
6. Emmison, *Morals*, p. 59.
7. Harrison, p. 36.
8. Emmison, *Disorder*, p. 229; Emmison, *Morals*, p. 275.
9. Emmison, *Morals*, p. 275.
10. John Christopher Coldeway, "Early Essex Drama" (Ph.D. diss., University of Colorado, 1972), p. 37.
11. *C.S.P.D.* 1633–34, pp. 275–276.
12. Christopher Hill, *Society and Puritanism*, 2nd ed. (New York, 1967), pp. 190–191.
13. Thomas, *Religion*, p. 65.
14. Emmison, *Disorder*, pp. 113–114.
15. Coldeway, "Drama," p. 156.
16. Keith Wrightson, "The Puritan Reformation of Manners" (Ph.D. diss., Cambridge University, 1973), pp. 24–41.
17. T. H. Curling, "The Gild of All Saints, Moreton," *Transactions of the Essex Archeological Society*, 2nd ser., 11 (1911), 223. For the general weakness of trade guilds in Essex, see Mrs. Gregory Nicholson, "A Nativity Play in Essex," *Essex Review*, 43 (1934), 89.
18. Bod. MS. Top. Essex, c. 18, fol. 24r; Felix Hull, "Court Rolls of the Manor of Gt. Dunmow," *Essex Review*, 49 (1940), 155.
19. J. E. Oxley, *The Reformation in Essex to the Death of Mary* (Manchester, 1965), p. 64.
20. E.R.O., D/P 94/5/1, July 1596.
21. Thomas, *Religion*, pp. 62, 63.
22. Harrison, p. 36.
23. Emmison, *Morals*, p. 187.
24. John Strype, *Life of . . . Matthew Parker* (Oxford, 1821), pp. 303–306.
25. Coldeway, "Drama," pp. 68–76.
26. Ibid., p. 172.
27. Charles Phythian-Adams, in Peter Clark and Paul Slack, eds., *Crisis and Order in English Towns, 1500–1700* (London, 1972), pp. 73–80; R. C. Richardson, *Puritanism in North-west England* (Manchester, 1972), p. 117.
28. Thomas, *Religion*, p. 65.
29. John Rogers, *A Treatise of Love*, 3rd. ed. (London, 1637), p. 217. For Perkins, see Christopher Hill, *Puritanism and Revolution* (New York, 1964), p. 225.
30. Ibid., pp. 212–213.
31. Jeremy Dyke, *A Counterpoyson against Covetousness* (London, 1619), p. 41.
32. Richard Rogers, *Seven Treatises*, 3rd ed. (London, 1610), pp. 190–193, 496, 389.
33. Ibid., p. 496.
34. John Rogers, *Love*, pp. 62, 211.

35. Rogers, *Seven Treatises*, 3rd ed., p. 192.

36. Ibid., p. 195.

37. Arthur Hildersam, cited in Hill, *Society and Puritanism*, p. 285.

38. John Rogers, *Love*, p. 214.

39. Edward C. Banfield, *The Unheavenly City Revisited* (Boston, 1974), p. 61.

40. Rogers, *Seven Treatises*, 3rd ed., p. 574.

41. John Rogers, *Love*, pp. 213, 224.

42. Richard Rogers, *The Practice of Christianity* (London, 1623), p. 623; Rogers, *Seven Treatises*, 3rd ed., pp. 629-630.

43. Samuel Clark, *The Lives of Sundry Eminent Persons in the Later Age* (London, 1683), p. 59.

44. John Strype, *Life of . . . Aylmer* (Oxford, 1821), pp. 71-72.

45. Cotton Mather, *Magnalia Christi Americana* (Hartford, Conn., 1852), I, 335.

46. Joan Kent, "Attitudes of Members of the House of Commons to the Regulation of 'Personal Conduct' in Late Elizabethan and Early Stuart England," *Bulletin of the Institute of Historical Research*, 46 (May 1973), 44.

47. Emmison, *Disorder*, pp. 204-206.

48. Keith Wrightson, "Reformation of Manners," p. 106.

49. E.R.O., T/R 5/1/4, fol. 178v; D/P 264/8/3, fol. 81r; D/P 60/8/1, 11 September, 1678.

50. John Rogers, *Love*, pp. 213-214.

51. Dyke, *Counterpoyson*, pp. 23-24.

52. John Rogers, *Love*, p. 46.

53. Dedham Minutes, pp. 99-100.

54. Matthew Newcomen, *A Sermon Preached at the Funeral of . . . Samuel Collins* (London, 1658), p. 49.

55. Keith Wrightson and David Levine, "An Essex Village and the Courts, 1590 to 1650" (unpublished typescript, 1970).

56. Thomas Shepherd, "A Memoir of his own Life," in Alexander Young, ed., *Chronicles of the First Plantation of the Colony of Massachusetts Bay* (Boston, 1846), p. 515.

57. Peter Clark, *Provincial Society from the Reformation to the Revolution* (East Brunswick, N.J., 1977), pp. 175-177; Richardson, *Puritanism*, pp. 145-147.

58. T. G. Barnes, *Somerset: 1625-1640* (Cambridge, Mass., 1961), pp. 76-77.

59. For evidence on this point from Arthur Dent and others, see Laura S. O'Connell, "Anti-Entrepreneurial Attitudes in Elizabethan Sermons and Popular Literature," *Journal of British Studies*, 15 (Spring 1976), pp. 6-7.

60. Peter Clark, in Clark and Slack, *Crisis and Order*, p. 28.

61. Timothy Rogers, *The Roman-Catharist, or the Papist is a Puritan* (London, 1621), p. 2.

62. For examples of various uses of the term, see Hill, *Society and Puritanism*, pp. 13-29.

63. Timothy Rogers, *Roman-Catharist*, pp. 37-41.

64. John Rogers, *Love*, p. 153.

65. Hill, *Society and Puritanism*, p. 23.

66. John Bastwick, *The Confession of . . . John Bastwick* (London, 1641).

67. Albert Peel, ed., *The Seconde Parte of a Register* (Cambridge, 1915), II, 187-188; Strype, *Aylmer*, pp. 71-72.

68. Gifford, *Country Divinity*, sig. A ii-iii.

69. John Rogers, *Love*, p. 155; *The Doctrine of Faith*, 3rd ed. (London, 1629), p. 381.

70. Clark, *Lives*, p. 59.

71. E.R.O., Q/SR 84/28, 43; M. M. Knappen, ed., *Two Elizabethan Puritan Diaries* (Chicago, 1933), p. 71.

72. Patrick Collinson, *The Elizabethan Puritan Movement* (Berkeley, Calif. 1967), p. 171.

73. Dedham Minutes, p. 62.

74. Emmison, *Disorder*, pp. 109, 140, 188–189; *Morals*, pp. 66–67, 76, 98, 104–105, 118; Collinson, *Movement*, pp. 50, 352; Peel, *Seconde Parte*, II, 28–32.

75. E.R.O., Q/SR 118/32–33, 39–40.

76. Knappen, *Diaries*, p. 80.

77. E.R.O., Q/SR 64/44–45.

78. George Gifford, *A Dialogue between a Papist and a Protestant* (London, 1582), dedication, fol. 1.

79. E.R.O., Assize File 35/36/T/34.

80. *H.M.C.* Cecil, V, 394.

81. John Gerard, *The Autobiography of an Elizabethan*, trans. Philip Caraman (London, 1956), pp. 32–33.

82. Gifford, *Country Divinity*, pp. 20, 38, 41.

83. E.R.O., Q/SR86/34; E.R.O., Q/SR 64/44–45.

84. E.R.O., Q/SR 65/61. Gifford attributed a similar argument to his papist in *A Dialogue*, fol. 58.

85. Lambeth MS. 2442, fol. 7v.

86. E.R.O., D/AZ/1/3, fol. 212v.

87. E.R.O., D/ACA 31, fol. 22v; 42, fol 1; D/AEA 24, fol. 24; 27, fol. 154.

88. E.R.O., T/R 5/1/4, fol. 181.

89. E.R.O., D/AEA 29, fol. 76v.

90. Emmison, *Morals*, p. 70.

91. Ibid., p. 61.

92. Emmison, *Disorder*, pp. 141–142.

93. John Rogers, *Love*, p. 29.

94. D.W.L. 31/B/I/115.

95. E.R.O., D/AEA 26, fol. 43v.

96. Lambeth MS. 2442, fol. 8.

97. Gifford, *Country Divinity*, pp. 2–3.

98. Ibid., p. 29.

99. Ibid., pp. 4, 9.

100. Arthur Dent, *The Plaine Man's Path-Way*, (London, 1607), p. 25.

101. Gifford, *Country Divinity*, p. 52.

102. Thomas Hooker, *The Soules Preparation for Christ* (London, 1632), p. 29.

103. Ibid., p. 54.

104. Gifford, *Country Divinity*, p. 3.

105. John Rogers, *Love*, p. 46.

106. *H.M.C.* Cecil, V, 394.

107. Gifford, *A Dialogue*, dedication.

108. Strype, *Aylmer*, pp. 71–72.

109. E.R.O., D/B 3/3/155/5; 3/3/423/1; Collinson, *Movement*, pp. 376–377; William John Petchey, "The Borough of Maldon, Essex: 1500–1688" (Ph.D. diss., Leicester University, 1972), pp. 239, 244–246.

110. Peel, *Seconde Parte*, II, p. 33.

111. John Rogers, *Love*, p. 28.

112. Gifford, *Country Divinity*, pp. 47–48.

113. Ibid., p. 17.

114. Cited in Charles H. George and Katherine George, *The Protestant Mind of the English Reformation* (Princeton, 1961), p. 109.

115. Hooker, *Preparation*, p. 43.

7. Faction and Policy in Jacobean Essex

1. This summary represents a synopsis of what I was taught. The interpretive literature on the English Revolution is enormous. Useful introductions are provided by Lawrence Stone, *The Causes of the English Revolution, 1529–1642* (New York, 1972), and R. C. Richardson, *The Debate on the English Revolution* (London, 1977). The most systematic development of the Court-Country antagonism is to be found in H. R. Trevor-Roper, "The General Crisis of the Seventeenth Century," in Trevor Aston, ed., *Crisis in Europe, 1560–1660* (New York, 1967), pp. 63–102, and Perez Zagorin, *The Court and the Country* (New York, 1970).

2. T. G. Barnes, *Somerset, 1625–1640* (Cambridge, Mass., 1961); Alan Everitt, *The Community of Kent and the Great Rebellion* (Leicester, 1966); Derek Hirst, *The Representative of the People?* (Cambridge, 1975); J. S. Morrill, *Cheshire, 1630–1660* (Oxford, 1974), and *The Revolt of the Provinces* (London, 1976); and Conrad Russell, *Parliaments and English Politics, 1621–1629* (Oxford, 1979). For an attempt at a revisionist synthesis, see Robert Ashton, *The English Civil War: Conservatism and Revolution, 1603–1649* (London, 1978).

3. Hirst, *Representative*, passim. Hirst's work owes a good deal to the inspiration of J. H. Plumb, "The Growth of the Electorate in England from 1600 to 1715," *Past and Present*, no. 45 (1969), 90–116.

4. Russell, *Parliaments*, p. 2.

5. Christopher Hill, *Puritanism and Revolution* (New York, 1964), p. 20; *Century of Revolution* (New York, 1961), p. 100.

6. Thirsk, pp. 621, 865; Peter Laslett, *The World We Have Lost*, 2nd ed. (London, 1971), pp. 120–122; Keith Thomas, *Religion and the Decline of Magic* (New York, 1971), pp. 7–8.

7. So much is acknowledged by J. H. Hexter, otherwise a critic of the new revisionists. See J. H. Hexter, *Reappraisals in History*, 2nd ed. (Chicago, 1979), pp. 175–176.

8. Barbara Donagan, "The Clerical Patronage of Robert Rich, Second Earl of Warwick, 1619–1642," *Proceedings of the American Philosophical Society*, 120 (October 1976), 389–390; R. P. Stearns, *The Strenuous Puritan, Hugh Peter: 1598–1660* (Champagne, Ill., 1954), pp. 29–30; Hull, p. 283.

9. Lawrence Stone, *The Crisis of the Aristocracy* (Oxford, 1965), pp. 106, 760; *C.S.P. Ven.* 1610–1613, p. 368.

10. *D.N.B.*, "Robert Rich, Second Earl of Warwick"; A. P. Newton, *The Colonizing Activities of the English Puritans* (New Haven, 1914), p. 16.

11. After Rich's divorce from his wife, Penelope, in 1605, Archbishop Bancroft scornfully told him to go back "amongst his Puritans"; *H.M.C.* 7th Report, appendix, p. 527.

12. William Pemberton, *The Godly Merchant* (London, 1613), dedication; Arthur Dent, *The Ruine of Rome* (London, 1603), dedication.

13. Cyril Falls, *Mountjoy: Elizabethan General* (London, 1955), p. 88.

14. *C.S.P. Ven.* 1610–1613, p. 368; 1613–1615, pp. 209–211, 256, 332, 347, 366, 437.

15. *C.S.P. Ven.* 1615–1617, p. 437; 1617–1619, p. 224; Stone, *Crisis,* p. 367.

16. Newton, *Colonizing Activities,* pp. 27, 34–35.

17. Quintrell, pp. 16, 39–40.

18. *D.N.B.,* "Robert Rich."

19. William Gouge, *God's Three Arrows* (London, 1631), dedication.

20. S. R. Gardiner, ed., *Debates in the House of Lords,* 1621, Camden Society, 103 (London, 1870), 133.

21. *C.S.P.D.* 1603–1610, p. 581.

22. Arthur Wilson, *The History of Great Britain* (London, 1653), p. 162.

23. On the character and career of Henry Rich, see Barbara Donagan, "A Courtier's Progress: Greed and Consistency in the Life of the Earl of Holland," *Historical Journal,* 19, no. 2 (1976), 317–353.

24. Wilson, *History,* p. 162.

25. Donagan, "Clerical Patronage," p. 404; Edmund Calamy, *Funeral Sermon on . . . the Earl of Warwick* (London, 1658), p. 36; *D.N.B.,* "Robert Rich."

26. Donagan, "Clerical Patronage," p. 404; P.R.O., probate will of Robert Rich, Earl of Warwick (1658); Edward Hyde, Earl of Clarendon, *The History of the Great Rebellion* (Oxford, 1819), II, 281.

27. *D.N.B.,* "Robert Rich."

28. *C.S.P. Ven.* 1617–1619, p. 224; Frank W. Craven, *The Dissolution of the Virginia Company* (Oxford, 1932), p. 83.

29. Craven, *Dissolution,* pp. 129–136.

30. Shipps, p. 107; P.R.O., PROB 11/154/70.

31. Newton, *Colonizing Activities,* p. 64; *H.M.C.* 7th Report, appendix, p. 543.

32. Quintrell, p. 33. The official returns of members of Parliament are printed in *British Sessional Papers: House of Commons, 1878,* vol. 62, pt. 1.

33. Wallace Notestein, F. H. Relf, and H. Simpson, eds., *Commons Debates of 1621* (New Haven, 1935), IV, 104–105.

34. B.M. Egerton MS. 2651, fol. 24.

35. Barry E. Supple, *Commercial Crisis and Change in England: 1600–1642* (Cambridge, 1959), passim; Christopher Hill, *Century,* pp. 35–37.

36. *A.P.C.* 1619–1621, p. 79.

37. Fletcher, pp. 232–233, 240.

38. Notestein, Relf, and Simpson, *Commons Debates 1621,* III, 353.

39. Ibid., III, 11, 27, 36, 106, 353; William Cobbett, *Parliamentary History* (London, 1806), I, 1193, 1290.

40. Cobbett, *History,* I, 1197.

41. Wilson, *History,* p. 161.

42. Notestein, Relf, and Simpson, *Commons Debates 1621,* III, 470; Cobbett, *History,* I, 1311; Russell, *Parliaments,* p. 131; Christopher Thompson, "The Origins of the Politics of the Parliamentary Middle Group, 1625–1629," *Transactions of the Royal Historical Society,* 5th ser., 20 (1972), 76–77; Notestein, Relf, and Simpson, *Commons Debates 1621,* III, 471.

43. Notestein, Relf, and Simpson, *Commons Debates 1621,* III, 470; Cobbett, *History,* I, 1311; Russell, *Parliaments,* p. 131.

44. P.R.O., probate will of Robert Rich, Earl of Warwick (1658).

45. P.R.O., SP 14/117/104–105.

46. Notestein, Relf, and Simpson, *Commons Debates 1621,* III, 262, 433; Shipps, p. 54.

47. Notestein, Relf, and Simpson, *Commons Debates 1621,* IV, 415.

48. Russell, *Parliaments,* pp. 8, 20–21, 122, 413; Notestein, Relf, and Simpson, *Commons Debates 1621,* II, 405; III, 219–221, 343, 433; IV, 405.

49. Bod. MS. Top. Essex, e. 10/3, fol. 29.

50. Fletcher, p. 203.

51. Russell, *Parliaments,* p. 90.

52. Ibid., p. 8.

53. Mary F. Keeler, *The Long Parliament, 1640–1* (Philadelphia, 1954), p. 198; Robert C. Johnson, Maija J. Cole, Mary F. Keeler, William B. Bidwell, eds. *Commons Debates 1628* (New Haven, 1977–), II, 313. The loan of 1621 was also refused by Sir Harbottle Grimston, later to represent Colchester and serve as knight of the shire.

54. Peter Laslett, *The World We Have Lost,* 2nd ed. (London, 1971), pp. 120–123; Barnes, *Somerset,* p. 3.

55. Thomas Barnes, *The Court of Conscience* (London, 1623), pp. 14–15; Bod. MS. Firth, c. 4, p. 575; P.R.O., SP 14/138/89.

56. *A.P.C.* 1621–1623, pp. 224–225, 233.

57. Ibid., pp. 371–372, 397, 436; Bod. MS. Firth, c. 4, p. 575.

58. *A.P.C.* 1621–1623, p. 392; Bod. MS. Firth, c. 4, p. 589.

59. *A.P.C.* 1623–1625, p. 105.

60. Bod. MS. Top. Essex, e. 10/1, fol. 80.

61. *A.P.C.* 1621–1623, p. 377.

62. A single subsidy in Essex came to £2,418; Russell, *Parliaments,* p. 73.

63. Bod. MS. Firth, c. 4, p. 587.

64. Craven, *Dissolution,* pp. 153–216.

65. Christopher Hill, *The Century of Revolution* (New York, 1966), p. 58.

66. J. P. Kenyon, ed., *The Stuart Constitution* (Cambridge, 1966), p. 131, 145–146.

67. E.R.O., Morant MS. D/Y 2/7, fol. 19; Quintrell, p. 149.

68. Barnes, *Court,* p. 11.

69. Craven, *Dissolution,* p. 203.

70. Barnes, *Court,* dedication, pp. 14–15, 34, 144–145.

71. Morrill, *Cheshire,* pp. 22–23; Hirst, *Representative,* p. 146.

72. Hirst, *Representative,* p. 218.

73. Quintrell, pp. 21–22.

74. E.R.O., D/B 3/1/19, fol. 176v.; D/B 3/392, fols. 18, 53, 67; Hirst, *Representative,* p. 240.

75. Shipps, pp. 39–40; Hill, *Puritanism and Revolution,* pp. 240–242.

76. Russell, *Parliaments,* pp. 174, 181, 189. On this Parliament, see also S. I. Adams, "Foreign Policy and the Parliaments of 1621 and 1624," in Kevin Sharpe, ed., *Faction and Parliament: Essays on Early Stuart History* (Oxford, 1978), pp. 140–171.

77. Adams, "Foreign Policy," pp. 150–151; Thompson, "Origins," pp. 72–74; S. R. Gardiner, ed., *Debates in the House of Commons in 1625,* Camden Society, n.s. 6 (London, 1873), iii.

78. Russell, *Parliaments,* pp. 157–160, 181; Shipps, p. 43.

79. Shipps, pp. 44–45.

80. B.M. Harleian MS. 159, fol. 136.

81. Adams, "Foreign Policy," pp. 146–148, 171.

82. Shipps, p. 48; Adams, "Foreign Policy," p. 144. The first solid evidence we have about the personal association of Pym, Saye, and Warwick comes from the autumn of 1626, when Pym stood as trustee in the mortgage of Warwick's estate, and Warwick, Rich, and Barrington acted on behalf of Saye's son in a marriage negotiation; *C.S.P.D.* Addendum, 1625–1649, pp. 724–725; Thomas, "Origins," pp. 77–78, 81.

83. John Wing, *The Saint's Advantage* (London, 1624), "To the Christian Reader," pp. 33–37.

84. E.R.O., D/P 264/8/3, 1624, passim.

8. The War Years

1. In 1607, for example, a report to the House of Lords on enclosure and depopulation spoke of the need for the state to "vent" the increasing population "either by transferring to the wars or deducing of colonies"; Thirsk and Cooper, p. 109.

2. Bod. MS. Firth, c. 4, p. 107.

3. Thomas Barnes, *Vox Belli* (London, 1626), pp. 14–16.

4. E.R.O., Q/SR 245/25–26; 246/49.

5. *C.S.P.D.* 1623–1625, pp. 113, 282.

6. *D.N.B.,* "Robert Radcliffe, Fifth Earl of Sussex"; C. L'Estrange Ewen, "Robert Radcliffe, Fifth Earl of Sussex: Witchcraft Accusations," *Transactions of the Essex Archeological Society,* n.s. 22 (1940), 232–238, and portrait facing p. 294.

7. Bod. MS. Top. Essex, e. 10/1, fols. 79, 93; P.R.O. SP 14/181/53.

8. S. I. Adams, in Kevin Sharpe, ed., *Faction and Parliament: Essays on Early Stuart History* (Oxford, 1978), p. 170.

9. Bod. MS. Top. Essex, e. 10/1, fols. 98–99, 104; *V.C.H. Essex,* II, 223.

10. Bod. MS. Top. Essex, e. 10/1, fol. 98.

11. *A.P.C.* 1623–1625, pp. 407, 476; Bod. MS. Top. Essex, e. 10/1, fols. 100–101; P.R.O., SP 14/181/53.

12. E.R.O., Morant MS. D/Y 2/6, fol. 132.

13. *A.P.C.* 1623–1625, p. 448; *C.S.P.D.* 1623–1625, p. 456; 1625–1626, p. 253.

14. *C.S.P. Ven.* 1623–1625, pp. 419–420.

15. Derek Hirst, *The Representative of the People?* (Cambridge, 1975), p. 128.

16. B.M. Additional MS. 12,496, fol. 98.

17. Pierre du Moulin, *The Anatomy of Arminianism* (London, 1620), dedication; Christopher Hill, *Puritanism and Revolution* (New York, 1964), p. 240; P.R.O., probate will of Dame Ann Mildmay (1657).

18. *C.S.P.D.* 1623–1625, p. 271.

19. E.R.O., D/B 3/1/19, 210 v.; B.M. Additional MS. 12,496, fol. 98; Mary F. Keeler, *The Long Parliament* (Philadelphia, 1954), p. 274.

20 E.R.O., Morant MS D/Y 2/4, fols. 55, 59, 63, 83.

21. Christopher Thompson, "The Origins of the Politics of the Parliamentary Middle Group, 1625–1629," *Transactions of the Royal Historical Society,* 5th ser., 20 (1972), 75–76; Conrad Russell, *Parliaments and English Politics, 1621–1629* (Oxford, 1979), pp. 206–209.

22. John Preston, *The Saint's Qualification,* 2nd ed. (London, 1634), p. 269; S. R. Gardiner, ed., *Debates in the House of Commons in 1625,* Camden Society, n.s. 6 (London, 1873), 6.

23. William Cobbett, *Parliamentary History* (London, 1806), II, 12.

24. Gardiner, *Debates . . . 1625*, pp. 18–26.

25. Preston, *Saint's Qualification*, p. 294.

26. Gardiner, *Debates . . . 1625*, pp. 6, 9, 14, 26, 137.

27. Ibid., pp. 62–63, 90–91.

28. Thompson, "Origins," pp. 77–78.

29. Gardiner, *Debates . . . 1625*, pp. 127, 137; Thompson, "Origins," p. 77.

30. Russell, *Parliaments*, p. 208; Robin Clifton, "The Popular Fear of Catholics during the English Revolution," *Past and Present*, no. 52 (1971), 24.

31. Bod. MS. Top Essex, e. 10/2, fols. 5,8.

32. *A.P.C.* 1625–1626, pp. 153, 166; P.R.O., SP 16/6/38; *V.C.H. Essex*, II, 223–224.

33. Bod. MS Firth, c. 4, p. 154; P.R.O., SP 16/9/62; 17/13, 30.

34. P.R.O., SP 16/6/44.

35. P.R.O., SP 16/6/44, 60.

36. T. Birch, *The Court and Times of Charles the First*, ed. R. F. Williams (London, 1848), I, 49; *C.S.P. Ven.* 1625–26, p. 167.

37. P.R.O., SP 16/6/41, 41 I; *C.S.P. Ven.* 1625–26, p. 175.

'38. *C.S.P.D.* 1625–26, pp. 108–110; E.R.O., Morant MS. D/Y 2/7, fols. 271, 277.

39. P.R.O., SP 16/6/60, 76; SP 16/6/77.

40. E.R.O., D/P 264/8/3, July-November 1625.

41. P.R.O., SP 16/6/98, 116.

42. P.R.O., SP 16/6/98 I, II; *C.S.P.D.* 1625–26, p. 138; Bod. MS. Top. Essex 10/1, fol. 115; *V.C.H. Essex*, II, 225.

43. E.R.O., Barrington Papers, D/DBa/F5/1.

44. Hill, *Puritanism and Revolution*, p. 243; Birch, *Charles I*, I, 8.

45. P.R.O., SP 16/25/12, 12 I.

46. Shipps, p. 57; Thompson, "Origins," p. 81. This fact seems to me conclusive evidence against S. I. Adams's claim that Rich remained on close terms with Buckingham until well into 1627. There may, of course, have been some abortive attempt at reconciliation. See Adams, "Foreign Policy," p. 144.

47. Thompson, "Origins," p. 80.

48. P.R.O., SP 16/26/47; 29/23.

49. P.R.O., SP 16/39/3, 3 I; 54/47; 67/49, 49 I, 49 II; 72/44; 73/71; 75/48; 76/13, 13 I–II; 13 II; 76/22, 22 I–III; *C.S.P.D.* 1627–28, pp. 41–42, 221, 329–330. For the population estimates I have used the 1670 Hearth Tax returns, as tabulated by Burley, p. 337.

50. P.R.O., SP 16/34/62.

51. Keeler, *Long Parliament*, p. 268; Birch, *Charles I*, I, 161–162, 165.

52. P.R.O., SP 16/41/3; Birch, *Charles I*, I, 172; Gardiner, *England*, VI, 150; *C.S.P.D.* 1625–26, p. 485.

53. *C.S.P.D.* 1627–28, pp. 61, 204; John Rushworth, *Historical Collections* (London, 1659–1701), I, 428, 473.

54. P.R.O., SP 16/52/62–66; 54/47; 67/49 I–II; 73/71; 76/13; 76/22 II; *C.S.P.D.* 1627–28, pp. 41–42, 221, 329–330.

55. Birch, *Charles I*, pp. 149–150; P.R.O., SP 16/36/22; *C.S.P.D.* 1625–26, p. 433.

56. Shipps, p. 55. On the Feoffees, see Isabel M. Calder, ed., *The Activities of the Puritan Faction of the Church of England 1625–33* (London, 1957).

57. P.R.O., SP 16/210/44.

58. Cotton Mather, *Magnalia Christi Americana* (Hartford, Conn., 1852), I, 333–334, 346. The fullest account of Hooker's early career is to be found in George H. Williams et al., eds., *Thomas Hooker: Writings in England and Holland, 1626–1633,* Harvard Theological Studies, vol. 28 (Cambridge, Mass., 1975).

59. Mather, *Magnalia*, I, 335, 345, 355; P.R.O., SP 16/142/113.

60. P.R.O., SP 16/142/113.

61. R. P. Stearns, *The Strenuous Puritan, Hugh Peter: 1598–1660* (Champagne, Ill., 1954). p. 30.

62. Thomas Shepherd, "A Memoir of his own Life," in Alexander Young, ed., *Chronicles of the First Planters of the Colony of Massachusetts Bay* (Boston, 1846), p. 515.

63. P.R.O., SP 16/142/113.

64. Matthew Newcomen, *A Sermon Preached at the Funeral of . . . Samuel Collins* (London, 1658), p. 49: Shepherd, "Memoir," p. 514.

65. E.R.O., Q/SR 254/24–25.

66. B.M. Egerton MS. 2650, fol. 318.

67. Ogbu Uke Kalu, "The Jacobean Church and Essex Puritans" (Ph.D. diss. University of Toronto, 1972), pp. 358, 397.

68. A. E. Bland, P. A. Brown, and R. H. Tawney, *English Economic History: Select Documents* (London, 1914), p. 393.

69. William Gouge, *God's Three Arrows* (London, 1631), p. 12.

70. Hooker, *Writings,* p. 47; Gouge, *Arrows,* p. 172.

71. Barnes, *Vox Belli,* pp. 4–5, 7; Hooker, *Writings,* p. 47.

72. Perez Zagorin, *The Court and the Country* (New York, 1969), p. 345; Stephen Marshall, *Meroz Cursed* (London, 1643).

73. Gardiner, *Debates . . . 1625,* p. 5.

74. Barnes, *Vox Belli,* pp. 29–31, 40.

75. Hooker, *Writings,* pp. 48–49.

76. Ibid., pp. 118–119, 78–80.

77. Gouge, *Arrows,* pp. 75–76.

78. Mather, *Magnalia,* I, 337, 345.

79. Hill, *Puritanism and Revolution,* pp. 252–253; Stearns, *Strenuous Puritan,* pp. 34–35, 41.

80. Hooker, *Writings,* pp. 69–70.

81. I owe this point to Elizabeth Clark.

82. Bod. MS. Top. Essex, e. 10/2, fol. 60; P.R.O., SP 16/57/1; 76/13, 13 I–II; 92/86.

83. Barbara Donagan, "The Clerical Patronage of Robert Rich, Second Earl of Warwick, 1619–1642," *Proceedings of the American Philosophical Society,* 120 (October 1976), 408.

84. P.R.O., SP 16/76/13, 22, 22 I–III.

85. P.R.O., SP 16/57/1; Bod. MS. Firth, c. 4, pp. 297–305.

86. Birch, *Charles I,* I, 207.

87. Bod. MS. Firth, c. 4, pp. 300, 304.

88. P.R.O., SP 16/61/79.

89. J. S. Morrill, *Cheshire 1630–1660* (Oxford, 1974), pp. 12–14; Barnes, pp. 147, 268–269, 283, 293.

90. Bod. MS. Firth, c. 4, pp. 322–323.

91. Ibid., p. 325.

92. Barnes, pp. 251–252; Fletcher, pp. 185–186; Russell *Parliaments,* p. 324.

93. P.R.O., SP 16/59/19, 84; *C.S.P.D.* 1627–28, pp. 124–125, 132.

94. E.R.O., Morant MS D/Y 2/8, fol. 3; *A.P.C.* 1625–26, p. 212.

95. P.R.O., SP 16/59/84; Bos. MS. Top. Essex, e. 10/2, fols. 75–78.

96. *C.S.P.D.* 1627–28, pp. 132, 141; *A.P.C.* 1627, pp. 235, 295. Not all deserters were so lucky. At least one was hanged at the July Assizes. Bod. MS. Top. Essex, e. 10/2, fol. 79.

97. P.R.O., SP 16/59/31; 70/56; 71/29; Bod. Ms. Top. Essex 2/10, fols. 72–75.

98. *C.S.P.D.* 1627–28, p. 204; Birch, *Charles I,* p. 243; *V.C.H. Essex,* II, 225; G. A. Lowndes, "The History of the Barrington Family," *Essex Archeological Society Transactions,* n.s. 2, no. 3 (1879–1884), 23.

99. P.R.O., SP 16/56/69; 60/37; 14/215, p. 64.

100. P.R.O., SP 16/60/75; 61/33; 73/22; 74/104.

101. P.R.O., SP 16/64/26; 115/76, 79.

102. Birch, *Charles I,* I, 224.

103. Ibid., p. 260.

104. Ibid., pp. 251–252.

105. *C.S.P.D.* 1627–28, pp. 128, 247, 259, 471; *V.C.H. Essex,* II, 226.

106. Hill, *Puritanism and Revolution,* p. 255; Stearns, *Strenuous Puritan,* pp. 42–43; Mather, *Magnalia,* I, 416.

107. G. E. Aylmer, "Communication: St. Patrick's Day in Witham, Essex," *Past and Present,* no. 61 (1973), 140–141.

108. Bod. MS. Top. Essex, e. 10/2, fol. 111; P.R.O., SP 16/91/86.

109. Aylmer, "Communication," pp. 141–143; *A.P.C.* 1627–28, pp. 253, 260; P.R.O., SP 16/92/85, 85 I–V.

110. P.R.O., SP 16/91/86; *C.S.P.D.* 1627–28, pp. 509, 536; *A.P.C.* 1627–28, pp. 264, 282.

111. Russell, *Parliaments,* p. 338.

112. Bod. MS. Top. Essex, e. 10/3, fol. 11; *C.S.P.D.* 1625–1649, p. 727.

113. E.R.O., Morant MS. D/Y 2/4, fols. 9–11, 15.

114. Robert C. Johnson et al., eds., *Commons Debates 1628* (New Haven, 1977–), II, 169.

115. Colchester Castle, Colchester Assembly Book 1620–1646, fol. 36.

116. Ibid., fols. 73, 81, 81v.; E.R.O., Morant MS. D/Y 2/2, fols. 351–352.

117. Hirst, *Representative,* pp. 52, 200–201.

118. E.R.O., Morant MS. D/Y 2/4, fols. 139, 183; Hirst, *Representative,* p. 200.

119. E.R.O., Morant MS. D/Y 2/4, fol. 85.

120. See the sensible discussion of this matter by J. H. Hexter, in *Reappraisals in History,* 2nd ed. (Chicago, 1979), pp. 181–185.

121. E.R.O., D/Y, fols. 67, 85.

122. *H.M.C.* Buccleuch, III, p. 324.

123. Birch, *Charles I,* I, 323; *C.S.P. Ven.* 1626–1628, pp. 595, 605.

124. Birch, *Charles I,* I, 333; P.R.O. 16/94/35.

125. Hirst, *Representative,* pp. 200–201.

126. P.R.O., SP 16/94/35; Birch, *Charles I,* I, 332–333.

127. *C.S.P.D.* 1628–29, p. 217; Kalu, "Jacobean Church," p. 437.

128. P.R.O., SP 16/96/39, 39 I; Bod. MS. Firth, c. 4, pp. 455–457; Birch, *Charles I,* I, 331.

129. Johnson, *Commons Debates 1628,* II, 124.

130. B.M. Sloane MS. 826, fols. 97–99; B.M. Harleian MS. 37, fols. 226–227; Harleian MS. 1219, fols. 296–300, 320–322; Harleian MS. 1721, fols. 352–360v.

131. Johnson, *Commons Debates 1628*, II, 313.

132. John Rogers, *A Treatise of Love*, 2nd ed. (London, 1632), p. 233.

133. Johnson, *Commons Debates 1628*, II, 391.

134. P.R.O., SP 16/96/39, 39 I.

135. Johnson, *Commons Debates 1628*, IV, 156.

136. Russell, *Parliaments*, p. 381.

137. Johnson, *Commons Debates 1628*, IV, 120, 125, 156, 169.

138. G. M. Trevelyan, *England under the Stuarts*, 21st ed. (London, 1965), p. 137.

139. *C.S.P.D.* 1628–29, p. 217.

140. Russell, *Parliaments*, p. 396.

141. *C.S.P.D.* 1628–29, pp. 250, 259; E.R.O., Q/SR 264/108; 266/117.

142. Lowndes, "Barrington Family," p. 29.

143. *H.M.C.* 7th Report, appendix, p. 544.

144. Birch, *Charles I*, I, 390, 394, 396, 398, 401–402; *C.S.P.D.* 1628–29, p. 262.

145. P.R.O., SP 16/114/24; 120/28; *C.S.P.D.* 1628–29, pp. 323, 373, 415.

146. *H.M.C.* 7th Report, appendix, p. 544.

147. Ibid.

148. B.M. Egerton MS. 2645, fols. 5, 7; Wallace Notestein and Frances Helen Relf, *Commons Debates for 1629* (Minneapolis, 1921), pp. 12–31.

149. B.M. Egerton MS. 2645, fol. 13.

150. Russell, *Parliaments*, pp. 412–413.

151. B.M. Egerton MS. 2645, fol. 21.

9. Noble Professors

1. Christopher Hill, *Society and Puritanism* (New York, 1964); Lawrence Stone, *The Crisis of the Aristocracy* (Oxford, 1965).

2. B.M. Egerton MS. 2646, fol. 7v; 2650, fol. 318.

3. B.M. Egerton MS. 2645, fols. 186, 299, 301, 303.

4. Ibid., fol. 188; Shipps, pp. 370–373.

5. B.M. Egerton MS. 2645, fols. 98–99v., 106; Shipps, pp. 369–370.

6. B.M. Egerton MS. 2645, fol. 142v.

7. B.M. Egerton MS. 2644, fol. 196; 2645, fols. 31, 69, 142, 156, 309; 2646, fol. 3v.; 2650, fol. 247.

8. B.M. Egerton MS. 2645, fol. 142v.

9. Ibid., fol. 235.

10. B.M. Egerton MS. 2644, fol. 196; 2646, fol. 3v.

11. B.M. Egerton MS. 2643, fols. 1–3.

12. B.M. Egerton MS. 2650, fols. 247, 318.

13. Cotton Mather, *Magnalia Christi Americana* (Hartford, Conn., 1852), I, 305–306.

14. Giles Firmin, *The Real Christian* (London, 1670), pp. 67–68.

15. Edward Hyde, Earl of Clarendon, *History of the Rebellion and Civil Wars in England*, ed. W. Dunn Macray (Oxford, 1888), VI, 404.

16. B.M. Egerton MS. 2650, fols. 186, 189, 191v–194.

17. B.M. Egerton MS. 2646, fol. 104; 2648, fol. 84v.

18. B.M. Egerton MS. 2650, fol. 186.

19. B.M. Egerton MS. 2645, fol. 323.

20. *H.M.C.* 7th Report, appendix, p. 547.

21. E.R.O. D/DBa/A2, fols. 5v, 6v, 12, 14, 17–19, 26–27, 29v.

22. Mary Bohannon, "A London Bookseller's Bill: 1635–1639," *The Library,* 4th ser., 18, no. 4 (1938), 421–432.

23. B.M. Egerton MS. 2646, fol. 34.

24. B.M. Egerton MS. 2650, fol. 181.

25. B.M. Egerton MS. 2646, fol. 104; Bohannon, "London Bookseller's Bill," p. 419.

26. P.R.O., SP 14/170/54.

27. B.M. Egerton MS. 2644, fol. 211.

28. Ibid. fol. 269.

29. B.M. Egerton MS. 2646, fol. 17v; *H.M.C.* 7th Report, appendix, p. 548.

30. G. A. Lowndes, "The History of the Barrington Family," *Essex Archeological Society Transactions,* n.s. 2, no. 3 (1879–1884), 44.

31. B.M. Egerton MS. 2646, fols. 27, 27v, 30.

32. B.M. Egerton MS. 2644, fol. 219; Lowndes, "Barrington Family," pp. 31–34; P.R.O., PROB 11/268/362.

33. P.R.O., Egerton MS. 2645, fol. 319; 2646, fol. 40; P.R.O., SP 16/205/83.

34. B.M. Egerton MS. 2646, fols. 46; 29v, 31.

35. B.M. Egerton MS. 2645, fols. 112, 114v.

36. Ibid., fol. 324.

37. B.M. Egerton MS. 2650, fol. 181.

38. B.M. Egerton MS. 2645, fols. 327–327v.

39. B.M. Egerton MS. 2646, fol. 32v.

40. Ibid., fols. 17–17v.

41. E.R.O., D/DBa/Q6/1–3.

42. Bohannon, "London Bookseller's Bill," p. 419.

43. Conrad Russell, *Parliaments and English Politics, 1621–1629* (Oxford, 1979), p. xx.

44. B.M. Egerton MS. 2645, fol. 54; Shipps, pp. 366–367.

45. B.M. Egerton MS. 2645, fol. 323v; 2650, fols. 191–192v.

46. B.M. Egerton MS. 2645, fol. 33.

47. Sir John Eliot also addressed Sir Richard Knightley, Sir Francis Barrington's son-in-law, as "Brother"; B.M. Egerton MS. 2643, fols. 6, 14.

48. Perez Zagorin, *The Court and the Country* (New York, 1970), p. 102.

49. E.R.O., D/DBa/F5/1, 2.

50. John Rogers, *A Treatise of Love,* 2nd ed. (London, 1632), pp. 42–44.

51. B.M. Egerton MS. 2645, fols. 112, 142.

52. E.R.O., D/DBa/F5/2.

53. B.M. Egerton MS. 2645, fols. 235; 124; 115, 146, 154.

54. R. M. Smuts, "The Puritan Followers of Henrietta Maria in the 1630s," *English Historical Review,* 93, no. 366 (1978), 26–45.

55. Barbara Donagan, "A Courtier's Progress: Greed and Consistency in the Life of the Earl of Holland," *Historical Journal,* 19, no. 2 (1976), 317–353.

56. B.M. Egerton MS. 2645, fol. 309v, 324; *H.M.C.* 7th Report, appendix, p. 544.

57. Smuts, "Puritan Followers," pp. 36–37, 40.

58. Donagan, "Courtier's Progress," pp. 343–344.

59. P.R.O., SP 16/205/83; B.M. Egerton MS. 2645, fol. 324; 2646, fol. 34.

10. The Sins of Manasseh

1. E.R.O., Q/SR for years 1620–1639.

2. Calculated to the nearest pound from transcripts supplied by W. K. Jordan.

3. E.R.O., Q/S Ba 2/34, petition of Great Burstead.

4. John Rogers, *A Treatise of Love,* 3rd ed. (London, 1637), pp. 231–232.

5. E.R.O., Q/S Ba 2/34, petiton of Great Burstead; Q/S Ba 2/28, petition of Great Oakley; Q/S Ba 2/43, petition of Great Horkesley.

6. E.R.O., T/R 5/1/4, passim.

7. E.R.O., Q/S Ba 2/29, petition of the clothiers of Bocking.

8. Rogers, *Love,* p. 215.

9. E.R.O., Q/SR 259/24.

10. Rogers, *Love,* pp. 233–234.

11. The description of Henrietta Maria as the "daughter of a strange God" is Thomas Hooker's, quoted in Cotton Mather, *Magnalia Christi Americana* (Hartford, Conn., 1852), I, 345.

12. Thirsk, p. 821.

13. John Walters, "Grain Riots and Popular Attitudes to the Law: Maldon and the Crisis of 1629," in John Brewer and John Styles, eds., *An Ungovernable People: The English and their Law in the Seventeenth and Eighteenth Centuries* (New Brunswick, N.J., 1980), p. 51; John Walters and Keith Wrightson, "Dearth and the Social Order in Early Modern England," *Past and Present,* no. 71 (1976), 36; E.R.O., D/B 3/3/208. There were also protests in Colchester against the export of grain; E.R.O., Morant MS. D/Y 2/7, fol. 247; 2/9, fol. 357.

14. Bod. MS. Firth, c. 4, pp. 488–491.

15. Ibid., pp. 485–487; E.R.O., Q/SR 266/120–121.

16. P.R.O., SP 16/141/1; E.R.O. Q/SR 266/120–121; Bod. MS. Firth, c. 4, pp. 484–485.

17. *A.P.C.* 1628–29, pp. 401–402; Bod. MS. Firth, c. 4, pp. 487, 491–493, 497–500; pp. 493, 496–497.

18. E.R.O., Q/SR 266/120–121.

19. P.R.O., SP 16/141/16.

20. P.R.O., SP 16/142/113.

21. P.R.O., SP 16/141/16.

22. E.R.O., Q/SR 266/121.

23. E.R.O., D/B 3/3/208; *A.P.C.* 1629–30, pp. 24–25; Thomas Birch, *The Court and Times of Charles I,* ed. R. F. Williams (London, 1848), II, 17; Bod. MS. Firth, c. 4, p. 501.

24. Walters, "Grain Riots," pp. 75–82.

25. E.R.O., D/B 3/3/208; Walters, "Grain Riots," pp. 77–78.

26. Bod. MS. Firth, c. 4, pp. 501–504.

27. E.R.O., Assize File, 35/71/T/97.

28. Walter, "Grain Riots," pp. 76–77; Bod. MS. Firth, c. 4, pp. 502–505.

29. E.R.O., Stephen A. Warner, "Letters from a Lieutenancy Book," p. 18. (This pamphlet is a partial transcript of materials relating to the clothing crisis, from Bod. MS. Firth, c. 4.)

100. Newton, *Colonizing Activities,* pp. 258, 198.

101. Pym made precisely this argument in the Long Parliament; Newton, *Colonizing Activities,* p. 198.

102. Ibid., p. 41.

103. B.M. Egerton MS. 2645, fol. 245.

104. *Winthrop Papers,* II, 111, 114, 117.

105. Newton, *Colonizing Activities,* pp. 198, 283–285, 324.

106. E.R.O., D/DBa/02, 17 January, 25 January, 27 February 1632.

107. Newton, *Colonizing Activities,* pp. 114–117, 203–209.

108. E.R.O., Q/SR 267/18; 269/17; Bod. MS. Firth, c. 4, p. 539.

109. P.R.O., SP 16/238/39.

110. P.R.O., PC 2/41, p. 121.

111. P.R.O., SP 16/228/115; 250/66; 251/18; 258/53; *C.S.P.D.* 1633–34, pp. 289, 295, 402, 432, 436, 447, 456, 465–466, 507–508.

112. Hull, pp. 626–631; Birch, *Charles I,* II, 102; P.R.O., E 178/5287; *C.S.P.D.* 1629–1631, p. 321.

113. *C.S.P.D.* 1629–1631, pp. 84, 535; *C.S.P.D.* 1637–38, pp. 108, 311; P.R.O., PC 2/48/606.

114. *C.S.P.D.* 1631–33, p. 233; *C.S.P.D.* 1634–35, p. 189.

115. B.M. Stowe MS. 825, fol. 9.

116. P.R.O., SP 16/275/21.

117. *C.S.P. Ven.* 1632–36, pp. 299–300.

118. E.R.O., Q/SR 286/12.

119. C.S.P. Ven 1632–36, pp. 336–337.

120. Philip Lee Ralph, *Sir Humphrey Mildmay, Royalist Gentleman* (New Brunswick, N.J., 1947), p. 147; Archibald Clark, "The Forest of Waltham under the Tudors and Stuarts," *Essex Review,* 35 (1926), 137.

121. M. D. Gordon, "The Collection of Ship-Money in the Reign of Charles I," *Transactions of the Royal Historical Society,* 3rd ser. 4 (London, 1910), 155–157; *C.S.P.D.* 1634–35, p. 248.

122. B.M. Egerton MS. 2646, fols. 109, 111.

123. E.R.O., D/DEb 7/4.

124. This method of assessment was resisted in Theydon Garnon, where inhabitants without land refused to contribute; *C.S.P.D.* 1635, p. 481; *C.S.P.D.* 1635–36, pp. 6, 331; *C.S.P.D.* 1636–37, p. 3.

125. *C.S.P.D.* 1634–35, pp. 245, 248, 345, 464; *C.S.P.D.* 1635, pp. 66, 537, 556, 569, 580, 594; *C.S.P.D.* 1635–36, pp. 13, 331; *C.S.P.D.* 1636–37, pp. 3, 23, 56–57, 64, 214, 226, 231; Ralph, *Mildmay,* pp. 83–84.

126. P.R.O., SP 16/328/49; *C.S.P.D.* 1636–37, p. 183; Ralph, *Mildmay,* p. 80.

127. B.M. Harleian MS. 454 (Diary of Sir Humphrey Mildmay), fols. 9, 29v, 32–34, 41.

128. P.R.O., SP 16/337/34.

129. V. A. Rowe, "Robert, Second Earl of Warwick and the Payment of Ship Money in Essex," *Essex Archeological Society Transactions,* 3rd ser. 1 (Chelmsford, 1964–65), 160–62; *C.S.P.D.* 1636–37, pp. 197, 226, 231; Ralph, *Mildmay,* pp. 83–84.

130. *C.S.P. Ven.* 1636–37, pp. 124–125.

131. *C.S.P. Ven.* 1636–1639, p. 126.

132. Rowe, "Warwick," p. 162.

133. S. R. Gardiner, *History of England* (London, 1894–1896), VIII, 203, 211–217.

134. C. V. Wedgwood, *The King's Peace* (London, 1966), p. 124.

135. Gardiner, *England,* VIII, 205–208; Rowe, "Warwick," p. 162.

136. *C.S.P.D.* 1636–37, p. 183; Ralph, *Mildmay,* p. 80.

137. P.R.O., SP 16/7/27.

138. P.R.O., E 134/8 Car. I/ Mich. 18; E 134/8–9 Car. I/ Hil. 21; P/C 2/43/256, 258; P/C 2/50/278; SP 16/247/22–24; SP 16/248/4, 4 I–II.

139. Birch, *Charles I,* II, 272.

140. *C.S.P.D.* 1637, p. 132.

141. P.R.O., SP 16/358, pp. 56–57, 103, 116–117.

142. Ibid., passim.

143. Gordon, "Ship-Money," pp. 157–158.

144. Birch, *Charles I,* II, 283.

145. E.R.O., Q/SR 306/74a, 99; P.R.O., PC 2/50/401, 679.

146. Ralph, *Mildmay,* p. 148.

147. Barbara Donagan, "A Courtier's Progress: Greed and Consistency in the Life of the Earl of Holland," *Historical Journal,* 19, no. 2 (1976), p. 326.

148. P.R.O., SP 16/361/92.

149. *C.S.P. Ven.* 1636–39, p. 299.

150. Ibid., p. 300.

151. P.R.O., SP 16/350/54 I.

152. *C.S.P.D.* 1636–37, pp. 29, 545.

153. *Massachusetts Historical Society Collections,* 4th ser. 6 (Boston, 1863), 408.

154. E.R.O., D/DBa/F5/2, January 17, 1635.

155. *Massachusetts Historical Society Collections,* 4th ser. 6, p. 47.

156. *C.S.P.D.* 1637, pp. 544–545; Smith, pp. 51–54.

157. E.R.O., D/DBa/F5/2; *C.S.P.D.* 1636–37, p. 545.

158. Dr. Tyack has discovered cases of opposition to the railing of altars in thirty-three parishes. But these are only the cases that reached the church courts. Many more examples of noncompliance must have gone unreported because the churchwardens themselves opposed the new arrangements; Tyack, pp. 320–345.

159. P.R.O., SP 16/327/101.

160. *C.S.P.D.* 1635–36, p. 263; *L.J.,* IV, 156–158, 186.

161. *C.S.P.D.* 1636–37, pp. 242, 265; William Prynne, *A Quench-Coal* (London, 1637), pp. 351–356.

162. *C.S.P.D.* 1637, pp. 544–545.

163. E.R.O., T/B 211/1, fols. 18, 28.

164. B.M. Sloane MS. 922, fol. 92v.

165. *Calendar of State Papers, Colonial, 1574–1660,* p. 266.

166. E.R.O., T/B 211/1, fols. 18, 28.

167. Davids, p. 182; John Rushworth, *Historical Collections* (London, 1659–1701), II, 718, 720.

168. Gordon, "Ship-Money," p. 157.

169. E.R.O., T/B 211/1/39, trascribed in Shipps, pp. 406–408.

11. The Puritan Moment

1. Lawrence Durrell, *Bitter Lemons* (New York, 1958), p. 152.

2. E.R.O., Q/S Ba 2/47, petition of Hugh Harr.

3. E.R.O., Q/SR 418/74.

4. E.R.O., Assize File, 35/81/T/9–10.

5. Philip Lee Ralph, *Sir Humphrey Mildmay, Royalist Gentleman* (New Brunswick, N.J., 1947), p. 152.

6. M. D. Gordon, "The Collection of Ship-Money in the Reign of Charles I," *Transactions of the Royal Historical Society*, 3rd ser. 4 (London, 1910), 157.

7. *The Life of Stephen Marshall* (London, 1688), pp. 23, 28.

8. *H.M.C.* 7th Report, appendix, p. 549; John Nalson, *An Impartial Collection* (London, 1682), I, 279 (misnumbered 269); P.R.O., PC 2/52/444; Shipps, p. 209.

9. *H.M.C.* 7th Report, appendix, p. 549; E.R.O., D/Y 2/4/35.

10. B.M. Harleian MS. 454, fol. 30. For Neville's Laudianism, see the letter in praise of his activities from Robert Aylett to Dr. John Lambe, P.R.O., SP 16/350/54.

11. Nalson, *Collection,* I, 279 (misnumbered 269); *C.S.P.D.* 1639–40, pp. 608–609; *H.M.C.* 7th Report, appendix, p. 549.

12. B.M. Egerton MS. 2646, fol. 142.

13. *D.N.B.,* "Harbottle Grimston." The exchange of syllogisms, relating to the power of bishops, is appended to *The Order and Form of Church Government . . . Voted . . . 16 July, 1641* (London, 1641), n.p.

14. William Addison, *Essex Heyday* (London, 1949), pp. 35–37, 318–319.

15. Harbottle Grimston, *Mr. Grimston his Speech . . . concerning Troubles Abroad and Grievances at Home* (London, 1641), n.p.; William Cobbett, *Parliamentary History* (London, 1807), II, 542–544.

16. B.M. Harleian MS. 454, fol. 31v.

17. *C.S.P.D.* 1640, pp. 26, 155, 442, 540.

18. Harvard University, Houghton MS. Eng. 109.

19. *C.S.P.D.* 1640–41, pp. 30, 36, 43, 46.

20. *C.S.P.D.* 1640, pp. 83, 163, 165; *C.S.P.D.* 1640–41, pp. 30, 36, 43, 46.

21. *C.S.P.D.* 1640, pp. 342, 391, 432.

22. Ibid., pp. 163, 294, 450, 500; P.R.O., P/C 2/52/510.

23. *C.S.P.D.* 1640, p. 450; P.R.O., P/C 2/52/634.

24. *C.S.P.D.* 1640, pp. 622–623.

25. Ibid., p. 517.

26. Smith, p. 69.

27. Cotton Mather, *Magnalia Christi Americana* (Hartford, Conn., 1852), I, 416–417.

28. *C.S.P.D.* 1640, pp. 511–517; John White, *The First Century of Scandalous Malignant Priests* (London, 1643), p. 15.

29. E.R.O., Q/SR 311/4, 46–51; P.R.O., P/C/ 2/52/674; *C.S.P.D.* 1640, p. 551; *L.J.,* IV, pp. 307, 322.

30. Smith, pp. 140–143; E.R.O., Assize File, 35/81/T/14.

31. White, *Century,* p. 3; Smith, pp. 115–117; Davids, p. 230.

32. P.R.O., P/C 2/52/674; *C.S.P.D.* 1640, pp. 516–517; P.R.O., Carew Transcripts, 30/5/6, p. 361.

33. *C.S.P.D.* 1640, pp. 517, 551.

34. *H.M.C.* 12th Report, appendix 2, p. 261; Smith, pp. 69, 181–183.

35. P.R.O., Carew Transcripts, 30/5/6, p. 361.

36. E.R.O., D/Y 2/4/51; D/Y 2/8/73.

37. E.R.O., D/Y 2/4/35, 39.

38. Geoge Caunt, *Essex in Parliament* (Chelmsford, Essex, 1969), p. 30; Mary

Frear Keeler, *The Long Parliament, 1640–1641: A Biographical Study of its Members* (Philadelphia, 1954), pp. 45–46.

39. B.M. Harleian MS. 454, fol. 36.

40. John Wenlock, *To . . . Charles II* (London, 1662), p. 21.

41. Caunt, *Essex,* p. 27; Keeler, *Long Parliament,* pp. 262–263, 322–323.

42. Harbottle Grimston, *Mr. Grimston's Speech in the High Court of Parliament* (London, 1641), n.p.; Cobbett, *History,* II, 656–661.

43. *L.J.,* IV, pp. 100, 107, 109, 113, 183.

44. E.R.O., transcript 22 from Q/S Ba 241.

45. B.M. Harleian MS. 454, fol. 38v; E.R.O., Q/SR 312/58, 112.

46. *H.M.C.* 7th Report, appendix, p. 550; Smith, pp. 49, 88, 303.

47. Smith, p. 274; "Some Althams of Mark Hall in the Seventeenth Century," *Essex Review,* 17 (1908), 74–87; *Calendar of the Committee for Compounding,* Mary Anne Everett Green, ed. (London, 1889–1892), p. 879.

48. Ralph, *Mildmay,* pp. 103, 172; Davids, p. 456.

49. Smith, pp. 41, 255, 258; Ralph, *Mildmay,* pp. 197–198.

50. Richard Baxter, *Reliquiae Baxterianae* (London, 1696), I, 39.

51. Brian Manning, *The English People and the English Revolution* (London, 1978). See also his earlier seminal article, "The Nobles, the People, and the Constitution," in Trevor Aston, ed., *Crisis in Europe: 1560–1660* (Garden City, New York, 1967), pp. 261–284.

52. B.M. Harleian MS. 454, fols. 37–38v.

53. Sir Philip Warwick, *Memoirs of the Reign of King Charles* (London, 1702), p. 164.

54. B.M. Harleian MS. 454, fol. 40v.

55. E.R.O., Q/SR 306/126; 308/120; 309/11; 330/30; 312/67–73; 313/38.

56. Bruno Ryves, *Mercurius Rusticus* (London, 1646), p. 22; Josselin, p. 12.

57. *H.M.C.* 12th Report, appendix 2, p. 281.

58. C. A. Holmes, "The Eastern Association" (Ph.D. diss., Cambridge University, 1969), p. 83.

59. *C.S.P.D.* 1639–40, p. 594.

60. E.R.O., Q/S Ba 2/44, letter from Sir Francis Coke.

61. E.R.O., Q/SR 314/130; Ralph, *Mildmay,* p. 163.

62. B.M. Egerton MS. 2651, fol. 104.

63. Baxter, *Reliquiae,* I, 40.

64. Smith, p. 408.

65. Ryves, *Mercurius,* pp. 22–23.

66. Mather, *Magnalia,* I, 335; Ryves, *Mercurius,* pp. 23–26.

67. Ryves, *Mercurius,* pp. 23–26.

68. E.R.O., Q/S Ba 2/43, petitions of West ham and Great Horkesley.

69. *Three Petitions from . . . Colchester . . . Essex* (London, 1642); Harbottle Grimston, *Mr. Grimston's Speech . . . upon the Essex Petition* (London, 1642), n.p.; John Pym, *A Speech Delivered at a Conference, 15 January 1641* (London, 1642), p. 18; *L.J.,* IV, 523.

70. *L.J.,* IV, 523.

71. *Perfect Diurnall,* #311 (22–29 August 1642).

72. Grimston, *Speech . . . upon the Essex Petition.*

73. Pym, *Speech Delivered at a Conference,* pp. 17–18.

74. *H.M.C.* Beaufort, p. 23.

75. P.R.O., PC 2/52/634.

76. *Lord Willoughby of Parnham his Letter* (London, 1642); *L.J.*, V, 143; John Rushworth, *Historical Collections* (London, 1659–1701), IV, 479.

77. Holmes, pp. 39–47.

78. Thomas Barnes, *Vox Belli* (London, 1626), pp. 4–5, 7.

79. Stephen Marshall, *Meroz Cursed* (London, 1641/2), p. 8.

80. Josselin, p. 13.

81. Matthew Newcomen, *The Craft and Cruelty of the Churches' Adversaries* (London, 1642).

82. C. H. Firth, *Cromwell's Army* (London, 1902), p. 315.

83. Ryves, *Mercurius*, pp. 17–18, 30–31.

84. E.R.O., Q/S Ba 2/45, information of Jane Earle.

85. Ralph, *Mildmay*, p. 168; White, p. 45.

86. White, *Century*, pp. 3, 25; Smith, pp. 140–43; Davids, p. 237.

87. Smith, pp. 181–183.

88. Edward Symmons, *The Loyal Subject's Belief* (London, 1643), passim; Ryves, *Mercurius*, pp. 16–19.

89. E.R.O., D/DEb 15, fol. 23.

90. Holmes, pp. 45–47.

91. John Wenlock, *To . . . Charles II* (London, 1662), pp. 21–25.

92. Ryves, *Mercurius*, pp. 24–26.

93. E.R.O., Q/SR 314/92; 318/29; Q/S Ba 2/43, examination of Thomas Harvey; 2/47, examination of Gamaliel Jaie.

94. Ryves, *Mercurius*, pp. 24–26; Smith, p. 179.

95. Printed in *Archeologia*, 35 (1855), 311–334.

96. *Special Passages*, #15 (22–29 November 1642), 133; E.R.O., Q/SR 319/23–37.

97. *L.J.*, V, 300.

98. *H.M.C.* Braye, pp. 146–147; Ryves, *Mercurius*, p. 1; *Special Passages*, #3 (22–29 August 1642), 17.

99. *H.M.C.* Braye, pp. 146–147; Ryves, *Mercurius*, pp. 1–5.

100. *H.M.C.* Braye, p. 147.

101. Ryves, *Mercurius*, pp. 11–14.

102. Smith, p. 112; P.R.O., SP 16/229/123.

103. *Perfect Diurnall*, #11 (22–29 August 1642); *A Message Sent to the Parliament by Sir Thomas Barrington and Harbottle Grimston* (London, 1642), n.p.

104. E.R.O., Exams. and Recogs., 27 September 1642.

105. *Special Passages*, #3, p. 22; *C.S.P.D.* 1641–43, p. 377.

106. John Rous, *The Diary of John Rous*, ed. Mary Anne Everett, Camden Soc., 1st ser., 66 (London, 1856), 121.

107. Ryves, *Mercurius*, p. 15.

108. C. Fell Smith, *Mary Rich, Countess of Warwick* (London, 1901), pp. 113–114; Francis Peck, *Desiderata Curiosa* (London, 1735), II, bk. xii, 23–25.

109. *C.J.*, II, 736–737; Ryves, *Mercurius*, p. 5.

110. *C.J.*, II, 741.

111. *E.R.O.*, Colchester Exams. and Recogs., 27 September 1642.

112. *C.J.*, II, 738, 741, 753; Ralph, *Mildmay*, p. 161; E.R.O., Q/S Ba 2/47, printed order concerning the goods of Lady Rivers.

113. Ralph, *Mildmay*, p. 162; Smith, p. 183; Ryves, *Mercurius*, p. 13.

114. *L.J.*, VI, 19; *H.M.C.* 5th Report, appendix, p. 82; Ryves, *Mercurius*, p. 15.

115. *Special Passages,* #3, p. 22; Rous, *Diary,* p. 121; *C.J.,* II, 758.

116. *C.J.,* II, 758; Ralph, *Mildmay,* p. 162; E.R.O., Q/SR 319/23–40.

117. *H.M.C.* 5th Report, appendix, p. 21.

118. *C.J.,* II, 881.

119. Ryves, *Mercurius,* pp. 29–30; E.R.O., Colchester Exams. and Recogs., 27 September 1642.

120. *L.J.,* VI, 21.

121. For details, see William Hunt, "The Godly and the Vulgar" (Ph.D. diss., Harvard University, 1974), pp. 639–708.

122. Austin Woolrych, introduction to E. W. Ives, ed., *The English Revolution, 1600–1660* (New York, 1971), p. 19.

123. Hunt, "Godly," pp. 587, 605; *C.S.P.D.* 1641–1643, p. 357; B.M. Egerton MS. 2651, fol. 118; Ralph, *Mildmay,* p. 162; Holmes, pp. 41–47.

124. Philip Morant, *The History and Antiquities of the County of Essex* (Chelmsford, Essex, 1916), pp. xxiii–xxv.

125. Baxter, *Reliquiae,* I, 30.

126. Ibid., pp. 40–42.

127. For examples, see E.R.O., Colchester Exams. and Recogs., 9 July 1642.

128. This is only an impression, albeit a strong one; the matter needs more careful quantitative study.

129. Indicted for the plundering of Edward Church at Rucking were thirteen laborers, one glover, one tailor, one carpenter, and seven men without additions; E.R.O., Q/SR 316–324.

130. *H.M.C.* Braye, pp. 146–147.

131. *L.J.,* IV pp. 100, 107, 109, 113, 183.

132. Ryves, *Mercurius,* pp. 29–30.

133. On this class paranoia, see Christopher Hill, "The Many-Headed Monster," in *Change and Continuity in Seventeenth-Century England* (London, 1974), pp. 181–204.

134. Rous, *Diary,* p. 121; Ryves, *Mercurius,* p. 15.

135. Thomas Carte, *Letters Concerning England* (London, 1739), I, 14.

136. *H.M.C.* 5th Report, appendix, pp. 45–46.

137. Keith Thomas, *Religion and the Decline of Magic* (New York, 1971), p. 75.

138. See E.R.O., Q/SR for 1640–1642. This is especially remarkable in view of the riot that occurred at Hatfield Broad Oak as late as 1639.

139. For an account, see Macfarlane, *Witchcraft,* pp. 135–144.

140. Marshall, *Meroz Cursed,* p. 8.

141. Edward Symmons, *Scripture Vindicated* (Oxford, 1644), sig. A3.

12. Conclusion

1. *L.J.,* V, 43.

2. Stephen Marshall, *A Sacred Panegyric* (London, 1644), p. 21.

Index

Harvard Historical Studies

84. *Marvin Arthur Breslow*. A Mirror of England: English Puritan Views of Foreign Nations, 1618–1640. 1970.
85. *Patrice L. R. Higonnet*. Pont-de-Montvert: Social Structure and Politics in a French Village, 1700–1914. 1971.
86. *Paul G. Halpern*. The Mediterranean Naval Situation, 1908–1914. 1971.
87. *Robert E. Ruigh*. The Parliament of 1624: Politics and Foreign Policy. 1971.
88. *Angeliki E. Laiou*. Constantinople and the Latins: The Foreign Policy of Andronicus, 1282–1328. 1972.
89. *Donald Nugent*. Ecumenism in the Age of the Reformation: The Colloquy of Poissy. 1974.
90. *Robert A. McCaughey*. Josiah Quincy. 1772–1864: The Last Federalist. 1974.
91. *Sherman Kent*. The Election of 1827 in France. 1975.
92. *A. N. Galpern*. The Religions of the People in Sixteenth-Century Champagne. 1976.
93. *Robert G. Keith*. Conquest and Agrarian Change: The Emergence of the Hacienda System on the Peruvian Coast. 1976.
94. *Keith Hitchins*. Orthodoxy and Nationality: Andreiu Şaguna and the Rumanians of Transylvania, 1846–1873. 1977.
95. *A. R. Disney*. Twilight of the Pepper Empire: Portuguese Trade in Southwest India in the Early Seventeenth Century. 1978.
96. *Gregory D. Phillips*. The Diehards: Aristocratic Society and Politics in Edwardian England. 1979.
97. *Alan Kreider*. English Chantries: The Road to Dissolution. 1979.
98. *John Buckler*. The Theban Hegemony, 371–362 BC. 1980.
99. *John A. Carey*. Judicial Reform in France before the Revolution of 1789. 1981.
100. *Andrew W. Lewis*. Royal Succession in Capetian France: Studies on Familial Order and the State. 1982.
101. *Robert E. Sullivan*. John Toland and the Deist Controversy: A Study in Adaptations. 1982.
102. *William Hunt*. The Puritan Moment: The Coming of Revolution in an English County. 1983.